Women and infertility in sub-Saharan Africa:

A multi-disciplinary perspective

Women and infertility in sub-Saharan Africa: A multi-disciplinary perspective

J. Ties Boerma and Zaida Mgalla, editors

Royal Tropical Institute - The Netherlands

Royal Tropical Institute
KIT Publishers
P.O. Box 95001
1090 HA Amsterdam
The Netherlands
Telephone: 31 (20) 568 8272
Telefax: 31 (20) 568 8286
E-mail: publishers@kit.nl
Website: www.kit.nl

Design: Grafisch Ontwerpbureau Agaatsz BNO,
Meppel, the Netherlands
Photos: Ferry Herrebrugh. These photographs also
appeared in: Vogelzang J, Van den Hombergh P
and Bakker J (eds) (1997), *Images of Power*,
Nederlandse Vereniging voor Tropische
Geneeskunde, the Netherlands.
Map on p. 154: M. Rieff
Printing: Bariet, Ruinen, the Netherlands

ISBN 90 6832 116 1

*Photo cover: 'Dolls' to be carried by women on their
backs and cared for until the birth of the first child
(Kirdi or Fali, North-Cameroon / Nigeria border).*

Table of contents

Acknowledgements

The original idea for a study of infertility in sub-Saharan Africa from a multi-disciplinary perspective was born within the Tanzania-Netherlands project to support AIDS control in Mwanza Region Tanzania (TANESA project). Several chapters in this book are based on research carried out in the context of the TANESA project, and supported by the Netherlands Minister for Development Cooperation. Six of the chapters were presented and discussed at a USAID/MEASURE Evaluation/UNAIDS/CDC meeting on *HIV, STDs and infertility: key issues* in Arlington, Virginia, USA December 14-15 1998. This meeting was sponsored by USAID and UNAIDS. The publication has been made possible with partial support from the USAID Africa Bureau/Sustainable Development to the MEASURE Evaluation project. We are very grateful to Maria Khan at the University of North Carolina, who provided invaluable assistance with the editing, referencing and indexing of the chapters.

About the authors

John Blacker first became interested in demography when reading history at Oxford. After his BA he thus went on to a PhD at the London School of Economics. Having worked on censuses in Tanganyika, Zanzibar, Uganda and Kenya and teaching for two years at the LSE, in 1967 he became a Regional Adviser in Demographic Statistics with the UN Economic Commission for Africa, carrying out short-term advisory missions in about 20 African countries. After a return to the UK in 1973, a year with the WFS and two years at the Institute of Development Studies, University of Sussex, he joined the Centre for Population Studies at the London School of Hygiene and Tropical Medicine. Since retiring in 1992 he has worked as a consultant in demographic statistics.

Ties Boerma completed a medical degree and MSc (demography) at the University of Groningen, the Netherlands, and a PhD in medical demography at the University of Amsterdam. During his 15 years in international health, he has worked as primary health care adviser for UNICEF/WHO in eastern and southern Africa, as coordinator for health analysis for the Demographic and Health Survey programme (DHS) and for the TANESA project on AIDS in Tanzania. He is currently Director of the USAID-sponsored MEASURE Evaluation project and Research Associate Professor in the Maternal and Child Health Department of the University of North Carolina at Chapel Hill.

Pierre Buekens, MD, MPH, PhD, is Professor and Chair of the Department of Maternal and Child Health, School of Public Health, University of North Carolina at Chapel Hill. Dr Buekens is President of the Association of Teachers of Maternal and Child Health (ATMCH) and US editor of Paediatric and Perinatal Epidemiology. Dr Buekens' research interests include perinatal epidemiology and evaluation of perinatal services.

Bruno Dujardin, MD, DTMH, PhD, is Vice President of the School of Public Health and Professor at the Department of Policy and Health Systems, Université Libre de Bruxelles, Brussels, Belgium. He has worked extensively in Central America and Africa. His fields of interest are public health and epidemiology, health services management and evaluation, health district planning, maternal health, and decision making analysis.

Marjolein Gijsels received a PhD in linguistic anthropology at the University of Amsterdam in 1996. She has carried out research in D.R. Congo, Tanzania and Uganda, working on research topics including Swahili, oral literature, infertility and commercial sex work. Currently she works for the Medical Research Council (UK) Programme on AIDS in Uganda.

Aileen Jacobus is a nurse/midwife from Zimbabwe. She trained as a research midwife, and has worked on projects related to contraceptive use, teenage pregnancy and other reproductive health issues. For several years she has conducted clinical research on infertility and run the daily infertility clinic services in the teaching hospital in Harare Medical School, University of Zimbabwe. She has recently (June 2000) graduated as a M. Phil. student at the University of Oslo, where her thesis was on community perspectives on infertility.

Ulla Larsen completed her PhD in sociology and demography at Princeton University in 1985. In 1994 she joined the Department of Population and International Health at the Harvard School of Public Health, where she is an Associate Professor of Demography. Her major area of research interest is infertility and fertility decline in sub-Saharan Africa. Currently, she is working on a project on the incipient fertility decline in northern Tanzania.

Philippe Mayaud graduated as an MD (GP) in France in 1986 and obtained an MSc (clinical tropical medicine) at the London School of Hygiene and Tropical Medicine (LSHTM) in 1991. He worked for five years as a Medical Officer in STD clinics in French Guyana and a District Medical Officer in PHC settings in other parts of the Caribbean. In 1991 he joined the LSHTM; based in Mwanza, Tanzania, for 6 years, he collaborated on a large international STD/HIV intervention trial conducted by the African Medical Research Foundation (AMREF) and the LSHTM. Currently he is a clinical senior lecturer at LSHTM, and in charge of the MSc in sexually transmitted infections and HIV. He is supporting research on clinical, epidemiological and control aspects of STDs in Morocco, The Gambia, the Central African Republic, Tanzania and Uganda.

Zaida J. Mgalla trained as a teacher, receiving a BA in education (1988) from the University of Dar es Salaam, Tanzania, and an MA in Education (1994) from Murdoch University, Australia. Additional coursework has covered gender training and health systems research. Employed by the Tanzanian Ministry of Education and Culture since 1988, she was seconded to the TANESA project in 1994 as a researcher. Since 1996 she has been a coordinator in the Mwanza region of Tanzania for youth sexual and reproductive health and HIV/AIDS intervention programs supported by the TANESA project.

Xavier De Muylder received a medical degree in 1976 from the Catholic University of Louvain, Belgium, an MSc (physiology) from the University of Montreal, Canada, in 1983 and a PhD in 1996, with a dissertation on infertility in Africa. He is a specialist in obstetrics and gynaecology and was a Provincial Consultant on maternal health in Zimbabwe for four years. Currently he teaches reproductive medicine and maternal health at the Institute of Tropical Medicine in Antwerp, Belgium.

Robert Pool obtained a PhD in medical anthropology from the University of Amsterdam in 1989. He has carried out research in India, Cameroon, the Netherlands, Tanzania and Uganda. Topics have included food taboos, traditional aetiologies and interpretations of illness, mother and child health, witchcraft, euthanasia, traditional healers, sexually transmitted diseases and various socio-cultural aspects of HIV/AIDS. He is currently working with the Medical Research Council (UK) Programme on AIDS in Uganda.

Han Raggers received his MA degree in demography from Groningen University, the Netherlands, in 1987. He spent several years with the United Nations in the Marshall Islands and the Centro Latinoamericano de Demografía in Santiago, Chile. Since 1992 he has been a data processing specialist with the Demographic and Health Survey program.

Denise M. Roth Allen is a Mellon Postdoctoral Fellow (1999-2000) in the Office of Population Research, Princeton University. She received her Masters Degree in public health from the School of Public Health, University of California, Los Angeles (1988) and her doctorate in sociocultural anthropology at the University of Illinois, Urbana (1996). As part of the University of Michigan Population Fellows Program she served as a technical officer in the Division of Family and Reproductive Health at the WHO. She has carried out fieldwork on maternal and reproductive health issues in Tanzania and Liberia, and has served as a Peace Corps health volunteer in Gabon.

Johanne Sundby is a medical doctor and a specialist in gynaecology and community medicine. Her PhD (1994) was on the causes, care and consequences of infertility in Norway. Since 1992 she has worked in international reproductive health research on infertility, abortion and STDs. She has herself experienced infertility. At present she is an associate Professor in women's health and international health at the University of Oslo. In 1997-99 she led the Norwegian Commission on Women's Health.

Mark Urassa has completed an MA in demography at the University of Dar es Salaam and an MSc in medical demography at the London School of Hygiene and Tropical Medicine. Since 1994, he has worked as a research coordinator at the TANESA project in Mwanza, Tanzania.

Lilian Wambura holds a BSc in Home Economics and Human Nutrition from Sokoine University of Agriculture, Tanzania and in 1999 completed an MPH at the Royal Tropical Institute in Amsterdam. She works as a researcher on Reproductive Health issues in the TANESA project, Mwanza, Tanzania.

Ndatulu Robert Washija has been a research assistant at the Tanzania-Netherlands project to support AIDS control in Mwanza Region (TANESA) since 1994. He has worked on a range of qualitative studies on traditional healers and sexual behaviour among the Sukuma people in northwest Tanzania.

Richard White obtained a BSc in Physics, followed by an MSc in Medical Demography at the London School of Hygiene and Tropical Medicine (1996). He has worked at the London School's Center for Population Studies, analysing sexual behaviour data from the Global Program on AIDS surveys and modelling STDs and infertility in sub-Saharan Africa. Recently he moved within the School to the Infectious Disease Epidemiology Unit. There he is currently working on a project funded by UK DFID, modelling the effectiveness of STD treatment/IEC intervention trials on HIV incidence in rural East Africa.

Basia Zaba is a senior lecturer at the Centre for Population Studies, London School of Hygiene and Tropical Medicine. She has worked on demographic analysis of population

11

change in the Caribbean and on indirect estimation techniques, particularly in the field of migration, but her current interests focus largely on measurement and modelling of reproductive health in Africa and Asia. She chairs the IUSSP committee on AIDS, and the development of the micro-simulation modelling used in this book owes much to intense discussion with other committee members.

Introduction

J. Ties Boerma and Zaida Mgalla

Reproductive health is now high on the agenda of international and national health programmes. It spans a range of health and population programme areas, including family planning, safe motherhood, infertility, and control of sexually transmitted diseases (STDs) and HIV. The potential benefit of combining these population and health issues under the umbrella of reproductive health lies in the interrelationships among the interventions and their ultimate effect on health. For instance, family planning programmes that prevent unwanted pregnancy are also likely to improve maternal and child health. Promoting condom use prevents both unwanted pregnancy and STD or HIV infection. Programmes that are successful in addressing underlying gender issues are likely to benefit many areas of reproductive health. A broad intervention package to improve reproductive health as a whole may thus have a much greater effect than the sum of the effects of the individual packages.

This book examines an element of reproductive health that is often neglected: while infertility is common in sub-Saharan Africa, it has received only piecemeal attention in research and health programmes. The main reason is the lack of feasible, affordable and effective treatment interventions. In addition, population and health programmes in Africa have primarily been oriented towards high fertility and high rates of population growth. Why address infertility?

This book argues that infertility is a major public health problem as well as a human rights issue with far-reaching consequences for the individual, the couple and, to a lesser extent, the health system. Furthermore, infertility is intertwined with many other elements of reproductive health. We contend that it is a logical part of a reproductive health programme. The chapters discuss infertility from the standpoint of different disciplines, including demography, clinical medicine, epidemiology, anthropology and public health. They illustrate the linkages of infertility to sexual and marital behaviour, to STDs and HIV, to maternal health and to family planning, from these different disciplinary perspectives. In bringing this material together, our intention is to provide information and increase awareness about infertility within reproductive health and other women's health programmes.

Infertility is an all-pervasive issue for those who experience it; realizing its importance to women, men and families can facilitate treatment, mitigate the consequences of infertility and help the achievement of other reproductive health goals.

Measurement of infertility

A range of terms and definitions are used to describe and measure impaired fertility in women, men and couples by clinicians, epidemiologists, demographers and anthropologists.

In this volume the following terms are used:

- *Sterility:* inability to conceive or to impregnate. This term often implies complete and permanent inability to conceive.

- *Infertility:* inability to produce a live birth. This term captures inability to conceive, impregnate or carry a pregnancy to term and live birth. Women who conceive but have subsequent abortions (pregnancy wastage) are considered infertile, just as women who are unable to conceive. Distinction is made between primary (has never given birth) and secondary infertility (cannot give birth following at least one live birth).

- *Childlessness:* not having a living child. A woman may have given birth to at least one live child but all have died. In populations with high levels of child mortality, the difference between the prevalence of childlessness and primary infertility is not trivial. For instance, in 27 national Demographic and Health Surveys (DHS) in sub-Saharan Africa, the median proportion of women 35-49 years who never had a live birth was 3.0%, while 4.5% had no living child. Demographers often use the term 'childlessness' to refer to primary infertile women.

Measuring the prevalence of infertility is difficult because it focuses on women who are still in their reproductive age span (women may still deliver a child before their menopause) and because it requires a delineation of a period of exposure to the risk of pregnancy. For clinical-epidemiological purposes the WHO Scientific Working Group on the Epidemiology of Infertility defined infertility as the inability of a woman, man or couple to have a conception after a period of two years of exposure without conception (WHO, 1975). Most clinicians, however, use a 12-month period of unprotected intercourse (Rowe *et al.*, 1993). A distinction is also made between inability to conceive and inability to carry a pregnancy through to term and have a live child.

Most estimates of the prevalence of infertility rely on data collected in cross-sectional surveys. In such surveys birth histories are collected from female respondents aged 15-49 (only in a few cases from male respondents). Methods have been developed to estimate the prevalence of primary and secondary infertility from such incomplete birth histories, that is, from women who may still bear additional children (Larsen and Menken, 1989). The duration of the period of exposure to the risk of pregnancy since marriage or the last birth is set at five to seven years, depending on the measure being used. If no detailed birth history is available, the proportion of women with an open birth interval of five years or longer is often used as an indicator of secondary infertility (Larsen, 1996).

Extrapolations from survey data need to take contraceptive use into account. While some women who use contraceptives are infertile, contraceptive users are, on the whole, more likely to be fertile than non-contracepting women. In any case, as contraceptive use increases it will become increasingly difficult to estimate infertility from survey data. In most sub-Saharan African countries this problem is still not insurmountable, as shown by the analysis of Ulla Larsen and Hans Raggers in Chapter 1.

All of these factors increase the difficulty of estimating the magnitude of the problem of infertility in sub-Saharan Africa. Using Larsen and Raggers' estimates of primary infertility, we estimate that about three to four million women in sub-Saharan Africa are currently affected. As voluntary childlessness is rare in most of sub-Saharan Africa, this is also likely to reflect the number of women (and couples) who see this as a health and social problem. A larger number of women can be considered to have secondary infertility, probably more than 13 million women. The extent to which these women (and couples) perceive this as a health and social problem will be smaller than 13 million, because some of these women may have already achieved, at least in part, their desired level of fertility. Data from infertility clinics show that about 40% of the infertility cases are primary infertility, while 60% concern secondary infertility (Favot et al., 1997; Cates et al., 1985; Giwa-Osagie et al., 1984; Moutsinga, 1973). This suggests there are about five to six million women for whom the problem of not being able to bear another child is sufficiently serious to justify a visit to an infertility clinic. Based on these calculations, we estimate that eight to ten million women in sub-Saharan Africa are currently suffering from infertility.

The definition of infertility has considerable impact on estimates of the prevalence of infertility and thus on evaluations of the success rate of infertility treatment. Marchbanks et al., (1989) analysed five different definitions of infertility in the USA. Three measures were based on a questionnaire and two on a life-event calendar (including pregnancy, births, sexual exposure, contraceptive use, etc.). For couples reporting no conception after two years of trying to conceive, the prevalence of infertility was 12.5%. For those who had consulted a physician (and reported no conception after two years of trying to conceive) it was 9.6 per cent, and when based on a physician's diagnosis (with no conception after two years) prevalence was 6.1%. Much higher levels of infertility were found using measures based on life-events (which is more comparable to demographic methods of estimation): 20.6% if no conception had occurred after 24 months of unprotected intercourse and 32.6% if no conception had occurred after 12 months of unprotected intercourse. The study also showed significant differences in subsequent conception rates, depending upon the definition used. The Marchbanks et al. (1989) study suggests that better measurement of infertility may be achieved by asking more direct questions about the couple's desire for a pregnancy. For example, surveys might ask directly if a woman is currently trying to have a first or a subsequent child. In the World Fertility Survey (WFS) married women were asked about their ability to have another child with their husband if they wanted one. The results were not considered a good indicator of actual inability to bear children (Vaessen, 1984). To obtain better estimates of infertility from such surveys, it would be worthwhile to add a question about efforts to conceive. In Rakai, Uganda, results obtained by using this question appeared useful (Ron Gray, personal communication).

Who pays the price: women or men?

Infertility may be due to the woman, the man or both. However, the indicator of infertility of the couple is the woman, whether infertility is the result of female or male factors. In sub-Saharan Africa male infertility is likely to be a significant factor, although data are limited, as discussed by Philippe Mayaud in Chapter 2. Even so, anthropological and demographic studies indicate that the majority of 'visible' infertility is likely to be associated with female factors. Women who do not bear children are often divorced, have multiple, life-time partners, and are therefore apt to have sexual intercourse with fertile partners at some point in their lives. Three chapters discuss these issues: Marjolein Gijsels, Zaida Mgalla and Lilian Wambura, in Chapter 8, Zaida Mgalla and Ties Boerma, in Chapter 7 and Ties Boerma and Mark Urassa, in Chapter 6. The anthropological studies in Chapters 7, 8 and 9 also describe the coping mechanisms in place to circumvent male infertility without breaking up the marriage, assuring for example that a woman will become pregnant from another man without the knowledge of her husband.

There is ample evidence that infertile women are paying a heavy price for not being able to fulfil the reproductive expectations of their husband, family, clan and community at large. For example, in Chapter 8 Gijsels *et al.* employ life histories to document the misery of 'barren' women in northwest Tanzania, which included public derogation, beatings and divorce. The low social status of infertile women is also illustrated by the reports of group discussions with Tanzanian men and women in Chapter 7 by Mgalla and Boerma, the interviews with women in a rural community in western Tanzania (Roth, Chapter 9) and by interviews with infertile women and men in the Gambia and Zimbabwe, presented in Chapter 11 by Johanne Sundby and Aileen Jacobus.

Relationships with other elements of reproductive health

Sexual behaviour and marriage

Anthropological studies have described the changes in marriage and sexual behaviour among infertile couples and infertile men. A man or a woman may be more likely to have extra-marital partners if no children have been born. Studies in Sierra Leone (Harrell-Bond, 1975) and Uganda (Southwold, 1973) suggest that husbands of infertile wives often had extra-marital partners, although it is not immediately clear to what extent their sexual behaviour can be attributed to the infertility per se. As noted, several chapters describe the secret arrangements made to assure a woman becomes pregnant in the event of suspected male infertility. In most societies infertility is also an important reason for divorce (Chapter 8; Nabaitu *et al.*, 1994; Solivetti, 1994; Reyna, 1975), while in other societies men may add another wife to their infertile union (David and Voas, 1981; Pool, 1972).

A few epidemiological and demographic studies lend further evidence to the anthropological studies. In population-based surveys, infertility has been associated with greater marital instability in Cameroon and Nigeria and with polygyny in Cameroon (Larsen, 1995). In rural Tanzania, infertile women also had more sexual partners and more marriages than fertile women, and HIV prevalence among infertile women was three times higher than among fertile women (Chapter 6; Favot *et al.*, 1997). The association between HIV and infertility is largely due to a fertility-reducing effect of HIV, but may also partly be a consequence of behaviours associated with infertility.

Primary infertility was very common in the 1950s and earlier. In Chapter 4, Richard White, Basia Zaba, Ties Boerma and John Blacker show that the high prevalence of primary infertility is likely to have been associated with a very early onset of sexual intercourse, often prior to menarche. An increase in age at first sex and sexual mixing patterns may have contributed to the pronounced decline in primary infertility that can be observed from about the middle of the 20th century. Chapter 5 (Ulla Larsen) shows that in the heart of the infertility belt as well, in the Central African Republic, primary and secondary infertility have declined considerably, although levels are still considerably higher than in most other parts of Africa.

STD and HIV

Reproductive tract infections including STDs are common in many parts of sub-Saharan Africa. First ecological studies (e.g. Romaniuk, 1968; Arya *et al.*, 1980) and later clinical research (Cates *et al.*, 1985) demonstrated the prominent role of STDs in the etiology of female infertility (Chapter 2). Both gonorrhoea and chlamydia infection may lead to pelvic inflammatory disease (PID), which may lead to scarring of the tubes of the female reproductive system and subsequent infertility.

The review of data from the first half of the 20th century in Chapter 4 shows that a high prevalence of STDs, notably gonorrhoea, is the most likely cause of the very high levels of primary infertility several decades ago. Microsimulations and evidence from in-depth studies suggests that the dramatic decline in primary infertility has largely been due to the introduction of antibiotics.

Current efforts to improve STD case management practices in health facilities are likely to reduce the risk of infertility following an STD among those who make use of modern health facilities (Chapter 2). A significant proportion of patients, however, do not make use of these facilities. Instead they practice self-treatment, buy drugs in shops or pharmacies or visit traditional healers (Chapter 8). Among traditional healers, many may have specialized in STD care. This was the case in rural Tanzania, as discussed by Robert Pool and Ndatulu Robert Washija in Chapter 10. These healers also have some biomedical knowledge and appeared to be keen on better collaboration with the modern health sector.

Maternal health

According to the estimates by Larsen and Raggers in Chapter 1, secondary infertility is common. In part, this is due to increased biological infertility caused by the aging of the woman. However, the number of women with secondary infertility is well in excess of what would be expected on the basis of natural infertility levels observed in historical populations in Europe and the USA (Bongaarts and Potter, 1983). The main culprit appears to be postpartum infection, and, to a lesser extent, postabortal infection. Reproductive tract infections, mostly STDs, can easily lead to PID during the puerperal period (Chapter 2), though there are few studies to confirm this. Caesarian section can also lead to postpartum infection and subsequent infertility, as shown in a study in Zimbabwe discussed by Xavier de Muylder, Pierre Buekens and Bruno Dujardin in Chapter 3.

Family planning

As early as the 1950s, Anne Retel-Laurentin (1974) tried to draw attention to the link between the problem of infertility and the acceptability and success of family planning programmes. She argued that attention to the problem of infertility would enhance the acceptability of family planning programs to African populations, especially those with high levels of infertility. At present, even with the success of family planning programmes, adolescent girls are still concerned with infertility: the consequences of not being able to bear children are devastating. These concerns are demonstrated clearly in interviews with women (Chapter 9) and in focus group discussions in Tanzania where use of modern contraceptives is still low (Chapter 7).

Interventions

Infertile women report high levels of health services utilization (Chapter 11). For instance, women attending a hospital infertility clinic in Tanzania reported they had visited on average 2.7 different kinds of modern health facilities and 5.9 traditional healers in connection with their infertility (Favot *et al.*, 1997). In a rural community in Tanzania, more than half of traditional healers reported that they specialized in dealing with infertility problems (Chapter 10). As Sundby and Jacobus report from their Zimbabwe and Gambia studies, women with infertility problems often present themselves with several other complaints and leave without the health worker diagnosing the cause underlying the visit. Not infrequently, inappropriate interventions, such as dilatation and curettage are performed. Repeated visits to modern and traditional health facilities represent a cost to women, couples or families as well as to the health system.

Addressing infertility should be part of reproductive health programmes. This should include both preventing infertility by preventing STDs and the timely and adequate treatment of these diseases. In some cases it is feasible to treat infertility even with limited resources. Health workers need to be better equipped to deal with infertility, if only to avoid inappropriate interventions and improve their counselling skills. At the societal level, there is a need to address the social dimension and enhance discussion about infertility as a reproductive health and social problem. In some settings the establishment of local organizations of women with infertility, such as the 'Kanyaleng' in the Gambia, may help women to help themselves (Chapter 11).

Overview of the chapters

The idea of studying women and infertility in sub-Saharan Africa from a multi-disciplinary perspective originated within the Tanzania-Netherlands project to support AIDS control in Mwanza Region (TANESA). Several chapters in this book are based on research carried out in the context of the TANESA project. Other chapters are based on a wide range of studies in different parts of sub-Saharan Africa. Some include original materials, others original analyses of survey data or critical reviews of the available literature on the subject.

In Chapter 1, Larsen and Raggers present the largest compilation of national and sub-national data on infertility in sub-Saharan Africa to date. It uses a well-established methodology to estimate the prevalence of primary and secondary infertility from cross-sectional survey data. National estimates for 29 nations are presented, including age patterns and trends in infertility, based on data from 42 nationally representative surveys between 1977 and 1996. Wide variations in the prevalence of infertility (primary and secondary) in sub-Saharan Africa can be seen. The Central African countries of Cameroon, the Central African Republic and Chad have the highest levels of infertility, while the East African countries of Burundi and Rwanda, as well as the West African country of Togo, have the lowest levels. For instance, at ages 30-34 the rate of infertility is 37% in the Central African Republic and 9% in Rwanda. In contrast to the relatively high prevalence of age-specific infertility documented beyond age 30 in each of the African countries analysed, primary infertility is relatively low in most of these countries. Indeed, the recent survey of countries with multiple surveys indicates that it is 3% or less in 18 of the 29 countries analysed. Most African women who become infertile from pathological causes do so after they have had at least one child. Even within countries infertility tends to vary greatly, with urban areas having higher levels than rural areas; some regions may have much higher levels. There is also a substantial effect of infertility on the total fertility level in many countries. In about half of the countries, the 'depressing' effect of the high prevalence of infertility on fertility exceeds one child per women.

Philippe Mayaud (Chapter 2) extensively reviews known etiological factors in male and female infertility in sub-Saharan Africa. Although a wide variety of conditions can cause infertility, evidence shows that the problem of female infertility in Africa is largely a consequence of tubal blockage, often caused by PID. Infertility in sub-Saharan Africa is often a consequence of many preventable factors resulting from neglected or improperly treated sexually transmitted infections in both men and women, as well as poorly performed medical interventions such as abortions, caesarean sections, deliveries or IUD insertions. Mayaud argues that greater emphasis should be placed on the adequate control of sexually transmitted infections (primary and secondary prevention) and the improvement of general gynaecological and obstetrical practices (primary and secondary prevention); such interventions should lead to a reduction in the incidence of infertility.

More research is needed on the role of postpartum infections in infertility, including the role of medical interventions on poor obstetric or postpartum care. Using a case control methodology in a hospital study in Zimbabwe, de Muylder, Buekens and Dujardin (Chapter 3) compare the rate of previous caesarean section among women with secondary infertility with a matched control group of fertile women. The results suggest that caesarean section can have a deleterious effect upon future fertility, and indicate the need for prophylactic measures.

In Chapter 4, White, Zaba, Boerma and Blacker describe historical trends in primary infertility and use a microsimulation analysis to assess the relative importance of factors that have contributed to a decline. The microsimulation model shows that the prevalence of sexually transmitted disease is the major causal factor for high levels of infertility in the past, in combination with early onset of sexual activity, not infrequently before the menarche. The introduction and use of antibiotics from the early 1950s onwards is likely to have been the main factor in the decline of primary infertility. In fact, there are relatively few examples in medical history of such a dramatic health effect of a medical intervention. In some populations, as in Zanzibar, the decline in primary infertility seems to have preceded the introduction of antibiotics. This decline may have been the result of changes in sexual behaviour leading to a reduction in STDs or epidemiological adaptation.

It is now forty years since Anne Retel-Laurentin undertook her groundbreaking studies on the very high levels of infertility in the eastern parts of Central African Republic. Larsen analyses data from the 1994-1995 DHS in Central African Republic in Chapter 5 to show that, even though infertility levels appear to be lower than in the 1950s, infertility is still higher than in all other African countries. Only Cameroon has similar levels of infertility. Primary infertility, measured by the 'percentage childless' after at least seven years of marriage, reaches 6%, and the 'percentage subsequently infertile' increases gradually with age from 18% at age 20-24 to 39% at age 30-34 and 78% at age 40-44 in Central African Republic. Infertility is more common in certain regions and among specific ethnic groups. There is also evidence of an association between infertility and multiple marriages as well as earlier onset of sexual intercourse, but not with the practice of female circumcision.

Using data from a cohort study in a rural area in northwest Tanzania, Boerma and Urassa examine the complex association between fertility status and HIV infection, marital instability and multiple sexual relationships (Chapter 6). HIV infection rates among infertile women were about three times higher than among fertile women. These results further corroborate the evidence of decreased fertility among HIV infected women, who in this study had only half the fertility of HIV-negative women. Part of the fertility difference may be due to infertility prior to HIV infection, as women with low fertility are more likely to divorce and may have more sexual partners. The effect of lower fertility on HIV incidence was, however, fairly small in this study population.

Qualitative research can provide insights into the consequences of infertility for women, men and couples. Four chapters deal with aspects of infertility among the Sukuma of Tanzania: three studies in Mwanza Region and one in Shinyanga Region. In Chapter 7, Mgalla and Boerma explore group discussions with men and women of different ages and backgrounds, in which a number of competing and complementary discourses about infertility are given. Traditional explanations easily blended with biomedical knowledge, as became clear when infertility was discussed as a possible side effect of modern contraceptives. The group discussions also revealed substantial gender differences in attitudes towards infertility, and particularly its consequences. Even though there is considerable awareness of the existence of male infertility, the consequences of the inability to have children are generally borne by women. This study points up the strong negative attitudes towards infertility, which perpetuate social injustice toward infertile women.

Gijsels, Mgalla and Wambura (Chapter 8) use life histories of infertile women in northwest Tanzania to describe the socio-cultural context of infertility and the impact of infertility on individual women's lives. The life histories illustrate the high value of children, the low social status of infertile women and how infertile women are discriminated against. The discrimination is greater if the woman is barren than if she has secondary infertility. Divorce, neglect by the husband, withdrawal of economic support and rejection by the husband's kin were common features of the life histories of the Tanzanian women.

Roth delineates the contextual issues related to fertility concerns in a small rural community in west-central Tanzania in Chapter 9. Women are concerned with their reproductive health, especially any risk to their ability to bear children. Interviews with women and a local traditional healer displayed a wide range of physical and spiritual risks to their reproductive health. Most of these conditions have no simple biomedical equivalent; women seek help from both traditional and modern health services to prevent and heal such conditions.

Pool and Washija focus specifically on traditional healers, STDs and infertility in Chapter 10. They found that, in spite of certain generalized misconceptions, knowledge of STDs and infertility was relatively high among traditional healers, particularly regarding etiology and prevention. Most traditional healers said they were keen on some form of collaboration with the modern health sector and incorporated aspects of biomedical knowledge into their own treatment practices. The number of traditional healers far exceeded modern health facilities in the study area, and healers were the most common source for the treatment of STDs and infertility. Almost one-fifth of the healers specialized in infertility and the causes of infertility they cited were very similar to those listed in Chapter 9.

While several of the previous chapters outline options that can be used to prevent infertility, Sundby and Jacobus discuss ways in which modern and traditional health services can mitigate its consequences, or possibly offer treatment (Chapter 11). They use data from the Gambia and Zimbabwe to assess the barriers women and men face in seeking health care for infertility. They also consider the infertility services that are practical at various levels of the health care system. They argue that a better understanding of constraints on care seeking and of the emotional and social needs of client's infertility, combined with better knowledge of appropriate infertility interventions, may improve infertility care even in resource-poor settings.

In summary, infertility is a substantial public health problem in sub-Saharan Africa, with an estimated 8-10 million women being affected. The significant social stigma attached to infertility strongly affects the lives of both the women and their partners. However, a great deal can be done. We can help prevent reproductive tract infections, particularly STDs, through sexual health education and promotion of condoms. We can reduce the consequences and spread of such infections by accessible, timely and effective treatment. We can provide low-cost treatment for infertile women and couples, even though success rates are likely to be low. We can mitigate the consequences of infertility for those who cannot be treated, by improving counselling and by addressing the issue of infertility in society at large. If we neglect female infertility, then we fail to address the full potential of reproductive health for women.

Bibliography

Arya OP, Taber SR and Nsanze H (1980), 'Gonorrhoea and female infertility in rural Uganda'. *American Journal of Obstetrics and Gynecology* 138: 929-32.

Bongaarts J and Potter RG (1983), *Fertility, biology and behaviour: an analysis of the proximate determinants*, Academic Press, New York.

Cates W, Farley TMM and Rowe PJ (1985), 'Worldwide patterns of infertility: is Africa different?' *Lancet* ii: 596-9.

David N and Voas D (1981), 'Societal causes of infertility and population decline among the settled Fulani of North Cameroon'. *MAN* 16: 644-64.

Favot I, Ngalula J, Mgalla Z, Klokke AH, Gumodoka B and Boerma JT (1997), 'HIV infection and sexual behaviour among women with infertility in Tanzania: a hospital-based study'. *International Journal of Epidemiology* 26: 414-9.

Giwa-Osagie OF, Ogunyemi D, Emuveyan EE and Akinla OA (1984), 'Etiologic classification of infertility in 250 couples'. *International Journal of Infertility* 29: 104-108.

Harrell-Bond BE (1975), *Modern marriage in Sierra Leone: a study of the professional group*, Mouton and Co., the Hague.

Hughes EC (ed.) (1972), *Obstetrics/gynecology terminology*, FA Davis Company, Philadelphia.

Larsen U (1995), 'Differentials in infertility in Cameroon and Nigeria'. *Population Studies* 48: 459-74.

Larsen U (1996), 'Childlessness, subfertility and infertility in Tanzania'. *Studies in Family Planning* 27: 18-28.

Larsen U and Menken J (1989), 'Measuring sterility from incomplete birth histories'. *Demography* 26: 185-201.

Marchbanks PA, Peterson HB, Rubin GL and Wingo PA (1989), 'Research on infertility: definition makes a difference'. *American Journal of Epidemiology* 130: 259-267.

Moutsinga H (1973), 'La sterilite feminine au Gabon en consultation gynecologique journaliere'. *Medicin d'Afrique Noire* 20: 103-109.

Nabaitu J, Bachengana C and Selley J (1994), 'Marital instability in a rural population in South-west Uganda: implications for the spread of HIV-1 infection'. *Africa* 64: 243-51.

Pool JE (1972), 'A cross-comparative study of aspects of conjugal behavior among women of 3 West African countries'. *Canadian Journal of African Studies* 6: 233-59.

Programme of Action of the 1994 International Conference on Population and Development (ICPD) (1995) (Chs I-VIII). *Population and Development Review* 21:187-213.

Retel-Laurentin A (1974), *Infécondité en Afrique noire: maladies et consequences sociales*, Masson et Co., Paris.

Reyna SP (1975), 'Age differential, marital instability, and venereal disease: factors affecting fertility among the Northwest Barma'. In: Nag M (ed.), *Population and social organization*, Mouton and Co., the Hague: 55-73.

Romaniuk A (1968), 'Infertility in tropical Africa'. In: Caldwell JC and Okonjo C (eds), *The population of tropical Africa*, Longmans, London: 214-24.

Rowe PJ, Comhaire FH, Hargreave TB and Mellows HJ (1993), *WHO manual for the standardized investigation and diagnosis of the infertile couple*, Cambridge University Press, Cambridge.

Solivetti LM (1994), 'Family, marriage and divorce in a Hausa community: a sociological model'. *Africa* 64: 252-71.

Southwold M (1973), 'The Baganda of Central Africa'. In: Molnos A (ed.), *Cultural source material for population planning in East Africa: Volume III, beliefs and practices*, East African Publishing House, Nairobi, Kenya: 163-73.

Vaessen M (1984), 'Childlessness and infecundity'. *WFS Scientific Studies No. 31*, International Statistical Institute, Voorburg, the Netherlands.

World Health Organization (1975), The Epidemiology of Infertility, Report of a scientific working group, Technical Report Series no. 582, Geneva.

Namji doll to be worn touching the belly (and fed) to induce pregnancy (Namji or Dawayo, Nigeria/Cameroon border)

1 Levels and trends in infertility in sub-Saharan Africa

Ulla Larsen and Han Raggers

The World Health Organization (WHO) has repeatedly called for research on infertility in Africa (WHO Technical Report Series, 1969 and 1975; WHO, 1988, 1992, 1994). From 1978 to 1985 WHO directed a worldwide clinical study to provide a standard approach for the investigation of infertile couples (WHO, 1987). This study found that infections from sexually transmitted diseases (STD), following either a childbirth or an abortion, were the major causes of infertility in sub-Saharan Africa (Cates et al., 1985). Couples were defined as 'infertile' if they had not conceived after more than one year of unprotected sexual activity. It is well known, however, that this medical definition of infertility is not very specific. That is, a substantial fraction of couples who are defined as 'infertile' because they have not conceived after one year of unprotected intercourse go on to have a live-birth without ever receiving any treatment (Collins et al., 1983). Thus, this medical definition will lead to higher estimates of infertility than would be obtained using a demographic definition (Menken et al., 1986). Furthermore, this WHO clinical study was based on a selective sample: it was unlikely that all infertile couples in the community would have sought clinical treatment; also, only couples with both partners diagnosed were enrolled in the study. Thus, inferences about the level, age pattern and trend of infertility in the community at large cannot be made from the WHO study. Another limitation is that this study of 'Africa' was actually confined to the four cities of Ibadan (Nigeria), Lusaka (Zambia), Nairobi (Kenya) and Yaounde (Cameroon).

No previous study has provided estimates of the prevalence of secondary infertility in sizeable areas of sub-Saharan Africa. A recent study of 17 sub-Saharan African countries found infertility (primary and secondary) to be prevalent in each country (Larsen, 1994). Only one of these countries, Cameroon, was located in Central Africa in the area traditionally referred to as the 'infertility belt', and the information on it was based on survey data collected in 1991 or earlier. Larsen (1994) showed that the prevalence of infertility spans a wide geographical area in sub-Saharan Africa, and that Cameroon exhibits the highest prevalence and Burundi the lowest. For example, at age 30 to 34, the proportion of people subsequently infertile reaches 41% in Cameroon and 11% in Burundi (Larsen, 1994). The reason for the low level of infertility found in Burundi is not well understood.

Ericksen and Brunette (1996) investigated infertility in 26 African countries. This study approximated infertility from the proportion of women with an open birth interval of five years, and the proportion of women with an open birth interval of seven years. They calculated two open birth interval measures to evaluate the impact of misplacement of the last birth on their proxy measure of infertility. However, it is well known that open birth interval measures do not capture the true proportion of people who are infertile (Larsen and Menken, 1989). These measures are sensitive to variations in other reproductive characteristics, to the chosen length of the open interval, e.g. whether it is set to five or seven years, and to sample size. Ericksen and Brunette (1996) presented one open birth interval estimate for all age groups, and hence no information about the age pattern of infertility was provided. Finally, they did not take into account the bias from contraception on estimates of infertility, and, therefore, falsely concluded that infertility is particularly prevalent in Zimbabwe and Botswana.

It is essential to estimate infertility both at the country and the regional level, and also by ethnic group across countries, because there is strong evidence to suggest that infertility is a local problem (Henin, 1982; Retel-Laurentin, 1974). For instance, in Kenya in the 1977/78 World Fertility Survey (WFS) the proportion subsequently infertile at age 35-39 reached 0.51 in the Coast region compared with 0.11 in the central region (Larsen, 1993). It is believed that infertility is particularly high in the Coast region because of the relatively high prevalence of STDs (e.g. gonorrhoea and chlamydia infection). In general, infertility appears to be particularly prevalent in the areas invaded in the 19th century by Arab slave traders, who are thought to have spread STDs (Romaniuk, 1968). Data about the prevalence of STDs in the community are not available, but it may be very useful to determine whether regional patterns of infertility follow hypothesized regional patterns of STDs. (For further details on Uganda, see Arya *et al.*, 1973, 1980 and Hunt, 1989; on Tanzania, see Henin, 1982). Knowledge about the regional distribution of infertility may facilitate more cost-effective campaigns aimed at preventing and treating infertility of pathological origin.

There is evidence that infertility decreased during the 1980s in Cameroon, Nigeria and Sudan, while remaining at about the same level in Ghana, Kenya and Senegal (a WFS from around 1980 and a Demographic Health Survey (DHS), from around 1990 were available for these six countries only; Larsen, 1994, 1995b). However, estimates of infertility from the 1989 DHS survey in Kenya were biased by contraceptive use among respondents, so that further analysis is needed to determine the trend of infertility in that country. In the present study the analysis of infertility in Kenya focuses on the issue of estimating infertility in the presence of substantial contraceptive use, i.e., the current use of modern contraceptives was estimated at 27% in the 1993 DHS survey. Contraceptive use has increased in numerous sub-Saharan African countries, and the bias this contributes to estimates of infertility is evaluated for each country analysed. The trend in infertility over time is assessed for each country with figures available from two or more nationally representative demographic surveys.

In the next decade, the resources spent on preventing HIV/AIDS and improving reproductive health should result in a reduction of STDs and hence a decline in infertility (e.g. Mayaud, Chapter 2; White *et al.* Chapter 4). Further extensions of medical services and preventive medicine might also indirectly lead to a decline in infertility. Such changes may be achieved in particular through a reduction in the incidence and prevalence of pelvic inflammatory disease (PID). There is evidence to suggest that the greater availability of penicillin has reduced childlessness in Zaire (Tabutin, 1982). An even more rapid rate of population growth may result. The effect of reductions in infertility on the fertility rate can be illustrated as follows: if infertility in Cameroon in the 1970s were lowered to the level found in Burundi in the 1980s (assuming that everything else remained the same), then the total fertility rate for women aged 20-44 in Cameroon would increase from 5.3 to 7.4 (Larsen, 1994). Thus, the prevalence of infertility in certain areas of sub-Saharan Africa, and the effective prevention or treatment of infertility are complex issues. Here we propose to assess the extent to which infertility suppresses fertility in sub-Saharan Africa.

Methods

Infertility can be due to the woman, the man or the couple as a unit (Sherris and Fox, 1983). However, it is usually not feasible to identify the source of the infertility from nationally representative surveys. Most demographic work on infertility has been based on data collected from women, and infertility of the couple has been inferred from the evidence of women's birth experiences (see, for example, Larsen, 1994; Larsen and Menken, 1989). In this chapter we will follow the tradition of inferring the couple's infertility from information concerning the birth histories of the women. Infertility is defined as the inability of a non-contracepting sexually active woman to have a live birth. Primary infertility describes infertility of women who have never had a live birth, and secondary infertility denotes infertility of women who have had at least one child (Pressat and Wilson, 1985).

Estimates of infertility are confined to ever-married women to increase the chance that all women investigated are in a union where regular sexual activity occurs. Onset of exposure is set at the month of entry into first marriage, and the end of exposure is set at the month of the survey or the month when sex last took place, whichever occurred first. Estimates of infertility are not sensitive to the age at initiation of sexual relations (Larsen and Menken, 1989). To ensure that most women engage in regular sexual intercourse, onset of exposure is set at the month of first marriage, instead of the month of first sexual act, although we recognize that month of marriage is not a well-defined concept in the sub-Saharan African context. The WFS surveys do not contain information about the month of last sex, and for these surveys exposure ends at the month of interview. To minimize the chance of classifying a woman who is not sexually active as infertile, we excluded from the WFS survey data all the women who reported that they practised terminal abstinence. The analysis is not restricted to currently married women because infertile women are more likely to be separated or divorced (Larsen, 1995a).

The level and age pattern of infertility (primary and secondary) are estimated using the 'subsequently infertile' estimator (Larsen and Menken, 1989). This measure provides age-specific estimates of infertility from incomplete birth histories. It uses all information available for a woman until she is of an age equal to her age at the time of censoring minus five. These last five years are used to determine her status (infertile or fertile) at the last observation five years before the censoring. She is considered infertile at the last observation if she has had no live births during these five years; otherwise she is considered fertile. A woman who has not given birth at age a or later is defined as being 'infertile subsequent to age a'. The index of the proportion subsequently infertile at age a is estimated as the number of women infertile subsequent to age a, divided by the total number of women observed at that age. All estimates are based on monthly dates, and sample weights are used in the calculations of infertility. The proportion subsequently infertile cannot be interpreted as being the true proportion sterile at the age at which the calculation was made. To estimate sterility an age correction is required, as discussed by Larsen and Menken (1989, 1991). Because taking the next step, estimating sterility from information about subsequent infertility, introduces an extra error, the present analysis is aimed at the analysis of infertility, and no age correction is made.

Secondary infertility is measured using the 'subsequently infertile' estimator based on women with at least one child. Primary infertility is measured by the proportion childless among women who entered their first marriage at least seven years before the end of exposure. Estimates of childlessness require at least seven years of exposure, otherwise they are sensitive to variations in fecundability (Larsen and Menken, 1989).

Data

The analysis is based on the following nationally representative surveys: the 1982 WFS and the 1996 DHS in Benin; the 1988 DHS in Botswana; the 1993 DHS in Burkina Faso; the 1987 DHS in Burundi; the 1978 WFS and the 1991 DHS in Cameroon; the 1994/1995 DHS in Central African Republic; the 1996/97 DHS in Chad; the 1996 DHS in Comoros; the 1980 WFS and the 1994 DHS in Côte d'Ivoire; the 1979 WFS, the 1988 and 1993 DHS in Ghana; the 1977/1978 WFS, the 1989 and 1993 DHS in Kenya; the 1977 WFS in Lesotho; the 1986 DHS in Liberia; the 1992 DHS in Madagascar; the 1992 DHS in Malawi; the 1987 and 1995/1996 DHS in Mali; the 1982 WFS in Mauretania; the 1997 DHS in Mozambique; the 1992 DHS in Namibia; the 1992 DHS in Niger; the 1981 WFS and the 1990 DHS in Nigeria and the 1986/1987 DHS in Ondo State; the 1983 WFS and the 1992 DHS in Rwanda; the 1978 WFS, the 1986 and 1992/1993 DHS in Senegal; the 1978 WFS and the 1989/1990 DHS in Sudan; the 1991/1992 and 1996 DHS in Tanzania; the 1988 DHS in Togo; the 1988/1989 and 1995 DHS in Uganda; the 1992 DHS in Zambia; and the 1988 and 1994 DHS in Zimbabwe (Demographic and Health Surveys, 1999; World Fertility Survey, 1984). Each of the WFS and DHS surveys contains complete birth histories, as well as information on the respondent's age and birth date, contraceptive use, marriage and cohabitation, and socioeconomic characteristics (Demographic and Health Surveys, 1999).

Analyses of DHS data quality associated with the preparation of the individual country reports demonstrate consistent and reliable reporting (for further detail, see the respective country reports listed above). A further assessment of the DHS-I data quality concluded that the birth history data were flawed, but the probable effects on fertility were minimal (Demographic and Health Surveys, 1990). For instance, it appeared that interviewers tended to misrecord the birth dates of some children to avoid asking the health questions (which are limited to births born within five years of the survey date). The extent of this problem of birth displacement is fairly minor. It rarely results in women being falsely classified as infertile. Birth dates from the more recent DHS-III should suffer less from the problem of displacement (Demographic and Health Surveys, 1990, 1994, 1996).

Information about women's ages and the birth dates of their children is less complete in the WFS than in the DHS surveys, i.e., more monthly dates are imputed, and there is concern about displacements of births to older women. In spite of some deficiencies, the WFS data are deemed reasonably accurate (World Fertility Survey, 1984) and were the most detailed, nationally representative, reproductive data collected in the late 1970s and early 1980s in sub-Saharan Africa. Information from the WFS and DHS surveys is comparable, enabling a comparative study of the level and age pattern of infertility in 29 countries and trend analyses of the data from the 13 countries that have conducted two or more surveys.

The thrust of this analysis concerns infertility of young and middle-aged women, i.e., women aged 25 to 49 years. Estimates of infertility rely on information about only the month or year of the last birth (or of marriage, if childless), the age of the woman and the date of her first marriage. Most women had their most recent child relatively close to the date of interview, which reduces the risk of an erroneous response. Furthermore, the interpretation of the results focuses more on directions and relative levels of infertility than on the actual values of the infertility estimates. For instance, data about childlessness are known to be particularly inaccurate. In sub-Saharan Africa, having children is very highly valued; barren women tend to hide their childlessness. Thus, childless women may avoid being interviewed, report 'Don't Know' to questions about children ever born or fail to distinguish between bearing and rearing children. Therefore, infertility estimates from 'childlessness' may be underestimated; these estimates provide merely the lower bounds of primary infertility. We emphasize that childlessness estimates are only rough summary statistics, so they should be interpreted with great caution (for a discussion of this problem, see Larsen, 1994).

Results

Potential bias from contraceptive use

As a first step, the potential bias in infertility estimates from contraception was ascertained. Information about the prevalence of contraception, as well as the type of method used, was available but there were usually no data about the duration of contraceptive use during the open birth interval. Therefore, we cannot distinguish the women who were infertile due to pathological causes from those contraceptive users who had successfully prevented a birth for more than five years. Consequently, estimates of infertility may be biased. In a simulation study, Larsen (1994) examined a number of different patterns of contraceptive use and their effects on infertility estimates. In general, the simulation results suggested, as expected, that estimates of infertility are much less sensitive to contraceptive spacing than to contraceptive stopping behaviour. The present study captures the range of bias in infertility estimates due to contraception by calculating lower and upper bound estimates of infertility. More specifically, we assumed that all current users of a modern contraceptive were fertile at the time of interview; a lower bound infertility estimate was thus obtained, because some contraceptors might have been infertile. Next, by ignoring the use of contraception, an upper bound estimate of infertility was obtained, because some effective contraceptors might have been falsely classified as infertile. The discrepancy between the lower and the upper bound estimates was examined to assess the countries where contraceptive use biases estimates of infertility. Table 1 presents age-specific estimates of infertility by country, as measured by the per cent subsequently infertile.[1] Modified infertility estimates, where all users of a modern contraceptive are considered fertile at date of interview, are presented in parentheses. We also calculated modified infertility estimates, in which all users of a contraceptive (whether a modern or a traditional method) were considered fertile at interview. There was no substantial difference between the estimates obtained when all users are included and the estimates obtained by classifying only modern contraceptive users as fertile at interview.

Table 1 Per cent infertility in women by age, based on the 'subsequently infertile' estimator[a]

Country, survey date	Age (years)						
	20-24	25-29	30-34	35-39	40-44	20-44	Sample size[b]
Benin 1982[c]	7 (7)	14 (14)	27 (27)	45 (45)	72 (72)	18 (18)	1,173
Benin 1996	4 (4)	8 (8)	18 (18)	40 (39)	66 (63)	13 (13)	3,107
Botswana 1988	8(6)	13(10)	25(18)	41(29)	56(47)	17(13)	1,063
Burkina Faso 1993	5 (5)	9 (9)	16 (15)	35 (34)	67 (66)	12 (12)	3,427
Burundi 1987	4 (4)	6 (6)	10 (10)	24 (24)	41 (41)	8 (8)	1,501
Cameroon 1978	20 (20)	29 (29)	42 (42)	54 (54)	68 (68)	31 (31)	4,204
Cameroon 1991	15 (14)	23 (22)	35 (33)	53 (50)	75 (73)	25 (24)	1,920
CAR[d] 1994/1995	17 (17)	26 (25)	38 (37)	55 (54)	76 (75)	29 (28)	3,138
Chad 1996/97	8 (8)	15(15)	27 (27)	51 (51)	78 (78)	18 (18)	4,121
Comoros 1996	11 (10)	17 (15)	28 (24)	45 (40)	68 (62)	21 (19)	1,361
Côte d'Ivoire 1980	10 (10)	15 (15)	25 (25)	40 (40)	62 (62)	18 (18)	2,775
Côte d'Ivoire 1994	9 (9)	15 (15)	26 (25)	43 (41)	66 (64)	19 (18)	3,952
Ghana 1979	7 (7)	11 (11)	20 (20)	38 (37)	64 (62)	15 (15)	3,225
Ghana 1988	5 (4)	8 (7)	16 (14)	32 (28)	51 (45)	10 (9)	1,633
Ghana 1993	7 (7)	13 (12)	23 (21)	41 (38)	62 (59)	16 (15)	2,656
Kenya 1977/1978	7 (7)	10 (10)	17 (16)	30 (29)	55 (53)	13 (13)	4,139
Kenya 1989	6 (5)	10 (8)	18 (14)	34 (26)	71 (59)	12 (9)	2,518
Kenya 1993	6 (5)	12 (9)	24 (17)	45 (32)	65 (52)	16 (12)	3,628
Lesotho 1977	13 (13)	23 (22)	35 (35)	53 (53)	76 (75)	27 (27)	2,149
Liberia 1986	10 (10)	16 (15)	26 (24)	39 (35)	52 (47)	18 (17)	2,229
Madagascar 1992	12 (12)	19 (18)	30 (28)	48 (45)	77 (74)	22 (21)	3,004
Malawi 1992	8 (8)	13 (13)	24 (23)	39 (37)	61 (59)	18 (17)	2,626
Mali 1987	7 (7)	14 (14)	20 (19)	35 (35)	53 (53)	14 (14)	1,434
Mali 1995/1996	7 (7)	11 (11)	19 (19)	39 (37)	70 (69)	15 (14)	5,869
Mauretania 1982	10 (10)	19 (19)	33 (33)	53 (52)	68 (68)	22 (22)	2,112
Mozambique 1997	11 (11)	20 (19)	33 (31)	51 (47)	73 (69)	23 (22)	4,621
Namibia 1992	8 (7)	16 (12)	27 (18)	43 (31)	68 (53)	22 (16)	1,856
Niger 1992	9 (9)	15 (15)	25 (25)	42 (41)	63 (62)	17 (17)	3,675
Nigeria 1981	12 (12)	21 (21)	35 (34)	50 (50)	71 (70)	23 (22)	5,234
Nigeria 1990	9 (9)	14 (13)	27 (26)	42 (40)	65 (63)	17 (17)	4,864
Ondo State 1986/1987	1 (1)	3 (3)	6 (5)	11 (10)	36 (34)	4 (3)	1,513
Rwanda 1983	3 (3)	5 (5)	12 (12)	26 (26)	50 (50)	9 (9)	2,856
Rwanda 1992	2 (2)	5 (4)	9 (9)	21 (20)	49 (46)	7 (7)	3,215
Senegal 1978	10 (10)	15 (15)	25 (25)	41 (41)	65 (65)	19 (19)	2,158
Senegal 1986	9 (9)	14 (14)	23 (22)	38 (38)	65 (63)	17 (17)	2,390
Senegal 1992/1993	7 (6)	12 (11)	21 (20)	38 (36)	64 (62)	15 (14)	3,314
Sudan 1978	11 (11)	19 (18)	33 (32)	52 (51)	72 (72)	21 (21)	2,213
Sudan 1989/1990	8 (7)	15 (14)	28 (27)	51 (49)	76 (74)	18 (18)	3,093
Tanzania 1991/1992	9 (8)	15 (14)	25 (23)	45 (42)	67 (63)	19 (18)	4,593
Tanzania 1996	9 (8)	14 (13)	23 (20)	41 (35)	66 (61)	18 (16)	3,914
Togo 1988	3 (3)	6 (5)	9 (8)	20 (19)	47 (46)	7 (6)	1,189
Uganda 1988/1989	11 (10)	15 (14)	23 (21)	41 (40)	70 (68)	17 (16)	1,598

Table 1, Continued

Country, survey date	Age (years)						
	20-24	25-29	30-34	35-39	40-44	20-44	Sample size[b]
Uganda 1995	9 (9)	13 (12)	22 (21)	41 (37)	64 (61)	16 (15)	3,098
Zambia 1992	8 (8)	13 (12)	21 (18)	37 (34)	64 (60)	16 (15)	3,381
Zimbabwe 1988	7 (6)	12 (10)	22 (17)	40 (31)	67 (55)	15 (13)	1,682
Zimbabwe 1994	9 (7)	15 (12)	26 (20)	47 (36)	72 (61)	19 (15)	3,005

[a] Estimates assuming all current users of a modern contraceptive are fertile at interview are shown in parentheses
[b] Unweighted
[c] Incomplete data set
[d] CAR = Central African Republic

Table 1 shows a discernible difference between the minimum and the maximum estimate of infertility in a number of countries, confirming that analyses of infertility need to consider the bias due to contraception. For example, in Kenya at age 35-39, the proportion subsequently infertile ranges from 0.29 to 0.30 in the 1977/1978 WFS, from 0.26 to 0.34 in the 1989 DHS and from 0.32 to 0.45 in the 1993 DHS. Thus contraception had a negligible effect on infertility estimates in the 1977/1978 WFS, a moderate effect on estimates in the 1989 DHS and a quite substantial effect on the 1993 DHS estimates. Obviously, the increased effects of contraception on estimates of infertility are due to the rapid rise in contraceptive prevalence in Kenya, e.g., the per cent of married women currently using a modern method rose from 4% to 18% to 27% in the 1977/1978 WFS, the 1989 DHS and the 1993 DHS data, respectively. The countries where contraception has the greatest impact on infertility estimates include Botswana, Comoros, Ghana, Kenya, Liberia, Namibia, Tanzania and Zimbabwe. These are countries where the prevalence of modern contraceptive methods among currently married women exceeds 10%. It is not possible to circumvent the bias due to contraception on infertility estimates by restricting the analysis to women who have never used contraception: in effect such women are selected for lower fertility and higher infertility (Larsen, Chapter 5).

Levels and age patterns

Figure 1 shows age-specific rates of infertility for the countries analysed to suggest the general pattern. The estimates presented are the lower bound estimates, where all current users of a modern method are considered fertile at interview. The most recent estimates are presented for the countries which have had more than one survey. The prevalence of infertility falls within a relatively wide range, being high in the Central African countries of Cameroon and Central African Republic, and low in the East African countries of Rwanda and Burundi and the West African country of Togo. For example, at age 35-39, the percentage infertile is 20 in Rwanda and 54 in Central African Republic. The age pattern of infertility varies also quite markedly between the countries analysed. For instance, in Burkina Faso infertility is relatively low up to age 35 years and increases quite rapidly at older ages, while in Liberia infertility is relatively high in people in their 20s but increases modestly in people in their 30s and 40s.

Figure 1   Age specific rates of infertility in the countries analysed

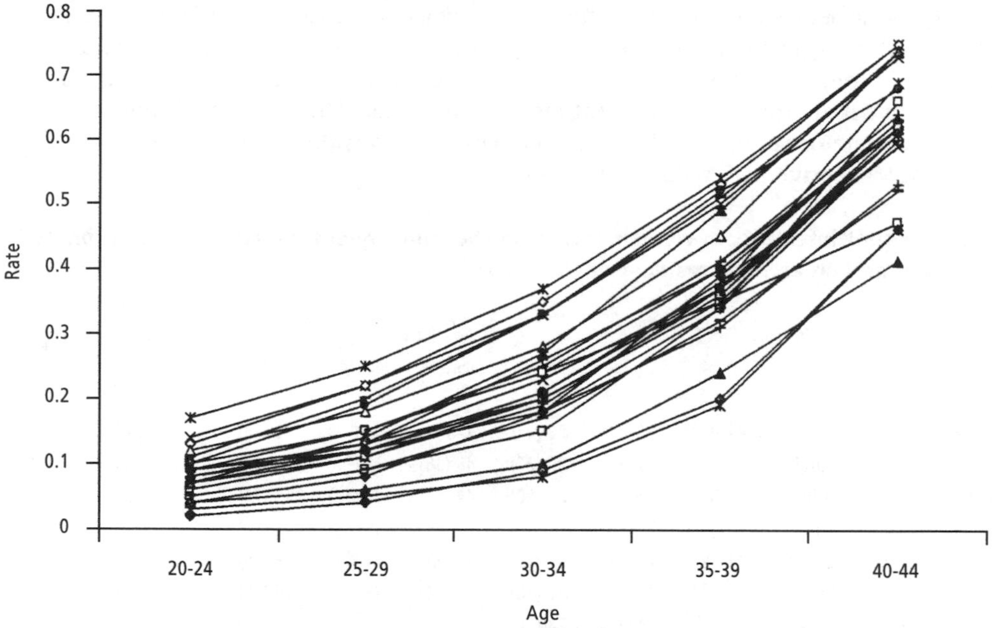

Trend in infertility

Inferences about the trend in infertility are made from estimates in which all modern contraceptive users are considered fertile at interview (Table 1). Hence, the decline in infertility may be overstated, because some contraceptors might be infertile: if this is the case, the estimates of infertility are apt to be too low. This bias is probably greater at the later survey dates, due to a general increase in contraceptive prevalence. The prevalence of infertility declined in eight countries (Benin, Cameroon, Nigeria, Rwanda, Senegal, Sudan, Tanzania and Uganda), it remained at about the same level in two countries (Côte d'Ivoire and Mali) and it increased in three countries (Ghana, Kenya and Zimbabwe). In Ghana and Kenya infertility declined from the early 1970s to the early 1980s and then increased to the late 1980s. The reader should recall that the infertility estimates are based on birth history data up to five years before survey date; if the survey was conducted in 1993, the estimates of the prevalence of infertility refer to 1988 and earlier. The increase in infertility in Ghana, Kenya and Zimbabwe is so substantial that it is presumably real, and not an artifact of erroneous reporting. Also, the number of cases analysed is great enough that the findings are not likely to be due to random fluctuations. Countries that show a trend towards declining infertility are located in both East and West Africa, as are the countries that show increases.

Differentials in infertility by urban and rural residence and by region

Infertility is more prevalent in urban than rural areas in the vast majority of countries analysed (Table 2), probably because of a higher incidence of STDs and subsequent PID. As expected, estimates of urban infertility are more affected by contraception because of the higher use of contraception in urban areas. However, the urban infertility estimates remain the higher, even when we consider all current users of a modern contraceptive as fertile at interview.

Table 2   Per cent infertility in women, based on the 'subsequently infertile' estimator, by age and urban/rural residence[a]

Country, survey date	Residence	Age (years) 20-24	25-29	30-34	35-39	40-44	20-44	Sample size[b]
Benin 1982[c]	Urban	9 (9)	15 (14)	29 (27)	42 (42)	71 (71)	18 (18)	228
	Rural	7 (7)	14 (14)	27 (27)	46 (46)	72 (72)	18 (18)	945
Benin 1996	Urban	5 (5)	9 (9)	22 (20)	44 (42)	67 (64)	15 (14)	889
	Rural	4 (4)	7 (7)	16 (16)	39 (37)	65 (63)	13 (12)	2,218
Botswana 1988	Urban	11 (8)	19 (14)	39 (23)	59 (33)	71 (41)	23 (15)	559
	Rural	7 (6)	10 (8)	20 (16)	37 (28)	53 (49)	15 (12)	504
Burkina Faso 1993	Urban	8 (8)	13 (11)	24 (20)	47 (41)	75 (71)	17 (15)	1,306
	Rural	5 (5)	8 (8)	14 (14)	33 (33)	66 (66)	11 (11)	2,121
Burundi 1987	Urban	11 (11)	18 (16)	30 (26)	56 (51)	76 (76)	20 (18)	197
	Rural	4 (4)	6 (6)	10 (10)	23 (23)	40 (40)	7 (7)	1,304
Cameroon 1978	Urban	22 (22)	37 (36)	48 (47)	57 (56)	69 (69)	36 (36)	978
	Rural	19 (19)	27 (27)	41 (41)	54 (54)	68 (68)	30 (30)	3,226
Cameroon 1991	Urban	17 (17)	28 (26)	40 (37)	57 (50)	84 (76)	28 (26)	1,010
	Rural	13 (13)	20 (20)	32 (31)	52 (50)	72 (71)	24 (23)	910
CAR 1994/1995	Urban	18 (17)	26 (25)	37 (36)	54 (51)	76 (74)	28 (27)	1,203
	Rural	17 (16)	26 (26)	39 (38)	55 (55)	77 (76)	29 (29)	1,935
Chad 1996/97	Urban	10 (9)	19 (18)	32 (32)	54 (53)	84 (84)	21 (20)	1,615
	Rural	7 (7)	14 (14)	26 (26)	50 (50)	77 (77)	18 (17)	2,506
Comoros 1996	Urban	12 (12)	16 (14)	28 (22)	46 (36)	68 (57)	21 (18)	355
	Rural	10 (10)	17 (16)	28 (25)	44 (41)	68 (64)	21 (19)	1,006
Côte d'Ivoire 1980	Urban	11 (11)	18 (18)	30 (30)	39 (39)	77 (77)	19 (19)	941
	Rural	9 (9)	14 (14)	23 (23)	40 (40)	59 (59)	18 (18)	1,834
Côte d'Ivoire 1994	Urban	12 (11)	20 (18)	30 (29)	46 (44)	68 (64)	21 (20)	1,645
	Rural	7 (7)	13 (13)	23 (23)	41 (40)	66 (64)	17 (17)	2,307
Ghana 1979	Urban	8 (8)	14 (13)	25 (24)	45 (44)	66 (64)	18 (17)	1,044
	Rural	6 (6)	10 (10)	19 (18)	35 (34)	63 (61)	14 (14)	2,181
Ghana 1988	Urban	7 (6)	12 (10)	25 (21)	41 (36)	54 (40)	15 (13)	512
	Rural	4 (4)	6 (6)	12 (11)	27 (24)	50 (48)	8 (7)	1,121
Ghana 1993	Urban	9 (9)	17 (15)	31 (27)	50 (45)	76 (69)	21 (18)	885
	Rural	6 (6)	11 (10)	19 (18)	36 (34)	57 (55)	14 (13)	1,771
Kenya 1977/78	Urban	14 (13)	21 (20)	42 (39)	60 (54)	86 (74)	25 (23)	654
	Rural	6 (6)	10 (9)	15 (14)	28 (27)	54 (52)	13 (12)	3,485
Kenya 1989	Urban	9 (8)	19 (13)	38 (23)	56 (30)	90 (44)	20 (14)	520

Table 2, Continued

Country, survey date	Residence	20-24	25-29	30-34	35-39	40-44	20-44	Sample size[b]
	Rural	6 (5)	9 (7)	16 (13)	31 (25)	68 (60)	11 (9)	1,998
Kenya 1993	Urban	13 (11)	24 (16)	46 (29)	79 (52)	81 (48)	28 (19)	449
	Rural	5 (4)	11 (8)	22 (15)	42 (30)	64 (52)	15 (11)	3,179
Lesotho 1977	Urban	17 (17)	27 (27)	42 (40)	67 (64)	88 (88)	33 (33)	168
	Rural	13 (13)	22 (22)	35 (34)	52 (52)	75 (74)	26 (26)	1,981
Liberia 1986	Urban	11 (10)	17 (16)	26 (23)	44 (37)	50 (46)	18 (16)	666
	Rural	10 (10)	16 (15)	26 (25)	37 (34)	53 (48)	18 (17)	1,563
Madagascar 1992	Urban	13 (12)	24 (20)	42 (34)	66 (53)	84 (77)	28 (23)	991
	Rural	12 (12)	18 (17)	27 (26)	44 (43)	76 (74)	20 (20)	2,013
Malawi 1992	Urban	11 (10)	15 (12)	23 (16)	37 (27)	77 (60)	18 (14)	243
	Rural	8 (8)	13 (13)	24 (23)	40 (38)	60 (59)	18 (17)	2,383
Mali 1987	Urban	8 (8)	15 (15)	27 (26)	48 (45)	56 (56)	15 (15)	562
	Rural	7 (7)	13 (13)	18 (18)	33 (33)	53 (53)	14 (14)	872
Mali 1995/1996	Urban	9 (8)	13 (12)	22 (20)	45 (40)	76 (70)	17 (15)	1,809
	Rural	6 (6)	10 (10)	19 (18)	37 (37)	68 (68)	14 (14)	4,060
Mauretania 1982	Urban	10 (10)	20 (20)	36 (36)	52 (52)	66 (66)	23 (23)	1,068
	Rural	10 (10)	18 (18)	32 (32)	53 (53)	70 (69)	22 (21)	1,044
Mozambique 1997	Urban	12 (11)	20 (17)	33 (27)	54 (40)	73 (60)	23 (19)	1,191
	Rural	11 (11)	20 (20)	33 (32)	50 (48)	74 (72)	23 (23)	3,430
Namibia 1992	Urban	13 (10)	25 (14)	42 (21)	68 (38)	81 (50)	33 (19)	624
	Rural	6 (6)	12 (10)	20 (17)	31 (27)	61 (55)	16 (14)	1,232
Niger 1992	Urban	11 (10)	16 (15)	24 (23)	36 (35)	58 (55)	17 (16)	1,405
	Rural	8 (8)	15 (15)	25 (25)	43 (42)	64 (63)	17 (17)	2,270
Nigeria 1981	Urban	11 (11)	21 (20)	37 (37)	56 (55)	79 (76)	23 (22)	1,383
	Rural	13 (13)	21 (21)	34 (34)	49 (49)	69 (69)	22 (22)	3,851
Nigeria 1990	Urban	8 (7)	14 (13)	30 (26)	50 (44)	69 (67)	18 (16)	1,714
	Rural	9 (9)	13 (13)	26 (25)	41 (39)	64 (63)	17 (17)	3,150
Ondo State 1986/1987	Urban	2 (2)	5 (5)	9 (7)	10 (6)	43 (38)	5 (4)	586
	Rural	1 (1)	2 (2)	5 (4)	12 (11)	33 (33)	3 (3)	927
Rwanda 1983	Urban	4 (4)	8 (8)	14 (14)	35 (35)	73 (73)	12 (12)	349
	Rural	3 (3)	5 (5)	12 (12)	25 (25)	49 (49)	9 (9)	2,507
Rwanda 1992	Urban	5 (5)	9 (8)	17 (14)	34 (30)	54 (52)	12 (10)	467
	Rural	2 (2)	4 (4)	9 (8)	21 (20)	48 (46)	7 (7)	2,748
Senegal 1978	Urban	12 (12)	18 (18)	29 (29)	42 (42)	73 (73)	21 (21)	694
	Rural	9 (9)	14 (14)	24 (24)	41 (41)	62 (62)	18 (18)	1,464
Senegal 1986	Urban	11 (10)	16 (15)	24 (23)	42 (41)	69 (63)	19 (18)	874
	Rural	8 (8)	13 (13)	22 (22)	36 (36)	62 (62)	16 (16)	1,516
Senegal 1992/1993	Urban	9 (8)	14 (13)	24 (21)	43 (37)	75 (69)	18 (16)	1,191
	Rural	6 (6)	10 (10)	19 (19)	36 (36)	58 (57)	13 (13)	2,123
Sudan 1978	Urban	10 (10)	17 (16)	34 (32)	59 (55)	76 (73)	22 (21)	949
	Rural	12 (12)	19 (19)	33 (32)	50 (49)	71 (71)	21 (21)	1,264
Sudan 1989/90	Urban	9 (8)	18 (16)	34 (32)	59 (55)	84 (81)	22 (21)	1,179
	Rural	7 (7)	13 (13)	24 (24)	44 (44)	69 (69)	16 (16)	1,914

Table 2, Continued

Country, survey date	Residence	Age (years) 20-24	25-29	30-34	35-39	40-44	20-44	Sample size[b]
Tanzania 1991/1992	Urban	12 (11)	21 (19)	35 (32)	54 (51)	76 (69)	24 (23)	807
	Rural	8 (8)	13 (13)	22 (21)	42 (40)	64 (61)	17 (16)	3,786
Tanzania 1996	Urban	13 (13)	23 (20)	35 (29)	57 (43)	72 (64)	25 (21)	881
	Rural	7 (7)	12 (11)	20 (18)	38 (34)	65 (60)	16 (15)	3,033
Togo 1988	Urban	8 (8)	12 (11)	18 (15)	28 (28)	46 (46)	12 (11)	307
	Rural	2 (2)	4 (4)	7 (6)	19 (17)	47 (46)	5 (5)	882
Uganda 1988/89	Urban	13 (13)	17 (16)	25 (22)	44 (37)	89 (71)	19 (17)	240
	Rural	10 (10)	15 (14)	23 (21)	41 (40)	68 (68)	17 (16)	1,358
Uganda 1995	Urban	12 (11)	19 (16)	33 (26)	52 (39)	74 (59)	21 (17)	887
	Rural	9 (8)	13 (12)	21 (20)	40 (37)	63 (61)	16 (15)	2,211
Zambia 1992	Urban	10 (9)	16 (14)	23 (19)	43 (37)	64 (57)	17 (15)	1,493
	Rural	7 (7)	11 (11)	19 (18)	34 (32)	63 (61)	15 (14)	1,888
Zimbabwe 1988	Urban	8 (7)	15 (11)	32 (21)	59 (38)	81 (47)	19 (14)	511
	Rural	6 (6)	10 (9)	19 (16)	34 (29)	64 (57)	14 (12)	1,171
Zimbabwe 1994	Urban	12 (10)	24 (17)	42 (29)	66 (48)	93 (77)	27 (20)	799
	Rural	7 (6)	12 (9)	21 (17)	41 (32)	67 (57)	16 (13)	2,206

[a] Estimates assuming all current users of a modern contraceptive are fertile at interview are shown in parentheses
[b] Unweighted
[c] Incomplete data set

Infertility varies markedly by region (Appendix Table A.1). For instance, it is particularly prevalent in the northern region of Cameroon and in the eastern parts of Central African Republic, locations known to have had a particularly high prevalence of STDs in the past (Retel Laurentin, 1974; Larsen, 1995a). Burundi and Rwanda have relatively low infertility compared with the neighbouring countries of Uganda and Tanzania. We conclude that these low estimates of infertility in Burundi and Rwanda are probably valid, because in both countries: 1) the age-pattern of infertility increases gradually with age; 2) infertility is higher in urban compared to in rural areas; 3) each region (except Imbo in Burundi) has low infertility; 4) both primary and secondary infertility are low, as shown below. Low childlessness and high fertility have been reported in Burundi in several surveys in the 1970s (Frank, 1983). In Rwanda the total fertility rate was as high as seven in the 1950s (Page and Coale, 1972).

Primary infertility

Today, the prevalence of primary infertility, or the per cent childless after seven years of entry into first marriage, is relatively low throughout sub-Saharan Africa (Figure 2 and Table 3). Bongaarts and Potter (1983) consider that about 3% of all couples cannot have children. Using 3% as a threshold, we may conclude that primary infertility is currently a problem in only a few sub-Saharan African countries, primarily in Central and West Africa. These countries are located in the area traditionally denoted the 'infertility belt' and include Central African Republic,

Cameroon, Chad, Niger and Nigeria. The islands of Madagascar and Comoros also have elevated levels of primary infertility that reach 4%. These are the only two island countries analysed, and the finding that they have relatively high primary infertility might be seen as support for the hypothesis that impaired fertility is more prevalent in areas close to waterways (Romaniuk, 1968). Childlessness reaches 4% in Mozambique, the only eastern African country with elevated levels of primary infertility. Primary infertility is 4% in Lesotho and 5% in Mauritania (data from the 1977 WFS and the 1982 WFS respectively) and we cannot rule out that primary infertility may have declined in these two countries during the 1980s.

Figure 2   Rates of primary infertility in the countries analysed

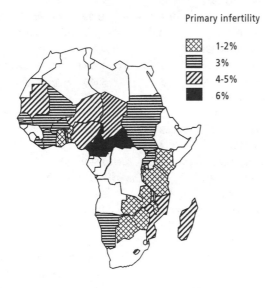

Primary infertility

- ▨ 1-2%
- ▤ 3%
- ▨ 4-5%
- ■ 6%

Table 3   Primary infertility (PI, in %) in all women childless at seven years or more since first marriage, and by urban/rural residence

Country, survey date, urban/rural	PI %	Nᵃ	Country, survey date, urban/rural	PI %	Nᵃ
Benin 1982[b]	3	1,264	Burundi 1987	2	1,436
Urban	4	242	Urban	3	198
Rural	3	1,022	Rural	2	1,238
Benin 1996	1	3,083	Cameroon 1978	11	4,513
Urban	2	845	Urban	13	1,001
Rural	1	2,238	Rural	11	3,512
Botswana 1988	2	984	Cameroon 1991	6	2,037
Urban	3	500	Urban	7	1,035
Rural	2	484	Rural	5	1,002
Burkina Faso 1993	3	3,574	CAR 1994/1995	6	3,338
Urban	4	1,332	Urban	6	1,309
Rural	3	2,242	Rural	6	2,029

Table 3, Continued

Country, survey date, urban/rural	PI %	N[a]	Country, survey date, urban/rural	PI %	N[a]
Chad 1996/97	5	4,445	Mali 1987	4	1,655
Urban	5	1,737	Urban	5	641
Rural	4	2,708	Rural	3	1,014
Comoros 1996	4	1,346	Mali 1995/1996	3	6,226
Urban	5	344	Urban	3	1,886
Rural	4	1,002	Rural	2	4,340
Côte d'Ivoire 1980	4	3,069	Mauretania 1982	5	2,509
Urban	4	1,042	Urban	6	1,293
Rural	4	2,027	Rural	4	1,216
Côte d'Ivoire 1994	3	4,081	Mozambique 1997	4	4,873
Urban	4	1,687	Urban	2	1,193
Rural	2	2,394	Rural	5	3,680
Ghana 1979	2	3,324	Namibia 1992	3	1,727
Urban	3	1,041	Urban	4	545
Rural	2	2,283	Rural	3	1,182
Ghana 1988	1	1,656	Niger 1992	4	4,231
Urban	1	509	Urban	5	1,559
Rural	1	1,147	Rural	4	2,672
Ghana 1993	2	2,610	Nigeria 1981	6	5,834
Urban	2	857	Urban	6	1,505
Rural	2	1,753	Rural	6	4,329
Kenya 1977	3	4,292	Nigeria 1990	4	5,127
Urban	6	664	Urban	4	1,696
Rural	2	3,628	Rural	4	3,431
Kenya 1989	2	2,558	Ondo State 1986/1987	1	1,468
Urban	4	518	Urban	1	565
Rural	2	2,040	Rural	0	903
Kenya 1993	2	3,597	Rwanda 1983	1	2,753
Urban	3	424	Urban	2	331
Rural	1	3,173	Rural	1	2,422
Lesotho 1997	4	2,317	Rwanda 1992	1	3,037
Urban	6	173	Urban	3	437
Rural	4	2,144	Rural	1	2,600
Liberia 1986	3	2,363	Senegal 1978	4	2,403
Urban	3	699	Urban	4	734
Rural	4	1,664	Rural	4	1,669
Madagascar 1992	4	3,010	Senegal 1986	4	2,536
Urban	3	957	Urban	5	886
Rural	5	2,053	Rural	4	1,650
Malawi 1992	2	2,759	Senegal 1992/1993	3	3,508
Urban	2	250	Urban	3	1,192
Rural	2	2,509	Rural	3	2,316

Table 3, Continued

Country, survey date, urban/rural	PI %	Nᵃ	Country, survey date, urban/rural	PI %	Nᵃ
Sudan 1978	5	2,365	Uganda 1988/1989	3	1,728
Urban	6	1,001	Urban	3	247
Rural	5	1,364	Rural	3	1,481
Sudan 1989/1990	3	3,262	Uganda 1995	3	3,182
Urban	4	1,218	Urban	3	868
Rural	2	2,044	Rural	3	2,314
Tanzania 1991/1992	2	4,624	Zambia 1992	2	3,489
Urban	4	797	Urban	2	1,512
Rural	2	3,827	Rural	3	1,977
Tanzania 1996	2	3,888	Zimbabwe 1988	1	1,691
Urban	4	867	Urban	1	495
Rural	2	3,021	Rural	2	1,196
Togo 1988	2	1,229	Zimbabwe 1994	2	2,974
Urban	4	305	Urban	2	760
Rural	1	924	Rural	1	2,214

ᵃ Unweighted

ᵇ Incomplete data set

It is well known that survey data about childlessness tend to understate the prevalence of childlessness in the community, as previously mentioned. We conclude that our estimates of childlessness or primary infertility are probably underestimates because comparison of the per cent subsequently infertile at ages 20-24 with the per cent childless reveals that the per cent subsequently infertile is substantially higher than the per cent childless. Of course, most African women initiate childbearing at relatively young ages, and it is plausible that many of the women who were subsequently infertile at ages 20-24 did indeed have a child at a younger age. Alternately, some childless women could have falsely reported that they have children, when they actually have foster children, and thus would be considered to have become subsequently infertile at a young age. It is difficult to speculate about the extent of underreporting of childlessness, but it would be possible to compare the survey data for childlessness with census data, and thereby gain some insight into the validity of survey data in this area. If the validity of information on childlessness does not vary over time, by region or by place of residence, then the observed patterns should be valid indicators of the differentials in childlessness and primary infertility. The following description of the differentials of primary infertility assumes that underreporting, if any, is uniform within countries.

Primary infertility declined very markedly from the late 1970s to the late 1980s or later in most of the countries in which two or more surveys had been conducted. For instance, in Cameroon - the country with the greatest decline - primary infertility declined from 11% in the 1978 WFS to 6% in the 1991 DHS. Furthermore, the 1991

DHS in Cameroon estimated the proportion childless to be 4% for women aged 30-34 and 10% for women aged 45-49 at survey, suggesting that primary infertility continues to decline in that country. It should also be noted that primary infertility remained at 2% in the 1991/1992 and 1996 DHS in Tanzania, and at 3% in the 1988/1989 and 1995 DHS in Uganda. However, in Tanzania and Uganda primary infertility was quite low at the time of the first survey and there was little room for further reductions. Primary infertility in Ghana was reported to be 2%, 1% and 2% in the 1977 WFS, 1988 DHS and 1993 DHS data, respectively; in Zimbabwe it was 1% and 2% in the 1988 DHS and 1994 DHS, respectively. When we analyse the age pattern of childlessness there is no evidence to suggest that younger women have more childlessness in either Ghana or Zimbabwe (results not shown). The pattern of increasing total primary infertility may indicate a reversal in the trend that warrants close monitoring in the next few years. Finally, virtually no childless woman married for more than seven years reported that she was currently using contraception in any of the countries analysed (Table 3), which suggests that contraception does not bias estimates of primary infertility.

Primary infertility is higher in urban areas in most of the countries analysed (Table 3). The countries with elevated levels of childlessness show some regional variation (Table A.2). For instance, in the 1991 DHS survey the per cent childless found in Cameroon was 7% in the North compared to 3% in the West and Littoral region. The decline in childlessness is also regional, as seen in Cameroon, where the West and Littoral region had a total per cent childless of 17% in the 1978 WFS and 3% in the 1991 DHS, compared to the Northwest and Southwest regions which had 4% childless on both survey dates.

Secondary infertility

The prevalence of secondary infertility varies greatly from country to country in sub-Saharan Africa, as illustrated in Figure 3 and Table 4. Secondary infertility, as presented in Figure 3, is measured by the per cent subsequently infertile of parous women aged 20 to 44: current users of a modern contraceptive are considered fertile at interview. The Central African countries of Cameroon and Central African Republic rank among the countries with the highest prevalence of secondary infertility, with percentages of 20% and 25%, respectively. Secondary infertility is also prevalent in Lesotho, Mozambique and Mauretania, where the percentages are 25%, 21% and 21%, respectively. The lowest levels of secondary infertility are found in the East African countries of Burundi and Rwanda, as well as in Togo, West Africa, where secondary infertility is only about 5%. The remaining countries analysed have secondary infertility in the middle range, from 10% to 18%. Secondary infertility is generally higher in urban than rural areas, and there are substantial variations in secondary infertility by region within countries (Table A.3).

Figure 3   Rates of secondary infertility in the countries analysed

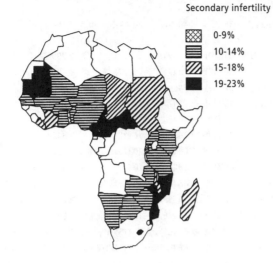

Secondary infertility

▨ 0-9%
▤ 10-14%
▨ 15-18%
■ 19-23%

Table 4   Per cent secondary infertility in women by age and urban/rural residence, based on the 'subsequently infertile' estimator and parous women[a]

Country, survey date, urban/rural	Age (years)						Sample size[b]
	20-24	25-29	30-34	35-39	40-44	20-44	
Benin 1982[c]	5 (5)	11 (11)	25 (25)	44 (43)	71 (71)	16 (16)	1,065
Urban	5 (5)	12 (11)	24 (23)	35 (34)	72 (72)	14 (14)	205
Rural	4 (4)	11 (11)	25 (25)	45 (45)	71 (71)	16 (16)	860
Benin 1996	4 (3)	7 (7)	17 (17)	39 (38)	65 (63)	13 (12)	2,950
Urban	4 (4)	8 (8)	21 (19)	43 (41)	66 (64)	14 (14)	831
Rural	3 (3)	6 (6)	16 (15)	37 (36)	64 (62)	12 (12)	2,119
Botswana 1988	6 (4)	11 (8)	23 (16)	39 (27)	53 (43)	14 (10)	1,013
Urban	8 (6)	17(12)	38 (21)	59 (33)	71 (41)	20 (13)	524
Rural	5 (4)	8 (7)	18 (14)	34 (25)	49 (44)	12 (9)	489
Burkina Faso 1992/1993	4 (3)	7 (7)	14 (13)	33 (32)	66 (65)	11 (10)	3,208
Urban	7 (6)	12 (10)	24 (20)	47 (41)	75 (71)	16 (14)	1,216
Rural	3 (3)	6 (6)	12 (11)	31 (31)	64 (64)	10 (10)	1,992
Burundi 1987	3 (3)	5 (5)	9 (9)	23 (23)	40 (40)	7 (7)	1,386
Urban	11 (11)	16 (14)	28 (24)	53 (48)	72 (72)	19 (18)	186
Rural	3 (3)	4 (4)	8 (8)	22 (22)	39 (39)	7 (7)	1,200
Cameroon 1978	12 (12)	21 (21)	34 (34)	48 (48)	64 (64)	24 (24)	3,569
Urban	13 (13)	27 (26)	39 (38)	51 (50)	65 (65)	28 (27)	855
Rural	12 (12)	20 (20)	33 (33)	48 (48)	63 (63)	24 (24)	2,714
Cameroon 1991	11 (10)	18 (17)	30 (28)	49 (46)	72 (69)	21 (20)	1,736
Urban	11 (11)	22 (21)	35 (31)	53 (46)	84 (75)	23 (21)	897
Rural	10 (10)	16 (16)	28 (27)	48 (46)	67 (66)	20 (20)	839

Table 4, Continued

Country, survey date, urban/rural	Age (years) 20-24	25-29	30-34	35-39	40-44	20-44	Sample size[b]
CAR 1994/1995	14 (13)	23 (22)	34 (33)	51 (50)	74 (73)	26 (25)	2,799
Urban	15 (14)	23 (22)	34 (32)	50 (48)	73 (71)	25 (24)	1,087
Rural	13 (13)	22 (22)	34 (33)	52 (51)	74 (74)	26 (26)	1,712
Chad 1996/97	6 (6)	12 (12)	25 (25)	49 (49)	77 (77)	17 (17)	3,855
Urban	8 (7)	16 (15)	30 (29)	51 (50)	83 (83)	19 (18)	1,509
Rural	6 (6)	12 (11)	23 (23)	49 (49)	76 (76)	16 (16)	2,346
Comoros 1996	9 (9)	15 (13)	26 (23)	44 (38)	68 (62)	20 (18)	1,230
Urban	10 (9)	14 (11)	26 (20)	45 (35)	68 (56)	20 (16)	315
Rural	9 (9)	15 (14)	26 (23)	43 (39)	68 (63)	20 (18)	915
Côte d'Ivoire 1980	7 (7)	12 (12)	21 (21)	37 (37)	59 (59)	15 (15)	2,574
Urban	8 (8)	16 (15)	28 (28)	37 (37)	76 (76)	17 (17)	855
Rural	6 (6)	11 (11)	19 (19)	36 (36)	56 (56)	15 (15)	1,719
Côte d'Ivoire 1994	7 (7)	13 (13)	23 (23)	41 (39)	65 (63)	17 (16)	3,746
Urban	9 (8)	17 (15)	27 (26)	43 (41)	66 (62)	19 (17)	1,538
Rural	6 (6)	11 (11)	21 (21)	40 (39)	65 (63)	16 (15)	2,208
Ghana 1979	6 (6)	10 (10)	19 (18)	37 (35)	63 (61)	15 (14)	2,998
Urban	8 (7)	13 (12)	24 (22)	44 (43)	65 (63)	17 (16)	957
Rural	5 (5)	9 (9)	18 (17)	34 (33)	63 (60)	14 (13)	2,041
Ghana 1988	5 (4)	8 (7)	15 (13)	31 (27)	51 (45)	10 (9)	1,525
Urban	7 (6)	11 (10)	24 (20)	40 (34)	53 (39)	15 (13)	466
Rural	4 (3)	6 (6)	11 (10)	26 (24)	50 (48)	8 (7)	1,059
Ghana 1993	6 (6)	11 (10)	20 (18)	39 (36)	61 (58)	15 (14)	2,461
Urban	9 (8)	15 (13)	29 (24)	49 (43)	76 (69)	20 (18)	807
Rural	5 (5)	9 (8)	16 (16)	35 (32)	56 (54)	13 (12)	1,654
Kenya 1977/1978	5 (5)	9 (8)	15 (14)	28 (27)	54 (52)	12 (11)	3,926
Urban	10 (9)	17 (15)	38 (35)	56 (50)	85 (72)	21 (19)	592
Rural	4 (4)	8 (8)	13 (13)	27 (26)	53 (51)	11 (11)	3,334
Kenya 1989	5 (4)	9 (7)	17 (12)	32 (23)	68 (54)	11 (8)	2,382
Urban	6 (4)	17 (11)	36 (20)	54 (26)	90 (39)	18 (11)	497
Rural	4 (4)	8 (6)	15 (11)	29 (23)	65 (56)	10 (8)	1,914
Kenya 1993	5 (4)	11 (8)	23 (15)	44 (31)	65 (51)	15 (11)	3,499
Urban	10 (8)	22 (14)	45 (26)	80 (51)	82 (49)	27 (17)	419
Rural	4 (3)	10 (7)	20 (14)	41 (29)	63 (51)	14 (10)	3,080
Lesotho 1977	11 (11)	20 (20)	32 (32)	51 (51)	75 (74)	25 (25)	1,941
Urban	14 (14)	22 (22)	36 (35)	64 (61)	88 (87)	30 (29)	144
Rural	11 (11)	20 (19)	32 (32)	50 (50)	74 (73)	25 (25)	1,797
Liberia 1986	10 (9)	15 (14)	25 (23)	38 (34)	51 (46)	18 (17)	2,049
Urban	10 (10)	16 (15)	25 (21)	42 (34)	49 (45)	17 (16)	611
Rural	9 (9)	15 (14)	25 (24)	36 (33)	51 (47)	18 (17)	1,438
Madagascar 1992	9 (9)	15 (14)	25 (23)	44 (41)	75 (72)	18 (17)	2,769
Urban	12 (11)	23 (19)	41 (32)	65 (52)	83 (76)	27 (22)	916
Rural	8 (8)	13 (12)	21 (21)	39 (38)	73 (71)	16 (16)	1,853

Table 4, Continued

Country, survey date, urban/rural	Age (years) 20-24	25-29	30-34	35-39	40-44	20-44	Sample size[b]
Malawi 1992	7 (7)	13 (12)	23 (22)	39 (37)	60 (58)	17 (17)	2,498
Urban	10 (9)	15 (12)	23 (16)	37 (27)	77 (60)	18 (14)	233
Rural	7 (7)	12 (12)	23 (22)	39 (37)	60 (58)	17 (17)	2,265
Mali 1987	6 (6)	12 (12)	18 (17)	33 (32)	52 (52)	13 (13)	1,303
Urban	5 (5)	13 (12)	24 (23)	44 (41)	53 (53)	13 (13)	504
Rural	6 (6)	12 (12)	16 (16)	31 (31)	52 (52)	13 (13)	799
Mali 1995/1996	5 (5)	9 (9)	18 (17)	37 (36)	69 (68)	14 (13)	5,501
Urban	7 (7)	11 (10)	21 (18)	43 (38)	75 (69)	16 (14)	1,677
Rural	5 (4)	9 (8)	17 (17)	35 (35)	67 (67)	13 (13)	3,824
Mauretania 1982	8 (8)	17 (17)	32 (32)	52 (51)	67 (67)	21 (21)	1,910
Urban	9 (9)	18 (18)	34 (34)	49 (49)	64 (64)	22 (22)	957
Rural	8 (8)	17 (17)	30 (30)	53 (53)	69 (68)	21 (21)	953
Mozambique 1997	10 (9)	18 (17)	30 (28)	48 (44)	72 (68)	22 (21)	4,234
Urban	11 (10)	18 (15)	31 (24)	52 (38)	72 (59)	22 (18)	1,118
Rural	9 (9)	19 (18)	30 (29)	47 (45)	72 (70)	22 (22)	3,116
Namibia 1992	6 (5)	13 (9)	24 (16)	40 (28)	67 (51)	19 (13)	1,732
Urban	8 (6)	19 (11)	36 (18)	65 (35)	81 (49)	27 (15)	569
Rural	5 (4)	9 (8)	18 (15)	28 (24)	59 (52)	14 (12)	1,163
Niger 1992	6 (6)	13 (12)	23 (22)	41 (40)	63 (62)	16 (15)	3,415
Urban	7 (7)	12 (12)	21 (20)	34 (32)	57 (53)	14 (14)	1,294
Rural	6 (6)	13 (12)	23 (23)	42 (41)	64 (63)	16 (16)	2,121
Nigeria 1981	9 (9)	17 (17)	30 (30)	46 (45)	68 (67)	19 (19)	4,606
Urban	7 (7)	17 (16)	32 (32)	51 (50)	76 (73)	20 (19)	1,211
Rural	9 (9)	17 (17)	30 (30)	45 (44)	66 (65)	19 (19)	3,395
Nigeria 1990	6 (6)	11 (11)	24 (23)	41 (38)	64 (62)	16 (15)	4,439
Urban	5 (5)	12 (10)	27 (23)	48 (42)	67 (65)	16 (14)	1,581
Rural	7 (7)	11 (11)	24 (23)	39 (37)	64 (62)	16 (15)	2,858
Ondo State 1986/1987	8 (7)	20 (16)	25 (21)	31 (28)	51 (49)	21 (17)	992
Urban	13 (11)	23 (19)	26 (20)	26 (15)	62 (55)	22 (17)	380
Rural	6 (4)	18 (13)	23 (20)	35 (34)	52 (52)	20 (17)	548
Rwanda 1983	2 (2)	4 (4)	11 (11)	25 (25)	49 (49)	9 (9)	2,626
Urban	2 (2)	5 (5)	12 (12)	34 (34)	73 (73)	11 (11)	341
Rural	2 (2)	4 (4)	11 (11)	24 (24)	48 (48)	9 (9)	2,305
Rwanda 1992	2 (2)	4 (4)	9 (8)	21 (20)	49 (46)	7 (7)	3,006
Urban	4 (3)	8 (6)	17 (13)	34 (29)	54 (52)	11 (9)	434
Rural	2 (2)	4 (4)	8 (8)	21 (19)	48 (46)	7 (7)	2,572
Senegal 1978	7 (7)	12 (12)	23 (23)	39 (39)	64 (64)	16 (16)	2,019
Urban	9 (9)	15 (15)	26 (26)	39 (39)	71 (71)	18 (18)	651
Rural	6 (6)	11 (11)	22 (22)	40 (40)	61 (61)	16 (16)	1,368
Senegal 1986	7 (6)	11 (11)	19 (19)	35 (35)	63 (61)	15 (14)	2,214
Urban	8 (7)	12 (11)	20 (18)	39 (37)	68 (61)	16 (15)	803
Rural	6 (6)	10 (10)	19 (19)	34 (34)	61 (61)	14 (14)	1,411

Table 4, Continued

Country, survey date, urban/rural	20-24	25-29	30-34	35-39	40-44	20-44	Sample size[b]
				Age (years)			
Senegal 1992/1993	5 (5)	10 (10)	19 (18)	37 (35)	64 (61)	14 (13)	3,112
Urban	7 (6)	13 (11)	23 (19)	41 (35)	75 (69)	17 (15)	1,108
Rural	4 (4)	9 (9)	18 (18)	35 (35)	57 (57)	12 (12)	2,004
Sudan 1978	8 (8)	15 (15)	30 (29)	50 (49)	71 (70)	19 (18)	1,977
Urban	6 (6)	14 (12)	31 (29)	57 (54)	75 (73)	19 (18)	849
Rural	9 (8)	16 (16)	30 (29)	46 (46)	68 (68)	19 (19)	1,128
Sudan 1989/1990	6 (6)	13 (12)	26 (25)	49 (47)	75 (74)	17 (16)	2,813
Urban	6 (6)	15 (14)	31 (29)	57 (53)	84 (81)	20 (19)	1,055
Rural	6 (6)	12 (12)	22 (22)	42 (42)	69 (69)	15 (15)	1,758
Tanzania 1991/1992	7 (7)	13 (12)	22 (21)	43 (40)	65 (62)	17 (16)	4,339
Urban	9 (9)	17 (16)	31 (29)	50 (47)	75 (68)	21 (20)	756
Rural	7 (7)	12 (11)	20 (19)	41 (38)	63 (60)	16 (15)	3,583
Tanzania 1996	7 (7)	12 (11)	21 (19)	40 (34)	65 (60)	16 (15)	3,708
Urban	11 (10)	20 (17)	33 (26)	55 (41)	70 (62)	23 (19)	817
Rural	6 (6)	10 (9)	19 (17)	37 (33)	64 (59)	15 (13)	2,891
Togo 1988	2 (2)	5 (4)	7 (6)	18 (17)	46 (45)	6 (5)	1,113
Urban	6 (5)	10 (8)	14 (11)	22 (22)	40 (40)	9 (8)	272
Rural	1 (1)	3 (3)	6 (5)	18 (16)	47 (46)	5 (4)	841
Uganda 1988/1989	8 (7)	12 (11)	19 (17)	37 (36)	66 (64)	14 (13)	1,498
Urban	11 (10)	14 (13)	21 (17)	39 (31)	89 (69)	16 (14)	223
Rural	8 (7)	12 (11)	19 (17)	37 (36)	65 (64)	14 (13)	1,275
Uganda 1995	7 (6)	11 (10)	21 (19)	39 (36)	63 (60)	14 (13)	2,900
Urban	10 (9)	17 (14)	31 (24)	51 (38)	73 (58)	19 (15)	820
Rural	6 (6)	11 (10)	20 (18)	38 (36)	63 (60)	14 (13)	2,080
Zambia 1992	7 (6)	12 (11)	20 (17)	36 (33)	63 (59)	15 (14)	3,210
Urban	9 (8)	15 (13)	23 (19)	43 (37)	64 (56)	17 (15)	1,429
Rural	5 (5)	10 (9)	17 (16)	33 (31)	63 (60)	14 (13)	1,781
Zimbabwe 1988/1989	6 (5)	10 (9)	21 (16)	39 (30)	66 (53)	14 (12)	1,605
Urban	7 (6)	14 (10)	32 (20)	59 (37)	81 (47)	19 (13)	484
Rural	5 (5)	9 (8)	17 (15)	33 (28)	61 (55)	13 (11)	1,121
Zimbabwe 1994	8 (6)	14 (11)	25 (19)	46 (35)	72 (61)	19 (14)	2,891
Urban	11 (9)	23 (15)	40 (27)	65 (46)	93 (77)	27 (19)	756
Rural	7 (5)	11 (9)	20 (16)	41 (32)	67 (56)	16 (13)	2,135

[a] Estimates assuming all current users of a modern contraceptive are fertile at interview are shown in parentheses
[b] Unweighted
[c] Incomplete data set

Depressing effect of infertility on fertility

To illustrate the effect of infertility in reducing fertility we estimated what each country's total fertility rate (TFR) would be for women aged 20-44, if infertility were at the level found in Burundi (one of the countries with the lowest level of infertility).

These simulated rates may be compared with the observed total fertility rates. Differences may be interpreted as indicators of the depressing effects of infertility on fertility assuming that all other reproductive characteristics remained the same. The discrepancies between observed and simulated TFRs range from about zero to more than two children (Table 5). In about half of the countries analysed, the depressing effect of infertility on fertility exceeds one child, suggesting that an unforeseen increase in fertility could follow if the documented decline in infertility in selected countries were to continue throughout sub-Saharan Africa.

Table 5   Observed total fertility rates[a] for ages 20-44, compared to simulated rates based on Burundi

| | Total fertility rate | | | | |
Country, survey date	Observed	Simulated	Country, survey date	Observed	Simulated
Benin 1982	6.1	7.5	Sudan 1989/1990	4.5	5.8
Benin 1996	5.5	6.5	Tanzania 1991/1992	5.3	6.0
Botswana 1988	4.2	4.6	Tanzania 1996	4.9	5.6
Burkina Faso 1993	5.9	6.6	Togo 1988	5.6	5.5
Burundi 1987	6.3	6.3	Uganda 1988/1989	6.2	7.3
Cameroon 1978	5.3	7.6	Uganda 1995	5.7	6.5
Cameroon 1991	4.9	6.5	Zambia 1992	5.2	5.8
CAR 1994/1995	4.2	5.9	Zimbabwe 1988	4.8	5.2
Chad 1996/97	6.6	7.2	Zimbabwe 1994	3.7	4.2
Comoros 1996	4.6	5.5			
Côte d'Ivoire 1980	5.8	6.9	[a] Observed TFRs for each country are from the respective		
Côte d'Ivoire 1994	4.8	5.8	WFS and DHS country reports		
Ghana 1988	5.6	5.6			
Ghana 1993	4.8	5.4			
Kenya 1977	6.8	7.3			
Kenya 1989	6.6	7.0			
Kenya 1993	4.6	4.9			
Liberia 1986	5.4	6.0			
Madagascar 1992	5.2	6.8			
Malawi 1992	6.2	7.1			
Mali 1987	5.7	6.4			
Mali 1995/1996	5.7	6.6			
Mozambique 1997	4.1	6.0			
Namibia 1992	4.6	5.1			
Niger 1992	6.0	7.1			
Nigeria 1990	5.0	5.9			
Ondo State 1986/1987	5.7	5.8			
Rwanda 1983	7.8	8.0			
Rwanda 1992	5.7	5.6			
Senegal 1978	6.0	7.2			
Senegal 1986	5.6	6.6			
Senegal 1992/1993	5.2	5.9			
Sudan 1978	5.3	7.0			

Discussion and conclusions

The main finding of this study is that there is a wide variation from country to country in the prevalence of infertility (primary and secondary) in sub-Saharan Africa. The Central African countries of Cameroon and Central African Republic have the highest levels of infertility, and the East African countries of Burundi and Rwanda, as well as the West African country of Togo, have the lowest levels. As an example, the per cent infertile, at ages 30-34, is 37% in Central African Republic and 9% in Rwanda. In contrast to the relatively high prevalence of age-specific infertility, beyond age 30, documented in each of the African countries analysed, childlessness or primary infertility is relatively low in most of these countries. For example, primary infertility (as measured in the most recent survey, for countries with multiple surveys), is 3% or less in 19 of the 29 countries analysed. This corresponds to the proportion of all couples unable to have children in any population in the world, currently deemed to be 3% (Bongaarts and Potter, 1983). Thus, most African women who become infertile do so from pathological causes after they have had at least one child. More detailed knowledge about the relationship between infertility and parity in sub-Saharan Africa is not available. A better understanding of the association between parity and infertility may provide clues to the effects of complications at delivery on subsequent infertility. If a relatively large proportion of couples became infertile after their first child, this would suggest that poor midwifery practice is an important cause of infertility.

Both primary and secondary infertility tend to be more prevalent in urban than in rural areas. The higher prevalence of infertility in urban areas could result, in part, from the movement of infertile women away from their rural residence of origin to a more urban area. Other factors may be suggested by the substantial regional variations in secondary infertility, as well as in primary infertility, seen in the countries with levels of primary infertility exceeding 3%. Romaniuk (1968) has theorized that infertility is more prevalent in the areas that participated in the Arab slave trade, suggesting that Arab slave traders spread STDs to the indigenous people causing the relatively high prevalence of STDs seen in these countries today. Hunt (1989) has developed a model of migrant labour and STDs to explain the prevalence of HIV/AIDS in Africa. With many others, Romaniuk and Hunt believe that multiple sex partners and high risk behaviour of migrant labourers and traders have increased STD prevalence. Multiple analyses have applied this kind of model in analyses of HIV/AIDS, but no systematic analysis has used this model to investigate the regional distribution of infertility in sub-Saharan Africa. Such an analysis could be done based on the regional distribution of primary and secondary infertility presented in this study, as well as on auxiliary information about migration, trading, sexual behaviour and STDs.

The main idea of the labour migration model is that industrial development in Africa has been based largely on a migrant labour system, and that labour concentrations are generally confined to urban locations. The combination of large concentrations of migrant male workers and long periods of familial separations have led to a breakdown in family and sexual patterns, and led to a rapid increase in prostitution and STDs. As a result, infertility is predicted to be higher in the areas with high concentrations of male migrant workers, even though there should also be a spread of STDs and subsequent infertility through the return of male migrant workers to their home villages, i.e., to the areas known as labour reserves. This theory could explain why infertility is usually higher in urban than in rural areas. Also, Rwanda and Burundi serve as labour reserves for the labour concentration in Uganda, and infertility is substantially lower in Burundi and Rwanda compared with Uganda. To test the labour migration model, more detailed information is needed about the labour and migration history of each husband and wife.

Regional boundaries are often ethnic boundaries and, to better understand the spatial distribution of infertility, both regional and ethnic variations should be analysed. For example, the Tutsi and the Hutu people live predominantly in Rwanda and Burundi. In recent years many Tutsi and Hutu in Rwanda have migrated into Tanzania to the Lake Victoria area (the Tutsi predominantly go to the Kagera region, and the Hutu predominantly go to the Kigoma region). The Haya people live in the Lake Victoria area of Tanzania (especially the Kagera region) and are known to have low fertility and, presumably, high infertility. However, it has been observed that when a Haya marries a Tutsi, and to a lesser extent a Hutu, they often have more children than would be expected. Indeed, there is a saying which recommends Hayas with difficulties in having children to find a Tutsi partner. To assess the validity of the folklore about ethnicity and fertility and to enhance the general understanding of ethnic and regional variations in infertility, further ethnographic analyses will be required.

Analyses of infertility based on nationally representative surveys (like the present study) or on censuses increase our knowledge about the levels and differentials of infertility. However, to better understand why some people suffer more from infertility at a young age, in-depth analyses at the micro level are needed. The etiology of infertility is quite well known, but contextual analyses of the social and cultural factors linked to enhanced infertility are lacking for sub-Saharan Africa. It is also not well known how infertility affects a couple - the man, the woman and the relationship between them - as regards social stigma and ostracism. Nor is it known how the implications of infertility for the individuals concerned vary from society to society. It has been reported that the limited health care services in sub-Saharan Africa are currently burdened by women seeking help for infertility. However, relatively little is known about the health care utilization of infertile people, or about the services offered to infertile women and men by the modern health care sector or by traditional healers. More knowledge about the current health care use and services may help to reduce the incidence of infertility at a young age.

On a positive note, it must be remembered that the prevalence of infertility (primary and secondary) has declined in eight of the 13 countries analysed in which multiple surveys have been conducted. This decline in infertility is often attributed to the increased use of antibiotics. However, infertility did increase in three countries from the late 1980s to the early 1990s (in Ghana, Kenya and Zimbabwe). These increases were quite substantial, especially considering that they happened over a period of only five years. It is particularly disconcerting that the increase in infertility occurred in the countries of Ghana, Kenya and Zimbabwe. In the context of sub-Saharan Africa, these three countries rank highly as regards the effectiveness of some of their public health programs. Indeed, the most recent DHS surveys (Demographic and Health Surveys, 1999) show that in Ghana, Kenya and Zimbabwe the per cent of children fully immunized reached 55%, 79% and 80%, respectively; the current use of modern contraceptives of married women was 10%, 27% and 42%, respectively; and the per cent of women receiving antenatal care for births born in the five years immediately before survey was 86%, 95% and 93%, respectively. Clearly, public health interventions aimed at preventing infertility take very different forms than do childhood vaccination programs or family planning programs. Nevertheless, efforts to expand programs designed to inform and educate the public about high risk behaviour, and to expand family planning programs to include reproductive health, appear to have been ineffective in reducing infertility in Ghana, Kenya and Zimbabwe. However, since these interventions were implemented mainly after the International Conference on Population and Development in Cairo and the 'Programme of Action' in 1994, we can hope to see further reductions in infertility in the results of future analyses in years to come.

Table A.1 Per cent infertility in women by age and region, based on the 'subsequently infertile' estimator[a]

Country, survey date and region	Age (years)						Sample size[a]
	20-24	25-29	30-34	35-39	40-44	20-44	
Benin 1982[b]							
Atacora	8 (8)	16 (16)	30 (30)	54 (54)	90 (90)	20 (20)	361
Atlantique	6 (6)	18 (18)	37 (37)	53 (53)	83 (83)	23 (23)	192
Borgou	10 (10)	15 (15)	26 (25)	43 (43)	74 (74)	19 (18)	268
Mono	4 (4)	8 (8)	19 (19)	34 (34)	53 (53)	13 (13)	352
Benin 1996							
Atacora	4 (4)	9 (8)	21 (19)	39 (37)	51 (50)	13 (12)	586
Atlantique	5 (4)	8 (7)	20 (20)	45 (45)	72 (69)	14 (14)	501
Borgou	4 (4)	8 (8)	15 (15)	31 (29)	52 (44)	11 (11)	576
Mono	4 (4)	6 (6)	15 (15)	36 (36)	57 (57)	12 (12)	541
Oueme	2 (2)	6 (6)	15 (15)	40 (38)	82 (79)	12 (12)	426
Zou	5 (5)	10 (10)	21 (21)	49 (48)	77 (76)	17 (17)	477
Burkina Faso 1993							
Ouagadougou	9 (8)	13 (11)	26 (22)	51 (44)	72 (65)	17 (15)	741
North	6 (6)	10 (10)	16 (16)	37 (36)	67 (67)	14 (14)	521
East	2 (2)	4 (4)	10 (10)	29 (29)	54 (54)	7 (7)	552
West	9 (9)	15 (14)	22 (21)	43 (42)	87 (85)	18 (17)	814
Central/South	3 (3)	5 (5)	10 (9)	26 (25)	60 (60)	8 (8)	799
Burundi 1987							
Imbo	6 (6)	10 (9)	13 (11)	43 (40)	76 (76)	10 (9)	246
Mumirwa	2 (2)	4 (4)	4 (4)	11 (11)	22 (22)	4 (4)	162
Mugamba	4 (4)	5 (5)	11 (11)	25 (25)	44 (44)	8 (8)	123
Plateaux Centraux	4 (4)	6 (6)	12 (12)	24 (24)	45 (45)	8 (8)	757
Depressions	4 (4)	7 (7)	8 (8)	29 (29)	31 (31)	8 (8)	213
Cameroon 1978							
Yaounde & Douala	19 (19)	30 (29)	44 (42)	63 (60)	80 (79)	32 (31)	614
North	28 (28)	41 (41)	59 (59)	66 (66)	71 (71)	41 (41)	1,076
Central, South, East	23 (23)	34 (34)	43 (43)	56 (56)	73 (73)	36 (36)	1,133
West & Littoral	10 (10)	17 (17)	28 (28)	42 (42)	60 (60)	21 (21)	667
Northwest, Southwest	9 (9)	16 (16)	27 (27)	45 (45)	64 (64)	19 (19)	674

Table A.1, Continued

Country, survey date and region	20-24	25-29	30-34	35-39	40-44	20-44	Sample size[a]
Cameroon 1991							
Yaounde & Douala	15 (14)	25 (23)	42 (37)	64 (57)	81 (72)	26 (24)	489
North	18 (18)	26 (26)	36 (36)	52 (52)	72 (72)	27 (27)	600
Central, South, East	17 (17)	28 (28)	41 (41)	63 (62)	91 (89)	32 (32)	300
West & Littoral	8 (7)	14 (13)	25 (21)	45 (38)	66 (62)	18 (16)	278
Northwest, Southwest	9 (8)	16 (15)	27 (25)	48 (43)	68 (62)	20 (18)	253
CAR 1994/1995							
RS I	16 (16)	27 (27)	41 (41)	62 (62)	84 (83)	31 (30)	530
RS II	14 (14)	22 (21)	31 (30)	41 (40)	63 (63)	24 (24)	540
RS III	10 (10)	15 (15)	25 (25)	41 (41)	65 (65)	19 (19)	568
RS IV	23 (23)	36 (36)	50 (49)	66 (63)	82 (76)	38 (37)	484
RS V	22 (22)	34 (33)	52 (51)	66 (65)	89 (89)	38 (37)	455
Bangui	19 (18)	28 (27)	38 (36)	57 (54)	77 (77)	29 (27)	561
Chad 1996/97							
Batha	7 (7)	8 (7)	19 (19)	41 (41)	66 (66)	14 (14)	171
B.E.T.	20 (20)	33 (33)	40 (40)	32 (32)	100 (100)	29 (29)	49
Biltine	2 (2)	6 (6)	15 (15)	38 (38)	48 (48)	9 (9)	98
Chari-Baguirmi	12 (12)	18 (18)	27 (27)	48 (48)	74 (74)	21 (21)	459
Gura	10 (10)	24 (24)	44 (44)	76 (76)	82 (82)	28 (28)	199
Kanem	3 (3)	7 (7)	14 (14)	34 (34)	75 (75)	11 (11)	171
Lac	7(7)	11 (11)	20 (20)	53 (53)	85 (85)	17 (17)	123
Logone Occidental	4 (4)	8 (8)	15 (15)	35 (35)	73 (73)	10 (10)	237
Logone Oriental	6 (6)	9 (9)	24 (24)	50 (50)	76 (76)	16 (16)	277
Mayo-Kebbi	9 (9)	15 (15)	29 (28)	49 (49)	86 (86)	20 (20)	416
Mayen-Chari	7 (7)	16 (15)	27 (26)	49 (48)	72 (72)	18 (18)	413
Ouadda	6 (6)	15 (15)	30 (30)	58 (58)	88 (88)	17 (17)	352
Salamat	7 (7)	21 (21)	39 (39)	76(76)	100 (100)	22 (22)	154
Tandjil	8 (8)	14 (14)	25 (25)	56 (56)	90 (90)	18 (18)	277
N'djamna	11 (10)	21 (20)	37 (35)	58 (57)	80 (80)	22 (21)	725
Comoros 1996							
Grande Comore	13 (12)	21 (19)	33 (29)	49 (44)	72 (68)	24 (22)	777
Moheli	13 (13)	20 (19)	27 (27)	56 (53)	75 (75)	24 (23)	71
Anjouan	7 (7)	11 (10)	19 (17)	38 (32)	64 (55)	15 (14)	513
Côte d'Ivoire 1980							
Abidjan	11 (11)	20 (20)	34 (34)	43 (43)	81 (81)	21 (20)	443
Urban forest	10 (10)	15 (15)	26 (26)	38 (38)	75 (75)	17 (17)	297
Rural forest	11 (11)	16 (16)	26 (26)	44 (44)	65 (65)	20 (20)	1,207
Urban savanna	12 (12)	20 (20)	27 (27)	35 (35)	67 (67)	19 (19)	200
Rural savanna	6 (6)	10 (10)	17 (17)	32 (32)	51 (51)	13 (13)	627
Côte d'Ivoire 1994							
Abidjan	14 (12)	22 (20)	35 (32)	55 (51)	75 (69)	24 (22)	527
Urban forest	11 (11)	19 (18)	30 (30)	40 (40)	68 (66)	20 (20)	584
Rural forest	8 (8)	14 (14)	24 (23)	41 (40)	66 (64)	18 (17)	1,475

Table A.1, Continued

Country, survey date and region	Age (years) 20-24	25-29	30-34	35-39	40-44	20-44	Sample size[a]
Urban savanna	9 (9)	14 (14)	21 (20)	35 (34)	54 (53)	16 (16)	534
Rural savanna	6 (6)	12 (12)	22 (22)	41 (40)	66 (65)	16 (16)	832
Ghana 1979							
Western	8 (8)	12 (12)	22 (21)	49 (48)	79 (79)	18 (18)	249
Central	8 (7)	10 (10)	15 (15)	29 (29)	49 (49)	14 (14)	263
Greater Accra	12 (11)	18 (16)	28 (27)	55 (49)	87 (67)	22 (20)	363
Eastern	6 (6)	12 (12)	25 (24)	41 (40)	64 (62)	17 (17)	522
Volta	7 (7)	13 (12)	22 (22)	43 (42)	66 (66)	16 (16)	331
Ashanti	6 (6)	11 (10)	21 (20)	41 (40)	70 (70)	15 (15)	696
Brong-Ahafo	5 (4)	8 (7)	14 (13)	30 (29)	52 (50)	12 (11)	261
Upper & Northern	6 (6)	8 (8)	15 (14)	21 (21)	49 (49)	10 (10)	540
Ghana 1988							
Western	4 (4)	8 (8)	11 (11)	20 (19)	60 (60)	8 (8)	128
Central	6 (6)	10 (9)	20 (19)	34 (28)	64 (62)	12 (11)	175
Greater Accra	6 (5)	12 (9)	24 (19)	44 (39)	61 (46)	16 (13)	187
Eastern	4 (4)	6 (6)	17 (14)	34 (28)	55 (38)	11 (9)	219
Volta	5 (5)	8 (8)	18 (17)	30 (30)	35 (35)	11 (10)	178
Ashanti	6 (5)	11 (10)	21 (18)	46 (40)	71 (69)	13 (11)	283
Brong-Ahafo	6 (6)	6 (6)	7 (6)	16 (16)	43 (43)	8 (7)	215
Upper & Northern	1 (1)	3 (3)	8 (7)	17 (17)	31 (31)	4 (4)	248
Ghana 1993							
Western	9 (9)	19 (19)	33 (32)	47 (46)	58 (58)	20 (20)	219
Central	8 (8)	14 (12)	17 (15)	39 (35)	75 (75)	15 (14)	249
Greater Accra	9 (9)	19 (16)	39 (30)	63 (49)	89 (73)	24 (21)	321
Eastern	6 (6)	11 (11)	22 (21)	43 (40)	68 (67)	16 (15)	298
Volta	10 (10)	13 (13)	23 (22)	46 (44)	70 (68)	19 (18)	311
Ashanti	6 (6)	14 (14)	26 (24)	41 (38)	56 (52)	16 (15)	437
Brong-Ahafo	7 (5)	12 (10)	20 (18)	38 (34)	61 (52)	14 (13)	247
Upper & Northern	3 (3)	5 (5)	11 (10)	26 (26)	42 (42)	9 (8)	574
Kenya 1977/1978							
Nairobi	7 (6)	11 (9)	35 (28)	55 (38)	82 (47)	18 (14)	257
Central	4 (4)	7 (7)	10 (10)	19 (19)	43 (42)	9 (9)	677
Coast	13 (13)	22 (21)	33 (33)	53 (51)	69 (62)	24 (23)	353
Eastern	6 (5)	9 (8)	13 (12)	24 (21)	52 (49)	12 (11)	708
Nyanza	8 (8)	11 (10)	17 (17)	32 (32)	56 (55)	15 (15)	856
Rift Valley	5 (4)	9 (9)	16 (15)	29 (28)	58 (56)	12 (11)	749
Western	6 (6)	11 (11)	16 (15)	35 (33)	58 (58)	14 (13)	514
Kenya 1989							
Nairobi	10 (8)	21 (12)	42 (20)	61 (27)	95 (10)	23 (13)	240
Central	3 (2)	10 (4)	24 (12)	39 (23)	85 (63)	12 (6)	476
Coast	6 (6)	15 (15)	30 (29)	58 (48)	84 (80)	17 (16)	325
Eastern	6 (5)	6 (5)	15 (10)	33 (26)	73 (66)	10 (8)	288
Nyanza	10 (9)	14 (13)	18 (17)	29 (25)	69 (67)	14 (13)	431

Table A.1, Continued

Country, survey date and region	20-24	25-29	30-34	Age (years) 35-39	40-44	20-44	Sample size[a]
Rift Valley	5 (4)	8 (7)	13 (10)	17 (12)	70 (70)	9 (7)	367
Western	3 (3)	6 (5)	12 (11)	29 (28)	47 (34)	8 (7)	391
Kenya 1993							
Nairobi	13 (11)	24 (17)	52 (34)	80 (58)	70 (39)	31 (22)	126
Central	7 (4)	17 (9)	30 (13)	51 (28)	68 (46)	21 (11)	513
Coast	8 (7)	15 (14)	29 (23)	44 (35)	62 (58)	18 (16)	517
Eastern	4 (3)	10 (7)	24 (16)	43 (29)	49 (40)	14 (10)	533
Nyanza	7 (6)	12 (10)	22 (17)	44 (35)	73 (52)	16 (13)	644
Rift Valley	5 (5)	10 (7)	20 (14)	37 (26)	57 (52)	13 (10)	836
Western	4 (4)	9 (8)	17 (15)	44 (36)	84 (68)	13 (11)	459
Lesotho 1977							
Lowlands	13 (13)	22 (22)	34 (33)	53 (52)	76 (73)	26 (26)	911
Foothills	12 (12)	24 (24)	38 (38)	53 (52)	75 (75)	27 (27)	516
Orange river valley	10 (10)	17 (17)	31 (31)	50 (50)	73 (73)	23 (23)	276
Mountains	16 (16)	25 (25)	38 (37)	58 (58)	84 (84)	29 (29)	374
Liberia 1986							
Sinoe	10 (10)	13 (13)	21 (21)	39 (38)	63 (55)	16 (16)	375
Grand Gedeh	9 (9)	13 (13)	20 (20)	34 (32)	54 (50)	16 (15)	429
Montserrado	12 (11)	19 (17)	33 (30)	48 (40)	58 (53)	21 (19)	344
Rest of country	10 (10)	16 (15)	25 (24)	37 (33)	49 (45)	17 (16)	1,081
Madagascar 1992							
Antananarivo	6 (6)	14 (12)	27 (23)	48 (42)	72 (69)	17 (15)	1,020
Fianarantsoa	9 (9)	16 (16)	25 (25)	45 (45)	87 (87)	18 (18)	648
Toamasina	12 (12)	16 (16)	26 (26)	45 (43)	87 (75)	21 (20)	344
Mahajanga	18 (17)	25 (24)	34 (33)	46 (46)	68 (68)	27 (27)	385
Toliary	23 (23)	29 (28)	42 (41)	62 (60)	81 (81)	33 (33)	323
Antsiranana	19 (19)	23 (22)	33 (31)	42 (39)	77 (74)	26 (25)	284
Mali 1987							
Kayer	11 (11)	17 (17)	30 (30)	50 (50)	52 (52)	18 (18)	166
Koulikoro	7 (7)	16 (16)	25 (24)	45 (44)	59 (59)	16 (16)	186
Sikasso	5 (5)	10 (10)	14 (14)	27 (27)	63 (63)	11 (11)	343
Segou	8 (8)	17 (17)	20 (20)	33 (33)	57 (57)	15 (15)	226
Mopti	7 (7)	11 (11)	14 (14)	30 (30)	44 (44)	13 (13)	275
Timbuktu							
Gao							
Bamako	10 (10)	16 (16)	26 (23)	39 (35)	37 (37)	16 (15)	212
Mali 1995/1996							
Kayer	8 (8)	13 (13)	23 (23)	47 (46)	78 (78)	18 (17)	897
Koulikoro	7 (7)	12 (12)	21 (21)	39 (38)	69 (69)	15 (15)	1,041
Sikasso	5 (5)	9 (9)	17 (16)	34 (32)	59 (56)	12 (12)	1,015
Segou	6 (6)	10 (10)	17 (16)	32 (31)	66 (65)	13 (13)	996
Mopti	5 (5)	9 (9)	17 (17)	36 (36)	73 (73)	13 (13)	779
Timbuktu	4 (4)	8 (7)	15 (15)	35 (33)	78 (70)	11 (10)	251

Table A.1, Continued

Country, survey date and region	20-24	25-29	30-34	Age (years) 35-39	40-44	20-44	Sample size[a]
Gao	10 (9)	16 (16)	29 (28)	51 (50)	73 (73)	20 (20)	301
Bamako	10 (10)	14 (12)	26 (23)	53 (46)	84 (74)	19 (17)	589
Mauretania 1982							
Hodh oriental	15 (15)	22 (22)	33 (33)	28 (28)	15 (15)	21 (21)	108
Hodh occidental	15 (15)	22 (22)	37 (37)	66 (66)	92 (92)	28 (28)	89
Assaba	12 (12)	20 (20)	37 (37)	62 (62)	36 (36)	23 (23)	149
Gorgol	8 (8)	18 (18)	35 (35)	54 (54)	82 (82)	22 (22)	308
Brakna	11 (11)	19 (19)	32 (32)	61 (61)	57 (57)	22 (22)	205
Trarza	5 (5)	17 (17)	29 (29)	49 (49)	76 (76)	22 (22)	237
Adrar	8 (8)	11 (11)	20 (20)	32 (32)	59 (59)	18 (18)	97
Nouadhibu	8 (8)	23 (23)	37 (37)	63 (63)	72 (72)	24 (24)	67
Tagant	7 (7)	14 (14)	29 (29)	52 (52)	65 (65)	18 (18)	53
Guidimaka	12 (12)	23 (23)	41 (40)	69 (66)	73 (67)	25 (24)	252
Tiris Zemmour	7 (7)	15 (15)	36 (36)	44 (44)	36 (36)	19 (19)	44
Inchiri	12 (12)	22 (22)	41 (41)	50 (50)	77 (77)	28 (28)	33
Nouakchott	10 (10)	18 (18)	33 (33)	49 (49)	69 (69)	21 (21)	470
Mozambique 1997							
Niassa	9 (9)	16 (16)	30 (29)	48 (48)	71 (71)	22 (21)	412
Cabo Delgado	20 (20)	30 (30)	35 (35)	37 (37)	57 (57)	29 (29)	351
Nampula	14 (14)	27 (27)	44 (44)	60 (60)	92 (92)	31 (31)	558
Zambzia	10 (10)	19 (18)	34 (32)	44 (36)	54 (53)	20 (19)	435
Tete	2 (2)	8 (7)	17 (17)	42 (42)	64 (64)	10 (9)	249
Manica	5 (5)	11 (11)	20 (20)	32 (31)	46 (39)	13 (13)	437
Sofala	4 (4)	7 (7)	12 (11)	23 (23)	61 (55)	9 (8)	457
Inhambane	15 (15)	27 (25)	39 (34)	67 (56)	80 (72)	32 (29)	401
Gaza	12 (12)	23 (22)	32 (32)	56 (55)	80 (80)	26 (26)	480
Maputo	13 (13)	21 (17)	30 (27)	48 (41)	78 (71)	24 (21)	359
Cidade de Maputo	13 (12)	22 (18)	39 (25)	58 (35)	70 (47)	27 (20)	482
Namibia 1992							
Northwest	6 (5)	8 (8)	15 (13)	24 (22)	57 (52)	13 (12)	600
Northeast	7 (7)	13 (12)	18 (16)	30 (28)	60 (55)	14 (13)	602
Central	14 (11)	25 (22)	43 (32)	61 (45)	72 (62)	33 (26)	184
South	12 (10)	27 (14)	45 (22)	70 (38)	83 (50)	36 (20)	470
Niger 1992							
Niamey	10 (9)	14 (13)	21 (19)	34 (30)	67 (60)	16 (14)	660
Agadez	9 (9)	5 (15)	25 (25)	12 (12)	64 (64)	14 (14)	107
Diffa	20 (20)	31 (31)	39 (39)	52 (52)	50 (50)	28 (28)	80
Dosso	5 (5)	10 (10)	22 (21)	44 (39)	65 (58)	14 (13)	388
Maradi	8 (8)	13 (13)	22 (22)	39 (39)	61 (61)	17 (17)	669
Tahoua	8 (8)	15 (15)	23 (23)	43 (43)	60 (59)	17 (17)	644
Tillab	5 (5)	9 (9)	20 (20)	33 (33)	58 (58)	12 (12)	441
Zinder	12 (12)	22 (22)	36 (36)	52 (52)	74 (74)	24 (24)	686

Table A.1, Continued

Country, survey date and region	Age (years) 20-24	25-29	30-34	35-39	40-44	20-44	Sample size[a]
Nigeria 1981							
Northeast	15 (15)	30 (30)	45 (45)	59 (59)	73 (73)	28 (28)	1,159
Northwest	20 (20)	26 (26)	41 (41)	51 (51)	61 (61)	28 (28)	1,343
Southeast	8 (8)	18 (18)	33 (32)	53 (52)	77 (76)	21 (20)	1,432
Southwest	5 (5)	10 (10)	21 (21)	38 (37)	64 (62)	13 (13)	1,300
Nigeria 1990							
Northeast	15 (15)	24 (23)	35 (34)	45 (44)	68 (65)	25 (25)	1,245
Northwest	9 (9)	13 (13)	29 (29)	45 (45)	76 (76)	18 (18)	1,059
Southeast	6 (6)	11 (10)	24 (24)	43 (40)	62 (61)	15 (14)	1,233
Southwest	3 (3)	8 (7)	19 (16)	37 (31)	52 (49)	12 (10)	1,327
Rwanda 1983							
Kigali	2 (2)	5 (5)	10 (10)	21 (21)	53 (53)	8 (8)	480
Northwest	3 (3)	5 (5)	12 (12)	27 (27)	50 (50)	9 (9)	843
Southwest	3 (3)	5 (5)	11 (11)	20 (20)	39 (39)	8 (8)	357
Central, South	3 (3)	5 (5)	14 (14)	28 (28)	52 (52)	10 (10)	657
Northeast	4 (4)	6 (6)	11 (11)	27 (27)	52 (52)	10 (10)	514
Rwanda 1992							
Kigali	3 (3)	5 (5)	10 (9)	21 (19)	42 (40)	8 (7)	683
Northwest	2 (2)	3 (3)	7 (6)	15 (13)	38 (35)	5 (5)	842
Southwest	2 (2)	4 (4)	10 (9)	23 (21)	64 (59)	8 (7)	430
Central, South	3 (3)	6 (5)	11 (11)	28 (27)	59 (59)	8 (8)	763
Northeast	3 (3)	5 (5)	9 (9)	24 (24)	48 (46)	8 (7)	497
Senegal 1978							
West	9 (9)	15 (15)	25 (24)	39 (39)	69 (69)	18 (18)	621
Center	9 (9)	14 (14)	24 (24)	40 (40)	62 (62)	17 (17)	875
Northwest	10 (10)	19 (19)	29 (29)	45 (45)	60 (60)	21 (21)	358
South	12 (12)	16 (16)	28 (28)	45 (45)	67 (67)	21 (21)	304
Senegal 1986							
West	10 (10)	14 (13)	23 (22)	38 (37)	61 (55)	17 (16)	856
Center	8 (8)	13 (13)	20 (20)	39 (39)	70 (70)	16 (16)	871
Northwest	10 (10)	17 (17)	24 (24)	39 (39)	68 (68)	19 (19)	348
South	10 (10)	13 (13)	25 (25)	36 (36)	58 (55)	18 (18)	315
Senegal 1992/1993							
West	8 (7)	12 (11)	21 (18)	35 (30)	65 (61)	15 (14)	1,095
Center	5 (5)	10 (10)	19 (19)	41 (40)	67 (66)	14 (14)	1,261
Northwest	7 (7)	14 (14)	24 (23)	38 (36)	62 (55)	16 (16)	384
South	7 (7)	13 (13)	24 (24)	39 (39)	55 (55)	15 (15)	574
Sudan 1978							
Khartoum	9 (8)	16 (14)	31 (28)	57 (51)	80 (76)	22 (20)	415
Northern	13 (12)	20 (19)	28 (28)	61 (61)	94 (94)	23 (23)	168
Eastern	11 (11)	18 (18)	32 (32)	54 (54)	84 (84)	20 (20)	351
Central	8 (7)	15 (15)	30 (29)	46 (45)	63 (63)	18 (17)	541
Kordofan	13 (13)	19 (19)	38 (38)	54 (54)	67 (67)	23 (23)	255

Table A.1, Continued

Country, survey date and region	Age (years) 20-24	25-29	30-34	35-39	40-44	20-44	Sample size[a]
Darfur	15 (15)	23 (23)	39 (39)	51 (51)	69 (69)	26 (26)	483
Sudan 1989/1990							
Khartoum	10 (9)	19 (18)	35 (31)	60 (55)	88 (84)	24 (22)	650
Northern	9 (9)	15 (15)	26 (26)	42 (42)	81 (81)	18 (18)	219
Eastern	8 (8)	13 (13)	30 (29)	48 (46)	63 (63)	16 (16)	343
Central	7 (7)	13 (13)	28 (27)	51 (49)	68 (66)	17 (16)	861
Kordofan	5 (5)	11 (10)	19 (19)	40 (40)	67 (67)	13 (13)	480
Darfur	7 (7)	16 (16)	29 (29)	52 (52)	75 (75)	19 (19)	540
Tanzania 1991/1992							
Coastal	9 (9)	16 (16)	29 (27)	47 (45)	64 (60)	20 (19)	1,111
Northern Highlands	6 (6)	9 (8)	15 (12)	35 (29)	63 (56)	13 (11)	377
Lake	8 (8)	14 (14)	24 (23)	43 (42)	67 (66)	18 (17)	1,513
Central	7 (7)	13 (13)	28 (27)	53 (53)	71 (70)	20 (20)	372
Southern Highlands	7 (7)	12 (10)	20 (17)	40 (36)	58 (53)	15 (14)	608
South	15 (14)	22 (21)	29 (27)	47 (43)	73 (65)	26 (24)	612
Tanzania 1996							
Coastal	10 (10)	18 (16)	29 (26)	49 (43)	76 (69)	21 (19)	1,119
Northern Highlands	5 (5)	10 (8)	25 (16)	54 (32)	84 (52)	16 (11)	403
Lake	7 (7)	13 (12)	19 (18)	33 (31)	55 (54)	15 (14)	899
Central	7 (7)	10 (9)	20 (18)	36 (34)	58 (56)	15 (14)	362
Southern Highlands	9 (9)	13 (12)	22 (20)	41 (38)	71 (71)	18 (17)	500
South	13 (12)	17 (17)	24 (22)	40 (34)	66 (62)	21 (19)	631
Togo 1988							
Maritime	5 (4)	8 (7)	11 (9)	23 (23)	52 (52)	9 (8)	479
Des Plateaux	4 (4)	6 (6)	12 (11)	26 (23)	49 (45)	8 (8)	253
Centrale	2 (2)	4 (4)	4 (4)	10 (10)	7 (7)	3 (3)	124
De la Kara	4 (4)	4 (3)	8 (6)	18 (14)	39 (39)	6 (5)	160
Des Savanes	2 (2)	4 (4)	2 (2)	6 (6)	78 (78)	3 (3)	173
Uganda 1988/1989							
Central	5 (15)	20 (20)	27 (25)	36 (34)	66 (58)	20 (19)	588
Eastern	14 (14)	21 (20)	31 (30)	52 (51)	78 (78)	23 (23)	291
Northern	7 (7)	9 (9)	19 (19)	49 (49)	100(100)	11 (11)	62
Western	6 (5)	8 (7)	14 (12)	34 (33)	63 (63)	11 (10)	657
Uganda 1995							
Central	11 (9)	15 (13)	24 (21)	43 (36)	65 (57)	18 (15)	857
Eastern	12 (12)	17 (16)	27 (25)	43 (41)	58 (56)	20 (19)	906
Northern	8 (8)	11 (11)	21 (21)	47 (47)	83 (83)	15 (15)	523
Western	6 (5)	10 (9)	18 (16)	33 (30)	58 (55)	12 (11)	812
Zambia 1992							
Central	10 (10)	13 (13)	19 (18)	44 (43)	68 (68)	18 (17)	279
Copperbelt	8 (8)	15 (14)	22 (19)	39 (36)	64 (57)	16 (15)	721
Eastern	6 (6)	12 (11)	20 (19)	31 (30)	65 (63)	15 (14)	330
Luapula	8 (7)	11 (10)	20 (19)	42 (41)	71 (70)	16 (15)	295

Table A.1, Continued

Country, survey date and region	Age (years) 20-24	25-29	30-34	35-39	40-44	20-44	Sample size[a]
Lusaka	11 (11)	17 (15)	26 (19)	40 (30)	58 (46)	19 (16)	523
Northern	4 (4)	7 (7)	10 (10)	33 (33)	70 (68)	11 (11)	267
North-Western	12 (11)	22 (20)	23 (22)	39 (37)	68 (52)	20 (18)	191
Southern	5 (5)	9 (9)	19 (17)	29 (27)	45 (43)	12 (11)	457
Western	12 (12)	18 (18)	27 (26)	41 (41)	71 (70)	22 (22)	318
Zimbabwe 1988							
Manicaland	5 (5)	7 (6)	16 (14)	27 (23)	45 (36)	10 (9)	215
Mashonaland	6 (5)	9 (8)	22 (17)	36 (31)	62 (55)	13 (11)	564
Matabeleland North	12 (12)	17 (15)	20 (18)	37 (31)	73 (72)	20 (18)	172
Midlands	7 (7)	11 (11)	23 (21)	45 (35)	75 (50)	17 (15)	265
Masvingo	5 (5)	8 (7)	12 (7)	31 (18)	68 (54)	11 (8)	195
Harare/Chitungwiza	9 (7)	15 (11)	30 (21)	51 (37)	58 (54)	17 (13)	144
Bulawayo	8 (6)	23 (16)	43 (25)	73 (49)	86 (63)	27 (18)	127
Zimbabwe 1994							
Manicaland	6 (6)	11 (9)	20 (16)	41 (37)	69 (61)	15 (13)	274
Mashonaland	8 (7)	13 (10)	24 (17)	47 (35)	71 (59)	18 (14)	920
Matabeleland North	9 (8)	13 (11)	21 (18)	36 (30)	65 (58)	17 (15)	603
Midlands	7 (4)	12 (8)	23 (16)	43 (29)	79 (56)	18 (12)	349
Masvingo	9 (6)	15 (12)	25 (21)	43 (35)	58 (52)	19 (15)	317
Harare/Chitungwiza	10 (8)	25 (16)	41 (27)	67 (45)	97 (86)	25 (18)	281
Bulawayo	17 (14)	27 (22)	45 (35)	69 (61)	93 (88)	32 (26)	261

[a] Estimates assuming all current users of a modern contraceptive are fertile at interview are shown in parentheses
[b] Unweighted
[c] Incomplete data set

Table A.2 Per cent primary infertility (PI) in all women (women childless at seven years or more since first marriage), and by region

Country, survey date and region	PI	N[a]	Country, survey date and region	PI	N[a]
			Zou	1	468
Benin 1982[b]			Burkina Faso 1993		
Atacora	3	375	Ouagadougou	3	750
Atlantique	2	210	North	4	563
Borgou	5	298	East	1	588
Mono	3	381	West	4	861
Benin 1996			Central/South	2	812
Atacora	1	602	Burundi 1987		
Atlantique	2	476	Imbo	2	246
Borgou	2	584	Mumirwa	1	152
Mono	1	542	Mugamba	4	113
Oueme	1	411			

Table A.2, Continued

Country, survey date and region	PI	Nᵃ	Country, survey date and region	PI	Nᵃ
Plateaux Centraux	2	714	Urban forest	2	345
Depressions	1	211	Rural forest	4	1,360
Cameroon 1978			Urban savanna	6	216
Yaounde & Douala	2	246	Rural savanna	3	667
North	1	152	Côte d'Ivoire 1994		
Central, South, East	4	113	Abidjan	4	527
West & Littoral	2	714	Urban forest	3	618
Northwest,Southwest	1	211	Rural forest	2	1,522
Cameroon 1991			Urban savanna	3	542
Yaounde & Douala	5	478	Rural savanna	2	872
North	7	709	Ghana 1979		
Central, South, East	7	315	Western	2	260
West & Littoral	3	281	Central	3	268
Northwest, Southwest	4	254	Geater Accra	3	345
CAR 1994/1995			Eastern	1	510
RS I	6	563	Volta	3	329
RS II	5	570	Ashanti	2	729
RS III	4	593	Brong-Ahafo	2	266
RS IV	7	503	Upper & Northern	3	617
RS V	1	485	Ghana 1988		
Bangui	6	624	Western	2	132
Chad 1996/1997			Central	1	174
Batha	3	180	Greater Accra	2	191
B.E.T.	4	47	Eastern	1	225
Biltine	1	102	Volta	1	176
Chari-Baguirmi	6	499	Ashanti	0	282
Gura	7	209	Brong-Ahafo	1	219
Kanem	4	186	Upper & Northern	1	257
Lac	3	145	Ghana 1993		
Logone Occidental	1	263	Western	1	215
Logone Oriental	2	287	Greater Accra	2	191
Mayo-Kebbi	6	449	Eastern	2	294
Moyen-Chari	5	429	Volta	3	298
Ouadda	5	375	Ashanti	2	429
Salamat	6	173	Brong-Ahafo	2	255
Tandjil	4	305	Upper & Northern	1	257
N'djamna	5	796	Ghana 1993		
Comoros 1996			Western	1	215
Grande Comore	5	772	Central	3	250
Moheli	5	77	Greater Accra	2	300
Anjouan	3	497	Eastern	2	294
Côte d'Ivoire 1980			Volta	3	298
Abidjan	4	480	Ashanti	2	429

Table A.2, Continued

Country, survey date and region	PI	N[a]	Country, survey date and region	PI	N[a]
Brong-Ahafo	2	255	Mali 1978		
Upper & Northern	1	569	Kayer	7	197
Kenya 1977			Koulikoro	3	221
Nairobi	3	247	Sikasso	3	413
Central	2	659	Segou	3	252
Coast	5	371	Mopti	3	302
Eastern	2	718	Timbuktu	0	14
Nyanza	4	942	Gao	0	11
Rift Valley	2	778	Bamako	7	245
Western	2	550	Mali 1995/1996		
Kenya 1989			Kayer	4	1,001
Nairobi	3	247	Koulikoro	2	1,120
Central	1	454	Sikasso	2	1,087
Coast	2	346	Segou	2	1,026
Eastern	2	285	Mopti	2	799
Nyanza	3	472	Timbuktu	3	263
Rift Valley	2	382	Gao	3	318
Western	1	387	Bamako	3	612
Kenya 1993			Mauretania 1982		
Nairobi	3	122	Hodh oriental	8	115
Central	1	488	Hodh occidental	11	96
Coast	1	520	Assaba	4	166
Eastern	1	527	Gorgol	2	353
Nyanza	3	654	Brakna	2	235
Rift Valley	1	823	Trarza	3	285
Western	1	463	Adrar	9	120
Lesotho 1977			Nouadhibu	5	82
Lowlands	4	970	Tagant	7	64
Foothills	4	545	Guidimaka	5	309
Orange river valley	4	305	Tiris Zemmour	8	61
Mountains	5	420	Inchiri	0	36
Liberia 1986			Nouakchott	5	587
Sinoe	4	392	Mozambique 1997		
Grand Gedeh	2	456	Niassa	2	472
Montserrado	3	363	Nampula	5	627
Rest of country	3	1,152	Zambzia	5	457
Madagascar 1992			Tete	2	270
Antananarivo	2	976	Manica	1	469
Fianarantsoa	3	649	Sofala	1	485
Toamasina	4	347	Inhambane	6	408
Mahajanga	9	406	Gaza	5	476
Toliary	9	349	Maputo	1	348
Antsiranana	3	283	Cicade de Maputo	2	459

Table A.2, Continued

Country, survey date and region	PI	Nᵃ	Country, survey date and region	PI	Nᵃ
Namibia 1992			Center	3	947
Northwest	2	550	Northwest	5	375
Northeast	2	607	South	5	341
Central	5	172	Senegal 1992/1993		
South	4	398	West	3	1,091
Niger 1992			Center	2	1,363
Niamey	4	705	Northwest	3	420
Agadez	2	120	South	3	626
Diffa	8	91	Sudan 1978		
Dosso	3	461	Khartoum	5	442
Maradi	3	786	Northern	6	179
Tahoua	3	752	Eastern	4	382
Tillab	2	516	Central	5	604
Zinder	6	800	Kordofan	5	272
Nigeria 1981			Darfur	6	486
Northeast	8	1,355	Sudan 1989/1990		
Northwest	11	1,594	Khartoum	5	669
Southeast	3	1,561	Northern	5	224
Southwest	2	1,324	Eastern	3	379
Nigeria 1990			Central	3	918
Northeast	7	1,443	Kordofan	2	511
Northwest	5	1,194	Darfur	2	561
Southeast	1	1,241	Tanzania 1991/1992		
Southwest	1	1,249	Coastal	2	1,142
Rwanda 1983			Northern Highlands	1	361
Kigali	1	469	Lake	2	1,524
Northwest	1	823	Central	4	369
Southwest	3	336	Southern Highlands	1	608
Central, South	1	626	South	3	620
Northeast	1	495	Tanzania 1996		
Rwanda 1992			Coastal	3	1,115
Kigali	2	644	Northern Highlands	2	380
Northwest	1	798	Lake	2	882
Southwest	1	408	Central	2	369
Central, South	0	712	Southern Highlands	3	513
Northeast	0	475	South	3	629
Senegal 1978			Togo 1988		
West	4	655	Maritime	2	482
Center	4	959	Des Plateaux	2	264
Northwest	3	425	Centrale	1	135
South	5	364	De la Kara	3	160
Senegal 1986			Des Savanes	0	188
West	4	873			

Table A.2, Continued

Country, survey date and region	PI	N[a]	Country, survey date and region	PI	N[a]
Uganda 1988/1989			Zimbabwe 1988		
Central	4	624	Manicaland	1	217
Eastern	4	337	Mashonaland	1	585
Northern	1	76	Matabeleland North	4	175
Western	2	691	Midlands	2	263
Uganda			Masvingo	1	195
Central	2	854	Harare/Chitungwiza	1	138
Eastern	4	937	Bulwayo	0	118
Northern	4	562	Zimbabwe 1994		
Western	3	829	Manicaland	1	273
Zambia 1992			Mashonaland	1	948
Central	5	291	Matabeleland North	2	594
Copperbelt	2	741	Midlands	2	329
Eastern	2	350	Masvingo	2	320
Luapula	3	318	Harare/Chitungwiza	2	262
Lusaka	2	529	Bulwayo	2	248
Northern	1	291			
North-Western	3	206			
Southern	2	443			
Western	3	320			

[a] Unweighted
[b] Incomplete data set

Table A.3 Per cent secondary infertility in women by age and region, based on the 'subsequently infertile' estimator and parous women[a]

Country, survey date and region	Age (years)						Sample size[b]
	20-24	25-29	30-34	35-39	40-44	20-44	
Benin 1982[c]							
Atacora	6 (6)	14 (14)	28 (28)	52 (52)	89 (89)	18 (18)	331
Atlantique	4 (4)	16 (16)	36 (36)	56 (56)	84 (84)	22 (22)	176
Borgou	6 (6)	10 (10)	23 (22)	39 (39)	69 (69)	15 (15)	238
Mono	2 (2)	6 (6)	17 (17)	33 (33)	53 (53)	11 (11)	320
Benin 1996							
Atacora	3 (3)	8 (7)	20 (18)	37 (36)	49 (48)	12 (11)	561
Atlantique	4 (3)	7 (6)	19 (19)	45 (44)	72 (69)	14 (13)	467
Borgou	3 (3)	7 (7)	14 (14)	30 (28)	52 (44)	10 (10)	542
Mono	4 (4)	6 (6)	15 (15)	36 (35)	57 (57)	12 (12)	513
Oueme	2 (2)	5 (5)	15 (15)	39 (37)	82 (79)	12 (12)	412
Zou	5 (5)	9 (9)	20 (20)	47 (46)	75 (75)	16 (16)	455

Table A.3, Continued

Country, survey date and region	20-24	25-29	30-34	Age (years) 35-39	40-44	20-44	Sample size[b]
Burkina Faso 1993							
Ouagadougou	7 (6)	12 (10)	26 (22)	51 (44)	72 (65)	16 (14)	717
North	3 (3)	7 (7)	14 (13)	34 (34)	64 (64)	11 (11)	504
East	1 (1)	4 (3)	9 (8)	28 (28)	54 (54)	6 (6)	545
West	5 (5)	11 (11)	19 (18)	40 (39)	85 (85)	14 (14)	784
Central/South	1 (1)	4 (4)	8 (8)	26 (25)	60 (60)	7 (6)	779
Burundi 1987							
Imbo	4 (4)	8 (7)	12 (10)	41 (37)	72 (72)	8 (7)	241
Mumirwa	1 (1)	3 (3)	4 (4)	11 (11)	22 (22)	3 (3)	160
Mugamba	2 (2)	5 (5)	6 (6)	18 (18)	34 (34)	5 (5)	117
Plateaux Centraux	3 (3)	4 (4)	10 (10)	24 (23)	45 (45)	7 (7)	743
Depressions	3 (3)	5 (5)	8 (8)	29 (29)	31 (31)	7 (7)	210
Cameroon 1978							
Yaounde & Douala	14 (14)	24 (23)	39 (37)	58 (56)	78 (77)	26 (25)	565
North	14 (14)	28 (28)	49 (49)	58 (58)	64 (64)	28 (28)	888
Central, South, East	12 (12)	23 (23)	32 (32)	46 (46)	67 (67)	25 (25)	987
West & Littoral	5 (5)	12 (12)	24 (24)	39 (39)	57 (57)	16 (16)	629
Northwest, Southwest	6 (6)	13 (13)	24 (24)	42 (42)	62 (62)	16 (16)	645
Cameroon 1991							
Yaounde & Douala	11 (11)	21 (18)	39 (33)	61 (53)	80 (71)	22 (20)	459
North	11 (11)	19 (19)	30 (30)	46 (46)	66 (66)	20 (20)	554
Central, South, East	12 (12)	22 (22)	34 (33)	57 (56)	89 (88)	26 (25)	278
West & Littoral	5 (5)	12 (11)	23 (19)	44 (37)	66 (61)	16 (14)	268
Northwest, Southwest	6 (6)	14 (13)	26 (23)	46 (40)	65 (59)	17 (16)	244
CAR 1994/1995							
RS I	12 (11)	22 (21)	35 (35)	59 (59)	82 (81)	26 (25)	493
RS II	10 (10)	17 (17)	26 (25)	36 (35)	60 (60)	19 (19)	511
RS III	6 (6)	12 (12)	21 (21)	39 (39)	63 (63)	15 (15)	539
RS IV	18 (17)	31 (30)	44 (43)	62 (59)	80 (74)	32 (31)	451
RS V	14 (14)	27 (27)	46 (45)	60 (59)	86 (86)	30 (30)	409
Bangui	14 (13)	25 (24)	35 (33)	54 (51)	75 (75)	25 (23)	524
Chad 1996/1997							
Batha	4 (4)	5 (5)	16 (16)	38 (38)	63 (63)	12 (12)	156
B.E.T.	17 (17)	28 (28)	33 (33)	27 (27)	100 (100)	25 (25)	45
Biltine	2 (2)	6 (6)	16 (16)	38 (38)	48 (48)	10 (10)	93
Chari-Baguirmi	9 (9)	14 (14)	23 (23)	45 (45)	73 (73)	18 (17)	426
Gura	7 (7)	20 (20)	41 (41)	75 (75)	80 (80)	25 (25)	185
Kanem	2 (2)	6 (6)	14 (14)	34 (34)	75 (75)	11 (11)	162
Lac	4 (4)	9 (9)	20 (20)	53 (53)	85 (85)	16 (16)	116
Logone Occidental	4 (4)	8 (8)	15 (15)	37 (37)	73 (73)	11 (11)	232
Logone Oriental	5 (5)	9 (9)	24 (24)	49 (49)	76 (76)	16 (16)	259
Mayo-Kebbi	6 (6)	13 (13)	25 (25)	47 (46)	86 (86)	18 (18)	385
Mayen-Chari	6 (6)	14 (14)	25 (25)	49 (49)	72 (72)	18 (18)	388

Table A.3, Continued

Country, survey date and region	Age (years) 20-24	25-29	30-34	35-39	40-44	20-44	Sample size[b]
Ouadda	4 (4)	13 (13)	29 (29)	57 (57)	88 (88)	15 (15)	324
Salamat	4 (4)	18 (18)	36 (36)	75 (75)	100 (100)	20 (20)	145
Tandjil	5 (5)	11 (11)	21 (21)	53 (53)	89 (89)	16 (16)	264
N'djamna	10 (9)	20 (18)	35 (33)	57 (55)	79 (79)	21 (20)	675
Comoros 1996							
Grande Comore	10 (9)	18 (16)	31 (26)	47 (42)	71 (67)	21 (19)	739
Moheli	7 (7)	15 (14)	23 (23)	52 (49)	71 (71)	19 (18)	65
Anjouan	5 (4)	9 (8)	18 (16)	38 (32)	64 (55)	14 (12)	501
Côte d'Ivoire 1980							
Abidjan	7 (6)	17 (16)	32 (32)	40 (40)	81 (81)	17 (17)	421
Urban forest	8 (8)	13 (13)	24 (24)	36 (36)	72 (72)	15 (15)	291
Rural forest	7 (7)	13 (13)	22 (22)	40 (40)	61 (61)	16 (16)	1,156
Urban savanna	6 (6)	15 (15)	24 (24)	35 (35)	67 (67)	15 (15)	187
Rural savanna	3 (3)	7 (7)	14 (14)	30 (30)	48 (48)	11 (11)	605
Côte d'Ivoire 1994							
Abidjan	10 (9)	19 (17)	31 (28)	51 (46)	75 (68)	21 (19)	505
Urban forest	8 (8)	16 (16)	27 (27)	38 (38)	68 (66)	17 (17)	565
Rural forest	6 (6)	12 (12)	22 (22)	40 (39)	65 (63)	16 (16)	1,447
Urban savanna	7 (7)	12 (12)	19 (18)	34 (33)	52 (51)	14 (14)	518
Rural savanna	4 (4)	9 (9)	20 (20)	39 (38)	64 (63)	14 (14)	813
Ghana 1979							
Western	6 (6)	9 (9)	20 (20)	48 (47)	79 (79)	16 (16)	244
Central	5 (5)	8 (8)	13 (13)	27 (27)	49 (49)	12 (12)	255
Greater Accra	9 (8)	16 (15)	27 (26)	54 (48)	86 (64)	20 (18)	348
Eastern	6 (6)	11 (11)	24 (23)	41 (39)	64 (62)	17 (16)	515
Volta	5 (5)	11 (10)	19 (19)	40 (39)	61 (61)	14 (13)	322
Ashanti	3 (3)	10 (9)	20 (19)	40 (38)	69 (69)	14 (13)	678
Brong-Ahafo	4 (3)	7 (7)	13 (12)	29 (28)	52 (50)	11 (10)	258
Upper & Northern	3 (3)	6 (6)	12 (12)	18 (18)	49 (49)	8 (7)	522
Ghana 1988							
Western	4 (4)	8 (8)	10 (10)	18 (16)	60 (60)	8 (8)	126
Central	6 (5)	8 (7)	19 (17)	34 (28)	64 (62)	11 (10)	173
Greater Accra	4 (3)	11 (8)	22 (17)	40 (35)	59 (44)	14 (11)	181
Eastern	4 (4)	5 (5)	15 (13)	34 (28)	55 (38)	10 (8)	217
Volta	5 (5)	8 (8)	18 (17)	30 (30)	35 (35)	11 (10)	177
Ashanti	5 (5)	11 (9)	21 (18)	46 (40)	71 (69)	13 (11)	280
Brong-Ahafo	5 (5)	6 (6)	6 (5)	13 (13)	43 (43)	7 (7)	211
Upper & Northern	0 (0)	3 (3)	8 (7)	17 (17)	31 (31)	4 (4)	247
Ghana 1993							
Western	8 (8)	17 (17)	30 (30)	45 (45)	57 (57)	19 (19)	216
Central	6 (5)	11 (9)	14 (12)	38 (35)	75 (75)	13 (12)	241
Greater Accra	7 (7)	17 (15)	37 (29)	62 (48)	89 (73)	23 (19)	314
Eastern	4 (4)	9 (9)	20 (19)	40 (37)	67 (66)	14 (13)	290

Table A.3, Continued

Country, survey date and region	20-24	25-29	30-34	35-39	40-44	20-44	Sample size[b]
Volta	8 (7)	10 (9)	19 (18)	44 (42)	70 (67)	16 (15)	301
Ashanti	5 (4)	12 (11)	23 (21)	39 (36)	56 (51)	14 (13)	426
Brong-Ahafo	6 (5)	10 (9)	18 (16)	38 (34)	61 (52)	13 (11)	240
Upper & Northern	3 (2)	4 (4)	9 (9)	24 (24)	41 (41)	7 (7)	566
Kenya 1977/78							
Nairobi	5 (4)	8 (6)	30 (23)	50 (32)	82 (45)	14 (10)	252
Central	2 (2)	5 (5)	9 (9)	18 (17)	42 (41)	7 (7)	665
Coast	8 (8)	18 (17)	29 (29)	50 (47)	67 (60)	19 (18)	336
Eastern	5 (4)	8 (7)	12 (11)	23 (20)	52 (48)	11 (10)	699
Nyanza	5 (4)	8 (8)	14 (14)	30 (30)	55 (54)	12 (11)	823
Rift Valley	3 (3)	7 (7)	14 (13)	28 (27)	57 (54)	10 (9)	740
Western	5 (5)	9 (9)	14 (13)	34 (31)	57 (56)	12 (12)	502
Kenya 1989							
Nairobi	7 (5)	19 (11)	41 (18)	61 (26)	95 (10)	21 (11)	231
Central	2 (1)	9 (3)	23 (10)	37 (20)	82 (55)	11 (5)	470
Coast	5 (4)	14 (14)	30 (28)	57 (48)	84 (80)	16 (15)	317
Eastern	4 (3)	5 (4)	13 (9)	33 (25)	73 (66)	9 (7)	284
Nyanza	8 (6)	12 (11)	15 (15)	28 (24)	69 (67)	12 (11)	412
Rift Valley	4 (3)	8 (6)	11 (8)	10 (5)	46 (46)	7 (5)	360
Western	3 (2)	5 (4)	11 (10)	27 (25)	41 (27)	7 (6)	385
Kenya 1993							
Nairobi	9 (7)	21 (14)	51 (33)	80 (58)	70 (39)	29 (20)	120
Central	6 (4)	16 (8)	28 (11)	50 (25)	67 (43)	20 (10)	508
Coast	7 (6)	14 (12)	27 (22)	42 (33)	60 (56)	17 (14)	509
Eastern	3 (2)	9 (6)	23 (15)	41 (28)	49 (40)	13 (9)	529
Nyanza	4 (3)	10 (8)	20 (15)	43 (34)	73 (52)	14 (11)	622
Rift Valley	4 (4)	9 (6)	20 (14)	37 (26)	57 (52)	12 (9)	824
Western	3 (2)	8 (6)	16 (14)	44 (35)	84 (68)	12 (10)	453
Lesotho 1977							
Lowlands	9 (9)	18 (18)	31 (30)	50 (50)	76 (73)	23 (22)	869
Foothills	8 (8)	22 (22)	36 (35)	50 (49)	73 (73)	24 (24)	494
Orange river valley	6 (6)	14 (13)	27 (27)	47 (47)	71 (71)	20 (19)	262
Mountains	11 (11)	20 (20)	34 (33)	55 (55)	83 (83)	25 (25)	354
Liberia 1986							
Sinoe	5 (5)	8 (8)	18 (18)	37 (37)	63 (55)	13 (12)	359
Grand Gedeh	7 (7)	11 (11)	18 (18)	32 (30)	53 (49)	14 (13)	420
Montserrado	9 (8)	17 (15)	31 (28)	47 (38)	58 (53)	19 (17)	331
Rest of country	8 (7)	14 (13)	24 (22)	35 (32)	49 (45)	15 (14)	1,044
Madagascar 1992							
Antananarivo	5 (4)	13 (11)	25 (21)	47 (40)	71 (68)	16 (13)	1,001
Fianarantsoa	6 (6)	12 (12)	21 (21)	40 (40)	85 (85)	14 (14)	624
Toamasina	9 (9)	12 (11)	21 (20)	41 (38)	87 (73)	16 (16)	326
Mahajanga	9 (9)	16 (16)	26 (24)	40 (39)	64 (64)	19 (18)	349

Table A.3, Continued

Country, survey date and region	20-24	25-29	30-34	Age (years) 35-39	40-44	20-44	Sample size[b]
Toliary	16 (16)	21 (20)	35 (33)	54 (53)	77 (77)	26 (25)	296
Antsiranana	16 (16)	19 (18)	27 (25)	37 (34)	75 (72)	22 (21)	274
Mali 1987							
Kayes	5 (5)	11 (11)	22 (22)	41 (41)	48 (48)	11 (11)	154
Koulikoro	4 (4)	13 (13)	23 (23)	44 (43)	58 (58)	14 (14)	180
Sikasso	3 (3)	6 (6)	9 (9)	21 (21)	62 (62)	7 (7)	336
Segou	7 (7)	16 (16)	20 (20)	32 (32)	55 (55)	14 (14)	221
Mopti	5 (5)	9 (9)	14 (14)	30 (30)	44 (44)	11 (11)	266
Timbuktu[d]							13
Gao[d]							13
Bamako	5 (5)	13 (12)	24 (21)	39 (34)	37 (37)	12 (11)	199
Mali 1995/1996							
Kayes	5 (5)	10 (10)	20 (20)	44 (44)	77 (77)	14 (14)	861
Koulikoro	5 (5)	11 (10)	20 (20)	39 (38)	69 (69)	14 (13)	1,016
Sikasso	3 (3)	7 (7)	15 (14)	32 (30)	56 (54)	10 (10)	999
Segou	4 (4)	8 (8)	14 (14)	30 (29)	64 (63)	11 (11)	971
Mopti	3 (3)	7 (7)	15 (15)	34 (34)	72 (72)	11 (11)	757
Timbuktu	3 (3)	6 (6)	13 (13)	33 (31)	77 (67)	9 (9)	246
Gao	6 (6)	12 (12)	26 (25)	49 (48)	71 (71)	17 (17)	290
Bamako	7 (7)	12 (11)	25 (21)	52 (45)	84 (73)	17 (15)	572
Mauretania 1982							
Hodh oriental	9 (9)	17 (17)	29 (29)	28 (28)	15 (15)	16 (16)	99
Hodh occidental	10 (10)	17 (17)	33 (33)	65 (65)	92 (92)	23 (23)	81
Assaba	9 (9)	18 (18)	36 (36)	62 (62)	36 (36)	21 (21)	144
Gorgol	6 (6)	17 (17)	34 (34)	54 (54)	82 (82)	21 (21)	301
Brakna	8 (8)	16 (16)	30 (30)	60 (60)	57 (57)	19 (19)	198
Trarza	3 (3)	15 (15)	28 (28)	48 (48)	75 (75)	20 (20)	232
Adrar	4 (4)	8 (8)	15 (15)	27 (27)	57 (57)	13 (13)	90
Nouadhibu	4 (4)	18 (18)	28 (28)	55 (55)	71 (71)	18 (18)	65
Tagant	2 (2)	6 (6)	19 (19)	50 (50)	65 (65)	12 (12)	51
Guidimaka	8 (8)	19 (19)	36 (35)	65 (62)	66 (59)	20 (20)	240
Tiris Zemmour	4 (4)	12 (12)	31 (31)	37 (37)	36 (36)	15 (15)	42
Inchiri	12 (12)	22 (22)	41 (41)	50 (50)	77 (77)	28 (28)	33
Nouakchott	6 (6)	14 (14)	30 (30)	47 (47)	68 (68)	17 (17)	451
Mozambique 1997							
Niassa	8 (8)	14 (13)	29 (27)	47 (47)	71 (71)	20 (20)	403
Cabo Delgado	12 (12)	24 (24)	31 (31)	34 (34)	55 (55)	23 (23)	310
Nampula	10 (10)	23 (23)	40 (40)	56 (56)	91 (91)	27 (27)	529
Zamb,zia	7 (7)	16 (15)	30 (27)	38 (30)	46 (45)	16 (15)	417
Tete	1 (0)	7 (6)	17 (17)	42 (42)	64 (64)	9 (9)	245
Manica	5 (4)	10 (10)	18 (18)	29 (27)	39 (31)	12 (11)	432
Sofala	4 (3)	7 (6)	11 (11)	23 (22)	61 (54)	8 (8)	443
Inhambane	10 (10)	23 (21)	37 (32)	66 (55)	80 (72)	29 (26)	65

Table A.3, Continued

Country, survey date and region	Age (years) 20-24	25-29	30-34	35-39	40-44	20-44	Sample size[b]
Gaza	7 (7)	18 (17)	27 (27)	53 (52)	79 (79)	22 (22)	463
Maputo	13 (12)	18 (16)	29 (25)	47 (40)	77 (71)	23 (20)	347
Cidade de Maputo	11 (11)	20 (16)	38 (23)	56 (33)	69 (45)	25 (18)	468
Namibia 1992							
Northwest	4 (3)	6 (6)	14 (12)	23 (21)	55 (50)	12 (10)	585
Northeast	5 (5)	12 (11)	17 (15)	29 (27)	59 (54)	13 (12)	585
Central	9 (7)	21 (19)	40 (29)	59 (43)	69 (58)	29 (23)	172
South	10 (8)	25 (12)	43 (20)	69 (36)	83 (49)	34 (18)	453
Niger 1992							
Niamey	6 (6)	11 (9)	20 (18)	32 (28)	67 (60)	13 (11)	632
Agadez	8 (8)	13 (13)	22 (22)	11 (11)	64 (64)	12 (12)	105
Diffa	10 (10)	23 (23)	33 (33)	49 (49)	50 (50)	20 (19)	73
Dosso	2 (2)	7 (6)	18 (17)	42 (38)	63 (55)	11 (10)	377
Maradi	6 (6)	12 (12)	21 (21)	38 (38)	60 (60)	15 (15)	653
Tahoua	5 (5)	13 (12)	21 (21)	42 (42)	60 (59)	14 (14)	622
Tillab	4 (4)	7 (7)	18 (18)	33 (33)	58 (58)	11 (11)	432
Zinder	8 (8)	18 (18)	31 (31)	50 (50)	74 (74)	19 (19)	646
Nigeria 1981							
Northeast	8 (8)	22 (22)	38 (38)	53 (53)	71 (71)	20 (20)	1,077
Northwest	10 (10)	18 (18)	32 (31)	42 (42)	51 (50)	18 (18)	1,213
Southeast	6 (5)	15 (14)	29 (28)	48 (47)	74 (73)	17 (17)	1,392
Southwest	3 (3)	8 (8)	19 (19)	37 (36)	63 (61)	11 (11)	1,270
Nigeria 1990							
Northeast	9 (8)	16 (16)	27 (26)	39 (38)	64 (60)	18 (17)	1,152
Northwest	4 (4)	8 (8)	25 (25)	42 (42)	75 (75)	14 (13)	1,005
Southeast	5 (5)	10 (9)	24 (23)	42 (40)	61 (61)	14 (14)	1,217
Southwest	3 (2)	7 (6)	18 (15)	37 (31)	52 (49)	11 (9)	1,314
Rwanda 1983							
Kigali	1 (1)	4 (4)	10 (10)	21 (21)	53 (53)	7 (7)	473
Northwest	1 (1)	4 (4)	11 (11)	26 (26)	49 (49)	8 (8)	833
Southwest	1 (1)	4 (4)	10 (10)	19 (19)	36 (36)	6 (6)	347
Central, South	1 (1)	5 (5)	13 (13)	28 (28)	52 (52)	9 (9)	648
Northeast	2 (2)	5 (5)	9 (9)	25 (25)	51 (51)	8 (8)	507
Rwanda 1992							
Kigali	2 (1)	4 (4)	9 (8)	21 (19)	42 (40)	6 (6)	671
Northwest	1 (1)	2 (2)	6 (6)	14 (13)	37 (35)	4 (4)	830
Southwest	1 (1)	3 (3)	10 (8)	23 (20)	64 (59)	7 (6)	425
Central, South	2 (2)	5 (5)	11 (10)	27 (27)	59 (59)	8 (8)	759
Northeast	2 (2)	5 (4)	9 (9)	24 (24)	48 (46)	7 (7)	493
Senegal 1978							
West	6 (6)	11 (11)	22 (21)	36 (36)	66 (66)	15 (15)	600
Center	6 (6)	10 (10)	21 (21)	39 (39)	61 (61)	14 (14)	838
Northwest	9 (9)	17 (17)	28 (28)	43 (43)	60 (60)	19 (19)	350

Table A.3, Continued

Country, survey date and region	Age (years) 20-24	25-29	30-34	35-39	40-44	20-44	Sample size[b]
South	8 (8)	13 (13)	27 (27)	45 (45)	67 (67)	18 (18)	288
Senegal 1986							
West	6 (6)	11 (10)	20 (18)	35 (33)	58 (52)	13 (12)	819
Center	5 (5)	10 (10)	17 (17)	36 (36)	68 (68)	13 (13)	844
Northwest	6 (6)	13 (13)	21 (21)	37 (37)	67 (67)	15 (15)	333
South	5 (5)	9 (9)	21 (21)	32 (32)	58 (55)	14 (14)	301
Senegal 1992/93							
West	5 (5)	10 (9)	20 (16)	34 (29)	64 (61)	13 (12)	1,063
Center	4 (4)	8 (8)	18 (17)	40 (39)	67 (66)	12 (12)	1,232
Northwest	5 (5)	11 (10)	21 (21)	38 (37)	55 (55)	13 (13)	556
South	5 (5)	11 (11)	20 (20)	35 (33)	61 (55)	13 (13)	373
Sudan 1978							
Khartoum	5 (4)	12 (10)	28 (24)	54 (49)	79 (75)	18 (16)	392
Northern	6 (6)	15 (14)	23 (22)	57 (57)	93 (93)	17 (17)	157
Eastern	6 (6)	12 (12)	28 (28)	54 (54)	84 (84)	15 (15)	329
Central	5 (4)	12 (11)	28 (26)	44 (43)	62 (62)	14 (14)	516
Kordofan	9 (9)	15 (15)	32 (32)	49 (49)	66 (66)	18 (18)	242
Darfur	9 (9)	18 (18)	33 (33)	46 (46)	64 (64)	20 (20)	453
Sudan 1989/90							
Khartoum	6 (6)	16 (14)	32 (27)	57 (52)	87 (83)	20 (18)	614
Northern	4 (4)	11 (11)	23 (23)	38 (38)	81 (81)	14 (14)	209
Eastern	6 (6)	12 (12)	28 (27)	48 (46)	63 (63)	14 (14)	334
Central	5 (5)	11 (11)	26 (25)	50 (47)	68 (66)	15 (14)	835
Kordofan	4 (4)	9 (9)	18 (17)	37 (37)	66 (66)	12 (12)	470
Darfur	5 (5)	14 (14)	25 (25)	49 (49)	74 (74)	16 (16)	526
Tanzania 1991/92							
Coastal	8 (7)	15 (14)	27 (26)	46 (44)	64 (60)	19 (18)	1,085
Northern Highlands	5 (5)	9 (8)	14 (11)	35 (29)	63 (56)	13 (11)	374
Lake	7 (6)	13 (12)	22 (21)	41 (40)	65 (64)	16 (15)	1,475
Central	3 (3)	8 (8)	23 (22)	47 (47)	69 (69)	15 (15)	360
Southern Highlands	6 (6)	11 (10)	20 (17)	40 (36)	58 (53)	14 (13)	602
South	12 (11)	19 (18)	26 (24)	45 (40)	72 (64)	23 (21)	593
Tanzania 1996							
Coastal	8 (8)	16 (14)	27 (24)	49 (42)	76 (69)	20 (18)	1,085
Northern Highlands	3 (3)	8 (7)	24 (15)	54 (32)	84 (52)	15 (10)	394
Lake	6 (5)	11 (10)	17 (16)	32 (30)	55 (54)	13 (13)	882
Central	5 (5)	9 (7)	18 (16)	34 (32)	57 (55)	13 (12)	352
Southern Highlands	7 (7)	11 (10)	20 (18)	40 (37)	71 (71)	16 (15)	488
South	10 (10)	16 (15)	22 (20)	38 (32)	63 (59)	19 (17)	607
Togo 1988							
Maritime	3 (3)	6 (5)	9 (8)	21 (21)	52 (52)	7 (6)	467
Des Plateaux	1 (1)	3 (3)	9 (9)	21 (18)	49 (45)	5 (5)	247
Centrale	1 (1)	4 (4)	4 (4)	10 (10)	7 (7)	3 (3)	123

Table A.3, Continued

Country, survey date and region	20-24	25-29	30-34	Age (years) 35-39	40-44	20-44	Sample size[b]
De la Kara	1 (1)	2 (1)	7 (5)	18 (14)	35 (35)	4 (4)	156
Des Savanes	2 (2)	4 (4)	2 (2)	6 (6)	78 (78)	3 (3)	171
Uganda 1988/89							
Central	10 (10)	16 (15)	22 (20)	31 (29)	62 (52)	16 (15)	566
Eastern	9 (9)	16 (16)	26 (24)	47 (46)	74 (74)	18 (18)	276
Northern	7 (7)	9 (9)	19 (19)	49 (49)	100 (100)	11 (11)	61
Western	4 (3)	7 (6)	12 (10)	32 (30)	61 (61)	9 (8)	647
Uganda 1995							
Central	9 (7)	13 (11)	22 (19)	42 (34)	65 (57)	16 (13)	833
Eastern	8 (8)	15 (14)	24 (23)	41 (39)	58 (55)	17 (16)	872
Northern	5 (5)	9 (9)	20 (20)	47 (46)	83 (83)	13 (13)	498
Western	3 (3)	8 (7)	17 (15)	31 (28)	57 (53)	10 (10)	793
Zambia 1992							
Central	6 (6)	11 (11)	17 (17)	44 (42)	68 (68)	15 (15)	267
Copperbelt	7 (7)	14 (13)	21 (19)	39 (36)	63 (56)	15 (14)	705
Eastern	5 (5)	11 (10)	20 (18)	31 (30)	65 (63)	14 (13)	321
Luapula	4 (4)	8 (7)	18 (17)	40 (39)	70 (68)	13 (12)	283
Lusaka	10 (9)	16 (13)	25 (18)	40 (30)	58 (46)	18 (15)	512
Northern	3 (3)	6 (6)	10 (10)	32 (32)	68 (66)	10 (10)	266
North-Western	10 (9)	19 (18)	21 (19)	38 (36)	68 (52)	18 (16)	185
Southern	3 (3)	8 (7)	17 (15)	29 (26)	45 (43)	10 (9)	446
Western	9 (9)	16 (15)	25 (24)	39 (39)	70 (70)	20 (19)	308
Zimbabwe 1988							
Manicaland	4 (4)	7 (6)	16 (14)	27 (23)	45 (36)	10 (8)	213
Mashonaland	5 (4)	8 (7)	21 (16)	35 (31)	61 (54)	12 (10)	556
Matabeleland North	9 (9)	13 (11)	15 (13)	34 (28)	71 (70)	16 (14)	165
Midlands	5 (5)	9 (9)	21 (18)	43 (32)	72 (42)	15 (12)	258
Masvingo	4 (3)	8 (7)	12 (7)	31 (18)	68 (54)	10 (8)	193
Harare/Chitungwiza	8 (6)	14 (10)	29 (20)	51 (37)	58 (54)	16 (12)	142
Bulawayo	8 (6)	23 (16)	43 (25)	73 (49)	86 (63)	27 (18)	126
Zimbabwe 1994							
Manicaland	5 (5)	11 (9)	19 (16)	40 (36)	69 (61)	15 (13)	271
Mashonaland	8 (6)	12 (10)	23 (17)	47 (34)	71 (59)	18 (14)	908
Matabeleland North	7 (6)	11 (10)	20 (17)	35 (29)	65 (57)	16 (13)	592
Midlands	6 (3)	11 (7)	22 (15)	42 (28)	79 (56)	17 (11)	344
Masvingo	7 (5)	13 (10)	24 (19)	41 (33)	58 (51)	17 (13)	312
Harare/Chitungwiza	9 (7)	23 (15)	39 (25)	66 (44)	97 (86)	24 (16)	273
Bulawayo	14 (11)	25 (19)	42 (32)	67 (58)	93 (88)	29 (23)	254

[a] Estimates assuming all current users of a modern contraceptive are fertile at interview are shown in parentheses
[b] Unweighted
[c] Incomplete data set
[d] Too few observations to calculate the 'subsequently infertile' estimator

Acknowledgements

This chapter is based on a paper presented at a UNAIDS/USAID/ MEASURE Evaluation/CDC meeting on 'Infertility, STDs and HIV: problems and prospects', Arlington, Virginia, December 14-15 1998. Some of the findings presented in this chapter were published in an article entitled 'Primary and Secondary Infertility in sub-Saharan Africa' in *International Journal of Epidemiology* 2000 29: 285-291.

Note

1. The estimates of age-specific infertility presented by Larsen (1994) are based on yearly counts. Therefore, they differ slightly from the estimates presented in this chapter, which are based on monthly counts. Improvements in data quality justify the use of monthly counts, e.g. there are fewer imputed monthly dates in the recent DHS surveys than in the WFS surveys.

Bibliography

Arya OP, Nsanzumuhire H and Taber SR (1973), 'Clinical, cultural and demographic aspects of gonorrhea in a rural community in Uganda'. *Bulletin of the World Health Organization* 48: 587.

Arya, OP, Taber SR and Nsanze H (1980), 'Gonorrhea and female infertility in rural Uganda'. *American Journal of Gynecology* 138: 929-32.

Bongaarts J and Potter RG (1983), *Fertility, biology, and behaviour: an analysis of the proximate determinants*, Academic Press, New York.

Cates W, Farley TMM and Rowe PJ (1985), 'Worldwide patterns of infertility: is Africa different?' *Lancet* 2(8455): 596-98.

Collins JA, Wrixon W, James LB, and Wilson EH (1983), 'Treatment-independent pregnancy among infertile couples'. *New England Journal of Medicine* 309: 1201-1206.

Demographic and Health Surveys (1990), 'An assessment of DHS-I data quality'. In: *DHS Methodological Reports* No.1, Institute for Resource Development, Macro International Inc., Calverton, MD, USA.

Demographic and Health Surveys (1994), 'An assessment of the quality of health data in DHS-I surveys'. In: *DHS Methodological Reports* No. 2, Macro International Inc., Calverton, MD, USA.

Demographic and Health Surveys (1996), 'Accuracy of DHS-II demographic data: gains and losses in comparison with earlier surveys'. In: *DHS Working Papers* No. 19, Macro International Inc., Calverton, MD, USA.

Demographic and Health Surveys (1999), 'Summary of demographic and health surveys as of April, 1999', Macro International Inc., Calverton, MD, USA. DHS (Demographic and Health Surveys) for all years mentioned in the text have been carried out under the sponsorship of Macro International Inc., Calverton, Maryland, USA. See also HYPERLINK http://www.macroint.com/dhs

Ericksen K and Brunette T (1996), 'Patterns and predictors of infertility among African women: a cross-national survey of twenty-seven nations'. *Social Science and Medicine* 42: 209-20.

Frank O (1983), 'Infertility in Sub-Saharan Africa'. In: *Center for Policy Studies Working Papers*, No. 97, The Population Council, New York, USA.

Henin RA (1982), 'Fertility, infertility and sub-fertility in Eastern Africa', Nairobi Population Studies and Research Institute, University of Nairobi.

Hunt CW (1989), 'Migrant labour and sexually transmitted disease: AIDS in Africa'. *Journal of Health and Social Behaviour* 30: 353-74.

Larsen U (1993), 'Levels, age patterns and trends of sterility in selected countries south of the Sahara'. In: IUSSP *International Population Conference* Vol. 1, Montreal: 593-605.

Larsen U (1994), 'Sterility in Sub-Saharan Africa'. *Population Studies* 48: 459-74.

Larsen U (1995a), 'Differentials in infertility in Cameroon and Nigeria'. *Population Studies* 49: 329-46.

Larsen U (1995b), 'Trends in infertility in Cameroon and Nigeria'. *International Family Planning Perspectives* 21: 138-42.

Larsen U and Menken J (1989), 'Measuring sterility from incomplete birth histories'. *Demography* 26: 185-202.

Larsen U and Menken J (1991), 'Individual-level sterility: a new method of estimation with application to sub-Saharan Africa'. *Demography* 28: 29-49.

Menken J, Trussell J and Larsen U (1986), 'Age and infertility'. *Science* 233: 1389-94.

Page H and Coale A (1972), 'Fertility and child mortality south of the Sahara'. In: Ominde SH and Ejiogu CN (eds), *Population growth and economic development in Africa*, Heinemann, London: 51-67.

Pressat R and Wilson C (1985), *The dictionary of demography*, Blackwell, New York.

Retel-Laurentin A (1974), 'Sub-fertility in black Africa - the case of the Nzakara in Central African Republic'. In: Adadevoh BK (ed.), *Subfertility and infertility in Africa*, Caxton Press, Ibadan: 69-80.

Romaniuk A (1968), 'Infertility in tropical Africa'. In: Caldwell JC and Okonjo C (eds), *The population of tropical Africa*, Longmans, London: 214-24.

Rowe PJ and Vikhlyaeva EM (eds), (1988), *Diagnosis and treatment of infertility*, Hans Huber Publishers, Toronto.

Sherris J and Fox G (1983), 'Infertility and sexually transmitted disease: a public health challenge'. In: *Population Reports* Series L, No.4: L113-L151.

Tabutin D (1982), 'Évolution Régionale de la Fécondité dans l'Ouest du Zaire'. *Population* 37: 29-50.

World Fertility Survey: Major Findings and Implications (1984), Alden Press, Oxford.

World Health Organization (1969), *Technical Report Series* No. 435, Geneva.

World Health Organization (1975), The Epidemiology of Infertility. Report of WHO Scientific Group on the Epidemiology of Infertility, *Technical Report Series* No. 582, Geneva.

World Health Organization (1987), 'Infections, pregnancies, and infertility: perspectives on prevention'. *Fertility and Sterility* 47: 964-68.

World Health Organization (1992), 'Reproductive health: a key to a brighter future'. In: Khanna J, van Look PFA and Griffin PD (eds), *Biennial Report 1990-1991*, Geneva.

World Health Organization (1994), 'Challenges in reproductive health research'. In: *Biennial Report 1992-1993*, Geneva.

Vodun cult figure said
to improve fertility;
cavities hold magic
substances to be applied
to the body (Fon, Benin)

2 The role of reproductive tract infections

Philippe Mayaud

Worldwide, the World Health Organization (WHO) estimates that 60 to 80 million couples may be infertile (Fathalla, 1992). Infertility has long appeared to be an immense problem for individuals, couples and communities in sub-Saharan Africa. However, measurement of the public health impact has been constrained by the lack of investigative facilities to determine its aetiologies, by scarce therapeutic resources, and by the stigma attached in Africa to this devastating physical and social condition.

Reproductive tract infections (RTIs), including sexually transmitted infections (STIs), appear to contribute enormously to the burden of ill-health, particularly among women in sub-Saharan Africa (World Bank, 1993). This chapter reviews some of the known etiological factors of male and female infertility in sub-Saharan Africa. It will focus specifically on the role of STIs (including HIV), poor obstetrical management and adverse pregnancy outcomes in the patho-physiological mechanisms leading to infertility. In addition, relevant policy and research recommendations will be given.

Definitions

Infertility can be defined in several ways (see also the Introduction). For clinico-epidemiological purposes, Belsey distinguishes three categories, each with different processes and aetiologies, all of which may lead to childlessness (Belsey, 1976), and each of which has distinct implications for the amelioration or prevention of infertility (Meheus, 1992).
- inability to conceive or impregnate, i.e. *infecundity* or *infertility*, terms often used interchangeably in the medical literature;
- inability to carry pregnancy to term, i.e. *pregnancy wastage*, which includes both spontaneous abortion and stillbirth;
- failure of a live birth to survive, i.e. *infant* or *child loss*.

The magnitude and distribution of the various forms of infertility in sub-Saharan Africa is presented by Larsen and Raggers in Chapter 1. This chapter focuses on the first category listed above, the 'inability to conceive'.

Over 25 pathogens, including bacteria, viruses, protozoal agents, fungal agents and ecto-parasites, can be transmitted via the sexual route (Piot and Holmes, 1990), causing STIs. Most infect the reproductive tract as their primary site, although not all may have sexual transmission as their dominant route of spread. For example, in countries with low standards of hygiene, the hepatitis B virus is mainly transmitted horizontally between siblings. The most important bacterial STIs include gonorrhoea (*Neisseria gonorrhoeae*), chlamydia infection (*Chlamydia trachomatis* strains D-K and L1-L3), chancroid (*Haemophilus ducreyi*) and syphilis (*Treponema pallidum*), while the most important viral infections include HIV, *Herpes simplex* type-2, Hepatitis B virus, and Human Papilloma viruses. The most frequent protozoal agent is *Trichomonas vaginalis*.

Reproductive tract infections (RTIs) have been defined to include STIs as well as infections that are non-sexually transmitted. The latter group consist of endogenous infections, such as bacterial vaginosis or vulvovaginal candidiasis caused by an overgrowth of organisms that can be present in the genital tract of healthy women, and iatrogenic infections which are associated with improperly performed medical procedures. These procedures can include unsafe abortions, poor delivery practices, pelvic examinations and IUD insertions (Wasserheit, 1989a; Wasserheit and Holmes, 1992; Meheus, 1992).

Infertility

Reproductive anatomy and endocrinology

The female genital tract is divided into the lower genital tract (vulva, vagina and cervix) and the upper genital tract (uterus, fallopian tubes and ovaries). The upper tract is usually sterile and shielded from infections by the cervix and cervical mucus which act as fairly effective mechanical and chemical barriers (Sweet *et al.*, 1986; Meheus, 1992). The ovaries are situated in the open peritoneal cavity, and there is communication between the normally aseptic uterine cavity and the lining of other vital organs such as the liver and intestines. The male genital tract comprises of the organs of sperm production (testes) and transport structures or ducts (epididymis, vas deferens, urethra) with satellite structures that contribute to the quality and quantity of sperm (prostate, seminal glands). The hypothalamo-pituitary-gonad axis plays a central role in causing the secretion of hormones by testes and ovaries, in inducing the maturation of spermatozoa and ova and in the normal development of sexual organs. The female menstrual cycle also depends upon this system for its induction and maintenance.

Causes

Following from the above summary of reproductive systems, there are two main mechanisms of infertility: inappropriate hormonal or endocrine functions which prevent spermatogenesis, egg release or fertilization; and damage to the epithelium or the organs themselves, preventing sperm transport or emission, or impeding implantation of a fertilized egg.

From the medical and public health viewpoint, there are 'core' causes of infertility that are for the most part untreatable since they arise from chromosomal, congenital and endocrinological abnormalities. However, some causes are 'acquired': they result from infectious, environmental and occupational factors. These can usually be prevented or corrected (Cates *et al.*, 1985).

Gender factors

Infertility is a disease of couples and can result from female factors, male factors, or couple factors, and a certain proportion of 'unknown' factors.

Female infertility, PID and STI in Africa

Female infertility factors

Previous literature reviews of the global epidemiology of infertility have attempted to ascertain the distribution of causal factors (Belsey, 1976; Sherris and Fox, 1983). In studies of infertile couples in Denmark, Israel, USA and Singapore (so called 'developed' countries), female factors accounted for 50-70% of all cases of infertility. Ovulation disorders accounted for 20-30% of these cases, tubal factors for 15-25%, uterine factors for 10% and a 'hostile' cervical environment for 5%. Endometriosis is a condition in which endometrial tissue grows on genital structures other than the uterus, causing adhesions and fibrosis: this disease may be present in 10 to 15% of cases (Sherris and Fox, 1983). This pattern does not seem to have changed recently (Symonds and Symonds, 1998).

A few, more limited, studies have investigated infertile couples in developing countries, including sub-Saharan Africa; most focused on female partners only. The lack of uniformity in data collection and the variation in patient selection among these studies makes it difficult to compare data. Thus, in the early 1980s, the WHO sponsored a multicentre research project spanning 35 medical centres in 25 countries throughout the developed and developing world (Cates et al., 1985). Over 5,800 infertile couples completed the investigation, including 842 from four urban centres in Africa: Nigeria, Zambia, Kenya and Cameroon. The results of the WHO study and the results of studies undertaken in Africa after that study are presented in Table 1. Figure 1 shows the distribution of infertility factors in couples in 'developed' countries compared with African countries (Percentages sum to more than 100 due to multiple causes of infertility).

Table 1 Causes of infertility in couples or women seeking treatment in African clinics

Country, year of study, (reference)	No. of couples	Causes of infertility (% of couples)			
		Male factors	Female factors	Male + female	Unknown
Nigeria, NA (Chukudebulu et al., 1979)[a]	114	48	50	4	2
Africa, 1979-1984; Africa/WHO, 1985 (Cates et al., 1985)	842	43	45	35	5
South Africa, 1986 (Wiswedel and Allen, 1989)	904	36	62	NA	2.4
Gabon, 1988 (Collet et al., 1988)	304[b]	NA	88	NA	12
Ethiopia, 1987/1988, (Sudik et al., 1989)	101[b]	NA	61	NA	39
Senegal, 1983-1989 (Cisse et al., 1992)	429	25	75	NA	NA
South Africa, NA (Chigumadzi et al., 1998)	100	21	NA	NA	NA

NA: not available

[a] Cited in Sherris and Fox, 1983

[b] Women, rather than couples

Source: Based on a literature review of studies in Africa in the 1980s and 1990s

(Format adapted from Sherris and Fox, 1983)

Tubal factors

Some earlier studies (1960-1980) conducted in Kenya, Gabon and Nigeria suggested that fallopian tube damage, or tubal factor infertility (TFI) might have a predominant role among the causes of female infertility in Africa (Sherris and Fox, 1983). The WHO study confirmed this by recording a higher proportion of women with TFI in sub-Saharan Africa compared with women from developed countries (64% and 27% respectively; Cates *et al.*, 1985). More recent series conducted in specialized clinics from Senegal (Cisse *et al.*, 1992), Gabon (Collet *et al.*, 1988), Ethiopia (Sudik *et al.*, 1989) and South Africa (Wiswedel and Allen, 1989; Chigumadzi *et al.*, 1998) have confirmed that the high rates of tubal damage or tubal occlusion, ranging from 57% to 83%) are a primary cause of female infertility (Table 1, Figure 1).

TFI is far more frequently reported as an underlying cause of female infertility in sub-Saharan Africa than in other regions of the world (Figure 2). The WHO multicentre study reported a two- to three-fold higher level of either bilateral tubal occlusion or other tubal damage in sub-Saharan Africa than in Asian, Eastern Mediterranean or Latin American regions (Cates *et al.*, 1985).

Table 1, Continued

Causes of female infertility
(as % of total female infertility)

Tubal factors	Ovulation disorders	Cervical factors	Uterine factors	Endo-metriosis	Multiple female causes	Other causes
50	24	0	14	0	NA	10
85	26	NA	NA	1	NA	NA
57	29	7	6	4	43	NA
83	32	29	6	NA	NA	NA
66	18	NA	NA	NA	NA	NA
80	NA	NA	NA	NA	NA	NA
77	21	0	21	0	NA	NA

Figure 1 Causes of infertility: developed countries versus sub-Saharan Africa

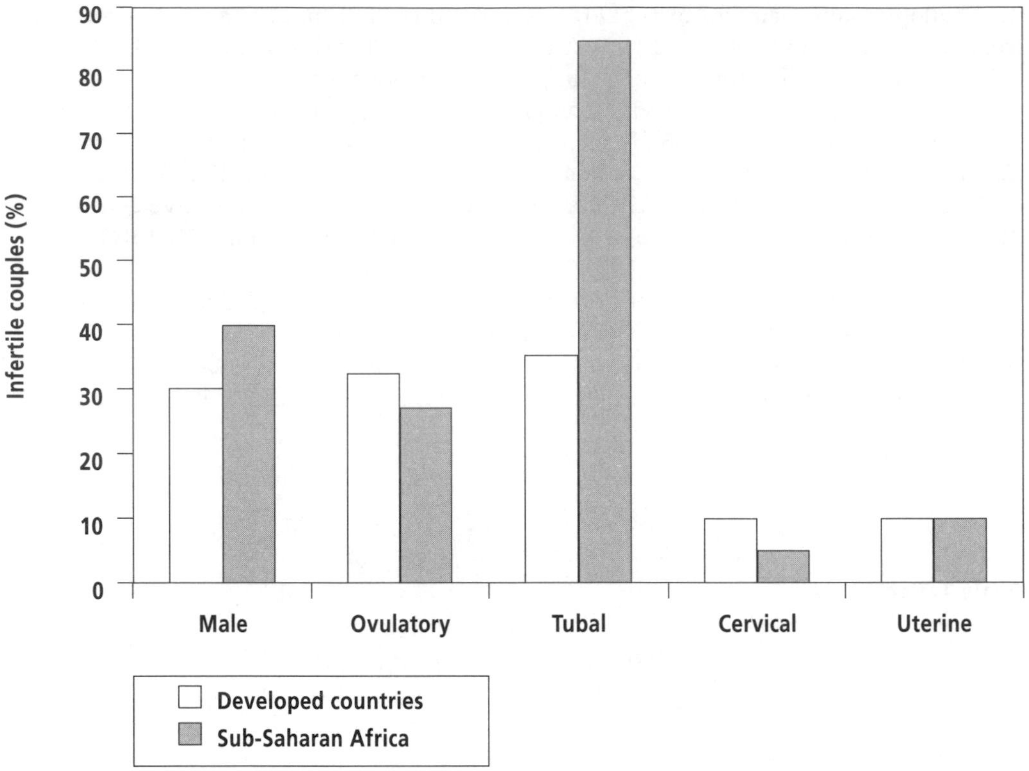

Source: Cates et al., 1985

The major cause of tubal blockage leading to infertility is pelvic inflammatory disease (PID) – a condition resulting from an infection, often originating in the cervix, which spreads to the upper reproductive tract causing extensive scarring of the fallopian tubes. Numerous studies worldwide have established a link between PID and tubal infertility (Muir and Belsey, 1980; Cates et al., 1990; Meheus, 1992; Cates et al., 1993). Landmark cohort studies conducted in Sweden have demonstrated that, over a period of 20 years, a woman with PID is likely to become permanently infertile if the initial disease is severe, if treatment is delayed, or if she has suffered multiple episodes of PID. In developed countries, an estimated 15-20% of women who develop PID become permanently infertile (Westrom, 1980; Westrom and Mardh, 1990). Results of a few African studies have confirmed the link between PID and tubal pathology (De Muylder et al., 1990; Cates et al., 1990; Meheus, 1992; Cates et al., 1993).

Ovulation disorders
The same studies identify ovulation or hormonal factors to have a role in infertility in about 20-30% of women. (Table 1, Figure 1). Moreover, hormonal or endocrine factors were found to be important in a study of 2,047 female partners of infertile couples in Nigeria (Kuku et al., 1987). Over 50% of the women had some abnormality of serum

Figure 2 Fallopian tube damage as cause of female infertility, by region

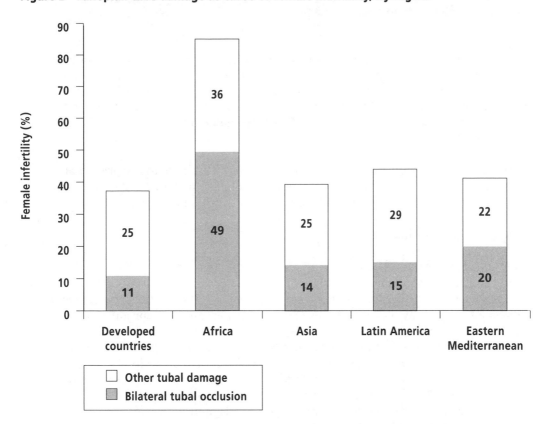

level of one or more of the hormones studied: hyperprolactinaemia was found in 26% and low progesterone serum levels - indicative of anovulation or severe ovulatory problems - were found in a further 17.5%. Postpartum hypopituitarism, caused by necrosis of the pituitary gland (Sheehan's syndrome), may be one cause of hyperprolactinaemia and prolonged amenorrhoea in sub-Saharan Africa. In a series of 40 cases over five years in Niamey, Niger, 60% of patients with this condition did not have any living children (Cenac *et al.*, 1991). Prolonged breast-feeding, a frequent occurrence in many parts of sub-Saharan Africa, is a natural cause of extended postpartum infertility. Breast-feeding maintains high levels of prolactin which prevents secretion of ovulatory hormones. The pattern of suckling also appears to play a role in the duration of this phenomenon (Huffman, 1983).

Uterine and cervical factors
In recent African studies, uterine and cervical factors are found to be involved in 10% to 20% of cases of female infertility; these results are comparable with studies from the developed world (Figure 1). As in industrialized countries, these factors include congenital abnormalities of the cervix or uterus but may also, more frequently, result from induced abortion, childbirth, or invasive medical procedures such as hysterosalpingography or curettage (Sherris and Fox, 1983; Wasserheit, 1989a; Meheus, 1992). The role of 'hostile cervical mucus', in which female antibodies have

been shown to immobilize sperm in the cervix or to cause sperm to stick together, has been insufficiently investigated in Africa.

Other factors
The frequency of endometriosis as an etiological factor in infertility has not been appropriately and systematically investigated in Africa. However, reports suggest that the figure may be low: endometriosis has been found in 1% of infertile women in the WHO multicentre study (compared with 6% and 10% in developed and Asian countries, respectively) and in 4% of infertile women from Cape Town (Wiswedel and Allen, 1989).

Alcohol, tobacco, drugs and environmental pollutants are potentially preventable factors of infertility in industrialized countries (Sherris and Fox, 1983). Data are lacking to ascribe a causative role to any of these factors in Africa.

Special conditions in Africa

Genital tuberculosis
Following an initial pulmonary infection, *Mycobacterium tuberculosis* may spread to the pelvic organs by the hematogenous route causing inflammation, scarring and adhesions which may block the tubes of any other parts of the reproductive tract. Little is known about the prevalence of genital tuberculosis (TB) due to its asymptomatic nature. A study conducted in Nigeria found that 0.2% of 4,700 specimens of pre-menstrual curettings harboured *M tuberculosis* (Gini and Ikerionwu, 1990). Another study in South Africa's Free State - an area of high prevalence and incidence of pulmonary TB - found that 20% of women in an infertility ward had genital TB (Oosthuizen *et al.*, 1990). Given the link between HIV and the occurrence of TB, the incidence of genital TB can be expected to increase in areas where both diseases are common, and its role in infertility should be more closely investigated.

Parasitic diseases
Parasitic infections are extremely prevalent in many parts of sub-Saharan Africa. There are anecdotal reports that infertility can result from genito-urinary schistosomiasis, caused by *Schistosoma haematobium* (Mouktar, 1966; Bullough, 1976; Maghoub, 1982), or from other worm infestations such as filariasis or *Enterobius vermicularis* infection (Neri *et al.*, 1986). The mechanisms are unclear but presumably involve the mechanical blockage and tissue inflammation surrounding the granulomatous lesions induced by eggs or worms in the cervix, uterine cavity, tube or pelvic peritoneum.

Nutritional factors
A balanced diet plays an important role in the onset of menarche and the maintenance of fertility by helping to maintain proper hormonal balance (Mosley, 1979; van der Spuy, 1985). The effects of acute starvation on ovarian functions during some of the world's largest famines (e.g. in Ethiopia in the mid 1970's) have been well documented (Sherris and Fox, 1983). These effects are believed to be temporary and reversible with improved diet. Women living under conditions of chronic under-nutrition do nevertheless succeed in becoming pregnant, suggesting the existence of adaptative mechanisms in basal metabolic rate and hormonal functions (van der Spuy, 1985). The

main documented impact of malnutrition on fertility is an increase in adverse pregnancy outcomes, foetal wastage and sequelae in the infant (van der Spuy, 1985).

Female genital mutilation

The WHO has recently produced a review (WHO, 1998 Reproductive Health website) of the health effects of female genital mutilation (FGM). Infection at the time of operation, interference in the drainage of urine and vaginal secretions, and postpartum wound infection may complicate FGM. These may result in ascending infections, leading to PID and scarring of the fallopian tubes. There is evidence that the rate of PID is higher among women with clitoridectomy than in women who have not undergone genital mutilation. Also, the rate of PID in infibulated women is three times that in women with clitoridectomy alone.

Pelvic inflammatory disease

As mentioned earlier, the problem of female infertility in Africa is largely a consequence of tubal blockage, often caused by pelvic inflammatory disease, a clinical entity that shall be described in more details now.

Definition

Pelvic inflammatory disease (PID) is a clinical syndrome among women resulting from infection of the uterus, fallopian tubes, ovaries, peritoneal surfaces and/or contiguous structures (CDC, 1993). The PID 'gold standard' diagnosis, however, relies on invasive procedures such as laparoscopy (Jacobson and Westrom, 1969; Morcos *et al.*, 1993) and endometrial histopathology (Kiviat *et al.*, 1990) which are frequently unavailable in developing countries. There is therefore a lack of data on the role of PID in infertility in resource-constrained African countries.

Epidemiology and risk factors

While the true incidence of PID in Africa is not known, several hospital-based surveys have indicated that it is a significant problem. Between 17 and 40% of gynaecological admissions may be related to pelvic infection (Meheus, 1992). Risk factors that lead to the development of PID or its sequelae have been studied in industrialized countries mainly, and have been summarized in a few recent reviews (Washington *et al.*, 1991; Bosu, 1997; Aral and Wasserheit, 1998); see Table 2.

Socio-demographic factors

Young, unmarried women with low levels of education, employment or income are at increased risk of STI and PID.

Sexual behaviour

Multiple sex partners, high frequency of sexual intercourse, young age at first intercourse, and the rate of acquiring new partners are all risk factors for STI and PID (Grodstein and Rothman, 1994; Washington *et al.*, 1991).

Contraceptive practice

The relationship between the use of oral contraception (OC) and the risk of PID is still undetermined. There have been reports of increased risk of chlamydial infection in some settings (Washington *et al.*, 1985), though a recent study found OC to protect against chlamydial PID among sex workers in Nairobi (Kimani *et al.*, 1996). Chemical barrier methods (e.g. vaginal spermicides) and mechanical barriers (condoms, diaphragms, cervical cap) reduce the risk of PID when consistently and correctly used during sexual activity (Kelaghan *et al.*, 1982), although recent studies have failed to confirm this protective effect (Aral and Wasserheit, 1998).

Table 2 Factors associated with the development and progression of PID[a]

Risk variables	Acquiring STI	Developing PID	Developing PID sequelae
Socio-demographic factors			
Young age	+	+	-
Low socioeconomic status	+	+	0
Marital status (unmarried)	+	+	0
Residence (urban)	+	0	0
Sexual behaviour			
Number of partners	+	+	0
Young at first coitus	+	+	0
Frequency of sexual intercourse	+	+	0
Rate of acquiring new partners	+	+	0
Contraceptive practice			
Barrier	-	-	-
Oral contraception	+	-	0
Intrauterine device	0	+	+
Health care behaviour			
Evaluation of symptoms	+	+	+
Compliance with treatment	+	+	+
Sex partner referral	+	+	+
Other			
Douching	0	+	0
Smoking	+	+	0
Substance abuse	+	0	0
Menstrual cycle	+	+	0

[a] Variables may be associated with increased risk (+), decreased risk (-), or no association may be reported (0)
Source: Adapted from Washington *et al.*, 1991; Bosu, 1997

Douching
Frequent vaginal douching could increase risk (Wolner-Hanssen *et al.*, 1990; Paisarntantiwong *et al.*, 1995) by altering the protective vaginal ecosystem and by flushing lower genital micro-organisms into the uterine cavity.

Menses/hormonal factors

The observation that onset of symptoms of chlamydial and/or gonococcal salpingitis develops significantly more often within seven days of onset of menses than 7-14 days afterwards (Sweet *et al.*, 1986) has led to various hypotheses about the role of hormonal factors. This role may include a protective effect of progesterone during the second (luteal) phase of the menstrual cycle. This hormone may induce production of bacteriostatic cervical mucus, and inactivate the endometrium, inhibiting bacterial attachment.

Health care behaviour

Early treatment-seeking behaviour, compliance with therapy and abstinence from sex during treatment may be the most important factors associated with a decreased risk of development of complications (Aral and Wasserheit, 1998).

Microbial causes of PID

The cause of PID in industrialized countries is polymicrobial, involving bacteria, endogenous flora and, perhaps, viruses (Eschenbach *et al.*, 1975). Numerous studies have established the role of cervical STI organisms in PID (Westrom and Mardh, 1990). *N gonorrhoeae* and *C trachomatis* have been isolated from the lower genital tract in as many as 85% of women with acute PID (Westrom and Mardh, 1990). While the course of gonococcal PID is often more acute, chlamydia-associated PID tends to be less clinically severe, though no less destructive. This has led researchers to coin the concept of 'silent PID' (Westrom and Mardh, 1990). Endogenous microbial agents are more commonly isolated in clinically severe, often suppurative cases than in mild PID. In about 20% of visually verified cases of clinical PID, no organisms have been isolated (Westrom and Mardh, 1990).

The cause of PID in Africa is not completely understood because of the lack of laboratory facilities, but *N gonorrhoeae* is implicated in 15-50% of PID cases and *C trachomatis* in 30-70% (Grech *et al.*, 1973; Burchell and Welgemoed, 1988; Wessels *et al.*, 1991; Marais *et al.*, 1991; Meheus, 1992; Sinei *et al.*, 1997). Studies from southern and eastern parts of Africa have shown even higher isolation rates for both organisms. Several case control studies measuring chlamydial and gonococcal antibodies (Mabey *et al.*, 1985; Frost *et al.*, 1987; Kelver and Nagani, 1989; DeMuylder *et al.*, 1990) in acute PID or salpingitis cases further support the major role of these pathogens in the development of PID.

The role of *Mycoplasma* species in PID is unclear. *Mycoplasma hominis* was recovered in 81% of 91 patients with gonococcal PID compared with 72% of 'control' patients with uncomplicated gonorrhoea in the US (Eschenbach *et al.*, 1975). Another study isolated *Mycoplasma* species in 61% of 50 patients with pelvic sepsis and in 77% of 50 matched controls without signs or symptoms of PID (Brown and Cruickshank, 1976). Serological evidence suggests that *Mycoplasma hominis* may be involved in up to 30% of PID cases (Westrom and Mardh, 1990), although it has rarely been isolated from the fallopian tubes (Mann *et al.*, 1996). *Mycoplasma genitalium* is believed to play a more prominent role in the pathology of PID. The evidence for its involvement includes its adherence to fallopian-tube epithelial cells in culture and a serological response in up to 30% of women with acute PID but no evidence of other STIs in UK patients (Taylor-Robinson and Furr, 1998). *Mycoplasma* species may act as an opportunistic secondary pathogen, invading tissue that has already been compromised by a primary pathogen such as *C trachomatis*.

Pathogenesis of PID

The complex mechanism by which PID develops is not entirely clear. The polymicrobial cause of PID suggests that cervical STI organisms primarily initiate an inflammatory tubal reaction, which is followed by secondary invasion of the primed tubal mucosa by the endogenous flora of the lower genital tract. Tissue destruction is mediated by cytokines, including tumor necrosis factor (TNF), interferon (INF) and interleukins (IL) (Westrom and Wolner-Hanssen, 1993). In-growing fibroblasts replace dead cells during the mucosal scarring process; this may eventually lead to occlusion or peritubal adhesions. Intratubal adhesions, mucosal and cilial damage can interfere with ovum and sperm transport through the fallopian tube. Various mechanisms have been postulated to explain the ascent of microbes into the upper genital tract. These include overgrowth of endogenous pathogens, uterine contractions during sexual intercourse, retrograde flow of infected menstrual blood, mechanical carriage by infected spermatozoa and active transport - involving a suction mechanism - at ovarian mid-cycle (Westrom and Wolner-Hanssen, 1993; Westrom and Mardh, 1990; Sweet, 1995; Keith *et al.*, 1984; Parsons and McGregor, 1997).

It has been suggested that the development of chlamydial PID is mediated by cellular immune responses. The findings of a recent prospective study of risk factors for chlamydial PID among sex workers in Nairobi lend support to this hypothesis. The independent risk factors identified included repeated *C trachomatis* infection, the presence of antibody to *C trachomatis* heat-shock protein 60 and the presence of the HLA-31 immunotype (Kimani *et al.*, 1996; Peeling *et al.*, 1997).

Endogenous infections

Several organisms constitute the 'normal' vaginal flora (Hillier and Holmes, 1990). Under certain circumstances which are not fully understood, overgrowth of such organisms can occur. This can produce a shift from a predominantly protective lactobacilli-dominated vaginal flora to large quantities of *Gardnerella vaginalis*, *Mycoplasma* species, and other anaerobic bacteria (such as *Mobiluncus* species, *Prevotella* species, *Peptrostreptococcus* species, *Bacteroides* species), resulting in bacterial vaginosis (BV).

The role of BV in the aetiology of PID has been controversial (Eschenbach, 1993; Faro *et al.*, 1993). Most organisms associated with BV have been recovered from the upper genital tract (Sweet, 1995). BV has been reported in 29% of 31 women with PID confirmed by laparoscopy and histology (Paavonen *et al.*, 1987). More recently, BV was reported to be present in 62% of women with laparoscopy-confirmed PID (Soper *et al.*, 1994). However, the definitive role of BV, either as an active component of PID or as a mere invader following tissue destruction, will be elucidated only by further studies which might include intervention trials.

Iatrogenic causes
Postpartum infection and sepsis

Endometritis is the most common maternal postpartum infection, responsible for 14 to 30% of maternal mortality in Africa (Meheus, 1992).

In one of the largest reported data series on vaginal deliveries in Africa, postpartum endometritis occurred in 20% of approximately 1,000 women in Nairobi, Kenya. In 35% of these cases there was an association with gonococcal or chlamydial infection (Plummer *et al.*, 1987). Antibiotic prophylaxis for *N gonorrhoeae*, given between 28 and 32 weeks of gestational age, has reduced postpartum infection rates by 50% in this population (Temmerman *et al.*, 1995; Gichangi *et al.*, 1997). Another important cause of sepsis is the entry of germs into the genital tract due to bad midwifery practice (e.g., from unwashed hands or unsterilized instruments) or the use of various foreign objects by untrained traditional birth attendants. Patients who have delivered by caesarean section face a higher risk of postoperative infectious morbidity, especially those women who have ruptured membranes during labour (see also Chapter 3). The most plausible mechanism is infection of the uterine cavity by organisms leaking from an infected amniotic cavity (Eschenbach, 1993; Soper, 1993). The bacteria involved in these infections are predominantly those of the patient's lower genital tract. Several studies from the USA (Faro, 1988; Soper, 1988; Soper, 1993) have shown that antibiotic prophylaxis before caesarean sections can reduce the risk of postpartum infection.

Postabortal infection and sepsis
The risk of developing ascending infection with sepsis, pelvic inflammation and tubal damage is substantial in women who have had abortions performed improperly (Eschenbach, 1993). In a review of several African studies, Ashworth found an incidence of incomplete abortion followed by sepsis of between 6 and 34%, more than 10 times higher than the rate in more developed countries (Ashworth, 1992). The WHO estimates that complications of unsafe abortions account for about 25% of maternal deaths in the developing world (WHO, 1998 Reproductive Health website).

IUCD insertion
Controversy has surrounded the role of intrauterine contraceptive devices (IUCDs) in PID. The insertion of IUCDs was associated with an increased risk of reproductive tract infection in Bangladesh (Wasserheit *et al.*, 1989b) and a 10-fold increase in incidence of acute PID in a British study (Vessey *et al.*, 1981). In the early 1990s, the WHO undertook a review of the evidence of the role of IUCDs in the development of PID (Farley *et al.*, 1992). The investigators found that the elevated risk of PID was confined to the first 20 days following insertion. The relative risk of complications during this period was 6.3 times that found at later times. PID risk was highest in the African region (6.2 cases per 1000 women-years of observation) than in the rest of the world (1.6 cases). The investigators concluded that exposure to STI, rather than the type of IUCD, was the major determinant of PID (Farley *et al.*, 1992). It is believed that organisms may be introduced into the endometrial cavity during IUCD insertion and that this may account for most IUCD-related PID. Prophylactic antibiotics given at the time of insertion might reduce the risk of PID (Sinei *et al.*, 1990).

Transcervical procedures
Various operative procedures such as cervical dilatation and curettage, tubal insufflation and hysterosalpingography (HSG) have been associated with PID (Westrom and Mardh, 1990; Soper, 1993). In Kenya, 44% of 150 women developed PID within one week of undergoing a HSG investigation for infertility (Lema and Majinge, 1993).

STIs and RTIs in African women

The development of PID is generally attributed to the high incidence and prevalence of undetected, untreated, or poorly treated STIs or endogenous infections in many African populations.

Classical STIs: gonorrhoea, chlamydia, syphilis and trichomoniasis
Surveillance of STIs is practically non-existent in many parts of sub-Saharan Africa, and most epidemiological data have come from prevalence studies. However, these surveys suffer from the disparity of population groups investigated, namely, students, antenatal clinic attenders, STI clinic attenders or commercial sex workers. Furthermore, due to their complexity and cost, very few surveys provide actual data on incident infections.

The most frequently utilized estimates of the magnitude of the STI problem among African women come from reviews of prevalence studies which are usually divided

Table 3 Selected studies of STIs among sub-Saharan female populations in the 1990s

Populations, country/area	Sample size	Gonorrhoea (%)	Chlamydia (%)	Trichomonas (%)	Bacterial vaginosis (%)
High risk populations					
STI clinic attenders					
Benin, Cotonou & Dangbo	192	5.7*	2.1*	11.5	NS[b]
Malawi, Blantyre	560	17.1	3.7	33.8	22.6
Tanzania, Mwanza	395	7.3	4.8	25.0	37.0
Sex workers					
Côte d'Ivoire, Abidjan	683	31.0	13.0*	NS	NS
Senegal, Dakar	374	16.0	12.6	46.0	NS
Zaire, Kinshasa	1,222	23.4	13.0	21.8	NS
Low-risk populations					
Antenatal clinics					
Côte d'Ivoire, Abidjan	546	3.7	5.5	13.2	NS
Gabon, Libreville	646	1.9	9.9	10.7	NS
Kenya, Nairobi	294	2.4	8.8	19.9	20.6#
Mozambique (R)[c]	201	7.0	7.9**	22.8	NA
Tanzania, Mwanza (R)[c]	964	2.1	6.6	27.4	15.0#
Tanzania, Mwanza	660	2.3	5.9	16.0	24.0
Zaire, Kinshasa	1,160	1.6	5.2	18.4	NS
Family planning clinics					
Kenya, Nairobi	550	2.1	3.8	10.0	NS
Tanzania, Dar Es Salaam	908	1.6	6.7	21.6	NS
South Africa, North Prov. (R)[c]	249	3.0*	12.0*	18.0	29.0
South Africa, Johannesburg	210	9.0*	18.0*	11.0	35.0#

into so-called 'high-risk' and 'low-risk' populations (Wasserheit, 1989a; Piot and Tezzo, 1990; DeSchryver and Meheus, 1990; Goeman *et al.*, 1991; Wasserheit and Holmes, 1992; Brunham and Embree, 1992). 'High-risk' populations include groups of women frequently exposed to STI pathogens by the nature of their occupation (sex workers), their environment (e.g. women living in mining communities) or their supposed sexual behaviour (STI clinic attenders). Among these groups, high STI prevalence rates are expected. 'Low-risk' populations, typically antenatal clinic or family planning clinic attenders, supposedly represent the less exposed female population; such women generally do not come into contact with health services for the single purpose of STI treatment. Aggregation of data from such surveys is complicated by the lack of comparability in size and sites, patient selection, methods used to diagnose the STIs, etc. However, during the 1990s, the WHO commissioned a number of studies seeking to evaluate the validity of newly introduced STI case management algorithms (Dallabetta *et al.*, 1998a). The very similar protocols, range of pathogens investigated and methods used allow direct comparison of results from these studies. Tables 3 and 4 summarize the findings of 17 key studies conducted on the African continent among 'high-risk' (6 studies) and 'low-risk' (11 studies) female populations.

Table 3, Continued

Candidiasis (%)	Syphilis (%)	Author, Year	
			[a] Diagnosis of: (i) N. *gonorrhoeae* by culture (except * by PCR); (ii) C. *trachomatis* by EIA (except * by LCR/PCR and ** by culture); (iii) T. *vaginalis* and C. *albicans* by wet mount;
32.3	2.1	Alary, 1998	(iv) bacterial vaginosis by Amsel's criteria (except # by
27.8	17.9	Costello-Daly 1998	observation of 'clue cells' on Gram-stained vaginal film only;
38.0	5.4	Mayaud, 1998[b]	(v) syphilis by dual reactivity on treponemal (TPHA or FTA Abs) and non-treponemal (RPR) tests.
NS	NS	Diallo, 1998	[b] NS: not studied
NS	29.4	Ndoye, 1998	[c] R: rural sites (all other sites urban)
NS	15.8	Vuylsteke, 1993[a]	
27.6	1.1	Diallo, 1997	
30.8	29.0	Bourgeois, 1998	
26.2	3.1	Thomas, 1996	
NA	14.6	Vuylsteke, 1993b	
14.3	10.1	Mayaud, 1995	
39.0	8.3	Mayaud, 1998d	
NS	1.1	Vuylsteke, 1993a	
NS	2.1	Temmerman, 1998	
7.5	3.9	Kapiga, 1998a	
NS	5.0	Schneider, 1998	
23.0	9.0	Fehler, 1998	

Table 4 Median prevalence of STIs among women in sub-Saharan Africa in the 1980s and 1990s (range in parentheses)

STI	High-risk populations Median % (range)		Low-risk populations Median % (range)		Low-risk WHO estimates 1995 Mean (%)
	1980s (%)	1990s (%)	1980s (%)	1990s (%)	
Chlamydia	14 (2-25)	8 (2-13)	8 (1-29)	7 (4-18)	7.1
Gonorrhoea	24 (7-66)	16 (6-31)	6 (0.3-40)	2.3 (1.6-9)	2.8
Trichomoniasis	17 (4-20)	28 (11-46)	12 (3-50)	18 (10-27)	14.1
Syphilis	15 (4-32)	8 (2-29)	8 (0.01-33)	4.4 (1-29)	3.9
Candidiasis	NS* (NS)	33 (28-38)	NS (NS)	27 (7.5-39)	NS
Bacterial vaginosis	NS (NS)	NS (NS)	Ns (NS)	22 (15-35)	NS

* NS = not studied

Sources: 1980s – Wasserheit & Holmes, 1992; 1990s, – see authors in Table 3; WHO 1995 – Gerbase *et al.*, 1998a

Median prevalence rates of 2.3% (range 1.6-9%) and 7% (range 4-18%) have been documented for gonorrhoea and chlamydial infection respectively, in 'low-risk' populations. Southern and eastern parts of the continent recorded the highest rates. Of note, the exception of Gabon in Central Africa which lies in the so-called 'infertility belt' of Africa and where combined low rates of gonorrhoea (1.9%) with high rates of chlamydia (9.9%) were observed. In the same populations, the median prevalence of active syphilis (*T pallidum* specific and non-specific dually reactive tests) was 4.4%, with varying prevalence rates ranging from 1% to 29% (Tables 3 and 4).

As expected, 'high-risk' groups had the highest rates of most STI pathogens, such as gonorrhoea, syphilis, or *T vaginalis*. However, the prevalence of *C trachomatis* did not markedly differ between STI clinic attenders and 'low-risk' populations. A major finding of these studies is the report that over 50% of cervical infections were truly 'asymptomatic'. Median prevalence rates obtained in the WHO algorithm validation studies are compared with earlier estimates obtained from a review of studies conducted among 'high-risk' and 'low-risk' African populations in the 1980s and early 1990s (Wasserheit and Holmes, 1992) and also with the most recent WHO estimates of mean prevalence rates (Gerbase *et al.*, 1998a, 1998b) (Table 4). All three estimates concur, confirming the very high prevalence of various STIs in female African populations.

Vaginal and endogenous infections
Vaginal infections (candidiasis, *T vaginalis*) were highly prevalent in both high-risk and low-risk groups in the WHO algorithm validation studies. *T vaginalis* appears to be the single most prevalent STI pathogen worldwide (Gerbase *et al.*, 1998a, 1998b) (Tables 3 and 4).

Until recently little was known about the prevalence of endogenous infections and bacterial vaginosis in sub-Saharan Africa. The lack of a well accepted standardized definition for BV in particular has contributed to this situation. Most studies conducted in the 1990s have used the traditional Amsel clinical criteria, which include observation of an adherent discharge, elevation of vaginal pH, detection of amine odour and presence of 'clue cells' on wet mount or Gram stain of vaginal fluid (Amsel *et al.*, 1983). These studies have reported a median BV prevalence of 22% (range 15-35%, Table 4). A more objective and useful classification of vaginal flora changes is now based on a scoring system for a Gram stain film of vaginal fluid (Nugent *et al.*, 1991). Studies using this method among pregnant and non-pregnant women on the African continent in the late 1990s reported prevalence rates of BV between 20% and 50% (Ledru *et al.*, 1992; Gaye-Diallo *et al.*, 1998; Gresenguet *et al.*, 1998; Sewankambo *et al.*, 1997; Govender *et al.*, 1996; Taha *et al.*, 1998; Mayaud *et al.*, 1998d).

Once believed to be a relatively benign though bothersome condition, BV has now been implicated in more serious complications, such as postpartum, postabortal, post surgical or post IUD-insertion ascending infections, leading to PID and subsequently infertility (Ison and Taylor-Robinson, 1997; Hillier and Holmes, 1990; Korn *et al.*, 1995; Blackwell *et al.*, 1994; Eschenbach, 1993; Soper *et al.*, 1994; Sweet, 1995). During pregnancy, BV can cause premature rupture of membranes resulting in pre-term birth and increased infant morbidity and mortality (Hauth *et al.*, 1995; Hay *et al.*, 1994; McGregor *et al.*, 1995; Hillier *et al.*, 1995; Govender *et al.*, 1996). Finally, an association has been found between vaginal flora changes, BV and increased prevalence and incidence of HIV (Cohen *et al.*, 1995; Sewankambo *et al.*, 1997; Taha *et al.*, 1998; Gresenguet *et al.*, 1998), making this a potentially serious public health problem.

Male infertility and STI in Africa

Male infertility factors

Male factors are thought to be the major cause of infertility in about 30% of all infertile couples worldwide and to contribute to infertility in a further 15% (Sherris and Fox, 1983). Male factors appear to contribute in a similar proportion to infertility in Africa, as they have been identified in between 21 and 48% of couples investigated in the recent African series (Table 1). The WHO multicentre study recorded a very similar rate of 43% in its African centres (Cates *et al.*, 1985). Investigations of infertile men in Africa have found more than 50% of men to suffer from azoospermia or oligospermia (absence or low sperm count), which in turn may have several causes. In a large proportion of male infertility cases (an estimated 30 to 50%), however, no demonstrable cause of infertility was found.

Varicocele (20%) was the most common cause identified among African men in the WHO study, and it was more common than among men from other regions of the world (Cates *et al.*, 1985). Similarly, other studies frequently reported varicocele (Modebe, 1989; Yeboah *et al.*, 1992; Cisse *et al.*, 1992). This condition, caused by a congenital defect of the testicular veins, allows excess blood to accumulate around the testes and to interfere with sperm production, possibly by altering spermatogenesis.

African studies have reported ductal causes, i.e. the blockage of conduits of semen transport, in 11% to 49% of cases. This finding - and the increased frequency of a past medical history of STI among infertile men (Yeboah *et al.*, 1992; Yeboah and Marmar, 1994; Bornman *et al.*, 1994) - point to untreated or poorly treated urethral infections as a possible cause. *N gonorrhoeae* and *C trachomatis* can multiply on the mucosal surface from their point of entry (urethra, rectum) and subsequently spread to other structures lined with susceptible epithelium. Such structures include the prostate gland, seminal vesicles, vas deferens and epididymis. This process may involve retrograde passage of infected urine or direct spread either by surface continuity or via the lymphatics. The inflammatory process causes prostatitis or epididymitis. In the absence of treatment, an abscess and infarction of the testicle may occur. Scarring will eventually develop, leading to blockage of the lumen and possible azoospermia. If both epididymes are blocked, infertility will result (Arya, 1998).

Genital tuberculosis is a 'classical' cause of male infertility, but it is very seldom reported. As in women, genital TB develops after a pulmonary infection and hematogenous spread to genital organs and is often asymptomatic. Other common bacterial or parasitic infections, such as filariasis and urogenital schistosomiasis, may affect the genital organs and cause much inflammation and scarring resulting in duct blockage. Lepromatous leprosy and mumps may cause bilateral inflammation of testes (orchitis). These aetiologies no longer appear to play a significant role in male infertility in Africa (Sherris and Fox, 1983).

In one small case control study in Nigeria, antisperm auto-antibodies were present in 44% of 50 infertile men compared with 4% among fertile 'controls' (Ekwere, 1995). These antibodies may be linked with other infectious processes (e.g. schistosomiasis) and cause sperm agglutination and necrosis. Chromosomal abnormalities, such as the Klinefelter's syndrome which includes testes atrophy and low testosterone production, are rarely reported in Africa.

Studies investigating sexual dysfunction in African men could not be found in the current medical literature, but several popular accounts have been published in the African media in recent years of men complaining of disappearing or 'snatched' penises. This possibly disguised account of male impotence has been conveniently attributed to 'witchcraft', and 'witches' or traditional healers have been arrested, beaten or killed in several countries of West Africa (Makossa, 1998). Just how widespread male impotence is, and what its role might be in couples infertility, are not known in Africa.

STIs in African men

Just as for women, infertility in men may largely result from untreated or poorly treated STIs. Few studies have documented the incidence and prevalence of STIs in representative samples of African men. There are no convenient samples of men coming into contact with health services for routine check ups; most men tend to use services only when they have an acute problem. Further, there is a paucity of research undertaken in accessible institutional cohorts such as factory workers, company employees, military personnel or students. Reasons given for this lack of data include the lack of research interest on the part of the scientific or public health authorities who perceive - often rightly - that the burden of STIs disproportionately affects women and children. As a result, little attention has been given to the problem of male sexual health in Africa. Finally, as in the case of female infertility, data from community-based studies are difficult and expensive to obtain, and have been collected in only a handful of sites (in Tanzania, Kenya and Uganda) in recent years.

Information on men with urethral discharge attending STI clinics suggests there is a high prevalence of gonorrhoea (commonly around or above 50%) and a lower prevalence (5-15%) of chlamydia infections (Mayaud et al., 1992; Moses et al., 1992; Alary et al., 1998; Dallabetta et al., 1998b) with frequent dual infections. Non-specific urethritis (NSU), after exclusion of cases of N gonorrhoeae and C trachomatis, accounts for about one quarter to one third of cases. In settings where it has been investigated, T vaginalis is not an infrequent pathogen, accounting for perhaps 2-20% of cases (Hoffman et al.,

1997; Mayaud et al., 1998d). There is always a relatively high proportion of men for whom no diagnosis of STI could be made, partly because of the frequency of prior self-treatment (Mayaud et al., 1992).

Community-based studies have reported very similar rates of N gonorrhoeae and/or C trachomatis among men and women (around 2-4% for each pathogen). The vast majority (>70%) of these infections were asymptomatic (Grosskurth et al., 1996; Wawer et al., 1997). In contrast with previously held knowledge, T vaginalis has been identified as one of the most frequent urethral pathogens in several large male population studies (Watson-Jones et al., 2000; Jackson et al., 1997; Wawer et al., 1997). The role of this organism on the pathogenesis of male infertility is not known.

The role of HIV in infertility

Epidemiological evidence points to an association between HIV and infertility. Several studies have reported a three-fold higher HIV prevalence among infertile women, e.g. in Gabon (Schrijvers et al., 1991) and Tanzania (Favot et al., 1997). In a cohort from a rural community in the Rakai District of Uganda, Gray and colleagues reported a 60% lower baseline pregnancy rate among HIV-positive women with concurrent syphilis compared to women without this combination of diseases (pregnancy rates of 8.5% and 21.4% respectively). They also reported a 32-34% reduction in pregnancy rate in women who either had active syphilis or were HIV positive (rates 14.6% and 14.2% respectively). Follow-up surveys showed evidence of a significantly lower incidence of pregnancy among HIV-infected women than in controls (23.5 vs 30.1 per 100 woman-years respectively) as well as a higher rate of pregnancy loss (18.5 vs 12.2% respectively) in these women (Gray et al., 1998). Earlier African studies also reported the negative impact of HIV on pregnancy outcomes (Temmerman et al., 1990; Taha et al., 1995).

The impact of HIV on male fertility has been less well documented, but a study in Bangui demonstrated that sperm count and motility was greatly affected in HIV-positive men. The effect was more pronounced in the more immuno-compromised individuals (Gresenguet et al., 1992).

Several conditions could explain these findings. First, women with frequent sexual contacts will be at increased risk of STIs and PID (and subsequent infertility) as well as increased risk of HIV. The observed association among diseases could result from this confounding effect. Second, sub-fertile women may modify their behaviour, attempting to prove fertility by increasing rates of partner changes, divorcing and/or by engaging in multiple partnerships as a means of survival. Third, HIV may modify the natural history of STIs and PID or alter the response to therapy, leading to higher rates of infertility among HIV-positive women who have acquired an STI. There is evidence that HIV does modify the natural course of PID, and that it induces a more severe clinical presentation and a higher frequency of tubo-ovarian abscesses (Kamenga et al., 1995; Sinei et al., 1997). However there is no evidence that prognosis, response to therapy and progression to infertility differ with HIV status (Sweet and Landers, 1997). Furthermore, HIV does not seem to influence the rate of IUD insertion-associated PID (Kapiga et al., 1998b; Sinei et al., 1998; Hicks, 1998). Fourth, the association could be explained by a direct effect of HIV on conception, though no evidence for this hypothesis yet exists despite the fact that the impact of HIV on pregnancy wastage is well documented. Immunoppression of the infected individuals seems to play a role at all stages since compromised immunity worsens rates of PID sequelae, rates of pregnancy wastage and sperm quality.

Programmatic, policy and research implications

It is not within the scope of this chapter to discuss all potential control options and recommendations in detail. Nevertheless, STI and RTI control programmes do play an important role in preventing infertility, which wil be briefly discussed.

Public health importance of STIs and RTIs

STIs and RTIs constitute an important public health and economical problem for three reasons:
- STIs and RTIs occur frequently, and have high prevalence and incidence rates;
- STIs and RTIs can have serious complications and sequelae;
- a number of STIs have been identified as facilitating the spread of HIV.

WHO has estimated that 333 million new cases of non-viral STIs occur each year in adults aged 15-49 years (Gerbase *et al.*, 1998a and 1998b). More than 80% of these cases occur in developing countries, a fact which partly reflects the global distribution of the world's population. However, there are substantial geographical variations in estimated prevalence and incidence. Sub-Saharan Africa, while accounting for 20% of the global STI estimates, displays the highest prevalence and incidence rates per capita for each of the four selected tracer STIs: gonorrhoea, chlamydia infection, syphilis and trichomoniasis (Gerbase *et al.*, 1998a and 1998b). Overall yearly incidence of those curable STIs in Africa is estimated at 254 per 1,000 population compared with between 77 and 91 per 1,000 for more developed countries (Gerbase *et al.*, 1998a). To a great extent, the reasons for this situation are associated with the lack of access to effective and affordable STI services in many African settings (Wasserheit and Holmes, 1992; Dallabetta *et al.*, 1998a).

STIs create an enormous burden of ill health and economic loss, particularly among women with more frequent and more severe complications (Over and Piot, 1993). The World Bank has estimated that STIs, excluding HIV, are the second commonest cause of healthy life-years lost by women in the 15-44 age group, outranked only by causes of maternal morbidity (Over and Piot, 1993; World Bank, 1993). The advent and increase of HIV infection has further highlighted the importance of STIs as a major health problem in developing countries. The enhancing effect of STIs on HIV transmission 'is no longer a hypothesis' (Cohen, 1998). Given the high prevalence and incidence of both STIs and HIV in Africa, thus far this epidemic has had the greatest impact on this continent. The World Bank, WHO and UNAIDS have therefore recommended that one of the most cost-effective ways to improve health in the world is to give high priority to the development of effective STI control programmes (World Bank, 1993; Piot and Islam, 1994; Gerbase *et al.*, 1998b).

STI/RTI control programmes

STI/RTI control programmes have three main objectives: to interrupt the transmission of STIs; to prevent the development of diseases, complications and sequelae; and to reduce the transmission of HIV infection (WHO/GPA, 1994; Meheus, 1998). These objectives can be achieved through primary prevention measures aimed at reducing the incidence of infection, or secondary prevention aimed at reducing the prevalence of STIs by shortening the duration of infection and disease. These actions in turn reduce the probability of complications, sequelae and disease transmission. In addition, tertiary prevention measures are intended to reduce the sequelae and impact of untreated or poorly treated infections and to provide rehabilitation.

Primary prevention of STIs

The objective of health promotion is to encourage behavioural changes in the general population or specific 'at risk' subgroups, to decrease exposure to, and transmission of, STIs. In particular, it is important to stress the role of educating men and women in STI symptom recognition and to promote early treatment-seeking behaviour, which is the only way to prevent the development of grave sequelae. For the individual patient, integral parts of syndromic STI case management include promotion of safer sexual behaviour, counselling to increase compliance with treatment, condom promotion and partner management in the form of notification and treatment (WHO/GPA, 1994).

To date, the development of effective STI vaccines has been very disappointing, except in the case of the hepatitis B virus (Barbosa-Cesnik *et al.*, 1997). Candidate vaccines for other viral STIs (herpes, human papilloma virus) are being developed and are promising. Immunogenic bacterial proteins which elicit protective immune responses have been identified in the case of *N gonorrhoeae* (Por, pili and Opa) and *C trachomatis* (major outer membrane protein: MOMP) and represent potential vaccine candidates, but no clinically tested vaccine is yet available. The main problem for *N gonorrhoeae* lies in its extreme antigenic variation and the escape mechanisms exhibited by the targeted proteins (Schulz, 1998).

STI case management

Traditionally, patients with STIs have been diagnosed and managed according to the etiological agents found in laboratory investigations. Ample evidence suggests that this technology-based method is inadequate and too expensive for the working conditions of many parts of the world, including primary care centres in sub-Saharan Africa (Adler, 1996). This system often results in inadequate or incomplete diagnosis, and may delay or prevent initiation of care. In addition, it often results in costly, ineffective and stigmatizing referral of patients to specialist centres. To address these limitations, the WHO has developed and advocated the *syndromic management approach* (WHO/GPA, 1994).

STI-associated syndromes are made up of easily identifiable groups of symptoms and clinical findings on which the health care providers can base a presumptive diagnosis. The use of clinical flowcharts simplifies management and allows time in the consultation to provide simple education messages, discuss partner notification and promote condoms. Antimicrobial therapy covering the majority of pathogens presumed to be responsible for the given syndrome in the specific geographical area is then provided at once.

The main advantages of using a syndromic approach in a primary health care setting is that it is quick and problem oriented, highly sensitive, and ensures high coverage of patients. The main disadvantage is the cost of overdiagnosis and overtreatment of many patients, especially women with vaginal discharge who are currently treated by targetting both vaginal and cervical pathogens, of greater public health importance. Although cervical infections are the most important from the public health viewpoint, they are not the most prevalent pathogens amongst women complaining of genital discharge who more often have vaginal infections. The syndromic approach, in this case, has been proven to lack specificity and has low (10-15%) positive predictive value (Dallabetta *et al.*, 1998a). The inclusion of sociodemographic or behavioural factors, combined in a risk score, in the flowchart for vaginal discharge has variable practical utility (Alary *et al.*, 1998; Bourgeois *et al.*, 1998; Costello-Daly *et al.*, 1998; Mayaud *et al.*, 1998b). Indeed, sensitivities range from 43 to 87% and specificities from 40 to 73%. Moreover, the risk-assessment approach is often improved when setting-specific risk factors are included. This suggests the approach requires careful evaluation in several settings, even within the same country, before it can be recommended for wide scale use. Further, an important pre-requisite for the good performance of syndromic STI case management is a reasonably well functioning primary health care system. This is particularly true as regards training, monitoring and supervision, aspects which ensure quality of care, and as regards provision of drugs to ensure the timely treatment of patients.

The gold standard diagnosis of PID, using laparoscopy (Jacobson and Westrom, 1969; Morcos *et al.*, 1993) and endometrial histopathology (Kiviat *et al.*, 1990) is rarely used outside research settings. The present WHO-recommended PID algorithm is based on the presence of lower abdominal pain and the result of a pelvic examination, with or without the presence of fever. Very few studies have attempted to evaluate this algorithm in developing countries. Based on studies from industrialized countries or from specialist African research centres (Kamenga *et al.*, 1995), STI experts have recommended the use of a combination of antibiotics against *N gonorrhoeae*, *C trachomatis*, and anaerobic bacteria.

Medical management usually suffices, but surgical management may be required to deal with pelvic abscesses and - in cases of failure to respond to antibiotics - pelvic masses, persistence of pain and ruptured tubo-ovarian abscesses (Bosu, 1997). There is no evidence that medical management of chronic cases will result in improved or restored fertility; only early management of the first episode of PID can have a significant preventative impact on the development of irreversible sequelae.

Early STI detection

The WHO recommends greater integration of STI services with Family Planning and Maternal and Child Health services (WHO/GPA/Van Praag, 1993). This offers the opportunity to provide screening or case finding strategies for women who consult for other reasons. Well-trained and sensitive staff can always question women about symptoms and offer a physical examination where possible. However, this strategy may not be very useful owing to the frequent symptomless nature of cervical infections and to the limited specificity of clinical signs. Screening on the basis of risk assessment alone, even in the absence of symptoms, has not proved useful in these populations (Thomas *et al.*, 1996; Mayaud *et al.*, 1998c; Kapiga *et al.*, 1998a; Schneider *et al.*, 1998). In developed countries, laboratories may be able to screen for *N gonorrhoeae* and/or *C trachomatis*. The weak surveillance of STIs and PID and scarcity of trained laboratory personnel and financial resources in Africa would limit the benefits of such a screening program.

Antimicrobial prophylaxis can be an alternative to case finding in settings where prevalence of treatable STIs is high and where laboratory or diagnostic facilities are lacking. This is particularly true among groups, such as pregnant women, at the highest risk for complications (Meheus, 1998). In women with a past history of poor pregnancy outcome attending antenatal services in Nairobi, mass treatment with a single intramuscular dose of ceftriaxone or a single oral dose of cefetamet-pivoxil at a gestational age between 28 and 32 weeks significantly decreased postpartum infections and low birth-weight rates (Temmerman *et al.*, 1995; Gichangi *et al.*, 1997).

African centres do not routinely screen or give prophylaxis for vaginal or endogenous infections. Given the evidence of the effect of these infections on pregnancy outcome and their potential role as risk factors for the development of PID following trans-cervical procedures, studies should be carried out to examine the public health impact, feasibility and overall cost-effectiveness of screening and/or presumptive treatment of vaginal infections.

Examination of male sexual partners of patients with PID is vital to reduce morbidity and prevent complications. One study demonstrated gonococcal, chlamydial infection or non-specific urethritis (NSU) in 59.7% of male partners of women with acute PID (Kamwendo et al., 1993). Only 32% of those men with gonococcal or chlamydial infection, and 8.5% of those with NSU, had symptoms of urethritis.

Partner notification is an integral part of the syndromic management advocated by WHO (WHO/GPA, 1994). Its success is highly variable in terms of return rates per index patient and differs according to sites and syndromes. Many settings achieve return rates of approximately 30%, in contrast with baseline rates of less than 5% achieved before the introduction of syndromic management (Winfield and Latif, 1985; Steen et al., 1996; Njeru et al., 1995; Mayaud et al., 1997a). Although the 'yield' of extra infections thus detected is often not known, it appears to be generally low, for genital discharge syndromes around 5-10 new cases per 100 contacts seen (Mayaud et al., 1998d).

Impact of STI control on PID and STIs
Primary, secondary and tertiary prevention strategies are all important in reducing STI, PID and their sequelae. A combination of these strategies has been most successful in some industrialized countries. Changes in the sexual behaviour and increased medical and public awareness of STIs have been responsible for a 40% decrease in the incidence of acute salpingitis in Sweden (Westrom, 1988). In Amsterdam, public health campaigns set up in response to the AIDS epidemic have been accompanied by a reduction of 50% in the incidence of PID within a few years (Coutinho et al., 1992). The authors ascribed this success to changes in sexual behaviour among the heterosexual population fol-lowing the campaigns, although gonorrhoea rates were already in decline (Coutinho et al., 1992). In another Swedish study, the decline in PID over 25 years was associated with a gradual fall in gonorrhoea and Chlamydia infection rates that started in the early 1980s (Kamwendo et al., 1998). The authors attribute this success to the combination of STI control activities, such as education, care, screening and partner notification.

There have been reports of declining STI incidence in parts of Africa, which could suggest that effective STI control programmes have been implemented. For example, Zambia reported a decline in total STI notified cases between 1985 and 1987 (Matondo, 1992). However, several external factors could bias these statistics: for example, decreased attendance due to the introduction of user fees, as observed in Nairobi (Moses et al., 1992). Simple STI control activities, such as those set up in the Mwanza Region of Tanzania, can achieve a substantial reduction (between 30 and 50%) in the incidence and prevalence of symptomatic STIs at the community level (Mayaud et al., 1997b).

Moreover, a 40% decrease in HIV incidence followed the introduction of a very cost-effective STI syndromic management intervention at the primary health care level in Mwanza (Grosskurth et al., 1995; Gilson et al., 1997). Whether this reduction in STIs will, in turn, lead to a reduction of PID and infertility will require monitoring.

Other reproductive health programmes

Family planning services can also provide integrated STI care, ensure adequate prevention of PID associated with IUD insertion (by encouraging aseptic techniques, STI screening or antimicrobial prophylaxis) and promote the prevention of infection and pregnancy through the use of contraceptives, of barrier methods (male and female condoms) and of microbicides. Finally, such centres should provide safe and accessible services for the termination of pregnancy.

Obstetric and surgical services should aim at reducing the incidence of iatrogenic RTIs by implementing Safe Motherhood programmes with emphasis on aseptic techniques performed by well-trained personnel. In view of their association with high rates of infection, indications for caesarean section or any transcervical procedures should be carefully assessed and the adjunction of antimicrobial prophylaxis considered.

Infertility management

Many African settings lack sophisticated solutions for the investigation and management of infertility, and existing services are usually confined to a few hospitals. Accessibility, waiting times and costs prevent infertile or subfertile couples from getting appropriate help in time. Primary care clinics, and family planning services in particular, may offer simple investigation services, such as history taking, physical examination, semen analysis or checking ovulation disorders, STI screening services and treatment, and counselling services. Clear guidelines to refer to hospitals that may be able to carry out further investigations (e.g., checking tubal patency with hysterosalpingography or laparoscopy) should also be developed. At such reference clinics, expert medical and surgical services may be available as well as counselling services. Such services should help to discuss the available options: for example, surgery, artificial insemination or *in-vitro* fertilization (IVF), or alternatively adoption or child fostering if therapy for infertility is unsuccessful. The priority that should be accorded to these services appears low however, given their questionable success rates, feasibility and cost in resource-constrained environment.

Policy and research challenges

The most pressing policy issue is the need to increase awareness among the public, health practitioners and decision makers about the link between STIs, poor management practices, and PID and infertility. Competition with other programs stands in the way of allocation of sufficient resources for specific measures to combat STIs or infertility. Therefore integration of services and application of proven cost-effective interventions (such as syndromic STI management) should be strongly promoted (Mayaud *et al.*, 1998a). Clearly, cultural and ethical issues concerning the status of women, attitudes of men and legal aspects of termination of pregnancy will also need to be faced and discussed if the devastating problem of infertility is to be effectively addressed.

Evaluation of the validity, impact and cost-effectiveness of several of the measures highlighted in this chapter is needed. These include the improvement of PID algorithms, and the relative roles of STI screening or presumptive treatment to curb complications associated with pregnancy, IUD insertion or transcervical procedures. The quest for simple, cheap and reliable diagnostic tests for gonorrhoea and chlamydia remains high on the policy and research agenda (Chernesky, 1997; Mayaud *et al.*, 1998a). The role of bacterial vaginosis and other endogenous infections and the potential role of tuberculosis in high HIV/TB prevalence settings on the development of PID and infertility also warrant further research. Finally, social science research is needed to understand the behavioural determinants of PID development, care-seeking behaviour and the role of sexual dysfunction in the aetiology of male infertility in Africa, a clearly under-researched area.

Conclusion

This review shows that infertility in sub-Saharan Africa is often the consequence of many preventable factors. It often results from neglected or improperly treated STIs in both men and women, and can also be a consequence of poorly performed medical interventions such as abortions, caesarean sections, deliveries or IUD insertions. PID is the main pathogenic mechanism by which infertility occurs in women. In men, the genital epithelium, spermatogenesis, and sperm quality are all affected by STIs. A greater emphasis therefore should be placed on the adequate control of STIs and the improvement of general gynaecological and obstetrical practices, both of which require primary and secondary prevention activities. Finally, the possibility of repair or treatment of infertility should also be emphasized as tertiary prevention.

Acknowledgements

The author is extremely grateful to the MEASURE Project for their support, and wishes to thank Prof. David Mabey, Sarah Hawkes, Basia Zaba and Rudiger Pittroff of the London School of Hygiene and Tropical Medicine, and Isabelle Favot for their comments on earlier drafts. An earlier version of this chapter was presented at a UNAIDS/USAID/ MEASURE Evaluation/CDC meeting on 'Infertility, STDs and HIV: problems and prospects', Arlington, Virginia, December 14-15, 1998.

Bibliography

Adler MW (1996), 'Sexually transmitted diseases control in developing countries'. *Genitourinary Medicine* 72: 83-8.

Alary M, Baganizi E, Guedeme A, *et al.* (1998), 'Evaluation of clinical algorithms for the diagnosis of gonococcal and chlamydial infections among men with urethral discharge or dysuria and women with vaginal discharge in Benin'. *Sexually Transmitted Infections* 74 (suppl. 1): S44-S49.

Amsel R, Totten PA, Spiegel CA, *et al.* (1983), 'Non-specific vaginitis. Diagnostic criteria and microbial and epidemiologic associations'. *American Journal of Medicine* 74: 14-22.

Aral SO and Wasserheit JN (1998), 'Social and behavioral correlates of pelvic inflammatory disease'. *Sexually Transmitted Diseases* 25: 378-85.

Arya OP (1998), 'Gonorrhoea'. In: Arya OP and Hart CA (eds), *Sexually transmitted infections and AIDS in the tropics*, CABI Publishing, Wallingford: 210-31.

Ashworth F (1992), 'Septic abortion'. In: Stabile I, Grudzinskas G and Chard T (eds) *Spontaneous abortion*, Springer, London: 119-32.

Barbosa-Cesnik CT, Gerbase A, Heymann D (1997), 'STD vaccines - an overview'. *Genitourinary Medicine* 73: 336-42.

Belsey MA (1976), 'The epidemiology of infertility: a review with particular reference to Sub-Saharan Africa'. *Bulletin of the World Health Organization* 54: 319-41.

Blackwell AL, Thomas PD, Wareham K and Emery SJ (1994), 'Health gains from screening for infection of the lower genital tract in women attending for termination of pregnancy'. *Lancet* 342: 206-10.

Bornman MS, Schulenburg GW, Boomker D, Chauke TR and Reif S (1994), 'Observations in infertile African males at an andrology clinic in South Africa'. *Archives of Andrology* 33: 101-4.

Bosu WK (1997), *Clinical profile and management of pelvic inflammatory disease in the Central Region of Ghana*, Dissertation for MSc Thesis, London School of Hygiene and Tropical Medicine, University of London, UK.

Bourgeois A, Henzel D, Dibanga G, *et al.* (1998), 'Prospective evaluation of a flowchart using a risk-assessment for the diagnosis of STDs in primary health care centres in Libreville, Gabon.' *Sexually Transmitted Infections* 74 (suppl. 1): S128-S131.

Brown IML and Cruickshank JG (1976), 'Aetiological factors in pelvic inflammatory disease in urban Blacks in Rhodesia'. *South African Medical Journal* 50: 1342-4.

Brunham RC and Embree JE (1992), 'Sexually transmitted diseases: current and future dimensions of the problem in the Third World'. In: Germain A, Holmes KK, Piot P and Wasserheit JN (eds), *Reproductive tract infections: global impact and priorities for women's reproductive health*, IWHC, Plenum Press, New York: 35-58.

Bullough CHW (1976), 'Infertility and bilharziasis of the female genital tract'. *British Journal of Obstetrics and Gynaecology* 83: 819-22.

Burchell HJ and Welgemoed NC (1988), 'Microbiology of acute pelvic inflammatory disease at Pelonomio Hospital, Bloemfontein'. *South African Medical Journal* 73: 81-2.

Cates W, Farley TM and Rowe PJ (1985), 'Worldwide patterns of infertility: is Africa different?' *Lancet* 2: 596-8.

Cates W Jr, Rolfs RT Jr and Aral SO (1990), 'Sexually transmitted diseases, pelvic inflammatory disease, and infertility: an epidemiologic update'. *Epidemiological Review* 12: 199-220.

Cates W Jr, Rolfs RT and Aral SO (1993), 'The pathophysiology and epidemiology of sexually transmitted diseases in relation to pelvic inflammatory disease and infertility'. In: Gray RH, Leridon H, and Spira A (eds), *Biological and Demographic Determinants of Reproduction*, Oxford University Press, Oxford: 104-125.

CDC (1993), 'STD treatment guidelines'. *Morbidity and Mortality Weekly*, Report 42: 75.

Cenac A, Soumana I, Develoux M, Touta A and Bianchi G (1991), 'Le syndrome de Sheehan en Afrique soudano-sahelienne, 40 observations'. *Bulletin de la Société de Pathologie Exotique* 84: 686-92.

Chernesky M (1997), 'How can industry, academia, public health authorities and the Sexually Transmitted Diagnostics Initiative (SDI) work together to help control sexually transmitted diseases in developing countries?' *Sexually Transmitted Diseases* 24: 61-63.

Chigumadzi PT, Moodley J and Bagratee J (1998), 'Infertility profile at King Edward VIII Hospital, Durban, South Africa'. *Tropical Doctor* 28: 168-72.

Cisse CT, Dao B, Afoutou JM, Mensah A, Diadhiou F and Wone I (1992), 'Sterilite conjugale au CHU de Dakar: profil épidemiologique et limites du bilan à propos de 429 cases'. *Dakar Medecine* 37: 151-7.

Cohen MS (1998), 'Sexually transmitted diseases enhance HIV transmission: no longer a hypothesis'. *Lancet* 351 (suppl. III): 5-7.

Cohen R, Duerr A, Pruithithada N, *et al.* (1995), 'Bacterial vaginosis and HIV seroprevalence among commercial sex workers in Chiang Mai, Thailand'. *AIDS* 9: 1093-7.

Collet M, Roniero J, Froot E, *et al.* (1988), 'Infertility in Central Africa: infection is the cause'. *International Journal of Gynaecology and Obstetrics* 26: 423-8.

Costello-Daly C, Wangel AM, Hoffman IF, *et al.* (1998), 'Validation of the WHO algorithm and development of an alternative scoring system for the management of women presenting with vaginal discharge in Malawi'. *Sexually Transmitted Infections* 74 (suppl. 1): S50-S58.

Coutinho RA, Rijsdijk AJ, van den Hoek JAR and Leentvaar-Kuijpers A (1992), 'Decreasing incidence of PID in Amsterdam'. *Genitourinary Medicine* 68: 353-55.

Dallabetta GA, Gerbase AC and Holmes KK (1998a), 'Problems, solutions, and challenges in syndromic management of sexually transmitted diseases'. *Sexually Transmitted Infections* 74 (suppl. 1): S1-S11.

Dallabetta GA, Behets F, Lule G, *et al.* (1998b), 'Specificity of dysuria and discharge complaints and presence of urethritis in male patients attending an STD clinic in Malawi'. *Sexually Transmitted Infections* 74 (suppl. 1): S34-S37.

DeMuylder X, Laga M, Tennstedt C, van Dyck E, Aelbers GNM and Piot P (1990), 'The role of *Neisseria gonorrhoeae* and *Chlamydia trachomatis* in pelvic inflammatory disease and its sequelae in Zimbabwe'. *Journal of Infectious Diseases* 162: 501-5.

DeSchryver A and Meheus A (1990), 'Epidemiology of sexually transmitted diseases: the global picture'. *Bulletin of the World Health Organization* 68: 639-54.

Diallo MO, Ettiegne-Traore V, Maran, M, *et al.* (1997) 'Sexually transmitted diseases and human immunodeficiency virus infections in women attending an antenatal clinic in Abidjan, Côte d'Ivoire'. *Int J STD & AIDS* 8: 636-38.

Diallo MO, Ghys PD, Vuylsteke B, *et al.* (1998), 'Evaluation of simple diagnostic algorithms for *Neisseria gonorrhoeae* and *Chlamydia trachomatis* cervical infections in female sex workers in Abidjan, Côte d'Ivoire'. *Sexually Transmitted Infections* 74 (suppl. 1): S106-S111.

Ekwere PD (1995), 'Immunological infertility among Nigerian men: incidence of circulating antisperm auto-antibodies and some clinical observations: a preliminary report'. *British Journal of Urology* 76: 366-70.

Eschenbach DA (1993), 'Bacterial vaginosis and anaerobes in obstetric-gynecologic infection'. *Clinical Infectious Diseases* 16 (suppl. 4): S282-7.

Eschenbach DA, Buchanan TM, Pollock HM, *et al.* (1975), 'Polymicrobial aetiology of acute pelvic inflammatory disease'. *New England Journal of Medicine* 293: 166-71.

Farley TMM, Rosenberg MJ, Rowe PJ, Chen J-H and Meirik O (1992), 'Intrauterine devices and pelvic inflammatory disease: an international perspective'. *Lancet* 339: 785-8.

Faro S (1988), 'Infectious disease relations to cesarean section'. *Obstet Gynecol Clinical North Am* 15: 685-95.

Faro S, Martens M, Maccato M, Hammill H and Pearlman M (1993), 'Vaginal flora and pelvic inflammatory disease'. *American Journal of Obstetrics and Gynecology* 169: 470-4.

Fathalla MF (1992), 'Reproductive health: a global overview'. *Early Human Development* 29: 35-42.

Favot I, Ngalula J, Mgalla Z, *et al.* (1997), 'HIV infection and sexual behaviour among women with infertility in Tanzania: a hospital-based study'. *International Journal of Epidemiology* 26: 414-19.

Fehler HG, Lyall M, Htun Ye, Muiznieks S, Khosa BD, Ballard RC (1998), 'Genital tract infections among women attending an urban family planning clinic'. *South African Journal of Epidemiology and Infect* 13(3): 79-82.

Frost E, Collet M, Reniers J, Leclerc A, Ivanoff B and Meheus A (1987), 'Importance of chlamydial antibodies in acute salpingitis in central Africa'. *Genitourinary Medicine* 63: 176-8.

Gaye-Diallo A, Wade A, Toure-Kane NC, *et al.* (1998), 'Bacterial vaginosis in Dakar (Senegal)'. *12th World AIDS Conference*, Geneva, June 28-July 3, 1998: Abstract No. 13285.

Gerbase AC, Rowley JT, Heymann DHL, Berkley SJF and Piot P (1998a), 'Global prevalence and incidence estimates of selected curable STDs'. *Sexually Transmitted Infections* 4 (suppl. 1): S12-16.

Gerbase AC, Rowley JT and Mertens TE (1998b), 'Global epidemiology of sexually transmitted diseases'. *Lancet* 351 (suppl. III) 2-4.

Gichangi PB, Ndinya-Achola JO, Ombete J, Nagelkerke NJ and Temmerman M (1997), 'Antimicrobial prophylaxis in pregnancy: a randomized, placebo-controlled trial with cefetamet-pivoxil in pregnant women with a poor obstetric history'. *American Journal of Obstetrics and Gynecology* 177(3): 680-4.

Gilson L, Mkanje R, Grosskurth H, *et al.* (1997), 'Cost-effectiveness of improved STD treatment services as a preventive intervention against HIV in Mwanza Region, Tanzania'. *Lancet* 350: 1805-09.

Gini PC and Ikerionwu SE (1990), 'Incidental tuberculous endometritis in premenstrual curettings from infertile women in eastern Nigeria'. *International Journal of Gynaecology and Obstetrics* 31: 141-4.

Goeman J, Meheus A and Piot P (1991), 'L'épidemiologie des maladies sexuellement transmissibles dans les pays en voie de développement à l'ère du SIDA'. *Annales de la Société Belge de Médicine Tropicale* 71: 81-113.

Govender L, Hoosen AA, Moodley P and Sturm AW (1996), 'Bacterial vaginosis and associated infections in pregnancy'. *International Journal of Gynaecology and Obstetrics* 55: 23-8.

Gray RH, Waver MJ, Serwadda D, *et al.* (1998), 'Population-based study of fertility in women with HIV-1 infection in Uganda'. *Lancet* 351: 98-103.

Grech ES, Everett JV and Musaka F (1973), 'Epidemiological aspects of acute pelvic inflammatory disease in Uganda'. *Tropical Doctor* 3: 123-7.

Grésenguet G, Bélec L, Hervé VM, Massanga M and Martin PM (1992), 'Anomalies quantitatives et qualitatives du sperme chez les individus africains infectés par le VIH1 (Quantitative and qualitative anomalies of sperm in African individuals infected with HIV)'. *Bulletin de la Société de Pathologie Exotique* 85: 205-7.

Grésenguet G, Kreiss JK, Chapko MK, *et al.* (1998), 'Bacterial vaginosis and HIV infection among STD patients in Central African Republic'. 12th World AIDS Conference, Geneva, June 28-July 3 1998: Abstract No. 13284.

Grodstein F and Rothman KJ (1994), 'Epidemiology of pelvic inflammatory disease'. *Epidemiology* 5: 234-42.

Grosskurth H, Mosha F, Todd J, *et al.* (1995), 'Impact of improved treatment of sexually transmitted diseases on HIV infection in rural Tanzania: randomised controlled trial'. *Lancet* 346: 530-6.

Grosskurth H, Mayaud P, Mosha F, *et al.* (1996), 'Asymptomatic gonorrhoea and chlamydial infection in rural Tanzanian men'. *British Medical Journal* 312: 277-80.

Hauth JC, Goldenberg RL, Andrews WW, *et al.* (1995), 'Reduced incidence of pre-term delivery with metronidazole and erythromycin in women with bacterial vaginosis'. *New England Journal of Medicine* 333: 1732-6.

Hay PE, Lamont RF, Taylor-Robinson D, *et al.* (1994), 'Abnormal bacterial colonisation of the genital tract and subsequent premature delivery and late miscarriage'. *British Medical Journal* 308: 295-8.

Hicks DA (1998), 'What risk of infection with IUD use' [Editorial]. *Lancet* 351: 1222-3.

Hillier S and Holmes KK (1990), 'Bacterial vaginosis'. In: Holmes KK, Mardh PA, Sparling PF and Wiesner PJ (eds), *Sexually transmitted diseases*, (2nd edition), McGraw Hill, New York: 547-59.

Hillier SL, Nugent RP, Eschenbach DA, *et al.* (1995), 'Associations between bacterial vaginosis and preterm delivery of a low birth-weight infant'. *New England Journal of Medicine* 333: 1737-41.

Hoffmann IF, Wallace A, Zimba D, *et al.* (1997), 'Trichomonas as a cause of urethritis in Malawi'. *12th Meeting of ISSTDR jointly held with 14th IUSTI - International Congress of Sexually Transmitted Diseases*, Seville, 19-22 Oct 1997: Abstract No. O237.

Huffman SL (1983), 'Maternal and child nutritional status; association with the risk of pregnancy'. *Social Science and Medicine* 17: 1529-40.

Ison CA and Taylor-Robinson D (1997), Bacterial vaginosis'. *International Journal of STD and AIDS* 8 (suppl. 1): 1-42.

Jackson DJ, Rakwar JP, Chohan B, *et al.* (1997), 'Urethral infection in a workplace population of East African men: evaluation of strategies for screening and management'. *Journal of Infectious Diseases* 175: 833-8.

Jacobson L and Westrom L (1969), 'Objectivized diagnosis of acute pelvic inflammatory disease'. *American Journal of Obstetrics and Gynecology* 105: 1088-98.

Kamenga MC, de Cock KM, St. Louis ME, *et al.*(1995), 'The impact of human immunodeficiency virus infection on pelvic inflammatory disease: a case-control study in Abidjan, Ivory Coast'. *American Journal of Obstetrics and Gynecology* 172: 919-25.

Kamwendo F, Johansson E, Moi H, Forslin L and Danielsson D (1993), 'Gonorrhoea, genital chlamydial infection, and nonspecific urethritis in male partners of women hospitalized and treated for acute pelvic inflammatory disease'. *Sexually Transmitted Diseases* 20: 143-6.

Kamwendo F, Forslin L, Bodin L and Danielsson D (1998), 'Programmes to reduce pelvic inflammatory disease the Swedish experience'. *Lancet* 351 (suppl. III): 25-28.

Kapiga S, Vuylsteke B, Lyamuya EF, Dallabetta G and Laga M (1998a), 'Evaluation of sexually transmitted diseases diagnostic algorithms among family planning clients in Dar es Salaam, Tanzania'. *Sexually Transmitted Infections* 74 (suppl. 1): S132-S138.

Kapiga SH, Lyamuya EF, Lwihula GK and Hunter DJ (1998b), 'The incidence of HIV infection among women using family planning methods in Dar es Salaam, Tanzania'. *AIDS* 12: 75-84.

Keith LG, Berger GS, Edelman DA, *et al.* (1984), 'On the causation of pelvic inflammatory disease'. *American Journal of Obstetrics and Gynecology* 149: 215-24.

Kelaghan J, Rubin GL, Ory HW and Layde PM (1982), 'Barrier-method contraceptives and pelvic inflammatory disease'. *Journal of the American Medical Association* 248: 184-7.

Kelver ME and Nagami N (1989), 'Chlamydia serology in women with tubal infertility'. *International Journal of Infertility* 34: 42-5.

Kimani J, Maclean IW, Bwayo JJ, *et al.* (1996), 'Risk factors for *Chlamydia trachomatis* pelvic inflammatory disease among sex workers in Nairobi, Kenya'. *Journal of Infectious Diseases* 173: 1437-44.

Kiviat NB, Wolner-Hanssen P, Eschenbach DA, *et al.* (1990), 'Endometrial histopathology in patients with culture-proved upper genital tract infection and laparoscopically diagnosed acute salpingitis'. *American Journal of Surgical Pathology* 14: 167-75.

Korn AP, Bolan G, Padian N, *et al.* (1995), 'Plasma cell endometritis in women with symptomatic bacterial vaginosis'. *Obstetrics and Gynecology* 85: 387-90.

Kuku SF, Akinyanju PA and Ojeifo JO (1987), 'Serum levels of gonadotropins, prolactin, and progesterone in infertile female Africans'. *International Journal of Fertility* 32: 393-8.

Ledru S, Meda N, Mohamed F, *et al.* (1992), 'Etiologic study of genitourinary infections in women of childbearing age in Bobo-Dioulasso, Burkina Faso, 1992'. *Sexually Transmitted Diseases* 23: 151-6.

Lema VM and Majinge CR (1993), 'Acute pelvic infection following hysterosalpingography at the Kenyatta National Hospital, Nairobi'. *East African Medical Journal* 70: 551-5.

Mabey DCW, Ogbaselassie G, Robertson JN, *et al.* (1985), 'Tubal infertility in The Gambia: chlamydial and gonococcal serology in women with tubal occlusion compared with pregnant controls'. *Bulletin of the World Health Organization* 63: 1107-13.

Maghoub S (1982), 'Pelvic schistosomiasis and infertility'. *International Journal of Gynaecology and Obstetrics* 20: 201-6.

Makossa E (1998), 'Enquête sur la rumeur qui tue'. *Actuel, Almanach 2001*, Hors Série: 180-5, Nova Press, Paris.

Mann SN, Smith JR and Barton SE (1996), 'Pelvic inflammatory disease'. *International Journal of STD and AIDS* 7: 315-21.

Marais NF, Wessels PH, Smith MS, Gericke A and Richter A (1991), '*Chlamydia trachomatis, Mycoplasma hominis* and *Ureaplasma urealyticum* infections in women. Prevalence, risks and management at a South African infertility clinic'. *Journal of Reproductive Medicine* 36: 161-4.

Matondo P (1992), 'National STD trends in Zambia: 1987-89'. *Genitourinary Medicine* 68: 192-3.

Mayaud P, Changalucha J, Grosskurth H, *et al.* (1992), 'The value of urine specimens in screening for male urethritis and its microbial aetiologies in Tanzania'. *Genitourinary Med* 68: 361-5.

Mayaud P, Grosskurth H, Changalucha J, *et al.* (1995), 'Risk-assessment and other screening options for gonorrhea and chlamydial infections in women attending rural Tanzanian antenatal clinics'. *Bulletin of the World Health Organization* 73(5): 621-630.

Mayaud P, Cleophas B, West B, *et al.* (1997a), 'Monitoring STD syndromic treatment effectiveness: experience of an integrated control programme in Mwanza, Tanzania'. *International Congress of Sexually Transmitted Diseases*'. Seville, 19-22 Oct 1997: Abstract No. O105.

Mayaud P, Mosha F, Todd J, *et al.* (1997b), 'Improved treatment services significantly reduce the prevalence of sexually transmitted diseases in rural Tanzania: results of a randomised controlled trial'. *AIDS* 11: 1873-80.

Mayaud P, Hawkes S and Mabey D (1998a), 'Advances in STD control in developing countries'. *Lancet* 351 (suppl. III): 29-32.

Mayaud P, ka-Gina G, Cornelissen J, *et al.* (1998b), 'Validation of a WHO algorithm with risk-assessment for vaginal discharge in Mwanza, Tanzania'. *Sexually Transmitted Infections* 74 (suppl. 1): S77-S84.

Mayaud P, Mosha F, Mugeye K, *et al.* (1998c), 'Asymptomatic STDs: How can routine health services tackle the problem in resource-poor countries?' *XIIth International Conference on AIDS/STDs*, Geneva, June 27-July 3, 1998: Abstract No. O237

Mayaud P, Uledi E, Cornelissen J, *et al.* (1998d), 'Risk scores to detect cervical infection in urban antenatal clinic attenders in Mwanza, Tanzania'. *Sexually Transmitted Infections* 74 (suppl. 1): S139-S146.

McGregor JA, French JI, Parker R, *et al.* (1995), 'Prevention of premature birth by screening and treatment for common genital tract infections: results of a prospective controlled evaluation'. *American Journal of Obstetrics and Gynecology* 173: 157-67.

Meheus A (1992), 'Women's health: importance of reproductive tract infections, pelvic inflammatory disease and cervical cancer'. In: Germain A, Holmes KK, Piot P and Wasserheit JN (eds), *Reproductive tract infections: global impact and priorities for women's reproductive health*, IWHC, Plenum Press, New York: 61-91.

Meheus A (1998), 'Control of STI, HIV and AIDS'. In: Arya OP and Hart CA (eds), *Sexually transmitted infections and AIDS in the tropics*, CABI Publishing, Wallingford: 397-418.

Modebe O (1989), 'Serum concentrations of pituitary and testicular hormones in infertile Nigerian males'. *International Journal of Fertility* 34: 408-10.

Morcos R, Frost N, Hnat M, Petrunak A and Caldito G (1993), 'Laparoscopic versus clinical diagnosis of acute pelvic inflammatory disease'. *Journal of Reproductive Medicine* 38: 53-56.

Moses S, Manji F, Bradley JE, *et al.* (1992), 'Impact of user fees on attendance at a referral centre for sexually transmitted diseases in Kenya'. *Lancet* 340: 463-6.

Mosley WH. (1979), 'The effects of nutrition on natural fertility'. In: Leridon H and Menken J (eds), *Fécondité naturelle'*. Ordina Editions, Liège, Belgium: 85-105.

Mouktar M (1966), 'Functional disorders due to bilharzial infection of the female genital tract'. *Journal of Obstetrics and Gynaecology of the British Commonwealth* 73: 307-10.

Muir DG and Belsey MA (1980), 'Pelvic inflammatory disease and its consequences in the developing world'. *American Journal of Obstetrics and Gynecology* 138: 913-28.

Ndoye I, Mboup S, De Schrijver A, *et al.* (1998), 'Diagnosis of sexually transmitted infections in female prostitutes in Dakar, Senegal'. *Sexual Transmitted Infections* 1998(74) (suppl. 1): S112-S117.

Neri A, Tadir Y, Grausbard G, Pardo J, Ovadia J and Braslavsky D (1986), '*Enterobius (Oxyuris) vermicularis* of the pelvic peritoneum a cause of infertility'. *European Journal of Obstetrics Gynaecology and Reproductive Biology* 23: 239-41.

Njeru EK, Eldridge GD, Ngugi EN, Plummer FA and Moses S (1995), 'STD partner notification and referral in primary level health centers in Nairobi, Kenya'. *Sexually Transmitted Diseases* 22: 231-5.

Nugent RP, Krohn MA and Hillier SL (1991), 'Reliability of diagnosing bacterial vaginosis is improved by a standardized method of gram stain interpretation'. *Journal of Clinical Microbiology* 29: 297-301.

Oosthuizen AP, Wessels PH and Hefer JN (1990), 'Tuberculosis of the female genital tract in patients attending an infertility clinic'. *South African Medical Journal* 77: 562-4.

Over M and Piot P (1993), 'HIV infection and sexually transmitted diseases'. In: Jamison DT, Mosley WH, Measham AR, Borbadilla JL (eds), *Disease control priorities in developing countries*, Oxford University Press, New York: 455-527.

Paavonen J, Teisala K, Heinonen PK, *et al.* (1987), 'Microbiological and histopathological findings in acute PID'. *British Journal of Obstetrics and Gynaecology* 94: 454-60.

Paisarntantiwong R, Brockmann S, Clarke L, *et al.* (1995), 'The relationship of vaginal trichomoniasis and pelvic inflammatory disease among women colonized with *Chlamydia trachomatis'*. *Sexually Transmitted Diseases* 22: 344-7.

Parsons A and McGregor JA (1997), 'Pathogens on the move: active uterine transport of cervico-vaginal fluid into the uterus and Fallopian tubes at ovarian mid-cycle'. *International Journal of STD and AIDS* 8 (suppl. 1): 22.

Peeling RW, Kimani J, Plummer F, *et al.* (1997), 'Antibody to chlamydial hsp60 predicts an increased risk for chlamydial pelvic inflammatory disease'. *Journal of Infectious Diseases* 175: 1153-8.

Piot P and Holmes KK (1990), 'Sexually Transmitted Diseases'. In: Warren KS and Mhamoud AAF (eds), *Tropical and geographical medicine* (2nd edition), McGraw-Hill International, New York: 894-910.

Piot P and Islam MQ (1994), 'Sexually transmitted diseases in the 1990s. Global epidemiology and challenges for control'. *Sexually Transmitted Diseases* 21(2 suppl.): S7-S13.

Piot P and Tezzo R (1990), 'The epidemiology of HIV and other sexually transmitted infections in the developing world'. *Scandanavian Journal of Infectious Diseases* 69 (Suppl.): 89-97.

Plummer FA, Laga M, Brunham RC, *et al.* (1987), 'Postpartum upper genital tract infections in Nairobi, Kenya: epidemiology, and risk factors'. *Journal of Infectious Diseases* 156: 92-8.

Schneider H, Coetzee DJ, Fehler HG, *et al.* (1998), 'Screening for sexually transmitted diseases in rural South African women'. *Sexually Transmitted Infections* 74 (suppl. 1): S147-S152.

Schrijvers D, Delaporte E, Peeters M, Dupont A and Meheus A (1991), 'Seroprevalence of retroviral infection in women with different fertility statuses in Gabon, western equatorial Africa'. *Journal of Acquired Immune Deficiency Syndrome* 4: 468-70.

Schulz TF (1998), 'Vaccination against STI, HIV and AIDS'. In: Arya OP and Hart CA (eds), *Sexually transmitted infections and AIDS in the tropics*, CABI Publishing, Wallingford: 419-425.

Sewankambo N, Gray R, Wawer M, *et al.* (1997), 'HIV-1 infection associated with abnormal vaginal flora morphology and bacterial vaginosis'. *Lancet* 350: 546-60.

Sherris J and Fox G (1983), 'Infertility and sexually transmitted disease: a public health challenge'. *Population Reports* Series L, No.4: L113-L151.

Sinei K, Cohen CR, Bukusi E, *et al.* (1997), 'The role of *Chlamydia trachomatis* in tubal factor infertility in Nairobi, Kenya'. *12th Meeting of ISSTDR jointly held with 14th IUSTI - International Congress of Sexually Transmitted Diseases*, Seville, 19-22 Oct 1997: Abstract No. P712.

Sinei SK, Morrison CS, Sekadde-Kigondu C, Allen M and Kokonya D (1998), 'Complications of use of intrauterine devices among HIV-1-infected women'. *Lancet* 35: 1238-41.

Sinei SKA, Schulz KF, Lamptey PR, *et al.* (1990), 'Preventing IUCD-related pelvic infection: the efficacy of prophylactic doxycycline at insertion'. *British Journal of Obstetrics and Gynaecology* 97: 412-9.

Soper DE (1988), 'Postpartum endometritis. Pathophysiology and prevention'. *Journal of Reproductive Medicine* 33 (suppl. 1): 97-100.

Soper DE (1993), 'Bacterial vaginosis and postoperative infections'. *American Journal of Obstetrics and Gynecology* 169: 467-9.

Soper DE, Brockwell NJ, Dalton HP and Johnson D (1994), 'Observations concerning the microbial aetiology of acute salpingitis'. *American Journal of Obstetrics and Gynecology* 170: 1008-17.

Steen R, Soliman C, Bucyana S, *et al.* (1996), 'Partner referral as a component of integrated sexually transmitted disease services in two Rwandan towns'. *Genitourinary Medicine* 72: 56-9.

Sudik R, Abbate Y and Andemariam S (1989), 'Problems in treatment of sterility in developing countries: experiences with sterility consultation in Gondar, Ethiopia'. *Zentralbl gynakol* 111(23): 1555-61.

Sweet RL (1995), 'Role of bacterial vaginosis in pelvic inflammatory disease'. *Clinical Infectious Diseases* 20 (suppl. 2): S271-5.

Sweet RL, Blankfort-Doyle M, Robbie MO and Schachter J (1986), 'The occurrence of chlamydial and gonococcal salpingitis during the menstrual cycle'. *Journal of the American Medical Association* 255: 2062-4

Sweet RL and Landers DV (1997), 'Pelvic inflammatory disease in HIV-positive women'. *Lancet* 349: 1265-6.

Symonds EM and Symonds IM (1998), 'Infertility'. In: Symonds EM and Symonds IM (eds), *Essentials of obstetrics and gynaecology*, Churchill Livingstone, London: 73-84.

Taha TE, Dallabetta GA, Canner JK, *et al.* (1995), 'The effect of human immunodeficiency virus infection on birth weight, and infant and child mortality in urban Malawi'. *International Journal of Epidemiology* 24: 1022-9.

Taha T, Kumwendo N, Liomba G, *et al.* (1998), 'Heterosexual and perinatal transmission of HIV-1: associations with bacterial vaginosis'. *12th World AIDS Conference*, Geneva, June 28-July 3 1998: Abstract No. 527/23347.

Taylor-Robinson D and Furr PM (1998), 'Update on sexually transmitted mycoplasmas'. *Lancet* 351 (suppl. III): 12-15.

Temmerman M, Kidula N, Tyndall M, *et al.* (1998), 'The supermarket for women's reproductive health: the burden of genital infections in a family planning clinic in Nairobi, Kenya'. *Sexually Transmitted Infections* 74: 202-4.

Temmerman M, Njagi E, Nagelkerke N, *et al.* (1995), 'Mass antimicrobial treatment in pregnancy: a randomized, placebo-controlled trial in a population with high rates of sexually transmitted diseases'. *Journal of Reproductive Medicine* 40: 176-80.

Temmerman M, Plummer FA, Mirza NB, *et al.* (1990), 'Infection with HIV as a risk factor for adverse obstetrical outcome'. *AIDS* 4: 1087-93.

Thomas T, Choudhri S, Kariuki C and Moses S (1996), 'Identifying cervical infection among pregnant women in Nairobi, Kenya: limitations of risk-assessment and symptom-based approaches'. *Genitourinary Medicine* 72: 334-8.

Van der Spuy ZM (1985), 'Nutrition and reproduction'. *Clinical Obstetrics and Gynaecology* 12: 579-604.

Vessey MP, Yeates D, Flavel R and McPherson K (1981), 'Pelvic inflammatory disease and the intrauterine device: findings in a large cohort study'. *British Medical Journal* 282: 855-7.

Vuylsteke B, Bastos R, Barreto J, *et al.* (1993), 'High prevalence of sexually transmitted diseases in a rural area in Mozambique'. *Genitourinary Medicine* 69: 427-30.

Vuylsteke B, Laga M, Alary M, *et al.* (1993), 'Clinical algorithms for the screening of women for gonococcal and chlamydial infection: evaluation of pregnant women and prostitutes in Zaire'. *Clinical Infectious Diseases* 17: 82-8.

Washington AE, Aral SO, Wolner-Hanssen P, Grimes DA and Holmes KK (1991), 'Assessing risk for pelvic inflammatory disease and its sequelae'. *Journal of the American Medical Association* 266: 2581-6.

Washington AE, Gove S, Schachter J and Sweet RL (1985), 'Oral contraceptives, Chlamydia trachomatis infection, and pelvic inflammatory disease: a word of caution about protection'. *Journal of the American Medical Association* 253: 2246-50.

Wasserheit J (1989a), 'The significance and scope of reproductive tract infections among third world women'. *International Journal of Gynaecology and Obstetrics* 3 (suppl.): 145-63.

Wasserheit JN, Harris JR, Chakraborty J, Kay BA and Mason KJ (1989b), 'Reproductive tract infections in a family planning population in rural Bangladesh'. *Studies in Family Planning* 20: 69-80.

Wasserheit JN and Holmes KK (1992), 'Reproductive tract infections: challenges for international health policy, programs, and research'. In: Germain A, Holmes KK, Piot P and Wasserheit JN (eds), *Reproductive tract infections: global impact and priorities for women's reproductive health*, IWHC, Plenum Press, New York: 7-33.

Watson-Jones D, Mugeye K, Mayaud P, *et al.* (2000), 'High prevalence of trichomoniasis in rural men in Mwanza, Tanzania: Results from a population-based study'. *Sexually Transmitted Infections;* 76: 355-362.

Wawer MJ, Sewankambo NK, Serwadda D, *et al.* (1997). 'Control of sexually transmitted diseases for AIDS prevention in Uganda: a randomised community trail'. Rakai Project Study Group. *Lancet;* 353: 525-35.

Wessels PH, Viljoen GJ, Marais NF, de-Beer JA, Smith M and Gericke A (1991), 'The prevalence, risks, and management of Chlamydia trachomatis infections in fertile and infertile patients from the high socioeconomic bracket of the South African population'. *Fertility and Sterility* 56: 485-8.

Westrom L (1980), 'Incidence, prevalence and trends of acute pelvic inflammatory disease and its consequences in industrialized countries'. *American Journal of Obstetrics and Gynecology* 138: 880-92.

Westrom L (1988), 'Decrease in incidence of women treated in hospitals for acute salpingitis in Sweden'. *Genitourinary Medicine* 62: 59-63.

Westrom L and Mardh PA (1990), 'Acute pelvic inflammatory disease'. In: Holmes KK, Mardh PA, Sparling PF, Wiesner PJ (eds), *Sexually transmitted diseases* (2nd ed.): 593-613, McGraw Hill, New York.

Westrom L and Wolner-Hanssen P (1993), 'Pathogenesis of pelvic inflammatory disease'. *Genitourinary Medicine* 69: 9-17.

Winfield J and Latif AS (1985), 'Tracing contacts of persons with sexually transmitted diseases in a developing country'. *Sexually Transmitted Diseases* Jan-Mar: 5-7.

Wiswedel K and Allen DA (1989), 'Infertility factors at the Groote Schuur Hospital Fertility Clinic'. *South African Medical Journal* 76: 65-6.

Wolner-Hanssen P, Eschenbach DA, Paavonen J, *et al.* (1990), 'Association between vaginal douching and acute pelvic inflammatory'. *Journal of the American Medical Association* 263: 1936-41.

World Bank (1993), *World Development Report 1993: Investing in Health*, Oxford University Press, New York.

WHO (1998), Reproductive health [1 screen; cited 1999 Feb], Available from: URL: http//www.who.int/rht/

WHO/GPA (Van Praag, E) (1993), 'Provision of STD services in Maternal and Child Health and Family Planning settings'. *Informal Technical Working Group Meeting on STD Activities in GPA*, Agenda Item No, IV, Background Paper No. 7, Geneva.

WHO/GPA (1994), *Management of sexually transmitted diseases*: WHO/GPA/TEM/94.1, WHO, Geneva.

Yeboah ED and Marmar JL (1994), 'Urethral stricture and semen quality'. *International Journal of Fertility and Menopausal Studies* 39: 310-5.

Yeboah ED, Wadhwani JM and Wilson JB (1992), 'Etiological factors of male infertility in Africa'. *International Journal of Fertility* 37: 300-7.

Nine *mwana hiti* (children of wood), traditionally
decorated and treated as children; symbols of
fertility used in the initiation of girls (Zaramo and
Kwere, Eastern Tanzania)

3 Caesarean section and infertility: a case-control study from Zimbabwe

Xavier De Muylder, Pierre Buekens and Bruno Dujardin

Caesarean section (CS) is a procedure that is widely used worldwide. It can be life-saving for the mother, foetus or both, but carries a risk of complications, the greatest of which is infection morbidity. These complications are a cause for concern because of the increasing rates of CS in many settings, including some African hospitals (De Muylder, 1993). For example, in Zimbabwe the CS rate was 6.0% in 1994, and was as high as 11.6% in one province (Central Statistical Office, Zimbabwe, and Macro International Inc., 1995).

One potential consequence of pelvic infection is tubal infertility; such infections may also cause pelvic adhesions, which have been suggested as another possible cause of infertility (Kemper at al., 1982). The relationship between CS and subsequent fertility is difficult to assess but cohort studies from Brazil, Finland, Scotland, Sweden and the U.S. have suggested a slight decrease in the fertility of women delivered by CS compared with those who had a vaginal delivery (Hemminki, 1996). The situation in Africa has remained largely unexplored. This is important because infertility is frequent in many African countries (Larsen and Raggers, Chapter 1). Our study compares the rate of previous CS among a group of secondary infertility patients to that of a matched control group of fertile women in a Zimbabwean Hospital.

Methods

All the patients in the study resided in the city of Gweru, Zimbabwe. They were referred to the Gynecology Clinic at the Gweru Provincial Hospital between March 1985 and August 1986 because of secondary infertility. Secondary infertility was defined as the absence of conception in a sample who had previously given birth and who had lived together with their partners, without any form of contraception, for more than 18 months after breast-feeding ended.

For every infertile patient, two control patients who delivered during the same week were recruited from the maternity ward. Patients were matched for four factors: age (+/- one year), number of previous deliveries, instruction level (five groups: illiterate; grade 1-3; 4-7; Form I-II; Higher) and height (<150 cm; 150-160 cm; >160 cm). Patients and controls living outside Gweru were excluded from the study.

All women were interviewed and examined. A complete obstetrical history was recorded for every patient, including history of previous pelvic infection, extrauterine pregnancy or dilatation and curettage. Special attention was paid to the history of pelvic infection. Postcaesarean sepsis was diagnosed after prolonged hospital stay (> seven days), high temperature after the fourth day, prolonged intravenous administration of antibiotics, pelvic pain or tenderness, evacuation of a purulent collection or the need for a second laparatomy. Pelvic inflammatory disease (PID) was diagnosed in cases with all of the following symptoms: temperature, abdominal pain with acute onset, abnormal uterine bleeding or abnormal vaginal discharge and relief with administration of antibiotics (oral or parenteral).

Matching was accounted for in the analysis, and cases with fewer than two controls were excluded. A stratified analysis with each stratum containing a case and two controls was carried out to compute odds ratios (OR) and 95% confidence intervals (CI) (Kleinbaum et al., 1982).

Results

During the study period, 116 infertile and 222 fertile patients were interviewed. Ten cases were matched with fewer than two controls and were excluded. The results presented pertain to 106 cases and 212 controls. Table 1 shows that the cases and controls were similarly distributed with respect to all matching factors.

Table 1   Demographic characteristics of 106 women with secondary infertility and 212 fertile controls

Age (years)	Cases		Controls	
	N	%	N	%
15-19		(-)	1	(0.5)
20-24	26	(24.5)	51	(24.1)
25-29	43	(40.6)	87	(41.0)
30-34	22	(20.7)	43	(20.3)
35-39	15	(14.2)	30	(14.1)
Parity				
1	63	(59.4)	126	(59.4)
2	34	(32.1)	68	(32.1)
3	9	(8.5)	18	(8.5)
Education				
Illiterate	7	(6.6)	14	(6.6)
Grade 1-3	15	(14.1)	30	(14.1)
Grade 4-7	50	(47.2)	100	(47.2)
Form I-II	19	(17.9)	38	(17.9)
Higher	15	(14.2)	30	(14.2)
Height (cm)				
< 150	16	(15.1)	32	(15.1)
150-160	65	(61.3)	130	(61.3)
> 160	25	(23.6)	50	(23.6)

Table 2 shows that a history of a previous CS was much more frequent among infertile patients than fertile women (17.9% and 8.5% respectively). It also indicates that in cases of secondary infertility CS occurred more frequently in the most recent pregnancy. Further, this table shows that a history of previous pelvic infection was also more common in infertile than fertile patients, but there was no statistically significant difference for ectopic pregnancy and abortion curettage.

Table 2 **Obstetrical and gynaecological history of study and control groups[a]**

	Cases		Controls		Odds ratio (95% CI[c])	
	N	%	N	%		
Previous CS[b]	19	(17.9)	18	(8.5)	2.33	(1.21-4.48)
CS at last delivery	18	(17.0)	14	(6.6)	2.83	(1.40-5.70)
Ectopic pregnancy	4	(3.8)	2	(1.0)	4.00	(0.83-19.20)
Abortion-curettage	12	(11.3)	22	(10.4)	1.11	(0.52-2.35)
Pelvic infection	73	(68.9)	43	(20.3)	11.30	(6.52-19.58)

[a] Study group: N=106; controls: N=212
[b] CS: caesarean section
[c] CI: confidence interval

Patients and controls were divided into five subgroups according to their history of previous CS and previous infection. The relationship of combinations of these two factors to fertility is presented in Table 3. The main difference appears to be that CS with postoperative sepsis was much more frequent in the infertile than in the fertile group. PID was also more common among infertile women. All infertile patients underwent a hysterosalpingography, which demonstrated tubal damage in 17 out of 19 women with CS and in 57 of the 87 women with no CS.

Table 3 **Relationship between mode of delivery and infection for study group and controls[a]**

	Cases		Controls		Odds ratio (95% CI[c])	
	N	%	N	%		
CS[b] with post-operative sepsis	12	(11.3%)	3	(1.4%)	11.50	(3.44-38.42)
CS without post-operative sepsis	4	(3.8%)	10	(4.7%)	0.80	(0.25-2.57)
CS without post-operative sepsis but with a PID later	3	(2.8%)	5	(2.4%)	1.25	(0.27-5.87)
No CS but PID later	58	(54.7%)	35	(16.5%)	8.05	(3.64-10.08)
No CS no PID	29	(27.4%)	159	(75.0%)	0.10	(0.06-0.17)

[a] Study group: N=106; controls: N=212
[b] CS: caesarean section
[c] CI: confidence interval

Discussion

The influence of the mode of delivery upon future fertility is difficult to estimate due to the many confounding factors. Women who delivered by CS have some characteristics that could put them at higher risk of other problems leading to infertility. Although we have matched for four potential confounding factors, the existence of residual confounding cannot be excluded.

A relatively small case-control study performed in the U.S. reported an OR of 1.2 (95% CI 0.4-3.7) of being infertile after CS (Holf *et al.*, 1990). The authors pointed out that a case-control study might underestimate this effect because women with a prior successful pregnancy who had a CS could be less motivated to seek care. This is less likely to happen in high-fertility African countries than in the U.S.

Cohort studies found that patients with a CS delivery tended to have fewer subsequent pregnancies or births than those with a spontaneous vaginal delivery (Hemminki, 1996). One of the published cohort studies reported secondary infertility rates, using a definition similar to the one in this study (Hemminki *et al.*, 1985). Secondary infertility occurred in 5.8% of the CS groups and in 1.8% of the vaginal delivery group. The size of the effect was similar to that we observed. However, the mechanism behind decreased fertility was not entirely clear.

Our data suggest that a history of a previous CS is much more frequently observed among secondary infertile patients than among fertile women of the same age, height, parity and social level. A possible link between CS, infectious morbidity, tubal damage and infertility is suggested because all but one CS were performed during the last delivery before the diagnosis of infertility, and most cases of infertility were of tubal etiology.

Pelvic infection (pelvic inflammatory disease, postabortal sepsis or postpartum sepsis) represents a well-known risk factor for infertility. Such antecedent infection was also much more frequent among infertile women in this study and could be an important confounding factor. However, it should be noted that among CS patients infection mainly arose during the days immediately after the CS, confirming a pathophysiological role for post CS sepsis. In some patients, the indications for CS (e.g. obstructed labour, amnionitis with foetal distress) could have been the origin of the postoperative infection. It is also plausible that the CS itself was the cause of the postoperative infection in many cases, or that it induced dissemination of a silent intra-uterine infection. Indeed, Plummer *et al.* (1987) have shown in Nairobi that the prevalence of gonococcal and chlamydial infection among women in labour was 6.7% and 20.8%, respectively, and that prevalence of postpartum upper genital tract infection was 20.3% after vaginal birth. Moreover, in case of CS, the presence of uterine contractions and the duration of labour are known to increase the subsequent risk of febrile morbidity (Eschenbach and Wager, 1980).

The data presented here show that 15 out of 37 CS were complicated by postoperative infection. This rate is consistent with the 31% rate of postoperative pelvic infection reported in Zimbabwe (De Muylder, 1989). Studies from industrialized countries have described comparable rates of postoperative infections (Kelleher and Cardozo, 1994; Neilsen, 1986). In our study, most CS were performed during labour and without any prophylactic antibiotherapy, which might decrease the frequency of postoperative infections (Reggiori *et al.*, 1996). It is thus possible that prophylactic antibiotics could decrease the risk of subsequent infertility.

The optimal CS rate in a community is always difficult to estimate. However it has been shown that CS in developing countries could be associated with higher mortality and morbidity rates, increased risk of uterine rupture during the next pregnancy, heavier socio-financial burden, and poorer acceptance by the population (De Muylder, 1993). This evidence has prompted some obstetricians to introduce strict guidelines for obstetrical management, to reduce CS rates in their communities. In a previous study, we reported that such a program could be successful without any adverse effect upon perinatal outcome (De Muylder and Thiery, 1990). The results of our present study, which suggest a deleterious effect of CS upon subsequent fertility, provide additional evidence for the adoption of such an obstetrical policy.

In conclusion, this study suggests the possibility that CS can have a deleterious effect upon future fertility. If confirmed by other studies, this observation should be taken into consideration in estimating the optimum frequency of use of CS in developing countries and a need to study possible prophylactic measures.

Acknowledgements

The authors thank E. Hemminki for her comments and suggestions. The material in this chapter was presented as a paper at a UNAIDS/USAID/MEASURE Evaluation/CDC meeting on 'Infertility, STDs and HIV: problems and prospects', Arlington, Virginia, December 14-15, 1998.

Bibliography

'Central Statistical Office [Zimbabwe] and Macro International Inc. (1995)'. *Zimbabwe Demographic and Health Survey, 1994*, Central Statistical Office and Macro International Inc., Calverton, Maryland.

De Muylder X (1989), 'Cesarean section morbidity at district level in Zimbabwe'. *Journal of Tropical Medicine and Hygiene* 92: 89-92.

De Muylder X (1993), 'Cesarean section in developing countries: some considerations'. *Health Policy and Planning* 8: 101-12.

De Muylder X and Thiery M(1990), 'The Cesarean delivery rate can be safely reduced in a developing country'. *Obstetrics and Gynecology* 75: 360-4.

Eschenbach B and Wager G (1980), 'Puerperal infections'. *Clinical Obstetrics and Gynecology* 23: 1003-37.

Hemminki E (1996), 'Impact of Cesarean section on future pregnancy a review of cohort studies'. *Paediatric and Perinatal Epidemiology* 10: 366-79.

Hemminki E, Graubard D, Hoffman H, Hosheer W and Fetterly K (1985), 'Cesarean section and subsequent fertility: results from the 1982 national survey of family growth'. *Fertility and Sterility* 43: 520-8.

Holf M, Daling J and Voigt I (1990), 'Prior Cesarean delivery in women with secondary tubal infertility'. *American Journal of Public Health* 80: 1382-3.

Kelleher C and Cardozo L (1994), 'Cesarean section: a safe operation?'. *Journal of Obstetrics and Gynecology* 14: 86-90.

Kemper T, Trinbos B and van Hall B (1982), 'Etiologic factors in tubal infertility'. *Fertility and Sterility* 37: 384-89.

Kleinbaum D, Kupper L and Morgenstern H (1982), *Epidemiologic research: principles and quantitative methods*, Van Nostrand Reinhold, New York: 394-6.

Nielsen T (1986), 'Cesarean Section: A controversial feature of modern obstetric practice'. *Gynecological and Obstetrical Investigation* 21: 57-63.

Plummer F, Laga H, Brunham R, *et al.* (1987), 'Postpartum upper genital tract infections in Nairobi, Kenya: epidemiology, etiology and risk factors'. *Journal of Infectious Diseases* 156: 92-98.

Reggiori A, Ravera M, Cocozza E, Andreata M and Mukasa F (1996), 'Randomized study of antibiotic prophylaxis for general and gynaecological surgery from a single centre in rural Africa'. *British Journal of Surgery* 83: 356-9.

The personification of fertility: round,
pregnant belly, large labium, hollow back with
pronounced buttocks; shrine-figure of wood
with sacrifice-patina (Lobi, Côte d'Ivoire)

4 Modelling the dramatic decline of primary infertility in sub-Saharan Africa

Richard G.White, Basia Zaba, J. Ties Boerma and John Blacker

Prior to the late 1960s primary infertility was very common in Africa. In a large area stretching across Central Africa - sometimes referred to as the 'infertility belt' of the continent - more than one in five women at the end of their reproductive period had never given birth or were childless (Retel-Laurentin, 1974). In many other parts of Africa, more than one in ten women were childless (Frank, 1983), a considerably higher figure than the 3% primary infertility risk accepted as the 'standard' level due to genetic, anatomic and endocrine factors (Bongaarts and Potter, 1983). The high prevalence of sexually transmitted diseases (STDs) has been identified as the main cause (Caldwell and Caldwell, 1983; Belsey, 1976).

During the past decade, a large number of national surveys have indicated that this situation has now radically changed. The prevalence of primary infertility among women in their forties have dropped to less than 5% in most African countries. They are now similar to, or only slightly higher than, levels in populations with almost no primary infertility due to STDs or other infections (Chapter 1). The main cause of the decline in primary infertility is thought to be the introduction of antibiotics, through the health system and through special campaigns - notably against yaws and venereal diseases - during the 1950s and early 1960s (Romaniuk, 1980; Caldwell and Caldwell, 1983; Belsey, 1976). On the other hand, there are current concerns about the early onset of sexual intercourse (particularly unprotected intercourse), the high prevalence of STDs, and the lack of sexual health services for youth, all of which may lead to an increased incidence of primary infertility in the future.

This chapter reviews the evidence for the historically high levels of primary infertility in sub-Saharan Africa and describes its decline during the past half century. Possible causes are discussed, including the introduction of antibiotics, the epidemiology of STDs and other infections, the changes in age at menarche, and abortions, as well as changes in sexual behaviour and patterns of marriage and first birth. A micro-simulation model is used to estimate the parameters required for high levels of primary infertility in the past and to assess the effect of changes in the determinants of the level of primary infertility. These include reduction in prevalence of sexually transmitted diseases (STD) among males, improved treatment of STD in females, changes in sexual behaviour and changes in age at menarche.

Indicators, risks and trends in primary infertility

In general, infertility should be studied as an attribute of couples, since either member could be responsible for the inability to bear a (live) child. However, if we want to differentiate between secondary infertility (SI), which follows the birth of one or more children, and primary infertility (PI), which is the inability to bear even one child, we need to focus on one sex only, as each member can bring different childbearing histories to the union. Because more information is available on the reproductive histories of women, they are the focus of this study.

Measurement issues

Primary infertility (PI) is defined here as the inability to give birth to a live child. The demographic measure of PI is childlessness among women at the end of their reproductive age span. This inevitably includes some women who were biologically capable of bearing a live child up to the menopause but did not stay in active sexual unions long enough to conceive, or who conceived but never carried a pregnancy to term (i.e. women who were not sterile). In populations in which virtually all women become sexually active, and spend most of their reproductive lives in sexual partnership, primary infertility at ages 50 and over is in fact a highly specific and sensitive indicator of primary sterility even if we use the stricter (largely immeasurable) biological definition. As we show later, in our default simulation, PI by age 50 (which is 9.1%) overestimates biological primary sterility (which is 8.8%) by just a fraction of a percentage point, or in proportional terms, by 3.4%. However, levels of primary infertility recorded in surveys can be affected by reporting errors; this depends on how accurately census and survey questions about childbearing were answered, and how data were subsequently classified. For example, women who lost all their live births may be misclassified as primary infertile.

Several other biases may lead to underestimation of primary infertility. Childless women, who might be more mobile, may be under-represented in sample surveys. In rural Tanzania, survey attendance was 13% lower among childless women than among women with children (Boerma et al., 1996). A barren woman may also be more likely to care for another woman's child and to report such a child as her own (Caldwell and Caldwell, 1983). This was found to occur in rural Tanzania, although on a relatively small scale (Boerma et al., 1996). Another bias that may occur in both surveys and censuses is underrepresentation of childless women because of their higher mortality. In Ethiopia mortality was higher among childless women, but the impact on estimates of infertility was small (Mammo and Morgan, 1986). On the other hand, the classic error of omitting dead children from a count of children ever born in surveys or censuses (Brass et al., 1968) would lead to overestimation of primary infertility.

Primary infertility risks and trends[1]

If excess PI (defined as that not due to genetic, anatomic or endocrine factors) is caused by STDs, the period of risk of becoming infertile starts at the initiation of sex and ends at the occurrence of the first birth. Surveys have shown that in most of sub-Saharan Africa, the median age at which these events occur is 16-17 and 19-20 years of age respectively (see Table 3). Extensive modelling of risk distributions of conception and STD infection lead us to believe that in populations with these mean ages for first sex and first birth, the external event leading to PI occurs on average between ages 18 and 19 years. Therefore, the prevalence of PI among women aged 45-49 years provides information about the risk of becoming infertile as it was about 30 years ago.

Table 1 summarizes trends in PI by birth cohort of women in selected populations. The tabulated data on proportions of childless women at ages 30 and over from various censuses and surveys have been reorganized to enable us to trace birth cohorts[2] of women as they are identified in each data source. Since very few first births occur after the age of 30, any variation in the proportions childless - as reported in enquiries at different dates after the cohort reached age 30 - are due either to misreporting and misclassification or to selective mortality of childless women. In general, we believe that data errors account for most of the discrepancies among the various sources pertaining to a particular cohort. The major sources of error appear to be, first, misreporting of women with no surviving children as childless and, second, the misclassification as childless of those with number of children not stated.

Table 1   Women with primary infertility by birth cohort in selected African populations (%)[a]

Population	Approximate birth cohort	Year of study	% PI	Year of study	% PI	Year of study	% PI
Congo, Bas Fleuve	1900-1910	1955	9.0				
	1910-1920	1955	11.5				
	1920-1925	1955	11.1	1975	8.8		
	1925-1930	1975	8.2				
	1930-1935	1975	2.9				
	1935-1940	1975	4.5				
	1940-1945	1975	2.8				
Congo, Kasai	1900-1910	1955	15.7				
	1910-1920	1955	16.9				
	1920-1925	1955	18.8	1975	19		
	1925-1930	1975	19.0				
	1930-1935	1975	15.3				
	1935-1940	1975	8.3				
	1940-1945	1975	5.6				
Congo, Equateur	1900-1910	1955	40.0				
	1910-1920	1955	40.7				
	1920-1925	1955	38.7	1975	37		
	1925-1930	1975	27.3				
	1930-1935	1975	17.6				
	1935-1940	1975	14.5				
	1940-1945	1975	9.4				
Congo, Tshuapa	1900-1910	1955	33.0				
	1910-1920	1955	38.4				
	1920-1925	1955	40.4	1975	43		
	1925-1930	1975	33.4				
	1930-1935	1975	21.7				
	1935-1940	1975	18.9				
	1940-1945	1975	14.0				
Senegal	1910-1915	1960	6.0				
	1935-1940	1985	4.6				
	1940-1945	1985	5.1	1995	2.0		
	1945-1950	1985	2.0	1995	2.1		
	1950-1955	1995	3.0				
Uganda	before 1903	1948	18.0				
	1938-1943	1988	4.7				
	1943-1948	1988	5.1	1995	2.0		
	1948-1953	1988	2.0	1995	2.1		
	1953-1958	1995	3.1				
Kenya	1917-1922	1962	4.8				
	1925-1930	1969	4.2				
	1938-1943	1988	2.7				
	1943-1948	1988	2.2				
	1948-1953	1988	2.1	1995	1.9		
Tanzania, mainland	before 1903	1948	17.0				
	1917-1922	1967	10.9				
	1922-1927	1967	11.3	1973	11.4		
	1927-1932	1967	10.6	1973	10.7		
	1932-1937	1991	3.7				
	1942-1947	1991	2.4	1996	1.8		
	1947-1952	1991	1.8	1996	1.7		
	1952-1957	1996	3.4				
Tanzania, Zanzibar	1902-1907	1948	26.4	1967	22.1		
	1907-1912	1967	19.8	1988	22.6		
	1912-1917	1967	19.7	1988	21.4		
	1917-1922	1967	17.0	1978	18.8	1988	21.2
	1922-1927	1967	16.3	1978	14.5	1988	19.0
	1927-1932	1967	15.3	1978	13.7	1988	14.7
	1932-1937	1967	13.9	1978	11.1	1988	13.3
	1937-1942	1978	8.6	1988	9.7		
	1942-1947	1978	7.2	1988	8.5		
	1947-1952	1988	6.6				
	1952-1957	1988	6.8				

[a] Subsequent studies pertaining to the same birth cohort are shown to the right in the same row

The most detailed trend data are available from western Congo (former Zaire) where surveys were carried out in 1955-1958 and 1975-1976 (Romaniuk, 1980; Tabutin, 1982). These are shown in Figure 1. PI in the two low-fertility provinces (Tshuapa and Equateur)[3] and in two mid to high fertility districts (Kasai and Bas-Fleuve) was fairly constant or slowly increasing among female birth cohorts between 1910 and 1925.[4] A dramatic decline occurred among women born in the 1930s, and this decline continues in subsequent cohorts. If we assume that the event leading to (excess) PI occurs around age 18, then the risk of PI has declined from 1950 onwards in these populations.

Figure 1   Trends in childlessness (%) by birth cohort, selected provinces, Western Congo DR

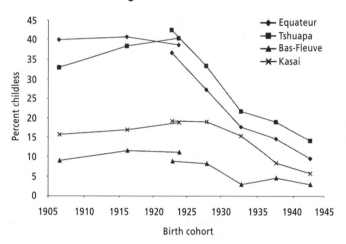

Data from other countries support the evidence from western Congo, although trends cannot be documented in as much detail. In Senegal, PI remained at about 6% from the 1910-1915 birth cohort and declined to 3% among women born in the 1950s. In Eastern Africa the decline in PI may have occurred in birth cohorts prior to 1925, as suggested by data from Kenya and Tanzania. Figure 2 illustrates the decline in Zanzibar and Pemba (Blacker, 1962), which furnishes a particularly good illustration of this general trend: there is a lot of overlapping information about the various birth cohorts from successive sources, which allows us to judge the quality of the data and the plausibility of the general trend.

Figure 2 Childless women in Zanzibar and Pemba (%)

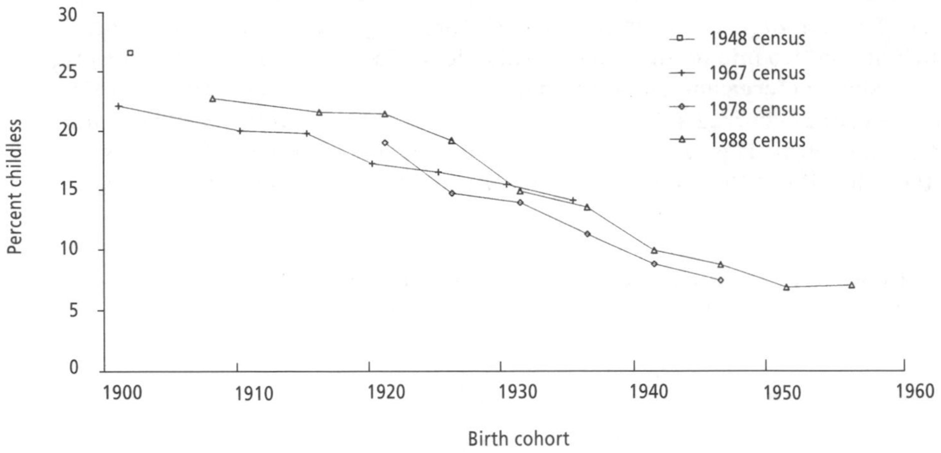

In Ethiopia trends derived from a single survey show a gradual decline in PI from just over 10% among women born in the 1920s to about 5% among women born in the 1940s (Mammo and Morgan, 1986). Data from Uganda also show a considerable decline.

In sum, there is ample evidence to show that the risk of PI has declined dramatically in sub-Saharan Africa, especially in those populations which previously had very high levels. The timing of the onset of the decline in risk of PI varied from place to place, but generally commenced in birth cohorts 1925 and beyond. This would correspond with a lowering of risk of STDs from the 1940s. While recent surveys indicate that the risk of PI has been very low virtually all over Africa since that time, in parts of Eastern Africa the decline appears to have started earlier. Moreover, the decline in PI appears to have been matched by a decline in SI (Larsen, 1995; Larsen, 1996).

Possible causes of high risks of primary infertility

Infertility was more common in Africa than in other parts of the world (Cates *et al.*, 1985; Frank, 1983).[5] A number of explanations have been put forward to account for the high level of infertility per se and the large variation in levels within Africa. STDs, other infectious diseases and behavioural factors have been considered as possible explanations.

Tropical diseases

Some tropical diseases have been shown to affect fertility. Schistosomiasis may cause salpingitis, but its epidemiological significance is not likely to be pronounced during the first two decades of life. That is, it should be more important as a cause of secondary than of primary infertility. Filariasis may have an indirect effect, since it may lower fertility in men, as a study in Gabon has suggested (Languillat *et al.*, 1978). It may reduce fertility in a population, but will only appreciably influence levels of childlessness in women in populations with very stable marriage patterns. In cultures where childlessness is viewed as grounds for divorce, the main effect of male infertility would be to lengthen the period of risk of PI in women. Malaria may affect fertility, mainly through increased foetal loss, but is not likely to have a strong effect on levels of PI *per se*. The geographical distribution of trypanosomiasis (sleeping sickness) partly overlaps with the zones of high levels of infertility in central Africa, but there is no evidence that suggests a causative relationship between sleeping sickness and PI.[6] Tuberculosis is also a possible cause of infertility, but is less likely to be a cause of PI in Africa (Belsey, 1976). Other conditions such as sickle cell disease, hormonal disorders, goitre and malnutrition are not likely to be important causes of PI (Belsey, 1976; Caldwell and Caldwell, 1983).[7]

Sexually transmitted diseases

STDs are considered to be the most probable cause of PI in sub-Saharan Africa, and ecological studies suggested a strong relationship between the two. In Congo, provinces with high levels of infertility also had a high prevalence of *Neisseria gonorrhoea* (gonorrhoea) and *Treponema palladum* (syphilis), (Romaniuk, 1968). In Uganda, Arya *et al.* (1980) compared women from two ethnic groups in a low fertility area and a high fertility area. Gonococcal cervicitis and clinical evidence of salpingitis were significantly more common in the low fertility area. Retel-Laurentin (1974) carried out several comparative studies of ethnic groups with high and low fertility rates and found large differences in the prevalence of STD.

Clinical studies have found an association between STD, pelvic inflammatory disease (PID) and infertility, predominantly tubal infertility (Cates *et al.*, 1993). Salpingitis with either gonorrhoea or *Chlamydia trachomatis* (chlamydia) has been causally related to tubal infertility in several studies in Sweden (Westrom, 1985). Serological studies in the Gambia and Zimbabwe have shown that infertile women more frequently experience gonorrhoea and chlamydia infections than pregnant women (Mabey *et al.*, 1985; de Muylder *et al.*, 1990). Earlier clinical studies of PID patients suggested a causal link with STD. For example, in Uganda, one-third of those hospitalized with acute PID were positive for gonorrhoea (Grech, 1973). Studies in Kenya and Gabon found that tubal occlusion was the main reason for PI (55-73% of cases) (Mati *et al.*, 1973; Chatfield *et al.*, 1970; Moutsinga, 1973).

Table 2 shows estimates of the risk of infection and subsequent infertility (Swinton *et al.*, 1992; Brunham *et al.*, 1994) based on a limited number of clinical studies and epidemiological modelling. According to these calculations, the overall risk of infertility as the result of a sexual relationship with an infected partner is around 5% per sexual relationship for either chlamydia or gonorrhoea. Once infected, the risk of infertility following a single episode is 12% (0.2 x 0.6) after untreated gonorrhoea and 18% (0.3 x 0.6) after untreated chlamydia infection. However, the risk of transmission of gonorrhoea is higher (50% to 60%) in the course of a 'typical' partnership compared with 30% for chlamydia. The clinical course of chlamydia salpingitis is often milder than that of gonorrhoea. Yet, it appears to cause more tubal damage than gonorrhoea and thus the risk of infertility is higher following chlamydia infection (Cates *et al.*, 1993). This may partly be explained by its milder course, which is associated with lower or delayed treatment. Its treatment also requires longer courses of antibiotics than the treatment of gonorrhoea.

Table 2   Estimated risk of infertility in women in sexual partnerships with
         ***Neisseria gonorrhoea* or *Chlamydia trachomatis* infected men**

	NG	CT
Risk of transmission within sexual partnership	0.5	0.3
Risk of progression to salpingitis/PID	0.2	0.3
Risk of untreated episode leading to infertility	0.6	0.6
Risk of infertility in sexual partnership with infected man	0.06	0.054

Source: Brunham *et al.*, 1994, Swinton *et al.*, 1992 (PID - pelvic inflammatory disease)

These data are somewhat difficult to interpret in the context of a behavioural model of fertility that models each coitus, as the infection risks quoted are 'per partnership' rather than 'per coitus'; no indication is given of the average coital frequency and duration of partnerships. Similarly, there is little direct evidence concerning the duration of a typical 'untreated episode'. If the overall likelihood of progression to salpingitis and infertility increases with the duration of infection, it would be useful to take into account the distribution of episode lengths. We would expect these to be linked to the probability of mutual reinfection within partnerships. Treatment with antibiotics reduces, but does not eliminate, the risk of infertility following an episode of PID. In Swedish studies the risk of infertility was reduced from almost 60% to less than 40% following untreated and treated PID/salpingitis respectively (Westrom, 1975).

Syphilis has also been considered a possible cause of high levels of infertility. Studies in Burkina Faso showed much higher infertility in populations with a high prevalence of syphilis (Armagnac and Retel-Laurentin, 1982). However, this may not be a satisfactory explanation for the high incidence of PI, as the main effect of syphilis on fertility is increased foetal loss. Belsey (1976) reviewed existing data and concluded there was no evidence that syphilis plays a part in the aetiology of infertility. If it does, its effect will occur through increased pregnancy wastage. This may lengthen the period during which the woman is at risk from gonorrhoea or chlamydia infection prior to a live birth, and thus indirectly increase the risk of infertility. A high prevalence of both sterilizing STDs and syphilis may consequently lead to higher levels of PI than would have occurred due to the high prevalence of sterilizing STDs alone.

Various factors may increase the risk of contracting STD during sexual intercourse, or increase the risk of sequelae following infection with a STD. These include age, previous episodes of PID, and the practice of douching (Cates *et al.*, 1990). It has been argued that pre-menarcheal sex carries a higher risk of STD because of the immaturity of the female genital tract (Duncan *et al.*, 1990). This may involve both immunological factors and to the risk of trauma (coital injury). Induced abortion is also a risk factor for subsequent reproductive tract infections (including STD) and may also be involved in causing infertility (Retel-Laurentin, 1967). Romaniuk (1980) did not consider induced abortion to be a major factor in the high levels of PI in the Democratic Republic of Congo in the 1950s and 1960s. But high levels of abortion among those pregnant for the first time would, at the very least, extend the 'at risk' period for PI. There is no ethnographic evidence that populations with very high levels of PI practice douching more frequently than populations with more moderate levels of PI.

Sexual behaviour

The previous section has indicated the importance of STD, especially gonorrhoea and chlamydia infection, as a cause of (excess) PI. To cause PI, a STD must occur before the first birth and can only occur after the initiation of sexual intercourse. In addition, if STD is a significant cause of PI, then STDs must be common in young women who must therefore be sexually active with STD infected men.

Large differences in the prevalence of PI among different ethnic groups have been observed (Retel-Laurentin, 1974; Romaniuk, 1980). For example, the Nzakara and related Zande peoples, who live across a broad zone in Central Africa, had extremely high levels of infertility, whilst neighbouring ethnic groups had much higher fertility (Retel-Laurentin, 1967; Romaniuk, 1980). Ethnicity can be considered a proxy for certain sexual practices, notably with respect to partnership formation, which may increase the risk of PI. Common features of populations with low fertility levels are permissiveness towards premarital (adolescent) sexual relations and marital instability (Retel-Laurentin, 1974).

Romaniuk (1980) suggested there was a pronounced tendency toward precocious marriage among populations suffering from high levels of infertility. For example, the Azande in southern Sudan had developed very high levels of infertility. Evans-Pritchard (1974) described their precocious sexuality in 1927-1930 and suggested this precocity was more common than it had been in the past.

Possible causes of the decline in primary infertility

If STD is the main cause of PI, then the dramatic decline in levels of PI can only have occurred either because of a rapid reduction in the incidence of STD at young ages (notably gonorrhoea and/or chlamydia infection) or because of a reduction of the sterilizing effects of STD. Epidemiological adaptation, improved treatment practices, and alterations in sexual behaviour may have brought about such changes.

Epidemiological adaptation

Historical data indicate that chlamydia, syphilis and gonorrhoea had been introduced to sub-Saharan Africa by the end of the 19th century. Retel-Laurentin (1974) argues that social disruption brought about by the slave trade and later labour migrations, including forced migrations, led to increased mixing of formerly endogamic ethnic groups and therefore to the spread of STDs. During the first part of the 20th century the risk of infertility was highest in areas which were exposed last to external influences, notably Central Africa. According to Caldwell and Caldwell (1983) the populations in such areas were very vulnerable to the newly introduced pathogens and so became victim to high risks of infertility. In some populations, the decline in PI appeared to have started as early as 1930. For example, data from subsequent censuses in Zanzibar suggest a decline from around 1935 (Figure 2), i.e. the approximate year when those cohorts born between 1910 and 1915 had reached the age of 18.5.

A process of population adaptation to these new diseases may have contributed to the decline of infertility. Recent studies suggest that some form of acquired immunity to chlamydia exists (Brunham et al., 1994). However, the very large differences in PI levels within Africa and the sharp tempo of the decline in PI suggest that other factors are more important.

Better treatment

Prior to the introduction of antibiotics, campaigns organized by colonial administrations using interventions such as mercury treatment achieved very limited success (Lyons, 1994). Expanding health systems and campaigns against specific diseases such as yaws, made antibiotics available for public health use in Africa during the late 1940s and 1950s. Yaws is a treponemal disease transmitted by skin-to-skin contact and was more common in rural populations with low socioeconomic and hygienic standards. The introduction of long-acting penicillin for the treatment of treponemal diseases in the late 1940s was the basis for large-scale campaigns covering entire populations. Most campaigns were conducted during 1955-1963 and were located mainly in West Africa. They covered almost 19 million people and led to a dramatic decline in the incidence and prevalence of yaws (Meheus and Antal, 1992). One single injection of long-acting penicillin would have been sufficient to cure gonorrhoea, but is likely to have been less effective for treatment of chlamydia. Therefore, it seems likely that most cases of PI were due mainly to gonorrhoea.

Some small-scale studies showed the direct impact of yaws and venereal diseases campaigns on infertility. In New Ireland (part of New Guinea in the Western Pacific) Ring and Scragg (1982) described a rapid increase in fertility following a mass penicillin campaign against venereal diseases in 1954. Childlessness remained as high as 25% among women over 40 years. However, a dramatic decline occurred in women aged 14-18 years at the time of the campaigns (Figure 3). Armagnac and Retel-Laurentin (1982) observed a less dramatic, but similar, fertility increase 15 years after a penicillin campaign in Burkina Faso.

Figure 3   Percent childless by birth cohorts: New Guinea, 1965

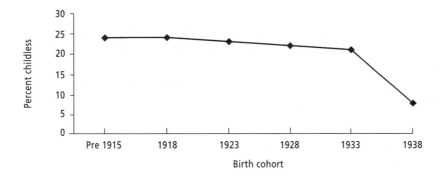

In Congo the rapid expansion of health services and penicillin campaigns against yaws and venereal diseases from the late 1940s were considered to have contributed significantly to the decline in infertility (Romaniuk, 1980). In other countries the decline was attributed to the increased availability and use of antibiotics through the formal and informal health system. In Ethiopia, the PI decline was thought to be associated with increased availability in shops of over-the-counter antibiotics which led to a reduction in gonorrhoea (Mammo and Morgan, 1986; Nordberg, 1974). However there are exceptions, the onset of the decline in PI in Ethiopia seems to have preceded the availability of antibiotics by almost two decades.

Changes in sexual and reproductive behaviour

There are only limited population data on changes in age at first sex and first birth for the period prior to 1950, but neither world fertility surveys (WFS) nor demographic and health surveys (DHS) seem to indicate substantial changes in sexual behaviour. During the period 1986-1996, 32 nationally representative DHS surveys were conducted in 25 countries in sub-Saharan Africa.[8] Retrospective data were collected on age at first sex, age at first marriage and age at first birth. The median age at first sex ranged from 15.0 years in Niger to 18.9 years in Namibia. The mean age at first intercourse among women aged 20-49 years was 16.9 years. There appears to have been very little change during the past 25-30 years (between 1955 and 1985): the mean age at first sex was 16.8 years among women aged 40-49 compared to 17.0 years among women aged 20-29 years (Table 3).

Table 3   Mean age at first sex, first marriage and first birth in DHS surveys[a] by woman's age, 1986-1996

	20-29 years	40-49 years	Change[b]
Age at first sex	17.0	16.8	+0.2
Age at first birth	19.3	19.5	-0.2
Age at first marriage	18.1	17.6	+0.5
Interval first sex-first birth	2.3	2.7	-0.4
Interval first sex-marriage	1.1	0.8	+0.3

[a] Average of 32 surveys in sub-Saharan Africa, 1986-1996
[b] younger minus older women

The mean age at first birth was 19.3 years among women aged 20-49 years in the 32 surveys, ranging from 18.0 years in Niger to 21.5 years in Rwanda. Comparing women aged 40-49 with those aged 20-29 years shows a small decline (0.2 years) in age at first birth. Marriage usually precedes first birth by about one and a half years. The mean age at first marriage was 17.8 years among women aged 20-49 years. Interestingly, one of the populations for which we have evidence of a relatively early fall in PI - Zanzibar - shows evidence of a significant rise in the median age at first birth: from 18.4 in the 1967 and 1978 censuses, to 20.2 years in 1988.

The interval between first sex and first birth in the 32 surveys has reduced from 2.7 to 2.3 years in the past 20 years.[9] In a few countries this interval exceeded three years among women aged 40-49 years (Niger, Mali, Central African Republic, Côte d'Ivoire,

Nigeria, Cameroon, Senegal, and Eritrea). Some of these countries had previously experienced high infertility rates, but others had not. A decrease in the gap between first sex and first birth could be due to higher fecundity at the time of first sex, or to higher proportions of early sexual encounters leading to regular sexual relationships.

In sum, the survey data suggest that relatively small changes in the interval between the first sexual act and the first birth have taken place after 1955.

Changes in age at menarche

Pre-menarcheal sex carries the risk of infection with STD and subsequent infertility, but not the risk of pregnancy. Therefore, changes in the age at menarche may affect the risk of PI. It has been suggested that the age at menarche has been declining in African girls during the past decades but evidence for this is circumstantial at best. Surveys in the 1950s in South Africa and Nigeria reported a mean age at menarche of 14-15 years (Burrell *et al.*, 1961; Oettle and Higginson, 1961; Ellis, 1950). Such studies were mostly carried out among secondary schoolgirls who represent a highly selective sample. A large population-based study of school girls in Transkei, South Africa, in the 1950s showed that the mean age at menarche was 15.0 years among girls from 'not poor' families and 15.4 years among girls from poor families (Burrell *et al.*, 1961).

Historical data from Europe and Asia provide some information on the possible tempo of a decline in age at menarche. In Norway, mean ages at menarche were 17.1 and 13.2 years in 1840 and 1950 respectively, an average decline of 0.35 years per decade (Gardner and Valandian, 1983). In Japan, mean age at menarche declined from 15.2 years in 1925 to 12.8 years in 1970, a decline of 0.96 years per decade (Nahamuru, 1986). Among minorities in China, a decline of 0.2-0.4 years per decade was observed between 1930 and 1970 (Ersheng *et al.*, 1994). In sub-Saharan Africa there is no evidence of a rapid decline of age at menarche. Several WFS surveys in the 1970s included questions on menarche to women of reproductive ages. The median age at menarche in African surveys ranged from 14-15.5 years, with little evidence of a decline. For example, in the 1977-1978 Kenya Fertility Survey, the median age at menarche was 14.5 years among women in both the 40-49 and 20-29 age groups. In the 1977 Lesotho Fertility Survey there was a minor decline from 15.3 years among women aged 40-49 to 15.1 years among women aged 20-29 years (Mpiti and Kalule-Sabiti, 1985).[10] However, estimates of dates of retrospectively reported events occurring in childhood may not be very reliable.

Anthropological studies suggest that the relationship between menarche and initiation of sex varies among ethnic groups. In some cultures menarche is related to female circumcision, in many others it is not. This may occur before or after menarche: in Nigeria, Wilson and Sutherland (1953) conducted 'tribal investigations' and reported that circumcision was usually performed prior to menarche. After the ritual the girls were considered to be ready for marriage. In other ethnic groups, the event of menarche is not given much attention, and there appear to be no specific sanctions against sexual intercourse preceding menarche.

Caldwell and Caldwell (1983) have argued that, in areas with low fertility, high levels of childlessness and a first birth at about 17 years of age, sexual activity must have started very early - perhaps at 10-12 years - and the first gonorrhoea infections must have been contracted at very young ages. This may have changed during the past decades as schooling and Christianization have rapidly increased. Sexual relations among schoolchildren, or between schoolgirls and adult men, have become less acceptable; this may have led to a reduction in precocious sexuality. Currently, these trends may be reversing, especially in urban areas where rapid societal changes take place and where parental authority over children's behaviour is thought to be diminishing.

In the following section microsimulations are used to estimate the parameters needed to reach the very high levels of childlessness observed in the past. They are also used to assess the potential contributions of antibiotic campaigns, changes in sexual behaviour, menarche and other factors to the decline in infertility.

The simulation model

Microsimulation modelling has proved invaluable to social science and bio-medicine whenever it is necessary to represent complex, interacting processes whose outcomes, but not all the intermediate determinants, can be measured. Mindel Sheps in the United States (Perrin and Sheps, 1964) and Hannes Hyrenius in Sweden (Hyrenius and Adolfsson, 1964) pioneered its application to fertility analysis. Barrett and Brass (1974) used microsimulation to study the effects of inter-woman fertility differentials on the estimation of SI. Santow (1978, 1979) has modelled fertility behaviour in populations of developed and developing countries to assess the contribution of abstinence, lactation and contraception to the size of the completed family. More recently, this method has been used to assess the validity of a deterministic model of fertility (Reinis, 1992), and to assess a method for determining whether couples were taking effective steps to limit fertility (Okun, 1993).

The modelling technique employed in this paper is a stochastic microsimulation, representing the life courses of a female cohort. The simulation process enables us to model individual women's reproductive lives, subjecting each woman to a series of chance events. The distribution and probability of occurrence of these events is bounded by defining a set of parameters which describe the processes at population level. In this case each run of the model has been used to generate a population of 10,000 women, whose lives are tracked between ages of 10 and 60 years. Each woman's reproductive potential is determined by her ages at menarche, sexual debut, menopause and death as shown in Appendix A. These are randomly selected from user-defined probability distributions.

The simulation steps through a woman's reproductive lifespan in 28-day cycles, corresponding to menstrual cycles as shown in Appendix B. In each 28-day step we determine the probability that a woman enters or leaves a sexual union, becomes pregnant, experiences a foetal death, live or stillbirth, becomes infected with an STD, experiences a cure or becomes infertile. The ages at which individual women experience these events are recorded in a population file, which can be saved to produce more detailed statistics and graphics. Population parameters and distributions (e.g. partnership length, variation in foetal death rates by age, probability that a male partner is infected) are set at the start of a simulation, but are determined randomly for each woman within the overall distribution. Thus, a clustering of events for a particular woman is due entirely to chance rather than to assumed behavioural traits. Although our model only records the events which befall women, it takes full account of sexual interactions and their results. It records all partnership formations and dissolutions (including those due to male mortality), infection and conception. There are two major simplifying assumptions implicit in male infection and partnership formation patterns: that there are always enough males in the population to satisfy the 'demands' of the women in terms of types of partnerships formed, and that the prevalence of STDs in males is an exogenous variable. It is this variable which essentially controls the level of STD in the female population. We ensure that STD incidence and duration in males are consistent with the chosen prevalence level. However, if we wanted to take account of any feedback effect of female prevalence to male incidence, we would have to iterate simulation runs, lowering or raising the male prevalence parameter to take account of female prevalence level changes in preceding runs.

In a real population, it would be practically impossible to distinguish between women who were fecund up to the menopause, and those who had become physically incapable of bearing children either because of a congenital defect or due to the sequellae of chlamydia or gonorrhoea. But in our simulations we can distinguish between these categories, and thus identify the contribution of STD-induced infertility and insufficient exposure to sexual activity to the overall proportion childless.

At the end of each run of 10,000 women's lives, certain population statistics are computed. These include population prevalence of STD, cohort percentage childless by age 50, levels of biologically defined PI and SI, the mean age at which women experience the STD-related event that renders them infertile, mean age at first birth, total fertility rate (TFR), and mean numbers of casual and cohabiting partnerships. Cohort statistics are computed by averaging the lifetime outcomes for individuals at age 50. Cross-sectional population statistics are found by allocating to each woman an 'age at survey', such ages being randomly distributed according to an overall stable population age model of a population growing at 2%. These data are saved permanently to allow comparison of simulation runs. A population size of 10,000 was chosen because this gave sufficiently large numbers to keep stochastic variability at acceptable levels.[11] Our model allows us to simulate the effects of biological factors (such as duration of STD episodes, male to female transmission risks, probabilities of foetal loss and progression from STD to infertility) as well as behavioural factors (age patterns of partnership formation, type and duration of partnerships and coital frequency patterns) and their interactions. Plausible default values were chosen for the biological and behavioural parameters to reflect the likely levels of these variables in a historical sub-Saharan African setting with moderately high levels of infertility. Two STDs were modelled in the default simulation: a 'generic' one causing sterilization, chosen to have characteristics intermediate between gonorrhoea and chlamydia; and syphilis, which increased foetal wastage.

In the default simulation, the age specific pattern of menarche and sexual debut are similar, starting around 12 years, with average ages around 16 years. This means that approximately half would experience sex before menarche. The mean age at PI in this population is 18.5 years, preceding by 15 months the mean age at first birth (19.8 years).

Mode of action of antibiotics

Our simulation model assumes that the principal mode of action of antibiotics, in their impact on STD and its sequellae, is through changes in the duration of episodes of disease. That is to say, whether taken specifically in response to recognized STD symptoms, or as part of a general campaign to treat STD or other infectious diseases, antibiotics shorten the average length of disease episodes in males and in females. They do not affect the likelihood of transmission of the infection in a single act of coitus, in which one of the partners is infected. Shorter disease duration has the following direct and indirect impacts:

- The prevalence of STD among the male partners of females entering sexual relationships is lowered. Since prevalence is proportional to duration, this would occur even if incidence rates among males remained unchanged (e.g. if males were assumed to contract STD only through contacts with a subpopulation of sex workers, in which the disease reservoir remained high).

- The incidence of STD among females would be lower, since their length of exposure to infected males in new or ongoing partnerships would be shorter.

- The overall progression from STD to PID would be lower, since the duration of STD episodes in females would be shorter.

- The lower prevalence in females (due to lower incidence and shorter duration) would lower the risk of reinfection of their male partners and thus lower incidence in men, further lowering male prevalence.

The last of these impacts is a feedback effect from females to males, and cannot therefore be captured directly in our 'single sex' model, which simulates only explicit transmission from males to females. However, we can estimate the approximate effect on male prevalence if we assume proportionality between this feedback effect and the direct change in female prevalence observed when the first three effects are modelled.

In a real population all the above changes would occur gradually and simultaneously, but our model allows us to partition the effects and estimate the separate contribution each of these would make to the overall change in female STD prevalence and to cohort levels of infertility. When all four direct and indirect effects are modelled, the model predicts that such a shortening of mean episode duration from one year (the default value) to half a year would produce an overall decline in female STD prevalence from 17.1% to 6.1% if we allow for all the postulated effects. This overall decline of 11.0 percentage points represents a proportionate decline in female STD prevalence of 64%. Proportion childless falls by 4.8 percentage points from 9.2% to 4.4%, a proportionate decline of 52%; SI drops by 31.6 percentage points, from 49.7% to 18.1%, a decline of 63.6%. Figure 4 shows the proportionate impact of each contribution to the overall change in STD prevalence and infertility.

Figure 4   Effect of 50% fall in sterilising STD episode duration

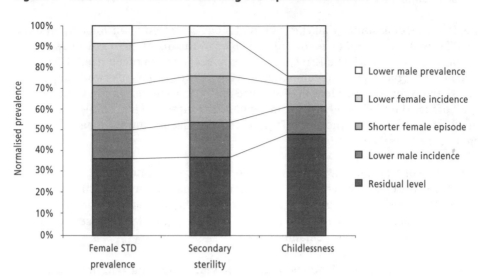

With respect to female STD prevalence and SI, it is the direct effect of shorter STD episodes in women that has the largest impact, accounting for about 35% of the overall change in each case. But for PI, the biggest impact, which accounts for almost half the overall change, is due to the decline in the proportion of new male partners who are infected with the sterilizing STD. This result highlights the importance of the first few sexual partnerships in a woman's life as determinants of PI and subsequent childlessness.

We have chosen to illustrate the effects of shorter episode duration by modelling the changes that result from a 50% fall in duration, from a year to half a year. This choice is somewhat arbitrary; there is little hard data to guide parameter choice.[12] The important result to note in the analysis is that, because episode duration influences so many of the determinants of PI, the proportionate decline in PI is likely to be bigger than the decline in episode duration. In subsequent simulations presented below, we do not postulate any feedback from changes in duration to changes in incidence: in effect, we neglect the last of the four effects explored above. This is a conservative approach, which assumes that only the direct effects of episode duration are observed. With only direct effects operating, however, the proportionate change in childlessness (from 9.2% to 6.0% - a decline of 35%) is proportionately smaller than the corresponding change in duration (50%).

Sensitivity analysis

Table 4 summarizes the results of a sensitivity analysis. This shows the effects, for selected outcome variables, of allowing each population parameter in turn to vary from its default value to a high and a low extreme. The default values chosen for the parameters yield realistic patterns of age-specific fertility and partnership formation, while producing a level of childlessness of slightly over 9%. This is higher than that currently observed, but was quite common in many African populations in the first half of this century. The total fertility in the default population is 5.6 births per woman by age 50. The high and low alternative values adopted represent the extremes of change that might be considered feasible over the 30 to 40-year period under consideration. The 'more favourable' parameter values represent the situation that most populations have moved towards, while the 'least favourable' might represent the worst-case situations of the countries most severely affected by PI in the past. The parameter changes are grouped into three catagories, illustrating the effects of changes in the timing of sexual debut relative to menarche, partnership patterns and disease severity.

Table 4 Sensitivity analysis

Default Value	Parameters	Extreme values	Prevalence of sterilizing STD (%)	Primary infertility Demo-graphic (%)	Primary infertility Bio-logical (%)	Secondary infertility (%)	Mean age at PI event (years)	Mean age at first birth (years)	TFR (births/woman)
	Default population value	-	17.1	9.2	9.0	49.7	18.6	19.6	5.6
	Timing of menarche & sexual-debut								
12-16 yr.	Menarche start and mean ages	10-14	17.8	7.9	7.7	51.1	18.7	18.9	5.7
		14-18	17.3	13.3	13.0	46.7	18.6	20.8	5.2
12-16 yr.	Sexual-debut start and mean ages	10-14	17.2	12.5	12.4	48.4	16.8	19.2	5.5
		14-18	16.8	7.3	7.2	50.9	20.0	20.6	5.6
	Early menarche, late sexual debut		15.7	6.6	6.5	50.0	21.1	20.3	5.6
	Late menarche, early sexual debut		18.2	15.3	15.2	46.2	17.6	20.4	5.2
	Partnership patterns								
75%	New partnerships casual	40%	17.2	8.8	8.6	50.3	17.9	19.0	5.9
		90%	16.5	10.4	10.2	47.8	18.6	20.1	5.3
12%	Peak monthly new union formation	3%	14.2	9.5	8.6	41.9	19.9	21.6	4.7
		18%	17.5	9.7	9.6	50.3	18.1	19.4	5.6
2	Relative coital frequency (CF) cohabiting / casual	3	18.1	8.4	8.1	50.1	19.0	20.0	5.6
		1	17.1	9.3	9.3	50.4	18.3	19.5	5.5
2	Relative male sterilising STD cas / coh	3	18.8	10.4	10.3	49.0	18.2	19.5	5.5
		1	17.5	7.7	7.6	51.2	18.3	19.7	5.7
	Low cas, low union entry, uneven CF, even STD		16.2	6.8	6.5	49.7	19.4	20.2	5.6
	High cas, high union entry, even CF, uneven STD		21.3	14.1	14.0	52.1	17.9	19.3	4.9

Biological

1.0 yr	Sterilising STD episode duration	0.5 yrs	9.4	6.9	6.7	33.6	18.3	19.8	6.4
		1.5 yrs	24.5	11.3	11.2	60.5	18.3	19.6	4.9
58%	Pregnancy wastage	50%	18.3	8.4	8.2	49.1	18.0	19.4	6.2
		66%	16.6	11.1	10.9	48.3	19.1	20.0	5.1
	Short episodes, low pregnancy wastage		8.7	6.6	6.3	33.5	17.7	19.6	6.8
	Long episodes, high pregnancy wastage		24.1	11.5	11.4	59.6	18.6	19.8	4.7
10%	Transmission of sterilising STD per coitus	5%	14.4	7.9	7.6	43.5	18.7	19.7	5.9
		15%	20.1	9.9	9.8	52.8	18.4	19.6	5.4
1.5%	Progression to infertility per month	1%	17.6	7.1	6.9	40.0	19.1	19.8	6.2
		2%	18.8	11.4	11.2	56.8	18.4	19.6	5.2
	Chlamydia: low transmission, high progression		13.8	8.6	8.5	52.3	18.6	19.7	5.5
	Gonorrhoea: high transmission, low progression		19.0	8.3	8.1	42.3	18.7	19.7	6.0
	Extreme combinations								
	All parameters favourable		**5.3**	**3.5**	**2.9**	**19.0**	**20.9**	**20.8**	**7.0**
	All parameters unfavourable		**32.0**	**34.2**	**34.2**	**52.1**	**17.2**	**19.9**	**3.0**

The first category in Table 4 shows that overall STD prevalence is not greatly affected by changes in timing of menarche and sexual debut, but that PI level is very sensitive to these factors. If the average age at sexual debut is less than menarche by two years, PI would be over 12%, if mean age at sexual debut is higher by two years, PI is under 8%. When both age distributions are varied simultaneously from their default positions, PI can be less than 7% when menarche precedes sex by up to four years, or over 15% if the situation is reversed. Since this model does not allow for increased susceptibility to PI among the sexually immature, the effects of precocious sexual activity on PI could well be higher than indicated here. Early sexual debut produces an earlier mean age at PI, but the mean age at PI is little affected by the mean age of menarche. Both menarche and sexual debut affect mean age at first birth to approximately the same extent. Age at sexual debut has little effect on SI, but when menarche is younger, higher levels of SI balance lower levels of PI. Thus, the total number of women becoming infertile before menopause is largely unaffected by age at menarche. Later menarche does reduce the TFR in the population due to the shorter fecund period and increased PI.

The next category shows the effects of changes in the postulated values in the partnership variables. In the default simulation, we assume that 75% of all new partnerships formed are casual unions of short duration (average three months) with relatively low coital frequency (initial daily frequency 0.25). This is in contrast to cohabiting partnerships, which have an average duration of over 18 years and an initially higher daily coital frequency of 0.5. Since we assume a gradual (exponential) decline in coital frequency with union duration, the mean coital frequency in casual and cohabiting unions over their entire duration is about 0.2 per day for both types of union under the default assumptions. At younger ages, when the average duration of cohabiting unions is short, coital frequency in cohabiting unions would be considerably higher than in casual unions. Our average coital frequency figure lies in the range reported by sexually active women in various African surveys. For example, recent sexual behaviour surveys (Cleland and Ferry, 1995) have found retrospectively reported coital frequency varies from 0.13 in Côte d'Ivoire to 0.24 in Tanzania and Zambia. Senkoro *et al.*, (1999) report a coital frequency of 0.2 among cohabiting couples in a Tanzanian cohort study.

Our default model also includes an assumption of differential risk of both types of STD among the male partners in casual and cohabiting unions, with prevalence and incidence among males in casual unions twice that in cohabiting unions. The average prevalence among all male partners in the population is much closer to that observed in cohabiting unions than in casual ones, due to the longer duration of cohabiting unions. The union re-formation rate after first union is dependent on age. The re-formation rate is lower at younger and older ages and reaches a maximum of 12% per month at age 25.

Allowing the proportion of casual partnerships to vary between 40% and 90%, a proportionate change of -46% and +20% causes the level of childlessness to vary between 8.8% and 10.4%. This is a proportionately smaller change (-5% to +13%) than that in the generating parameter. Lowering the proportion of casual partnerships lowers both the mean ages at first birth and at PI by approximately the same amount. The balance between casual and cohabiting partnerships has relatively little impact on SI, but TFR is considerably lower when the proportion of cohabiting unions is lower. This is because, under this assumption, women spend more of their lifetime outside of sexual relationships, since there is usually an appreciable delay between the end of one short partnership and the formation of the next one. A mean delay of about 1.5 years is assumed in our default model.

One of the more surprising findings of these simulations is the direct effect of proportion of casual partnerships on STD prevalence. This decreases slightly (from 17.1% to 16.5%) if the proportion of new unions which are short-lived casual partnerships is increased from the default level of 75% to 90%. This happens even though we have assumed STD prevalence among males in casual partnerships to be twice as high as that among male partners in cohabiting relationships. The reason for this counter-intuitive result is that coital frequency is assumed to be twice as high in cohabiting partnerships as in casual relationships. Thus, the overall decrease in coitus that would accompany an increase in the proportion of casual relationships would more than compensate for the increased average prevalence among all partners. A more realistic two-sex model which allowed for infection of men by women might produce a different result.

Union re-formation rates have an appreciable impact on overall STD prevalence and on levels of SI: lowering the monthly union re-formation rate by 75% (from 12% to 3%) decreases STD prevalence by nearly 20% and SI level by 17%. However, the effect of this variable on childlessness is small (3.1%), indicating again the importance of the first partnership in determining childlessness. The union re-formation rate also has an important impact on total fertility, which is more than 16% lower when the union re-formation rate is 75% lower. This is because childbearing is also curtailed when women spend more time between partnerships. In such circumstances we observe larger discrepancies between levels of childlessness (the demographic measure of PI) and the true 'biological' measure which can be obtained from our simulations. Childlessness exceeds PI by 0.9% (i.e., a proportionate excess of 10%) where the peak re-formation rate at age 25 is as low as 3% per month. The union re-formation rate is the only parameter in our simulation model that produces an appreciable difference between the demographic and biological measures of infertility.

We also investigated the effects of our assumptions about partnership duration (results not shown), but this had relatively little effect on either PI or SI, as the increase in exposure to risk due to increase in union duration is offset by the decrease in the number of partners. Again, this might not be the case in a more realistic, two-sex model, in which we might expect male prevalence to decrease in response to more stability in partnerships.

In the next four simulations shown in this catagory, the coital frequency and male partner STD prevalence in casual and cohabiting relationships were altered without changing the overall population level of these variables. The resulting simulations show that, in casual and cohabiting unions, slightly lower levels of PI are associated with higher differentials of coital frequency, but with lower differentials in prevalence of sterilizing STD. The coital frequency differential has very little impact on any of our outcome measures, but the balance of partner STD prevalence is more important, particularly with respect to overall female STD prevalence, PI, and thus childlessness.

When all the partnership variables are allowed to vary together, variations in childless-ness between 6.8% and 14.1% are produced. This indicates that, for the ranges considered here, partnership patterns have a level of impact on PI comparable to the timing variables considered in the top catagory.

The biological parameters considered in the third catagory govern the duration and transmission of STD and the severity of their consequences. In discussing the mode of action of antibiotics, we noted the importance of episode duration as a determinant of STD prevalence and infertility (see Figure 4). Here we note that if duration is assumed to be even longer than in our default model, very high STD prevalence figures for females will result, with correspondingly high levels of PI and SI. In fact, allowing for only direct effects, a 50% increase in episode duration will yield an increase of over 40% in female prevalence of STD, and an increase of PI and SI of over 20%. Conversely, the 50% increase in episode duration causes a drop of 13% in total fertility.

Next we explore the effects on PI of pregnancy wastage - foetal losses and stillbirths. In the default model we assume that the risk of foetal loss (including very early foetal losses which are not usually detectable in practice) follows the age pattern in the empirically-based model of Wood and Weinstein (1988). However, we assume that syphilis infection increases the risk of foetal loss (and stillbirth) by a factor of four. For uninfected women we assume that 5% of all pregnancies carried to term are stillbirths. Overall, this produces a level of pregnancy wastage of 58% when the prevalence of syphilis is 5% in cohabiting partners and 10% in casual partners. A variation of +/- 15% in the pregnancy wastage level results in changes in PI through a range of -10% and +20%, and total fertility by -/+ 10%, with very little effect on SI. Losing her first pregnancy exposes a woman to a significantly longer period of risk of PI, but losses of later pregnancies affect total fertility without increasing the risk of SI, as the period of exposure to risk is curtailed only by menopause. In these simulations we have assumed there is no causal relationship between syphilis, which increases propensity to foetal loss, and those STD which are associated with salpingitis/PID. If we adjusted the model in accordance with an assumption that syphilis is concentrated among women who also suffer from gonorrhoea or chlamydia, the overall impact of foetal loss on PI would be lower.

Combining the effects of foetal wastage with those of duration of STD episodes can produce PI levels of just over 6% (nearly 30% lower than in the default simulation), and as high as 11% (23% higher than in the default). The overall variation in SI is comparable, and ranges from 33% to 60%, i.e., from 30% lower to 20% higher than the default. When we combine a three-fold change in episode duration of a sterilizing STD with a similar scale of increase in syphilis, the total variation in childlessness is five percentage points. This is the same order of magnitude as the variation in childlessness produced by changing the relative timing of menarche and sexual debut by up to four years.

Finally, we investigate the implications of our assumptions about the nature of the 'generic' STD, by changing the parameters governing the per-coitus transmission probability and the monthly risk of an untreated episode of infection progressing to infertility. Although hard data about per coitus transmission probabilities are not available, particularly in an African context, we have made some rough estimates of the likely levels required to yield 'per partnership' transmission probabilities consistent with those given by Brunham et al. (1994). Their probability estimates are based on patients seen at STD clinics in Kenya. The mean interval between successive partnerships for female patients in that setting was 1.4 months, or 42 days. Assuming that half of this interval is spent in a sexual relationship and half in finding a new partner, and that the mean coital frequency within a relationship is about 0.2

(the average value within sexual partnerships in our default simulation) gives an average of 4.2 acts of coitus per partnership. At this rate, the per coitus transmission risk that yields a per partnership transmission risk of 0.5 (the estimate for gonorrhoea given by Brunham *et al.*, 1994) is 0.15, and the per coitus transmission risk which would yield a per partnership transmission risk of 0.3 (for chlamydia) is 0.08. In our simulated populations the average partnership durations are much longer than in the STD clinic population studied by Brunham *et al.*, but the partnership change rates are much lower. Thus, the basic reproduction number of the infections in our simulated populations would be broadly similar to those estimated in the Brunham study.

We have also modelled a higher monthly progression rate of 0.02 which, coupled with a mean duration of infection of one year, gives a per episode PI probability of 18%. This figure could be used to represent the joint probability of progression to PID and then to infertility for chlamydia. The lower rate (0.01) gives a per episode progression of around 12%, more appropriate for gonorrhoea.

Raising the transmission risk to 15% per coitus (an increase of 50%) increases the level of childlessness by just 0.7% (i.e. only 7.6%), and lowering transmission risk to 5% (a decrease of 50%) lowers PI by 1.3%. The effects of changing our assumptions about disease progression are modest. Lowering the monthly probability of progression by 33% lowers PI by 23%, but raising the progression by 33% raises PI by 24%.

Combining the transmission and progression rates appropriate to each disease shows that both the gonorrhoea and chlamydia disease profiles would produce a similar level of childlessness (8.3% and 8.6% respectively), slightly lower than that attributable to the 'generic' STD chosen for the default simulation. This would seem to imply that if gonorrhoea was the disease responsible for the very high levels of childlessness observed in a few populations in the past, its prevalence among males involved in casual unions in these populations might have been considerably higher than the 30% posited in our default scenario.

Returning to the 'generic' STD, we can investigate the maximum possible effect on PI of allowing all the possible biological and behavioural parameters to take on their extreme values. In the next pair of simulations PI ranges from just under 4% to over 34%, i.e., from 32% of its default value to nearly four times the default. The impact on SI is narrower, ranging from 19% to 52%. The high extreme has been observed in some African populations (Retel-Laurentin, 1974); it corresponds to a TFR of around three children and an STD prevalence among females of 32%. At the other extreme, TFR would be around seven children.[13] When disease linked factors have a minimum impact, excess childlessness over and above that expected from the usual level of genetic and endocrine complications is around half a percentage point. This is larger than the default difference, because in this scenario the rate of union re-formation is also lower. At this low level of infertility, the mean age at PI would be close to 21 years, almost the same as the mean age at first birth.

The overall effect of major changes in the grouped variables (timing effects, partnership patterns, disease severity and type) on STD prevalence, primary and secondary infertility, and total fertility is illustrated in Figure 5.

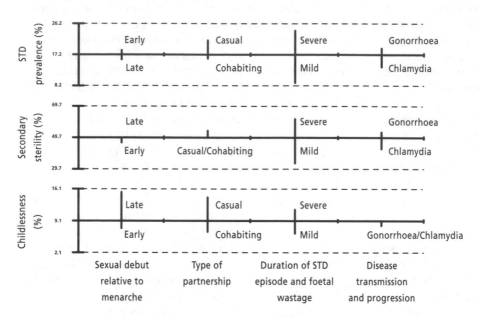

Figure 5 Summary of the effect of variation in biological and behavioural parameters on prevalence of STD, PI and SI

Discussion

Census and demographic survey data on childlessness show that PI must have been widespread during the first half of the 20th century. In some ethnic groups more than 20% of women did not bear children, as shown in the data from Zanzibar and selected provinces in the Congo. Even if we look at national level data, there are many examples (e.g. Tanzania and Uganda) of populations in which more than 10% of women had never born a child by the end of their reproductive life. More recently PI has fallen to around 5% in many African countries. The markedly higher levels of childlessness observed in certain African populations by the mid 1950s appear to be associated with three factors: proximity to trade routes (i.e. areas characterized by high mobility levels); the relatively recent introduction of venereal diseases; and most importantly, the absence of major restrictions on adolescent sexual behaviour coupled with high levels of marital instability. The first two factors influence the prevalence of STD, the last determines the initial age pattern of STD infection and pregnancy. The prevalence of sexually transmitted diseases appears to be the major causal factor: gonorrhoea, and perhaps chlamydia infection, have a more important role than syphilis. However, other diseases, such as trypanosomiasis and iodine deficiency, may have contributed to high levels of PI. Both anthropological data and modelling suggest that pre-menarcheal sex was fairly common and was a major contributing factor to the high incidence of PI in adolescence.

There is much current debate about the use of mass campaigns against STD (and indirectly against HIV). Literature reviews suggest that antibiotic treatment in the 1950s had a very dramatic and long-lasting effect on the risk of PI. Our models show that better treatment results in reducing the prevalence of STD by shortening episode duration of STD and, subsequently, by lowering incidence. Better treatment also reduces the risk of becoming infertile after contracting an STD, most probably by shortening the period in which disease progression can occur. However, the timing of the decline in childlessness in some populations suggests that part of the decline in PI may have preceded the introduction of antibiotics. Our models indicate that declines of this magnitude could be explained by changes in the timing of first sex relative to menarche.

The very high levels of infertility observed in several historical populations suggest that precocious sex was common. Although empirical evidence of substantial changes in sexual behaviour that may have caused the earlier declines in PI is limited, anecdotal evidence suggests that pre-menarcheal sex may have become less common, perhaps due to the expansion of Christianity and modern education. There is no evidence to contradict such a supposition, i.e., no evidence of a decline in age at first sex during the period 1940-1980. However, historical data on age at first sex are not very reliable as they are usually derived from retrospective reports by older women. A gradual decline in the age at menarche, such as would occur due to improved nutrition, would also have the effect of lowering the amount of pre-menarcheal sex if age at first sex remained constant.

Zanzibar is an interesting example of a population in which a shift in the relative ages of menarche and sexual debut is likely to have made an important contribution to the decline in PI. This island has experienced a pronounced rise in age at first birth (since at least the early 1950s), a corresponding fall in teenage childbearing, and a very large reduction in childlessness at the end of reproductive life. These changes started in the 1930s, a long time before antibiotics could have had an impact on STD prevalence.

As noted by Caldwell and Caldwell (1983), the populations most affected by the HIV/AIDS epidemic are not the same as those most affected by infertility, particularly primary infertility, in the past. Yet, populations with a sexual behaviour pattern that makes them vulnerable to high levels of PI are also predisposed to relatively high HIV incidence among adolescent girls who are having sex with older, infected men. With regard to the current epidemic of HIV/AIDS there are lessons to be learnt from the historic decline of PI.

The level of PI is sensitive to changes in the ages at which first intercourse occurs among girls, and to STD prevalence among their male partners. The longer the duration of the average episode of infection, the more marked will be the build up of STD prevalence by age in the population. A reduction in the age gap between sexual partners may therefore also have reduced the incidence of PI. In contemporary populations, those with a relatively narrow age gap between sexual partners are likely to experience less severe HIV epidemics than populations with wider partner age differences (Artzrouni, 1998).

Our simulation has highlighted two factors that could have an important bearing on trends in childlessness in the future. The use of hormonal contraception by nulliparous women and abortion of first pregnancies could lengthen the 'at risk' period for PI and cause childlessness to rise in the future. Both the spread of HIV in the past two decades, and the spread of STDs in the earlier part of this century, were associated with high human mobility; this, in turn, is associated with marital instability. Neither contraceptive use nor partnership duration have been explored in these simulations because there is no reason to suppose they have been relevant to historical change. But if the model is to be used to predict trends in childlessness in the future, more attention to such variables will be needed.

Acknowledgements

Our thanks to Michael Bracher, Philippe Mayaud, Rudi Pittroff and Ian Timaeus for comments on a draft. An earlier version was presented as a paper at a UNAIDS/ USAID/ MEASURE Evaluation/CDC meeting on 'Infertility, STDs and HIV: problems and prospects', Arlington, Virginia, December 14-15, 1998.

Notes

1. If not otherwise indicated, data have been derived from the WHO data base on infertility (World Health Organization, 1991).

2. The identification of birth cohorts in Table 1 is approximate, as in many cases the enquiries which identify women in conventional 5 or 10 year age groups are not exactly 5 or 10 years apart. Where the data are plotted on a graph (e.g. Figure 1) the data points are located on the X-axis at the mid-point of the cohort birth period.

3. In the 1955-1958 survey childlessness levels were highest in the northern part of the Democratic Republic of Congo, followed by Tshuapa and Equateur regions.

4. Childlessness was lower among the 1900-1910 birth cohort but a moderate selectivity bias is likely because of higher mortality among childless women than among other women.

5. Childlessness was also very common in Europe, North America and Australia (Rowland, forthcoming). In birth cohorts of women before 1920, often more than 15% remained childless. Late age at marriage and high proportions never married appear to be the key factors.

6. The sleeping sickness epidemic in Africa occurred during the early part of the 20th century. The disease was already known in maritime zones in the 1890s, and spread along the caravan trade routes. The peak expansion (and human toll) of trypanosomiasis was during 1906-1921; this may have had a temporary effect on fertility. But after the epidemic subsided fertility recovered quickly in populations with previously high fertility, suggesting a minor role of trypanosomiasis in infertility (Retel-Laurentin, 1974).

7. In particular, iodine deficiency disorders are common in some of the high infertility populations in Africa: for example, in northern Congo DR (Longombe and Geelhoed, 1997), although the evidence of a direct link at the population level is limited.

8. The countries are Benin, Botswana, Burkina Faso, Burundi, Cameroon, Comoros, Côte d'Ivoire, Eritrea, Ghana (2 surveys), Kenya (2), Liberia, Madagascar, Malawi, Mali (2), Namibia, Niger, Nigeria, Central African Republic, Rwanda, Senegal (2), Tanzania (2), Togo, Uganda (2), Zambia (2), Zimbabwe (2).

9. Note that means for age at first sex and age at first birth are not based on the same women. The former includes virtually all women, while the latter is based on all women who gave birth. The two groups are most similar in populations with low levels of PI.

10. During the past two decades several surveys of school girls have reported menarche occurring at ages below 14 years, but such studies were mostly based on reported age at menarche in samples of school girls. School surveys generally include a substantial proportion of girls who have not yet started to menstruate. The analysis therefore needs to be based on current status data (i.e. the girl's age and whether she has started to menstruate or not). Means based on reports by girls who have had their menarche are invariably biased downward.

11. In a series of 10 repeated runs simulating a population with the default parameter values, the cohort PI levels generated ranged from 8.96% to 9.03%, with a mean of 9.00% (well within 10% confidence limits for a simple binomial variable at this risk level: 8.63% to 9.36%). The variation in the cross-sectional STD prevalence was wider, ranging from 16.94% to 17.18%, with a mean of 17.06%, but still within the expected 10% confidence interval (16.44% to 17.68%).

12. Brunham et al. (1994) have calculated a likely range of 6 to 18 months for mean episode length for gonorrhoea and chlamydia.

13. Total fertility rates of eight and over were observed in Kenya in the 1970s.

Bibliography

Armagnac C and Retel-Laurentin A (1982), 'Relations between fertility, birth intervals, foetal mortality and maternal health in Upper Volta'. *Population Studies* 35: 218-34.

Artzrouni M (1998), 'A two-sex demographic model of the heterosexual spread of AIDS'. *IUSSP conference on modelling of HIV*, Copenhagen.

Arya OP, Taber SR and Nsanze H (1980), 'Gonorrhoea and female infertility in rural Uganda'. *American Journal of Obstetrics and Gynecology* 138: 929-32.

Barrett JC and Brass W (1974), 'Systematic and chance components in fertility measurements'. *Population Studies* 28: 473-493.

Belsey MA (1976), 'The epidemiology of infertility: a review with particular reference to sub-Saharan Africa'. *Bulletin of the World Health Organization* 54: 319-41.

Boerma JT, Urassa M and Isingo R (1996), 'Infertility and its association with sexual behaviour, STD and HIV infection in Tanzania'. paper presented at *IUSSP seminar: Innovative Approaches to the Measurement of Reproductive Health*, Manila, September 24-27, 1996.

Bongaarts J and Potter RG (1983), *Fertility, biology and behaviour: an analysis of the proximate determinants*, New York: Academic Press.

Blacker JCG (1962), 'Population growth and differential fertility in Zanzibar protectorate'. *Population Studies* 16: 258-66.

Brass W, Coale AJ, van de Walle E, Demeny P, Lorrimer F and Heisel D (1968), *The demography of tropical Africa*, Princeton University Press, Princeton, New Jersey.

Brunham RC, Nagelkerke NJD, Plummer FA and Moses S (1994), 'Estimating the basic reproductive rates of Neisseria gonorrhoea and Chlamydia trachomatis: the implications of acquired immunity'. *Sexually Transmitted Disease* 21: 353-6.

Burrell RJW, Healy MJR and Tanner JM (1961), 'Age at menarche in South African Bantu schoolgirls living in the Transkei reserve'. *Human Biology* 33: 250-61.

Caldwell JC and Caldwell P (1983), 'The demographic evidence for the incidence and cause of abnormally low fertility in tropical Africa'. *World Health Statistical Quarterly* 36: 2-34.

Cates W, Farley TM and Rowe PJ (1985), 'Worldwide patterns of infertility: is Africa different?' *Lancet* 2: 596-8.

Cates Jr W, Rolfs RT and Aral SO (1993), 'The pathophysiology and epidemiology of sexually transmitted diseases in relation to pelvic inflammatory disease and infertility'. In: Gray RH, Leridon H and Spira A (eds), *Biomedical and demographic determinants of reproduction*, Clarendon Press: Oxford: 101-125.

Cates Jr W, Rolfs RT and Aral SO (1990), 'Sexually transmitted diseases, pelvic inflammatory disease, and infertility: an epidemiologic update'. *Epidemiology Reviews* 12: 199-219.

Chatfield, *et al.* (1970), 'The investigation and management of infertility in East Africa: A prospective study of 200 cases'. *East African Medical Journal* 47: 212-216.

Cleland J and Ferry B (1995), *Sexual behaviour and AIDS in the developing world*, Taylor and Francis, London.

De Muylder X, Laga M, Tennstedt C, van Dyck E, Aelbers GNM and Piot P (1990), 'The role of Neisseria gonorrhoeae and Chlamydia trachomatis in pelvic inflammatory disease and its sequelae in Zimbabwe'. *Journal of Infectious Diseases* 162: 501-505.

Duncan ME, *et al.* (1990), 'First coitus before menarche and risk of sexually transmitted diseases'. *Lancet* 335: 338-340.

Ellis RWB (1950), 'Age at puberty in the tropics'. *British Medical Journal* I: 85-90.

Ersheng G, Jiang G and Jianguo T (1994), 'Analysis of menarche age of major minority nationalities in China'. In: *Ersheng G and Shah I (eds), Progress of social science research on reproductive health, Anthology of treatises of the International Symposium on Social Science Research on Reproductive Health*, China Publishing House: 44-51.

Evans-Pritchard EE (1974), *Man and woman among the Azande*, Faber and Faber, London.

Frank O (1983), 'Infertility in sub-Saharan Africa: estimates and implications'. *Population and Development Review* 9: 137-44.

Gardner J and Valandian I (1983), 'Changes over thirty years in an index of gynecological health'. *Annals of Human Biology* 10: 41-55.

Grech ES, Everett JV and Mukasa F (1973), 'Epidemiological aspects of acute pelvic inflammatory disease in Uganda'. *Tropical Doctor* 3: 123-127.

Hyrenius H and Adolfsson I (1964), *A Fertility Simulation Model*, University of Goteborg, Goteborg.

Languillat G, Albert M, Tursz A and Blot P (1978), 'Enquete sur l'etiologie de l'hypofecondite au Gabon oriental, I. Protocole et premiers resultats'. *Revue d'Epidemiologie et Sante* Publique 26: 237-57.

Larsen U (1995), 'Trends in infertility in Cameroon and Nigeria'. *International Family Planning Perspectives* 21: 138-42.

Larsen U (1996), Childlessness, 'subfertility and infertility in Tanzania'. *Studies in Family Planning* 27: 18-28.

Lyons M (1994), 'Sexually transmitted diseases in the history of Uganda'. *Genitourinary Medicine* 70: 138-45.

Mabey DCW, Ogbaselassia G, Robertson JN, Heckels JE and Ward ME (1985), 'Tubal infertility in the Gambia: chlamydial and gonococcal serology in women with tubal occlusion compared with pregnant control'. *Bulletin of the World Health Organization* 63: 1107-13.

Mammo A and Morgan SP (1986), 'Childlessness in rural Ethiopia'. *Population and Development Review* 12: 533-546.

Mati JK, *et al.* (1973), 'A second look into the problems of primary infertility in Kenya'. *East African Medical Journal* 50: 94-97.

Meheus A and Antal GM (1992), 'The endemic treponematoses: not yet eradicated'. *World Health Statistics Quarterly* 45: 237.

Moutsinga H (1973), 'La sterilité feminine au Gabon en consultation gynecologique journaliere'. *Medicin d'Afrique Noire* 20: 103-109.

Mpiti AM and Kalule-Sabiti I (1985), 'The proximate determinants of fertility in Lesotho'. *WFS Scientific Report* 78, International Statistical Institute, Voorburg, the Netherlands.

Nahamura I (1986), 'Changes of recollected menarcheal age and month among women in Tokyo over a period of 50 years'. *Annals of Human Biology* 13: 547-54.

Nordberg E (1974), 'Self-portrait of the average rural drug shop in Wellega Province, Ethiopia'. *Ethiopian Journal of Medicine* 12: 25-32.

Oettle AG and Higginson J (1961), 'The age at menarche in South African Bantu (Negro) girls'. *Human Biology* 33: 181-90.

Okun, BS (1993), 'Evaluating methods for detecting fertility control: the Coale-Trussell model and cohort parity analysis'. unpublished.

Perrin EB and Sheps MC (1964), 'Human reproduction: a stochastic process'. *Biometrics* 20: 28-45.

Reinis KI (1992), 'The impact of the proximate determinants of fertility: evaluating Bongaarts and Hobcraft and Little's methods of estimation'. *Population Studies* 46(2): 309-26.

Retel-Laurentin A (1967), 'Influence de certaines maladies sur la fecondite: un example Africain'. *Population* 22: 841-60.

Retel-Laurentin A (1974), *Infecondite en Afrique noire: maladies et consequences sociales*, Masson et Co., Paris.

Ring A and Scragg R (1973), 'A demographic and social study of fertility in rural New Guinea'. *Journal of Biosocial Science* 5: 89-121.

Romaniuk A (1968), 'The demography of the Democratic Republic of Congo'. In: Brass W, Coale A, Demenyet P *et al.*, *Demography of Tropical Africa*, Princeton University Press, Princeton.

Romaniuk A (1980), 'Increase in natural fertility during the early stages of modernization: evidence from an African case study, Zaire'. *Population Studies* 34: 293-310.

Rowland DT (forthcoming), 'Cross-national trends in childlessness.' In: Dykstra PA, Hagestad GO (eds), *Aging without children:* A cross-national handbook on parental status in late life. Newport, CT: Greenwood Press.

Santow G (1978), 'A microsimulation of Yoruba fertility'. *Mathematical Biosciences* 42: 93-117.

Santow G (1979), 'Models of contemporary Dutch family building'. *Population Studies* 33: 59-77.

Swinton J, Garnett GP, Brunham RC and Anderson RM (1992), 'Gonococcal infection, infertility, and population growth'. *IMA Journal of Mathematics Applied in Medicine and Biology* 9: 107-126.

Tabutin D (1982), 'Evolution regionale de la fecondite dans l'ouest du Zaire'. *Population* 1: 29-50.

Westrom L (1985), 'Influence of sexually transmitted diseases on sterility and ectopic pregnancy'. *Acta Europaea Fertilitatis* 16: 21-32.

Westrom L (1975), 'Effect of acute pelvic inflammatory disease on fertility'. *American Journal of Obstetrics and Gynecology* 121: 707-713.

Wilson DC and Sutherland I (1953), 'The age of the menarche in the tropics'. *British Medical Journal* Sep 12: 607-8.

Wood J and Weinstein M (1988), 'A model of age-specific fecundability'. *Population Studies* 42(3): 85-113.

Appendix A   Flow diagram of the top level of the microsimulation

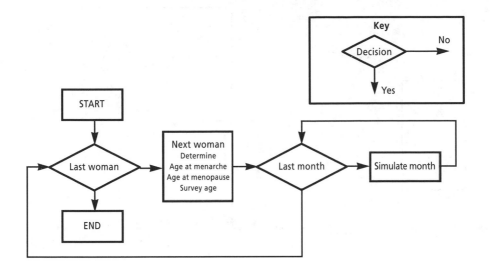

Each diamond represents a decision. If the decision is 'yes' the program follows the arrow pointing downward, if it is 'no' the program follows the arrow to the right. The details of the decisions programmed during a simulated month are shown in Appendix B.

Appendix B Flow diagram of a simulated month

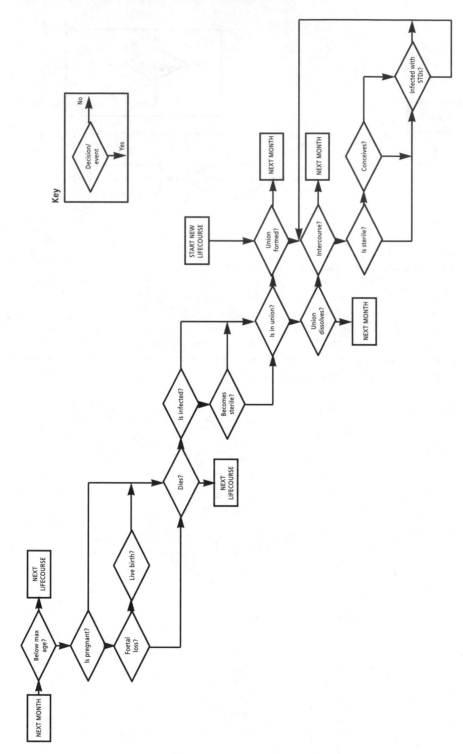

Each diamond represents a decision. If the decision is 'yes' the program follows the arrow pointing downward, if it is 'no' the program follows the arrow to the right.

'Dolls' to be carried by women on their backs and cared for until the birth of the first child (Kirdi or Fali, North-Cameroon/Nigeria border)

5 Primary and secondary infertility in Central African Republic

Ulla Larsen

Central Africa consists of six countries: Republic of the Congo, Gabon, Chad, Cameroon, Democratic Republic of the Congo and Central African Republic. The fertility of the population of this region is known to have been impaired before and during the 1970s (Page and Coale, 1972; Retel-Laurentin, 1974a, 1974b; Tabutin, 1982; Frank, 1983a, 1983b) but little is known about the extent of the problem today. Research on the demography of Central Africa has been hampered by the lack of nationally representative data. Demographic and Health Surveys (DHS) carried out a nationally representative survey in 11 sub-Saharan African countries in the late 1980s, but none of the countries surveyed were located in Central Africa. However, there are now opportunities for research using additional demographic data on Central Africa: a DHS survey was conducted in Cameroon in 1991 and 1997, in Central African Republic in 1994-1995, in Chad in 1996-1997 and in Congo in 1997 (DHS, 1998). By 1998, the data from Cameroon and Central African Republic DHS surveys were available for analysis. Further, an analysis of infertility in Cameroon documented a significant decline during the 1980s in both the proportion childless and in age-specific rates of infertility (Larsen, 1995a). It also showed that specific behaviour patterns are associated with higher levels of infertility, and that women's lives are hampered by their inability to reproduce (Larsen, 1995b). For example, women in Cameroon who initiate sexual relations before the age of 15 have significantly higher odds of infertility, and infertile women experience the many difficulties outlined in other chapters of this book. The aim of this chapter is to analyse infertility in Central African Republic, using the 1994-1995 DHS data (MOE and DHS, 1995). Specifically, the intent is to estimate the prevalence of primary and secondary infertility in Central African Republic, to identify subpopulations in which primary and secondary infertility are more prevalent, and to test five hypotheses about behaviour patterns associated with elevated risks of primary and secondary infertility. Infertility is defined as the inability of a non-contracepting sexually active woman to have a live birth (Pressat and Wilson, 1985). Primary and secondary infertility describe infertility of nulliparous and parous women respectively.

The importance of infection-related infertility in both men and women in Africa has been well documented (e.g. Cates *et al.*, 1985; Collet *et al.*, 1988). Female infertility at an early age is most frequently caused by pelvic inflammatory disease (PID). PID originates in the cervix; it can ascend to the upper reproductive tract blocking the fallopian tubes and leaving the woman unable to conceive. The most common causes of PID are sexually transmitted diseases (STD), such as gonorrhoea and chlamydia. Furthermore, when births or abortions are carried out under unhygienic conditions, the risk of PID is fairly high because microorganisms ascend more easily through a dilated cervix. Infertility might be due also to an inability to carry a pregnancy to term: for example, syphilis can infect the foetus causing intrauterine death, and malaria can infect the placenta and thereby impair foetal nutrition and increasing the risk of spontaneous abortion. Male infertility is usually due to the blockage of sperm ducts or disorders in sperm production which result in poor semen quality. The major cause of male infertility is an STD, such as gonorrhoea or chlamydia (Sherris and Fox, 1983). PID is treated easily with antibiotics, although the risk of becoming infertile is high after several incidences of infection (Westroem, 1975, 1980). The treatment of STDs, such as gonorrhoea and chlamydia, is often complicated by the existence of antibiotic-resistant strains of the disease organism. In general, Cates *et al.*

(1990) conclude that prevention of infection is the best way to reduce infertility. Currently, programs to reduce complications following childbirth are being implemented, e.g. the Safe Motherhood project under the direction of the World Health Organization.

Nationally representative demographic surveys, such as the DHS surveys, do not provide individual medical histories of diseases that can lead to infertility at a young age. For example, information in DHS surveys about whether a woman has had PID, and whether she has received treatment, is based on self-reports. Self-reported data about disease and treatment are known to be of poor quality, unreliable and invalid. Due to this lack of clinical data about women's health and medical history, population research on the causes of infertility must rely on proxy sources for health information. For example, geographical variations can provide clues to the presence of infertility-related environmental variations (such as the prevalence of chlamydia) or to cultural patterns (such as number of sexual partners) that affect sexual practices. Findings on differentials in infertility allow inferences about the causes of infertility to be made. The groups with the highest risk of infertility at a young age can be identified, and targets for medical interventions and educational campaigns can be determined.

The pressing concern about population growth may be one reason African policy makers traditionally have paid little attention to the prevention of subfertility and infertility. Another reason may be that STD and PID are non-fatal diseases and are not chronically debilitating. Hence, the limited resources available for health care have been used instead to treat illnesses such as malaria, diarrhoea and measles. However, the recent AIDS epidemic may change the public health priorities in Africa. Caldwell and Caldwell (1989) have suggested that one way to combat AIDS is to suppress STDs. STDs such as chancroid, syphilis, and genital herpes can increase the chance of HIV transmission through intercourse by as much as three to ten times (Liskin *et al.*, 1989; Over and Piot, 1990). Additionally, the population policy debate has recently put major emphasis on improving reproductive health for everyone, as outlined in the Programme of Action formulated at the International Conference on Population and Development (ICPD) in Cairo in 1994 (Population and Development Review, 1995). Thus, it is time to enhance the understanding of the level, trend, and differentials of infertility. The knowledge gained can be used to formulate and implement new public health programs that follow from the policy recommendations of the Cairo 1994 Programme of Action. In-depth information about the prevalence of infertility is also needed if we are to better understand and predict future levels of fertility and population growth.

Background

Central African Republic is located in Central Africa a little distance North of the equator (Figure 1). For governmental purposes, the country is divided into 16 counties (prefectures). To decentralize the public health decision making, the Ministry of Health has created five health regions (*Région Sanitaire* I-V). Each *Région Sanitaire* (RS) includes several prefectures, as shown in Figure 1. All the ethnic groups of Central African Republic are related; they are classified under the Eastern Nigritic People, Equatorial Cluster (Murdock, 1959). The Banda people live in the centre and in the river area of the country; the Baya live in the western areas; and the Nzakara and Zande peoples populate the eastern part of the country. The Zande also live in the neighbouring countries of northeastern Congo (former Zaire) and southwestern Sudan.

Figure 1   Central African Republic

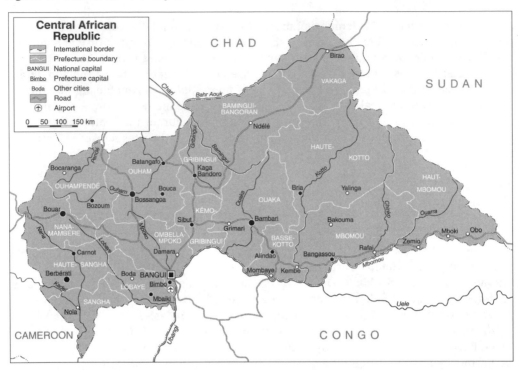

Central African Republic covers an area of 623,000 km² but, with fewer than three million people, it is quite sparsely populated. It became independent in 1960 and elected to have a multiparty political system in 1993. According to the 1988 census, the primary sector employs about 80% of the labour force, and there is almost no industry. The level of education is low: 55% of women and 29% of men reported that they had had no formal education, and 8% and 15% respectively indicated that they had attained secondary or higher education, in the 1994-1995 DHS survey (MOE and DHS, 1995). Modern amenities are rare. For example, based on households interviewed in the 1994-1995 DHS survey, 97% had no electricity, fewer than 1% had access to a flush toilet, and fewer than 2% had piped water in their house; only about 15% had access to a public tap. The 1959-1960 demographic survey and the censuses of 1975 and 1988 suggested that mortality declined during the 1970s and 1980s, even though the 1988 census indicated that life expectancy at birth was only about 50 years. The total fertility rate was 4.9 at the 1959-1960 demographic survey, 5.9 at the 1975 census, 6.1 at the 1988 census and 5.1 at the 1994-1995 DHS. An analysis of period fertility based on the 1994-1995 DHS data supports the finding that fertility increased in the late 1970s and early 1980s, and then declined from the late 1980s onwards According to Frank (1983b, p. 68) the total fertility rate from the 1959-1960 demographic survey was 4.6 for the Banda, 6.4 for the Baya, 3.0 for both the Banda and Nzakara, and (from a different survey in

1958-1960 by Retel-Laurentin (1974a, 1974b) 2.0 for both the Nzakara and the Zande. Retel-Laurentin studied the Nzakara of eastern Central African Republic in 1958-1959 and again in 1960. She documented the fact that the Nzakara have exceptionally low fertility, that women who have married more than once show particularly low fertility, and that STDs are a very important cause of the impaired fertility. She also called attention to the finding that an exceptional number of women were childless: 24% of Nzakara and Zande women (analysed as one group because of their similar ethnic origins) over the age of 40 reported that they had never borne a child (Retel-Laurentin, 1974b, p. 12). Preliminary findings from the 1994-1995 DHS data show that 26% of the Zande-Nzakara women aged 40-49 are childless, suggesting that the problem of impaired fertility has persisted, at least for this particular ethnic group. Muir and Belsey (1980) reported very substantial regional variations in childlessness in Central African Republic in the early 1960s. In their analysis, the proportion of childless women over age 50 was 10% in the West region, 15% in the Central region and 19% in the River region. There is no evidence to suggest that childlessness has recently declined in Central African Republic. Indeed, the proportion childless is 11% for women age 25-29 and 8% for women age 40-49 in the 1994-1995 DHS data (MOE and DHS, 1995). The level, age pattern and trend of secondary infertility in Central African Republic have never been investigated.

Hypotheses

Five hypotheses about a relationship between infertility and specific behaviour patterns have been formulated, based on Retel-Laurentin's seminal work in Central African Republic and on findings from research on the differentials of infertility in other areas of sub-Saharan Africa. For a more detailed discussion and review of previous work on infertility in sub-Saharan Africa, see Larsen (1989).

Hypothesis 1

The older the age at female circumcision the higher the risk of infertility. There is evidence to suggest that circumcised women suffer from severe pain, chronic pelvic and urinary tract infections, and, possibly, from impaired fertility (Toubia, 1994).

Hypothesis 2

Infertility is more prevalent in polygamous compared to in monogamous unions, and among women married more than once. Children are highly valued throughout sub-Saharan Africa. It is considered a man's right to have children, and if a union is childless or subfertile this tragic condition is often blamed on the woman (Caldwell and Caldwell, 1983). Thus, to achieve the number of children desired, a man may add another wife (usually a younger woman) to a subfertile or infertile union. If this pattern were to prevail, then the rate of infertility should be higher in polygamous unions than in monogamous unions. It has also been suggested that women in polygamous unions tend to have more partners themselves than women in monogamous unions, though this suggestion has not been empirically documented. If polygamous women were more promiscuous than monogamous ones, this would further increase the risk of disease and subsequent infertility among polygamous couples. In polygamous unions, infertility should be higher among first wives than later wives. However, the relationship between a woman's rank order and the presence of infertility may be complicated by other factors: some subfertile or childless unions may be dissolved, or divorced women may become higher rank order wives. In Larsen's (1989) multivariate analysis of infertility in Kenya using the 1977-1978 World Fertility Survey data, the risk of being infertile was higher among women in polygamous unions than those in monogamous unions, and was also higher among women married at least twice compared with women married only once. Similarly, Henin (1982) found evidence from the 1973 National Demographic Survey of Tanzania that infertility was relatively more prevalent in polygamous unions, and among women married more than once. However, neither of these studies investigated the relative risk of infertility in terms of a woman's place in the rank order in polygamous unions. Finally, an analysis of a random sample of rural men and women in eastern Uganda suggested that the prevalence of gonococcal infection was substantially higher for men and women in polygamous unions (Arya *et al.*, 1980).

It should be emphasized that a number of arguments support the contrary position, namely, that monogamous unions today have higher risks of infertility. For example, it is believed that husbands in monogamous unions are more likely to seek contacts with prostitutes (perhaps in particular during periods of pregnancy and postpartum abstinence), a group known to have an especially high prevalence of STDs (D'Costa *et al.*, 1985). Polygamous unions usually indicate some degree of wealth since the husbands have been able to pay more than one bride price, though it cannot be assumed that the bride price (in part or in total) was actually paid. If polygamous unions were more affluent, it might be expected that the men and women involved in them could better afford treatment for diseases associated with infertility, such as an STD or PID. If this were the case, polygamous unions should have lower risks of infertility.

Hypothesis 3

Infertility is related to sexual practices, such as number of partners and age at initiation of sexual relations. It has been hypothesized that sexual practices are associated with infertility because STDs, such as gonorrhoea and chlamydia, are known to be among the major causes of infertility in sub-Saharan Africa (Brunham and Embree, 1992; Cates *et al.*, 1985; Sherris and Fox, 1983). We hypothesize that infertility is more prevalent in exogenous than in endogenous unions, and that the relative risk of infertility is especially high if the woman has been paid to have sex. It is well known that prostitutes have particularly high incidence and prevalence of STDs (Brunham and Embree, 1992). Initiation of sexual relationships in the early teenage years is hypothesized to be associated with elevated risks of infertility for several reasons.

- Very young women often have sexual contacts with substantially older men who may be infected with an STD. In areas with especially high rates of HIV and AIDS, older men have begun to seek sexual contacts with virgin women to minimize the risk of HIV infection (Brunham and Embree, 1992).

- Women who have not yet fully matured often experience more physical difficulties in childbirth: the pelvic area is narrower, and vaginal delivery is difficult without tearing the tissue. Such complications at delivery can lead to infections, PID, and subsequent infertility.

- It is believed that the mucus in the reproductive tract of very young women is more susceptible to infections.

- It is conceivable that very young sexually active women have more induced abortions, which may cause damage to the reproductive system. Such abortions may be performed, for example, to postpone childbearing until schooling is finished, until a steady partner is found, or until a couple has the economic means to establish their own household. Induced abortions in sub-Saharan Africa are often carried out under very poor sanitary and medical conditions, and many women come into the hospitals with severe complications (Germain, 1989; Coeytaux, 1988).

- The younger the age at which a woman became sexually active, the more time she has had to contract a PID - either from an STD or from complications following an abortion or a delivery - and subsequently become infertile (see also White *et al.*, Chapter 4). In both developed and less developed countries, infertility appears to be higher among women who became sexually active in their early teens (see, for example, Duncan *et al.*, 1990; Kisekka, 1988; Westroem, 1975, 1980; Falahala, 1975; Grech *et al.*, 1973; Menken, 1972). In the multivariate models of infertility in Cameroon and Nigeria, women who had sex before age 15 had more than double the risk of infertility in comparison to women who became sexually active after age 20 (Larsen, 1995b). Also, in his analysis of subfertility in Tanzania, Henin (1982) found that women who initiated childbearing at very young ages had lower completed fertility than women who began childbearing at older ages. Brunham and Embree (1992), in their review of the literature on STDs, found that the risk of having antibodies to an STD pathogen is strongly correlated with the early onset of sexual activity, especially before menarche.

Hypothesis 4

Infertility, place of residence and migratory patterns. Hunt (1989) has developed a model of migrant labour and STDs to explain the prevalence of AIDS in Africa. We propose to test how well this model explains the prevalence of infertility which is, to a large extent, a sequel of STDs. Central to this model is the idea that industrial development in Africa has been based largely on a migrant labour system (Doyal, 1981). The combination of large concentrations of migrant male workers and long periods of familial separations has led to a breakdown in family and sexual patterns, and to an explosion of both prostitution and STDs (Murray, 1981). In light of this model we hypothesize that infertility is higher in those areas with high concentrations of male migrant labour; that infertility is especially high in male migrant workers and their (more or less) temporary partners, usually female prostitutes living near the centres of labour concentrations; and that there occurs a spread of infertility (and the underlying STDs) when male migrant labourers and female prostitutes return to their home villages, i.e., to the areas known as labour reserves. There is partial evidence to support the association between migrant labour movement and infertility. For instance, infertility is usually higher in urban compared to rural areas, particularly in capital cities (Larsen, 1995b).

Hypothesis 5

Infertility is not related to the individuals socioeconomic status. The existing evidence concerning the relationship between infertility and socioeconomic status is inconclusive. One might expect infertility to be higher among women with little or no education since they should be less informed about the major risk factors of infertility and about precautions to prevent it. Also, people with little or no cash income should have more difficulty receiving medical treatment of diseases such as STDs and PID that cause infertility. In general, poverty is associated with higher morbidity. However, a systematic association between infertility and socioeconomic status was not discerned in Larsen's (1995b) multivariate analysis of infertility in Cameroon and Nigeria. In the multivariate analysis of the prevalence of infertility in Kenya based on the 1977-1978 WFS data, neither the education of the woman, the education of her husband, nor his work status was associated with infertility (Larsen, 1989).

Methods

The level and age pattern of infertility is estimated by the subsequently infertile estimator (Larsen and Menken, 1989). This measure uses all information available for a woman up to the time that her age equaled her age at the time of the interview, minus five.The five years between these two points are used to determine her status as infertile or fertile at the point five years before the interview. She is considered infertile at that point if she has had no live births during the last five years before the interview, otherwise she is considered fertile. A woman who has not given birth at age a or later is defined as being infertile subsequent to age a. The index of the proportion subsequently infertile at age a is estimated as the number of women infertile subsequent to age a, divided by the total number of women observed at that age. Estimates of infertility are based on ever married women to assure that most women are engaged in regular sexual unions. However, the sample analysed is not restricted to currently married women, because there is evidence to suggest that women with impaired fertility are more likely to be abandoned by their husbands. Also, we do not have information about dates of marriage dissolution or about dates of entry into second or higher order marriages. Secondary infertility is measured by subsequently infertile estimates from parous women. Primary infertility is measured from the proportion childless among women who have been married for at least seven years. Alternate estimates of primary infertility are based on women married for at least five years, to make the samples analysed for primary and secondary infertility more comparable. There is evidence to suggest that estimates of childlessness are sensitive to variations in fecundability when based on five years of exposure (Larsen and Menken, 1989). Sample weights are used to estimate the prevalence of primary and secondary infertility, and in each table the presented sample size or women years of exposure represents the weighted observations.

To take into account simultaneously the effects of several covariates on age-specific rates of infertility, an individual level approach is required. Otherwise, we encounter the classic problem in life table analyses of too few cases in each subgroup to obtain precise estimates of the proportion infertile by age. In clinical practice a woman (or couple) is considered infertile if she has not conceived within a period of twelve months of unprotected intercourse. However, this twelve-month criterion does not lead to a measure sufficiently specific for demographic research on infertility (Menken *et al.*, 1986). In response to this difficulty, we developed a new method of assigning the status of fertile or infertile to individual women at a particular age. An age at onset of infertility can be assigned using the information about subsequent infertility (Larsen and Menken, 1991). This procedure involves determining the womans age at last live birth (or marriage, if childless) and designating this as $a-1$. The designation interval, designated as D, is defined as the earliest single year age interval for which no subsequent birth is observed, provided that the woman was observed for at least four subsequent years (i.e. that her age at interview was at least $a+4$) in which case D equals a. If the survey took place before age $a+4$, then D is not defined and the woman is considered fertile when last observed (five years prior to her age at the time of the interview).

A hazards model approach is used to analyse simultaneously the effects of several socioeconomic, cultural and demographic factors on secondary infertility. The relationship of the hazard rate to age and the explanatory variables is estimated using discrete logistic regression (Allison, 1995). The prevalence of secondary infertility is defined as the proportion of women with at least one child who are infertile at a given age (i.e., the proportion secondarily infertile). The dependent variable is the log odds of being infertile exactly five years before the survey, exactly ten years before, etc. Each woman contributes to the prevalence of secondary infertility analysis one observation for every fifth year, counting back from the survey to age at marriage. All the predictor variables are categorical, so they are entered into the logistic regression analysis as dummy variables, where there are one fewer dummy variables than the number of categories. The estimated coefficients for each dummy variable are converted into relative odds of secondary infertility, i.e., the odds that a woman in a particular category is secondarily infertile relative to the odds that a woman in the omitted (or reference) category is secondarily infertile. Variables are entered into the model using stepwise regression. The multivariate analysis of primary infertility is based on the odds of being childless after at least five years of marriage, and is estimated using logistic regression

Results

The results in this section are presented under several headings. First, estimates of the prevalence of primary and secondary infertility are given, and subgroups with particularly high infertility are identified. Next, multivariate models of primary and secondary infertility are presented, and findings are discussed with reference to the five hypotheses outlined above. Each hypothesis is tested in a model which includes a number of variables used to operationalize the hypothesis. The effects of age and birth cohort are controlled in each of the multivariate models. A final model includes all the variables analysed in the multivariate analysis. The analysis is based on the 1994-1995 DHS for Central African Republic, and covers a nationally representative sample of 5,884 women aged 15 to 49 (MOE and DHS, 1995).

Prevalence of primary infertility

The differentials of primary infertility, or the percentage childless by background characteristics, are the same for women in CAR (Central African Republic) married more than five years as for women married more than seven years, though a slightly lower percentage of the latter are childless, i.e., 6.2% versus 7.0% (Table 1). Fewer than 1% of current contraceptive users and fewer than 3% of women who have ever used contraception are defined as having primary infertility, suggesting that estimates of primary infertility are not biased by the use of contraception. Women married more than once have higher primary infertility than women married only once. The Zande-Nzakara have particularly high primary infertility compared to other ethnic groups. Women who were circumcized before age five have higher primary infertility than those who were not, though only 31 women were circumcised before age 5, so this finding may be due to chance. Women born after 1960 have lower primary infertility than women born before that year, particularly with reference to childlessness after seven years of marriage.

Table 1   Demographic characteristics of ever married women in CAR who have never had a live birth (%)

Variable		Time since first marriage[a]			
		5+ years		7+ years	
Ever married women		7.0	(3,790)	6.2	(3,380)
Contraceptive use	Ever	2.5	(1,522)	1.8	(1,339)
	Never	10.0	(2,268)	9.1	(2,041)
Current use	Yes	.9	(549)	.6	(474)
	No	8.0	(3,241)	7.1	(2,906)
Ethnic group	Haoussa	6.2	(180)	6.1	(163)
	Sara	3.9	(206)	2.4	(184)
	Mboum	5.5	(253)	4.4	(226)
	Gbaya	5.6	(1,107)	5.3	(1,000)
	Mandjia	6.9	(387)	5.1	(346)
	Banda	9.3	(990)	8.4	(883)
	Ngbaka-Bantou	4.7	(293)	4.9	(260)
	Yakoma-Sango	7.5	(187)	5.7	(158)
	Zande-Nzakara	14.9	(100)	15.1	(88)
	Endogenous[b]	6.3	(2,819)	5.7	(2,539)
	Exogenous[c]	9.1	(971)	7.6	(841)
Region	Ombella-Mpoko	4.7	(354)	4.4	(314)
	Lobaye	6.4	(237)	6.4	(216)
	Mambere-Kabei	8.1	(332)	7.8	(295)
	Sangha-Mbaere	2.2	(86)	1.2	(80)
	Nana-Maméré	3.0	(190)	2.7	(176)
	Ouham-Pendé	5.7	(329)	5.1	(292)
	Ouham	4.1	(335)	3.3	(298)
	Kemo	10.6	(156)	9.2	(135)
	Nana-Gribizi	6.4	(129)	5.8	(118)

Table 1, Continued

Variable		Time since first marriage[a]			
		5+ years		7+ years	
	Bamingui-Bangoran & Vakaga	5.9	(79)	4.4	(70)
	Ouaka	7.2	(258)	6.4	(229)
	Basse-Kotto	7.1	(278)	6.1	(241)
	Mbomou & Hautte-Mbomou	15.2	(177)	15.5	(163)
	Hautte-Kotto	10.5	(103)	9.8	(95)
Residence	Capital	8.1	(748)	6.4	(657)
	Other urban	5.9	(740)	5.5	(678)
	Rural	7.0	(2,302)	6.4	(2,045)
Times married	1	4.4	(2,358)	3.5	(2,069)
	2+	11.3	(1,427)	10.5	(1,306)
Marital status	Monogamous	6.7	(2,244)	6.1	(1,962)
	Polygamous	7.6	(975)	6.5	(885)
	Formerly married	7.1	(571)	6.2	(533)
Birth cohort	Before 1960	7.1	(1,534)	7.1	(1,527)
	1960 and after	6.9	(2,257)	5.5	(1,853)
Age at circumcision	Uncircumcised	6.4	(1,984)	5.6	(1,754)
	0-4	12.0	(36)	11.1	(31)
	5-9	7.6	(560)	7.3	(510)
	10+	7.6	(1,210)	6.5	(1,084)
Education	None	7.2	(2,217)	6.8	(2,027)
	Primary	7.0	(1,167)	5.7	(1,011)
	Secondary	5.5	(407)	3.8	(342)
Husband's education	None	7.5	(1,144)	7.0	(1,064)
	Primary	6.5	1,350)	5.7	(1,195)
	Secondary	6.3	(990)	5.1	(844)

Source: MOE and DHS (1995)

[a] Sample size shown in parentheses
[b] Husband and wife belong to the same ethnic group
[c] Husband and wife belong to different ethnic groups

Prevalence of subsequent infertility and bias from contraception

The percentage subsequently infertile (primary or secondary) by age increases gradually from 17.7% of women at age 20-24 to 77.5% at age 40-44. In all, 30.0% of women age 20-44 are subsequently infertile (Table 2). Women who have ever used contraception, as well as women who are currently using, have lower subsequent infertility at all ages in comparison with women who have never used contraception or who are not currently using. This finding suggests that, as expected, fertile women are more likely to contracept and that relatively few fertile contracepting women are falsely classified as subsequently infertile. We conclude that contraceptive use does not bias estimates of the level and age pattern of subsequent infertility because almost the same estimates are obtained when all current contraceptors are considered fertile at interview. For example, the percentage subsequently infertile for all women age 20-44 is 30.0%, against 29.0% when all current contraceptive users are considered fertile at interview.

Table 2   All subsequently infertile women in CAR, by age and contraceptive use (%)

Age group	All women	Contraceptive use		Currently contracepting		Modified all women	
		Ever	Never	Yes	No	1[a]	2[b]
20-24	17.7	10.2	22.3	4.5	19.7	14.6	17.1
25-29	26.6	19.2	30.7	9.7	28.6	20.4	25.7
30-34	39.0	31.2	42.8	17.1	41.0	29.3	37.7
35-39	56.4	50.8	58.7	30.2	58.0	41.7	54.7
40-44	77.5	75.9	78.1	58.8	78.2	57.5	75.6
Total (20-44)	30.0	21.4	34.7	9.9	32.4	23.1	29.0
Sample size[c]	32,465	11,417	21,049	3,452	29,013	32,465	32,465

Source: MOE and DHS (1995)

[a] All ever contraceptors considered fertile at date of interview
[b] All current contraceptors considered fertile at date of interview
[c] Total women-years of exposure

Prevalence of secondary infertility

Secondary infertility (subsequent infertility of women with at least one child) increases from 13.6% at age 20-24 to 75.3% at age 40-44. In all 26.5 of women age 20-44 are secondarily infertile (Table 3). Secondary infertility is higher at all ages for women married more than once, compared to women married only once. The Banda and Zande-Nzakara have higher secondary infertility than all the other ethnic groups analysed, though the Mandjia also have a fairly high level of secondary infertility.

Table 3 **All subsequently infertile CAR women who have borne at least one child, by age and background characteristics (%)**

		Age group						
		20-24	25-29	30-34	35-39	40-44	Total (20-44)	Sample size[a]
All women		13.6	22.3	34.3	52.9	75.3	26.5	27,925
Ethnic group	Haoussa	12.7	16.2	23.5	43.3	87.3	19.7	1,022
	Sara	12.1	18.5	30.5	42.8	70.6	22.8	1,505
	Mboum	8.4	11.1	17.5	41.0	73.3	17.1	2,101
	Gbaya	11.4	18.3	30.2	45.7	64.2	22.2	8,045
	Mandjia	13.2	25.6	42.3	66.9	90.2	31.4	3,114
	Banda	18.7	30.7	44.4	60.8	80.3	34.7	7,439
	Ngbaka-Bantoua	7.8	16.6	24.0	49.3	77.6	20.3	2,264
	Yakoma- Sango	12.7	20.1	32.2	56.2	65.7	23.1	1,282
	Zande-Nzakara	21.9	31.8	42.1	59.0	91.7	34.2	650
	Endogenous[b]	13.5	22.2	34.2	52.2	76.4	26.9	21,203
	Exogenous[c]	15.5	24.7	36.4	58.0	73.8	27.1	5,727
Times married	Once married	10.1	17.0	30.3	50.4	72.2	22.6	17,031
	Twice married	20.4	32.5	42.3	58.7	83.6	34.6	10,229
Marital status	Monogamous	11.5	18.2	29.7	48.3	73.4	23.0	14,734
	Polygamous	13.6	23.2	33.8	50.0	71.4	25.4	7,124
	Formerly married	22.5	34.4	48.2	68.2	86.9	0.3	5,412
Residence	Bangui	15.1	25.4	37.0	54.9	75.8	26.7	5,052
	Other urban	13.2	19.3	31.7	50.6	73.3	25.4	6,019
	Rural	13.1	22.3	34.5	53.3	75.9	26.8	16,853
Women born	Before 1960	14.2	22.5	34.3	52.9	75.3	30.0	21,379
	After 1960	12.8	21.4					6,545
Region	Ombella-Mpoko	14.3	24.1	37.3	63.6	82.5	28.5	2,576
	Lobaye	11.7	18.2	27.5	58.5	85.0	24.6	1,978
	Mambere-Kabei	12.3	16.1	25.3	36.1	55.9	20.4	2,528
	Sangha-Mbaere	11.1	20.4	30.8	58.2	79.0	25.1	758
	Nana-Maméré	11.1	18.6	28.8	36.8	68.8	22.4	1,389
	Ouham-Pendé	6.5	12.1	20.0	42.8	65.0	17.0	2,594
	Ouham	8.9	14.1	25.2	37.9	62.6	18.2	2,521
	Kemo	18.3	27.9	45.6	63.2	82.0	35.9	1,110
	Nana-Gribizi	10.2	22.7	38.6	53.8	71.4	25.9	997
	Bamingui-Bangoran & Vakaga	15.3	21.8	31.0	43.7	65.5	24.7	527
	Ouaka	21.4	34.8	46.7	65.7	81.4	37.9	2,056
	Basse-Kotto	13.2	26.8	46.8	61.5	88.3	33.0	2,016
	Mbomou & Hautte-Mbomou	31.3	40.1	54.3	70.8	87.5	45.0	1,433
	Hautte-Kotto	28.1	36.4	56.2	81.1	96.7	43.5	694
Age at circumcision	Uncircumcised	11.4	19.1	29.9	50.6	74.6	23.1	14,137
	0-4	21.4	25.9	35.4	39.2	78.8	30.0	231
	5-9	18.4	28.2	41.1	53.2	69.5	32.8	4,558
	10+	14.6	24.2	37.1	56.2	80.3	28.4	8,987

Table 3, Continued

| | | \multicolumn{7}{c}{Age group} | | | | | | |
		20-24	25-29	30-34	35-39	40-44	Total (20-44)	Sample size[a]
Education	None	13.7	22.0	33.3	51.6	75.4	27.9	18,706
	Primary	14.1	22.4	36.5	56.7	73.6	24.5	7,214
	Secondary	11.2	24.4	41.5	73.6	-	20.0	2,004
Husband's	None	14.7	24.2	36.9	55.6	79.3	31.3	10,586
education	Primary	12.6	19.9	28.7	45.6	71.7	23.2	9,360
	Secondary	13.3	24.0	39.6	64.3	72.3	23.6	5,108

Source: MOE and DHS (1995)

[a] Women years of exposure
[b] Husband and wife belong to the same ethnic group
[c] Husband and wife belong to different ethnic groups

Multivariate analysis of primary infertility

The multivariate analysis of primary infertility confirms findings from the analysis of primary infertility divided by subgroups. For example, women married more than once have higher odds of experiencing primary infertility than women married only once (Table 4; only the significant results from the full model shown). However, the Zande-Nzakara do not have higher odds of primary infertility in the multivariate analysis in which the effects of covariates are controlled. The Banda is the only ethnic group for which elevated risks of primary infertility are seen in the multivariate analysis. Women married to a man from the same ethnic group (denoted endogenous) have significantly lower odds of having primary infertility than women married to a man from a different ethnic group (denoted exogenous). When the effects of covariates are controlled, there is no evidence of a declining trend in primary infertility. In each of the multivariate models, women born before 1960 (i.e., women over age 35 at survey) do not have significantly higher odds of being childless than women born after 1960.

Table 4   Relative odds[a] of being childless for CAR women married at least five years, by selected characteristics

Variable	Category	Relative odds	P[b]	Sample size
Times married	Once	0.41	***	1,948
	Two or more	1.00		1,237
Marriage type	Endogenous	0.68	*	2,430
	Exogenous	1.00		223
	Formerly married	1.00		532
Money for sex	Yes	2.09	*	77
	No	1.00		1,821
	Missing	1.00		1,287
Ethnicity	Mandjia	1.00		291
	Banda	1.46	*	923
	Zanda-Nzakara	1.00		94
	Other	1.00		1,877
Region	Mambere-Kabei	1.72	*	299
	Kemo	2.36	**	94
	Mbomou & Hautte-Mbomou	3.34	***	188
	Hautte-Kotto	1.00		117
	All other	1.00		2,487
Education	None	1.64		1,947
	Primary	1.00		933
	Secondary	1.00		305

Source: MOE and DHS (1995)

[a] Relative odds obtained from full model that also included age at survey, birth cohort, problems due to circumcision, age at circumcision, marital status, where partner sleeps, age at first sex, religion, residence, duration of residence, husband's education, type of roof material, type of floor material, occupation, husband's occupation and income. None of these variables were significantly associated with the dependent variable at the .05 level. These variables are not included in the model presented.

[b] * .05 level of significance; ** .01 level of significance; *** .001 level of significance

Multivariate analysis of secondary infertility

The risk of secondary infertility is higher for women married more than once, and for formerly married women (Table 5; only the significant effects seen in the full model are shown). From the data available we cannot discern whether infertile women are in fact more likely to separate and divorce, or whether separated and divorced women have been falsely classified as being infertile because they are not in a regular sexual union. The risk of secondary infertility is higher in those who are younger at first sex, and also in women who have received money for sex. In the multivariate analysis, the Mandjia and Banda have significantly higher odds of secondary infertility compared with all other ethnic groups. Education of the woman is not associated with secondary infertility, while women whose husbands have had primary education are at lower risk of secondary infertility. Finally, the odds of being secondarily infertile are more than three times higher for women born after 1960 than for those born earlier.

The documented differentials of primary and secondary infertility remained virtually unchanged when the multivariate analysis was extended to include a variable related to contraception (data not shown). Women who had ever used contraception have significantly lower odds of primary, as well as secondary, infertility.

Table 5 **Relative odds[a] of being subsequently infertile for CAR women with at least one child, by background characteristics[b]**

Variable	Category	Relative odds	P	Sample size
Age at survey	25-29	1.00		2,619
	30-34	2.40	***	2,086
	35-39	7.13	***	1,395
	40-44	16.72	***	788
	45-49	93.36	***	377
Birth cohort	Before 1960	1.00		5,057
	1960 and after	3.05	***	2,208
Times married	Once	.61	***	4,552
	Twice or more	1.00		2,713
Partner sleeps	With her	.73	***	5,493
	Elsewhere	1.00		1,772
Marriage type	Endogenous	1.00		5,666
	Exogenous	1.00		213
	Formerly married	1.39	***	1,386
Age at first sex	<15	1.87	***	2,327
	15-19	1.29	*	4,408
	20+	1.00		530
Money for sex	Yes	1.47	*	141
	No	1.00		3,824
	Missing	1.00		3,300
Ethnicity	Mandjia	1.30	**	707
	Banda	1.33	***	2,114
	Zande-Nzakara	1.00		198
	Other	1.00		4,246
Duration of residence	Always	1.00		3,892
	0-4	1.00		785
	5-9	1.00		486
	10+	.78	***	1,820
	Do not know	1.00		282
Region	Mambere-Kadei	.73	***	706
	Kemo	1.00		213
	Mbomou & Hautte-Mbomou	1.00		379
	Hautte-Kotto	1.39	*	238
	All other	1.00		5,729
Husband's education	None	1.00		2,709
	Primary	.89	*	2,534
	Secondary	1.00		2,022
Roof material	Straw & bamboo	1.36	***	5,102

Table 5, Continued

Variable	Category	Relative odds	P	Sample size
	Tin & cement	1.00		2,163
Floor material	Tiles & cement	1.25	*	1,036
	Other	1.00		6,229
Occupation	Professional & clerical	1.78	***	173
	Sales	1.00		1,075
	Agriculture (self)	1.00		5,101
	Other	1.00		916
Husband's occupation	Professional & clerical	1.00		773
	Sales	1.00		385
	Agriculture (self)	.85	**	4,033
	Other	1.00		2,074
Income	< 25,000	1.00		2,488
	25 - 49,999	1.00		758
	50 - 99,999	.86	**	3,520
	100,000+	1.00		499

Source: MOE and DHS (1995)

[a] Relative odds obtained from full model that also included problems due to circumcision, age at circumcision, marital status, religion, residence and education. None of these variables were significantly associated with the dependent variable at the .05 level. These variables are not included in the model presented.

[b] * .05 level of significance; ** .01 level of significance; *** .001 level of significance

Discussion

In Central African Republic, primary infertility, measured by the percentage childless after at least seven years of marriage, was found to be 6%. The percentage subsequently infertile was seen to increase gradually with age from 18% at age 20-24 to 78% at age 40-44. In Cameroon, the other Central African country for which we have information about the prevalence of infertility, 6% have primary infertility; subsequent infertility rates are 14% and 70% at age 20-24 and age 40-44 respectively (Larsen, 1995a). Thus, the prevalence of primary infertility is the same in Central African Republic and in Cameroon, but the proportion subsequently infertile is higher at all ages in Central African Republic. It should be noted that primary infertility, and the proportion subsequently infertile by age, are lower in each of the 29 sub-Saharan African countries analysed by Larsen and Raggers (Chapter 1) than in Central African Republic and in Cameroon. Hence, impaired fertility is still higher in Central Africa, in the area traditionally referred to as the infertility belt.

The present analysis does not find any evidence of a decline in infertility by birth cohort in Central African Republic. Specifically, the multivariate analysis shows that the odds of primary infertility are not different for women born before 1960 than for women born in 1960 or later, though the latter group has significantly higher odds of secondary infertility. To better discern the trend in infertility further analyses of survey or census data from the 1960s, 1970s or 1980s would be required. However, the findings of Muir and Belsey (1980) that childlessness is lower in the West region than in the River region is replicated in this analysis, suggesting that regional variations in childlessness have prevailed for several decades. It is not clear precisely which areas they include in the West and River regions but this study has found the lowest childlessness in the western regions, and the highest in the eastern regions. The prevalence of primary infertility is especially high in the regions of Mbomou and Hautte-Mbomou, and the multivariate models have shown these regions to also have higher odds of primary infertility. Secondary infertility is prevalent in the eastern regions of Hautte-Kotto, Mbomou and Hautte-Mbomou, as well as in the regions of Kemo and Ouaka (see Figure 1). The region of Hautte-Kotto still has relatively high odds of secondary infertility when multivariate models are used for analysis. Thus, the areas with especially high infertility today are the same areas with unusually high levels of infertility in the late 1950s and early 1960s according to the seminal work of Retel-Laurentin (1974a, 1974b). The findings in this study suggest that educational campaigns aimed at informing people about high risk behaviour, as well as medical interventions aimed at treating diseases known to lead to infertility, might be more effective if they targeted these eastern regions of Central African Republic.

With respect to the hypotheses, we found that female circumcision and age at circumcision are not associated with either primary or secondary infertility. Even women who reported medical problems after their circumcision did not have higher odds of primary or secondary infertility in the final models, which control for covariates. The 1994-1995 DHS survey for Central African Republic does not include information about the type of circumcision, e.g., Sunna, Intermediate or Pharaonic, and it is plausible that only the more severe forms of incision result in subfertility and infertility. We recommend further studies of the association between infertility and the type of circumcision before drawing conclusions about the health impact of the practice and its harmful effects on the ability of women to reproduce.

Women married more than once are at higher risk of both primary and secondary infertility. However, after accounting for the rank order of the woman and other covariates, there is no difference in risk of primary or secondary infertility between women in monogamous unions and those in polygamous unions. Women who reported that their husband usually slept in their house had significantly lower secondary infertility than women whose husband slept elsewhere. The latter finding may reflect various factors. First, in polygamous unions the husband tends to sleep more often in the house with the younger and more fertile wife, i.e., the wife of higher rank order. Second, unions in which the husband is away for extended periods, e.g., for work, may be at higher risk of secondary infertility due to the husband's sexual contact with other women and the risks of STDs that this can involve. Higher infertility in women married more than once has also been reported in a multivariate analysis of Cameroon and Nigeria (Larsen, 1995b). Thus, there is further evidence for the notion that women's lives are severely affected by their ability to reproduce: their husbands may leave them if they are unable to have children. By contrast, there is no difference between the risks of primary and secondary infertility in women with co-wives and those women who are the sole wife, when the effects of covariates such as partner's sleeping arrangements are taken into account.

Sexual practices are associated with infertility. For example, age at first sex is not associated with primary infertility but women who initiate sexual relationships before age 20, and especially before age 15, have a higher risk of secondary infertility. The finding that age at first sex is associated with secondary infertility, but not with primary infertility, may reflect the fact that young women suffer more complications at childbirth and that poor midwifery leads to secondary infertility for some. Furthermore, women who have received money for sex have a higher risk of secondary infertility but not of primary infertility. The findings that young age at first sex and payment for sex are linked to higher secondary infertility, but not to primary infertility, may indicate that these women have been exposed to more STDs by a given age. They may simply have become unable to reproduce due to pathological causes at an age where they already had had at least one child. It is difficult to unravel the patterns among indicators of sexual practices and primary and secondary infertility from cross-sectional data. Further analyses of longitudinal data or individual event histories are warranted to enhance the understanding of the importance of sexual practices to subsequent infertility.

The hypothesis about migrant labour and infertility cannot be tested using the DHS data available. For instance, there is no information about durations of familial separations or on where the male migrants are concentrated. Also, questions that pertain to both wife and husband were limited to a subset of the sample of individual women interviewees. In the multivariate models women who had lived fewer than five years at their current residence, and women who did not know how long they had lived at their current residence, had higher odds of secondary infertility. This finding may indicate that women who had changed residence recently had an increased risk of contact with an STD infected partner. Neither primary nor secondary infertility is associated with place of residence in Central African Republic.

The relationship between infertility and socioeconomic status is not clear. Women with no education had higher odds of primary infertility, while education of the woman was not associated with the risk of secondary infertility; as noted, those whose husbands had primary education had lower odds of both sorts of infertility. Furthermore, the woman's occupation was not associated with primary infertility, though women with professional and clerical jobs had higher risks of secondary infertility than women in other occupations (sales, agriculture and others). The variable related to income was not associated with primary infertility. However, answers to questions about income are notoriously poor, and in Central African Republic an important part of a person's income is likely to be in kind rather than cash. To obtain more evidence about the association between socioeconomic status and infertility it may be fruitful to estimate the odds of primary and secondary infertility for a range of socioeconomic indicators (education and occupation of wife and husband, income, etc.) derived from all the DHS surveys for Africa. So far, different studies have used different indicators of socioeconomic status, and therefore it is difficult to draw inferences across studies about socioeconomic status and infertility.

In Central African Republic the level of education is low, modern amenities are rare, and the country ranks low with respect to most indicators of economic development. The lack of economic prosperity has often been attributed to its low population density. However, this study did not find any evidence to suggest that the high burden of infertility will be reduced in the near future. This is despite the fact that impaired fertility of pathological origin is recognized both as a major public health concern and as a problem for the individual women and men who cannot have the children they desire. At best, one may hope for an enhanced public awareness of the behavioural factors leading to infertility at a young age, and that the emerging family planning programs will be enabled to provide services covering a broad range of reproductive health needs.

Acknowledgements

This research was made possible by an award from the William F. Milton Fund.

Bibliography

Allison PD (1995), *Survival analysis using the SAS system: a practical guide*, SAS Institute Inc., Cary, North Carolina.

Arya OP, Taber SR and Nsanze H (1980), 'Gonorrhea and female infertility in rural Uganda'. *American Journal of Gynecology* 138: 929-932.

Brunham RC and Embree JE (1992), 'Sexually transmitted diseases: current and future dimensions of the problem in the Third World'. In: Germain A, *et al.* (eds), *Reproductive Tract Infections*, New York, Plenum Press: 269-297.

Caldwell JC and Caldwell P (1983), 'The demographic evidence for the incidence and course of abnormally low fertility in tropical Africa'. *World Health Statistics Quarterly* 36: 2-34.

Caldwell JC and Caldwell P (1989), 'The social context of AIDS in sub-Saharan Africa'. *Population and Development Review* 15: 185-235.

Cates W, Farley TTM and Rowe PJ (1985), 'Worldwide patterns of infertility: is Africa different?' *Lancet* 2: 596-598.

Cates W, Rolfs RT and Aral SO (1990), 'Sexually transmitted diseases, pelvic inflammatory disease, and infertility: an epidemiologic update'. *Epidemiologic Review* 12:199-220.

Coeytaux FM (1988), 'Induced abortion in sub-Saharan Africa: what we do and do not know'. *Studies in Family Planning* 19: 186-190.

Collet M, Reiners J, Frost E, Gass R, Yvert F, Leclerc A, Roth-Meyer C, Ivanoff B and Meheus A (1988), 'Infertility in Central Africa: infection is the cause'. *International Journal of Gynecology and Obstetric* 26: 423-428.

D'Costa LJ, Plummer FA and Bowmer I (1985), 'Prostitutes are a major reservoir of sexually transmitted diseases in Nairobi, Kenya'. *Sexually Transmitted Diseases* 12: 64-67.

DHS (Demographic and Health Surveys) for all years mentioned in the text have been carried out under the sponsorship of Macro International Inc., Calverton, Maryland, USA. See also HYPERLINK http://www.macroint.com/dhs and DHS (1998). Summary of Demographic and Health Research. Macro International Inc., Calverton, Maryland.

Doyal L and Pennell I (1981), *The political economy of health*, South End Press, Boston.

Duncan ME, *et al.* (1990), 'First coitus before menarche and risk of sexually transmitted diseases'. *Lancet* 335: 338-340.

Falahala FL (1975), 'Enquête sur la fécondité dans la province de l'est du Cameroon'. *WHO Report AFR/MCH/63.*

Frank O (1983a), 'Infertility in sub-Saharan Africa: estimates and implications'. *Population and Development Review* 9: 137-145.

Frank O (1983b), 'Infertility in sub-Saharan Africa'. *Center for policy studies working papers,* No. 97, The Population Council.

Grech ES, Everett JV and Mukasa F (1973), 'Epidemiological aspects of acute pelvic inflammatory disease in Uganda'. *Tropical Doctor* 3: 123.

Germain A (1989), 'The Christopher Tietze international symposium: an overview'. *International Journal of Gynecology and Obstetric Supplement* 3: 1-8.

Henin RA (1982), *Fertility, infertility and sub-fertility in Eastern Africa*, Population Studies and Research Institute, University of Nairobi, Nairobi.

Hunt CW (1989), 'Migrant labor and sexually transmitted disease: AIDS in Africa'. *Journal of Health and Social Behavior* 30: 353-374.

Kisekka MN (1988), 'Sexually transmitted diseases as a gender issue: examples from Nigeria and Uganda'. Paper presented at the Association of African Women for Research and Development, Dakar, Senegal.

Larsen U (1989), 'A comparative study of the levels and the differentials of sterility in Cameroon, Kenya, and Sudan'. In: Lesthaeghe RJ (ed.), *Reproduction and Social Organization in Sub-Saharan Africa*, University of California Press, Berkeley: 167-211.

Larsen U (1995a), 'Trends in infertility in Cameroon and Nigeria'. *International Family Planning Perspectives* 21: 138-142.

Larsen U (1995b), 'Differentials in infertility in Cameroon and Nigeria'. *Population Studies* 49: 329-346.

Larsen U and Menken J (1989), 'Measuring sterility from incomplete birth histories'. *Demography* 26: 185-202.

Larsen U and Menken J (1991), 'Individual-level sterility: a new method of estimation with application to sub-Saharan Africa'. *Demography* 28: 229-249.

Liskin L, Church CA, Potrow PT and Harris JA (1989), 'AIDS education - A beginning'. *Population Reports, Series L*, No 8.

Menken J (1972), 'The health and social consequences of teenage childbearing'. *Family Planning Perspectives* 4: 45-53.

Menken J, Trussell J and Larsen U (1986), 'Age and infertility'. *Science* 233: 1389-1394.

MOE (Ministry of Economics, Planning and International Cooperation), Direction des Statistiques Demographiques et Sociales Division des Statistiques et des Études Économiques, Central African Republic and Demographic and Health Surveys (DHS) (1995), *République Centrafricaine Enquête Démographique et de Santé 1994-95*. Macro International Inc., Calverton, Maryland.

Muir DG and Belsey MA (1980), 'Pelvic inflammatory disease and its consequences in the developing world'. *American Journal of Obstetrics and Gynecology* 138: 913-929.

Murdock GP (1959), *Africa: its people and their culture*, McGraw-Hill, New York.

Murray C (1981), *Families divided: the impact of migrant labour in Lesotho*, Cambridge University Press, Cambridge.

Over M and Piot P (1990), 'HIV infection and other sexually transmitted diseases'. In: Jamison DT and Mosley WH (eds), *Evolving health sector priorities in developing countries*, World Bank, Washington, D.C.: Chapter 10.

Page H and Coale A (1972), 'Fertility and child mortality south of the Sahara'. In: Minde SHO and Ejiogu CN (eds), *Population growth and economic development in Africa*, Heinemann, London: 51-67.

Population and Development Review (1995), Programme of action of the 1994 international conference on population and development (Chs I-VIII), *Population and Development Review* 21: 187-213.

Pressat R and Wilson C (1985), *The dictionary of demography*: Blackwell, New York.

Retel-Laurentin A (1974a), 'Sub-fertility in black Africa - the case of the Nzakara in the Central African Republic'. In: Adadevoh BK (ed.), *Subfertility and Infertility in Africa*, Caxton Press, Ibadan: 69-80.

Retel-Laurentin A (1974b), *Infécondité et maladies: les Nzakara République Centrafricaine*, Institut National de la Statistique et des Études Économiques, Paris.

Sherris J and Fox G (1983), 'Infertility and sexually transmitted disease: a public health challenge'. *Population Reports, Series L*, No 4.

Tabutin D (1982), 'Évolution régionale de la fécondité dans l'ouest du Zaire'. *Population* 37: 29-50.

Toubia N (1994), 'Female circumcision as a public health issue'. *New England Journal of Medicine* 331: 712-716.

Westroem L (1975), 'Effect of acute pelvic inflammatory disease on fertility'. *American Journal of Obstetric and Gynecology* 121: 707.

Westroem L (1980), 'Incidence, prevalence, and trends of acute pelvic inflammatory disease and its consequences in industrialized countries'. *American Journal of Obstetric and Gynecology* 138: 880.

Thought to be an altar piece for women who want children; the turtle (on her right side) symbolizes eternal life and is a messenger between the natural and the supernatural (Dogon, Kundou Gina, Mali)

6 Associations between female infertility, HIV and sexual behaviour in rural Tanzania

J. Ties Boerma and Mark Urassa

In Africa, female infertility still is an important public health problem despite decline in its levels over past decades (Cates et al., 1985; Larsen and Raggers, Chapter 1; White et al., Chapter 4). As outlined in earlier chapters, the inability to bear children may have far-reaching consequences for the individual or couple, and may also affect the health system and family planning programmes. Female infertility may be associated with HIV, STDs and sexual behaviour.

Infertility can be associated with non-infectious (e.g. endocrinological or anatomical abnormalities) or infectious causes. It has been estimated that between 50% and 80% of female infertility in sub-Saharan Africa is due to reproductive tract infections (Wasserheit and Holmes, 1992). The role of infections in the etiology of infertility is considerably more prominent in Africa than in other regions of the world. Gonorrhoea and chlamydia infections are the most common diseases that cause pelvic inflammatory disease, a condition that can lead to infertility (Meheus, 1992; Mabey et al., 1985; Mayaud, Chapter 2).

Anthropological and demographic studies in Africa have described the changes in marriage and sexual behaviour among infertile couples or infertile women. A man may be more likely to have extra-marital partners if his wife is unable to bear children (Buzzard, 1982; Harrell-Bond, 1975; Southwold, 1973). Others have described higher marital dissolution rates in childless marriages (Nabaitu et al., 1994; Parkin, 1966; Henin, 1969). In national survey data from Cameroon and Nigeria, infertility (including secondary infertility) was associated with greater marital instability (Larsen, 1995). In some settings infertility is not considered a reason for divorce (David and Voas, 1981; Pool, 1972; Parkin, 1966). However, men may then tend to marry one or more additional wives without divorcing the childless woman. Survey data from Cameroon have shown this association between infertility and polygamous unions (Larsen, 1995).

In 1994-1995 a hospital-based study was carried out among women attending an infertility clinic in the regional capital of Tanzania. These women were compared with women who had come to the same hospital to deliver their babies (Favot et al., 1997). Data on past sexual behaviour showed that infertile women had more marital breakdowns, more life-time sexual partners and almost three times higher HIV prevalence than fertile women.

Several studies in sub-Saharan Africa have shown that, in non-contracepting populations, HIV-positive women have lower fertility than HIV negative women, except in the youngest age groups. In the youngest women, the effect of 'group selection' for early start of sexual activity ensures that fertility is higher in the HIV infected individuals (Zaba and Gregson, 1998; Gray et al., 1998; Carpenter et al., 1997). In seven studies, the ratios of HIV-positive to HIV-negative women in terms of general fertility rates for women of all ages ranged from 0.6 to 0.9, and total fertility among HIV-infected women was 25% to 40% lower than that of HIV-negative women (Zaba and Gregson, 1998).

This study examines the association between fertility status and HIV infection, marital instability and multiple sexual relationships in a rural area in northwest Tanzania.

Data and methods

The study was carried out in Kisesa ward in Mwanza Region, Tanzania. The ward has a population of 20,000 and lies on average 20 kilometres east of the regional capital Mwanza, along the main road to Kenya. Kisesa ward includes six villages with a trading centre along the main road. More than 90 per cent of the population are Sukuma, the largest ethnic group in Tanzania. Farming is the main source of income, while petty trade in agricultural products (milk, tomatoes, maize, rice, fish etc.) is also common.

A demographic surveillance system is the basis of all research activities in Kisesa. In 1994 a baseline census was conducted. Follow-up visits were made every 4-5 months and by mid 1997, eight rounds had been completed (see also Boerma *et al.*, 1997). In August 1994 - July 1995 (first round) and again two years later (second round), a survey of all adults aged 15-44 years was carried out (open cohort). All eligible persons were listed using information from the most recent demographic round. They were asked to come to a central point in the village to be interviewed using a structured questionnaire and to give a blood sample for HIV testing. Eligibility was based on residence status. During the first round whole blood was collected; during the second survey all blood samples were collected on filter paper. The change was made to simplify logistics, reduce costs and try to maximize attendance, as in-depth research had suggested that finger pricks would be acceptable to more respondents than venapuncture. Home visits were made to encourage those who did not attend to come and in some cases interviews were conducted at home. All study participants were offered free medical treatment for health problems present at the time of the survey. During the second survey HIV counselling and testing was offered by a qualified counsellor, who followed up with those who wanted to know the HIV test results. Details on attendance, which was slightly over 80% in both rounds, have been presented elsewhere (Boerma *et al.*, 1999).

HIV testing was done in the regional laboratory that also had been used for other large studies in Mwanza Region. The test algorithm was based on two independent ELISA assays; Vironostika HIV-MIXT (Organon, Boxtel, the Netherlands) and Enzygnost HIV1/HIV2 (Behring, Marburg, Germany). Only samples with two positive ELISA tests were considered HIV positive.

Data were double entered using DBaseIV (Borland International, Scotts Valley, California, USA) and all analyses were done using Stata 4.0 (Stata Corporation, College Station, Texas, USA). In the prevalence analysis, results from all women who attended in either survey were combined into one file. The first round of results was used if a woman had attended twice. With regard to HIV incidence, seroconversion was assumed to have occurred in the interval between the two surveys. Data on births from the demographic surveillance system were used to calculate fertility rates.

Figure 1 Association between female infertility, HIV, STDs and sexual behaviour[a]

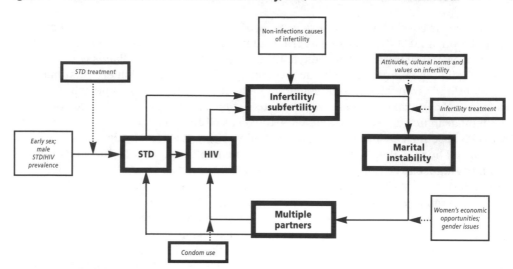

[a] Arrows with dotted lines indicate potential areas for interventions

Figure 1 shows possible associations between infertility or subfertility, sexual behaviour and STDs/HIV. This analysis will consider the association between HIV and fertility, and between fertility status and marital stability and sexual behaviour. Infertility is defined as the absence of a birth in the previous five years to a sexually active, non-contracepting woman with at least five years of exposure to the risk of pregnancy. Women with a birth in the last five years were considered fertile, women with no birth infertile or subfertile. Among these infertile women a distinction was made between those who have never given birth (primary infertility) and those who have given birth (secondary infertility). Women who were currently using contraceptives or women who had not been sexually active in the last year were excluded. We also excluded women who were pregnant at the time of the survey, but had not given birth in the last five years, as pregnancy does not indicate whether these women will actually have a live birth. Women who were currently using contraceptives were excluded, since we did not know whether they were fecund or not.

Contraceptive use is low in this part of Tanzania: in 1994 7% of women 15-49 years were using a modern method of family planning. Also, the desired family size is large: women's mean ideal number of children was 6.1 (Bureau of Statistics, 1995). Survey data on contraceptive use showed that 4.1% of women used a modern contraceptive in the first round and 6.0% in the second round.

The period of postpartum sexual abstinence is short: at four to five months postpartum 61% of women had started having sexual intercourse; by 11-12 months this figure has risen to 78%. The median age at first marriage was 19.1 years, and marriage is almost universal (98% of women 25-49 years had ever been married).

Qualitative methods were used to collect data on local bars, in particular their relationship to commercial sex. Local informants listed all bars, including traditional brew sales outlets called *pombe* shops. Previous research had shown that there is no clear distinction between commercial and non-commercial sex (Mgalla and Pool, 1997). Therefore, field workers and local informants listed all bar and *pombe* shop workers as well as women who tended to visit such places frequently to sell sex. In addition, all bar workers in a neighbouring urban ward were listed and interviewed as part of the planning for a health intervention for bar workers.

Results

HIV prevalence and incidence by parity

Table 1 presents HIV prevalence and incidence during 1994-1997 by parity and age of the woman. HIV prevalence is low among women under 20 years. Figure 2 shows the HIV prevalence by parity and age. At 20-24 and 25-29 years HIV prevalence is higher at lower parities (0 and 1), but differences are not large. HIV incidence was not markedly higher among women who were of parity zero during their first survey attendance, peaked at parity 2 and was lower from parity 4 onward. Differences by parity however were not statistically significant.

Table 1 **HIV prevalence and incidence in Tanzanian women 1994-1997, by parity and age (% HIV positive in parentheses)**

Parity	Prevalence					Incidence	
	15-19	20-24	25-29	30+	All	SC/year[a]	Incidence per 100 PY[b] (95% CI)
0	10/864	28/199	7/44	9/36	54/1143	7/896	0.8 (0.3-1.6)
	(1.2)	(14.1)	(15.9)	(25.0)	(4.7)		
1	7/159	28/353	27/118	8/72	70/702	6/527	1.1 (0.4-2.5)
	(4.4)	(7.9)	(22.9)	(11.1)	(10.0)		
2	0/25	15/290	20/168	13/98	48/581	7/474	1.5 (0.6-3.0)
	( )	(5.2)	(11.9)	(13.3)	(8.3)		
3	0/3	9/124	30/205	19/112	58/444	4/388	1.0 (0.3-2.6)
	( )	(7.3)	(14.6)	(17.0)	(13.1)		
4	0/1	4/26	17/154	23/172	44/353	1/359	0.3 (0.0-1.5)
	( )	( )	(11.0)	(13.4)	(12.5)		
≥5	-	0/10	14/143	60/1056	74/1209	10/1424	0.7 (0.3-1.3)
		( )	(9.8)	(5.7)	(6.1)		
All	17/1052	84/1002	115/832	132/1546	348/4432	34/4071	0.8 (0.6-1.2)
	(1.6)	(8.4)	(13.8)	(8.5)	(7.9)		
Gave birth between rounds	4/152	9/213	2/173	7/253	22/791	11/1592	0.7 (0.3-1.2)
	(2.6)	(4.2)	(1.2)	(2.8)	(2.8)		
Did not give birth	2/303	16/207	28/225	28/595	74/1330	23/2510	0.9 (0.6-1.4)
	(0.7)	(7.7)	(12.4)	(4.3)	(5.6)		

[a] SC/year: Seroconvertors per year

[b] PY: person years

Figure 2   HIV prevalence by parity and age, Kisesa women, 1994-1996

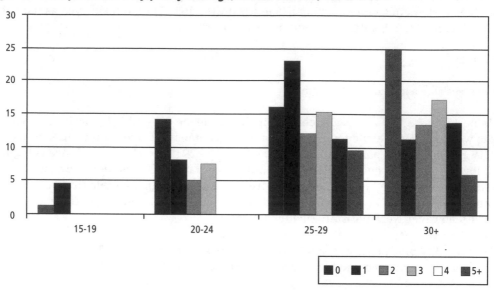

The two bottom rows of Table 1 compare HIV prevalence and incidence in women who gave birth between the two survey rounds and those who did not. Differences in HIV prevalence are large, especially at age 25-29 years. HIV incidence was only slightly higher among women who did not give birth between the survey rounds than among women who gave birth: 0.9 and 0.7 per 100 person years respectively. The incidence rate ratio is 1.3 (95% confidence interval 0.33-1.61, p=0.45).

Fertility by HIV status

Table 2 and Figure 3 show that fertility is much lower among HIV infected women. Young women, for whom fertility does not seem to differ with HIV status, appear to be an exception, but numbers of HIV infected women under 20 years are very small. The gap in age-specific fertility rates by HIV status increases with age. Overall, general fertility rate is 193 per 1,000 among HIV negative women and 94 per 1,000 among HIV infected women. Total fertility rates are 6.0 and 3.1 among HIV negative and HIV-positive women respectively.

Table 2   Fertility by HIV status, Kisesa 1994-1997

	HIV negative			HIV positive		
	Births/years		ASFR[a]	Births/years		ASFR
15-19	148	1382	105.6	2	11	177.0
20-24	393	1592	238.1	14	105	133.0
25-29	378	1417	255.4	16	167	95.9
30-34	311	1277	235.7	10	122	82.0
35-39	208	1004	202.1	5	67	75.0
40-44	93	826	108.9	3	50	59.6
45-49	14	241	58.2	0	8	0.0
All	1545	7739	193.2	50	530	94.3
TFR[b]			6.0			3.1

[a] ASFR: Age specific fertility rate
[b] TFR: Total fertility rate

Figure 3   Age-specific fertility rates, Kisesa, 1994-1997

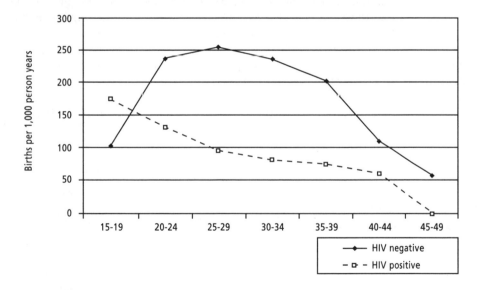

Prevalence of infertility

Primary infertility is not common in Kisesa (Table 3). About 3% of women aged 20-44 years who are sexually active, non-contracepting and have been exposed to the risk of pregnancy for at least five years have never had a live birth. A much larger proportion of such women have not had a birth in the last five years (24%). There is a very strong relationship with age. Among women aged 20-34 years 15.2% have secondary infertility and 18.7% have either primary or secondary infertility.

Table 3 Fertility and infertility by age, Kisesa 1994-1996[a]

Age group	N	Fertile %	SI[b] %	PI[c] %
20-24	252	88.1	7.1	4.8
25-29	736	82.7	13.0	4.2
30-34	627	76.9	21.1	2.1
35-39	430	68.1	30.2	1.6
40-44	391	48.9	49.4	1.8
All	2436	73.8	24.1	2.9

[a] Includes only ever-married women who commenced sexual intercourse at least five years prior to study, were not using contraceptives and had been sexually active in the last year

[b] SI: Secondary infertility

[c] PI: Primary infertility

Sexual behaviour by fertility

Table 4 compares selected variables related to sexual behaviour among fertile (birth in the last five years) and infertile women aged 20-34 years, as defined in Table 3. The comparison was limited to women 20-34 years: older women have much higher levels of secondary infertility, but the associated sexual behavioural consequences are less likely in this group. As a group, infertile women are more likely to be divorced and to have had more marital dissolutions. They are also more mobile, as indicated by a shorter duration of stay in the current residence.

Table 4 Sexual behaviour by fertility status, women 20-34 years, Kisesa, 1994-1996

	Fertile (%)	Infertile (%)	P-value
Number of women	1313	302	
Currently divorced	9.3	19.2	.000
At least 2 marital dissolutions (%)	3.9	8.6	.001
Two or more sexual partners in last year (%)	7.6	13.3	.002
STD in last year (%)	9.4	14.6	.007
HIV prevalence	8.4	21.8	.000
Lived here <5 years	20.4	29.5	.001
Age at first sex under 15	19.1	22.1	.410

P-value of chi square test of proportion fertile vs proportion infertile

With regard to sexual behaviour, there was no evidence of significant differences in recalled age at first sex, but infertile women more frequently reported multiple sexual partners in the last year. This significant difference in numbers of sexual partners was also present when women who had given birth in the last 6 or 12 months were omitted from the analysis (because they may have been practising postpartum abstinence). HIV prevalence was 8% among fertile women compared to 22% among infertile women. The odds ratio adjusted for age, education, and place of residence was 3.1 (95% CI 2.2-4.4). HIV incidence was also higher among infertile women (5 seroconversions in 554 person years of observation, i.e. incidence 0.9 per 100 person years, 95% CI 0.3-2.1) than among fertile women (13 seroconversions in 1931 persons, 0.7 per 100 person years, 95% CI 0.4-1.2), but this difference was not significant (incidence rate ratio 1.34, p=0.57).

Female bar workers

Using local informants, local field workers listed 365 women who were considered to be available for commercial sex. The majority of these women were working in the bars and *pombe* shops, and such women were common in all three areas. The mean age was just under 30 years (range 15-45 years). Infertility was more common among these women than among other women. Linking the women listed by the field workers to the serosurvey data showed that almost half had participated in at least one of the survey rounds. One-hundred and twelve women met the criteria in Table 3: the prevalence of infertility was 36% among those women, a proportion which was significantly higher than among other women (p=0.02). In other words, 6.3% of infertile women were listed as available for commercial sex, compared to 4.0% of fertile women. Among the 81 initially HIV negative bar workers who attended twice, HIV incidence was 4.5 per 100 person years (95% CI 1.7-18.2 per 100 person years).

Additional data were available from 77 female bar workers in the neighbouring town. Their mean age was 27 years (range 17-46 years). Most women had lived for several years in the area. The median duration of stay was about two and a half years. One in five bar workers had moved into the area during the last 6 months. Seventeen bar workers (22.1%) had never given birth and the mean number of children per woman was 2.1. Among the 50 women aged 24 years and over, four bar workers had never given birth (8%), and 27 bar workers (54%) had not given birth in the last five years. Fifty-two of the bar workers had been divorced at least once (73%), but 33 (46.5%) were currently in a union (mostly cohabitation without formal union). Only two of the bar workers regularly used modern contraceptives, but abortion may be fairly common. Condoms were used but not consistently. Several bar workers had a strong desire to have children (see Gijsels *et al.*, Chapter 8).

Discussion

Women may become HIV infected prior to the first pregnancy, during the postpartum period or during a period between births but outside the postpartum period. Data from Kisesa community show that HIV prevalence is somewhat higher among women with lower parity, but differences are fairly small. HIV incidence was highest at parity 2, but did not vary much by parity. Among women who gave birth in the two years between the rounds of the serosurvey, HIV incidence was slightly lower than among women who did not give birth. It is not possible with our data to discover whether the infection occurred before or after giving birth. Other studies have suggested that HIV incidence can be very high during the postpartum period. For example, in Malawi and Rwanda very high incidence has been reported during the postpartum period (Taha *et al.*, 1998; Leroy *et al.*, 1994). The Kisesa community cohort study showed that HIV prevalence was markedly higher among women with infertility than among fertile women: 8.4% versus 21.8% respectively. The findings were very similar to those of a hospital-based study in the regional capital where the HIV seroprevalence of women attending an infertility clinic was 18.2%, while non-primiparous women who came for delivery had a prevalence of 6.6% (Favot *et al.*, 1997). The odds ratio after adjustment for age, education and occupation was 2.7 (95% CI 1.4-5.3). Infertility is not uncommon in Kisesa; among women 20-34 years, secondary infertility stands at 15% and primary infertility at 3.5%.

As indicated by our conceptual framework (Figure 1), higher HIV prevalence among infertile women can occur for several reasons. Infertility may lead to divorce and sexual behaviour that puts women at greater risk of HIV (and other STDs). On the other hand, lower fertility may be a consequence of HIV infection, as has been shown in other studies (Zaba and Gregson, 1998). Fertility is reduced by approximately 50% among HIV-positive women in rural Kisesa, Tanzania. This is a larger fertility reduction than observed in other studies in the region (Zaba and Gregson, 1998). Lower fertility among HIV-positive women has been attributed to lower rates of conception and increased rates of pregnancy loss (Gray *et al.*, 1998). In part, this may be a direct effect of HIV infection, though it may also be associated with other past, or more recent, sexually transmitted infections such as gonorrhoea or syphilis, which tend to be more frequent among HIV infected women than among HIV negative women.

It may also be argued that part of the lower fertility observed among HIV-infected women reflects pre-existing lower fertility in this group. If that were true, HIV incidence should be higher among infertile women. In our study HIV incidence was only slightly higher among these women in comparison to fertile women; it was also not markedly higher among women who had not given birth during the two year interval between the two survey rounds. This suggests that pre-existing infertility plays a relatively minor role in explaining the observed differences in fertility among HIV-infected women.

Several indicators showed that sexual behaviour of infertile women differs from that of fertile women, including higher numbers of divorces and, therefore, higher numbers of sexual partners. This pertains to past marital sexual behaviour (e.g. a history of marital dissolution) as well as more recent behaviour (e.g. current marital status, sexual partners in the last year) rather than to pregnancy and delivery-related changes in sexual behaviour, such as postpartum sexual abstinence. The hospital-based study showed similar differences in marital and sexual behaviour (Favot *et al.*, 1997). However, it cannot be concluded that infertility causes differences in sexual behaviour. HIV and infertility-causing STDs both result from the same type of sexual behaviour, involving multiple partnerships or spouses with multiple partners. Differences in age at first sexual intercourse would have supported this hypothesis, but there was no such evidence.

It must be noted that very few women in the Kisesa community were aware of their HIV status. Voluntary counselling and testing facilities are not available in Kisesa but were offered during the second round of the serosurvey. Fewer than 1% of the survey respondents decided to make full use of these services to become aware of their HIV status. Therefore, changes in sexual or marital behaviour cannot be attributed to knowledge of HIV serostatus.

In sum, our study further corroborates evidence of decreased fertility among HIV infected women, whom we found to have only half the fertility rate of HIV negative women. As a result, HIV-infected mothers will have fewer babies than would be expected from calculations based on pre-AIDS fertility rates. Therefore there will be fewer HIV-positive newborns and fewer orphans when a woman dies prematurely of HIV/AIDS than would be expected otherwise. Part of the difference may be due to infertility that pre-dates HIV infection, but the Kisesa data suggest that this contribution would be relatively small. Women with reduced fertility have higher levels of HIV infection and more sexual partners than fertile women. The effect of HIV on fertility may indirectly increase the risk of divorce and also the risk of multiple partners, which may facilitate the spread of HIV. Specific interventions may be needed to address the behavioural consequences of infertility associated with HIV infection.

Acknowledgement

This study was carried out in the context of the Tanzania-Netherlands project to support AIDS control in Mwanza Region (TANESA), which is funded by the Netherlands' Minister for Development Cooperation. We are grateful to our colleagues of the TANESA project and the staff of the National Institute for Medical Research, Mwanza Centre, for their support during field work and data processing. Material in this chapter was presented at a UNAIDS/USAID/ MEASURE Evaluation/CDC meeting on 'Infertility, STDs and HIV monitoring: problems and prospects', Arlington, Virginia, December 14-15, 1998.

Bibliography

Boerma JT, Ngalula J, Isingo R, et al. (1997), 'Levels and causes of adult mortality in rural Tanzania with special reference to HIV/AIDS'. *Health Transition Review* 7 (suppl 2): 63-74.0

Boerma JT, Urassa M, Senkoro KS, et al. (1999), 'Spread of HIV in a rural area in Tanzania'. *AIDS* 13: 1233-1240.

Bureau of Statistics and Macro International Inc. (1995), *Tanzania knowledge, attitudes and practices survey 1994*, Planning Commission, Dar es Salaam and Macro International, Calverton, Maryland, USA.

Buzzard SA (1982), *Women's status and wage employment in Kisumu, Kenya*, PhD thesis, The American University, Washington, DC, University Microfilms International, Ann Arbor.

Carpenter L, Nakiyingi J, Ruberantwari A, Malamba S, Kamali A, and Whitworth J (1997), 'Estimates of the impact of HIV infection on fertility in a rural Ugandan population cohort'. *Health Transition Review* 7 (supplement 2): 113-126.

Cates W, Farley TMM, and Rowe PJ (1985), 'Worldwide patterns of infertility: is Africa different?' *Lancet* ii: 596-9.

David N and Voas D (1981), 'Societal causes of infertility and population decline among the settled Fulani of North Cameroon'. *MAN* 16: 644-664.

Favot I, Ngalula J, Mgalla Z, Klokke AH, Gumodoka B and Boerma JT (1997), 'HIV infection and sexual behaviour among women with infertility in Tanzania: a hospital-based study'. *International Journal of Epidemiology* 26: 414-9.

Gray R, Wawer M, Serwadda D, *et al.* (1998), 'Population-based study of fertility in women with HIV-1 infection in Uganda'. *Lancet* 351: 98-103.

Harrell-Bond BE (1975), *Modern marriage in Sierra Leone: a study of the professional group*, Mouton and Co., the Hague, Holland.

Henin RA (1969), 'The pattern and causes of fertility differentials in the Sudan'. *Population Studies* 23: 171-198.

Larsen U (1995), 'Differentials in infertility in Cameroon and Nigeria'. *Population Studies* 49: 329-346.

Leroy V, Van de Perre P, Lepage P, *et al.* (1994), 'Seroincidence of HIV-1 infection in African women of reproductive age: a prospective cohort study in Kigali, 1988-1992'. *AIDS* 8: 983-6.

Mabey DCW, Ogbaselassia G, Robertson JN, Heckels JE and Ward ME (1985), 'Tubal infertility in the Gambia: chlamydial and gonococcal serology in women with tubal occlusion compared with pregnant control'. *Bulletin of the World Health Organization* 63: 1107-13.

Meheus A (1992), 'Women's health: importance of reproductive tract infections, pelvic inflammatory disease and cervical cancer'. In: Germain A, Holmes KK, Piot P and Wasserheit JN (eds), *Reproductive tract infections: global impact and priorities for women's reproductive health*, IWHC, Plenum Press, New York: 61-91.

Mgalla Z and Pool R (1997), 'Sexual relationships, condom use and risk perception among female bar workers in north-west Tanzania'. *AIDS Care* 9: 407-416.

Nabaitu J, Bachengana C and Seeley J (1994), 'Marital instability in a rural population in south-west Uganda: implications for the spread of HIV-1 infection'. *Africa* 64: 243-251.

Parkin D (1966), 'Types of urban African marriage in Kampala'. *Africa* 36: 269-284.

Pool JE (1972), 'A cross-comparative study of aspects of conjugal behavior among women of three west African countries'. *Canadian Journal of African Studies* VI: 233-259.

Southwold M (1973), 'The Baganda of Central Africa'. In: Molnos A (ed.) *Cultural source material for population planning in East Africa, Volume III: Beliefs and practices*: 163-73, East African Publishing House, Nairobi, Kenya.

Taha TE, Dallabetta GA, Hoover DR, *et al.* (1998), 'Trends of HIV-1 and sexually transmitted diseases among pregnant and postpartum women in urban Malawi'. *AIDS* 12: 197-203.

Wasserheit JN and Holmes KK (1992), 'Reproductive tract infections: challenges for international health policy, programs and research'. In: Germain A, Holmes KK, Piot P and Wasserheit JN (eds), *Reproductive tract infections: global impact and priorities for women's reproductive health*, IWHC, Plenum Press, New York: 7-33.

Zaba B and Gregson S (1998), 'Measuring the impact of HIV on fertility in Africa'. *AIDS* 12 (suppl 1): S41-S50.

Reverse side of dolls (*Aku'amma*) carried by women who want to become pregnant, but also by women
who are already pregnant who want to insure themselves of a safe delivery and a beautiful baby. The high forehead and
the long neck with rings of fat are Ashanti ideals of beauty.
Designs on the reverse side are said to be fertility symbols. (Ashanti, Ghana)

7 The discourse of infertility in Tanzania

Zaida Mgalla and J. Ties Boerma

High fertility in sub-Saharan Africa needs to be interpreted in the context of a traditional religious belief system that is still active (Caldwell and Caldwell, 1987). Infertility should be considered in the context of similar discourses, as the inability to give birth is often interpreted as evidence of sin and disapproval. The mainly anthropological literature is relatively rich in description of the causes and, particularly, the consequences of infertility from the perspective of the infertile (Feldman-Savelsberg, 1994; Inhorn, 1994; Neff, 1994; and Gerrits, 1995). In a recent study in Pemba Island, Tanzania, Kielmann (1998) analysed the discourse on infertility through individual interviews and group discussions. She concluded that the absence of a biomedical discourse on infertility has created a particular kind of women's local knowledge on infertility and characterized the prevailing discourse as '... the simultaneous logic of greedy spirits and faulty organs.' (Kielmann, 1998: 153). There were signs of the development of a modernist discourse that individualizes and moralizes the problem of female infertility, mixed with a more traditional interpretation of the causes of infertility. Infertility was also considered to be a consequence of women's behaviour specifically, such as drinking, abortion and promiscuity. In this study attitudes to infertility, and the impact of infertility on women, are examined for another population in Tanzania where fertility is high and contraceptive use is low, i.e. used by fewer than 10% of women of reproductive age.

Focus group discussions

The study was carried out in two districts in Mwanza Region, northwest Tanzania during 1996-1997. This area is inhabited by the Sukuma people, the largest ethnic group in Tanzania. Since the main objective of our study was to gather insights on how the society views women and men with infertility, we opted for focus group discussions (FGDs) with a variety of participants. In total we conducted 12 FGDs with a total of 98 participants. Five group discussions were held with adolescents, three with boys and two with girls in secondary schools; four group discussions were carried out with middle-aged men and women (22-45 years); and three group discussions were held with older men (two) and older women (one) (over 45 years). All groups were living in the rural areas except the adolescents. Discussions were conducted in Swahili or in Sukuma or often both languages were used interchangeably. Each discussion was led by two or three moderators from the research team of whom at least one was fluent in the Sukuma language. All discussions were taped, transcribed and translated. Since the number of group discussions was small, analysis was done by 'hand'.

Causes of infertility

Initially, in the discussions about the causes of infertility an attempt was made to distinguish between primary and secondary infertility. This was difficult, since the causes are rather similar and the local terminology does not include a clear distinction. The two Swahili language terms for infertility are *ugumba* and *utasa*; according to the majority of participants in the group discussions these terms can be used inter-changeably, even though a barren woman is referred to as a *mgumba*. The same terms are used in the Sukuma language. In a series of interviews with infertile women, as part of another study among the Sukuma, a woman was generally considered infertile if she had not given birth after three years of trying to get pregnant. The terms *ugumba* and *utasa* generally refer only to female infertility, not to males. As is shown below, male infertility was acknowledged as a potential cause of a woman's inability to give birth, particularly in the younger age groups. Older men and older women were the most explicit: they did not consider it possible for a man to have the kinds of infertility suffered by women.

Participants in the various groups listed a number of anatomical or physiological abnormalities in the female reproductive system as causes of infertility. These included shortages of eggs or abnormalities of the uterus.

'A woman with infertility has no reproductive eggs (hana mayai).' (older women, adolescent/adult men)
'Some women are born without a womb. If God created you like that there is nothing you can do.' (women)
'Some women do not conceive because they have got a small opening to the womb for the sperm to pass through.' (older women)
'Surely conception can never happen with a deformed womb (mgongo umepinda).' (women).

Infertility was linked to *mchango* (in Swahili) or *nzoka* (in Sukuma). This concept is also discussed in Chapters 9 and 10. Although people describe *mchango* or *nzoka* in realistic terms (as a snakelike creature that lives in each person's abdomen), it is more likely to be seen as a metaphor for the balance between health and disease than as a living creature. The first group of quotations is from a group of middle-aged men, and the second from older men:

M (moderator): *'What causes infertility?'*
P (participant)1: *'This can be caused by mchango or what we call nzoka in Sukuma, which results into swelling of the stomach ... you can feel that the egg is matured and ready for being disposed. Then it keeps rotating in the lower abdomen making you feel that you are pregnant ... the woman does not get her menses regularly. These are mchango complications.'*
P2: *'eehh, mchango breaks the eggs.'*
M: *'Can a woman affected by mchango be able to get children in the future?'*
P1: *'If not detected early, it is not easy to treat.'*

P1: *'For some who have given birth that can still be affected by nzoka. The nzoka comes in the womb and disturbs, even though she was bearing children and stops thereafter. She becomes infertile.'*
M: *'You mean she was previously capable of giving birth and then she gets nzoka and cannot give birth anymore?'*
P1: *'Eeeh, she contracts nzoka, which feeds on the eggs, and she aborts frequently. Occasionally it may simply feed on the eggs and she is unable to conceive completely, even though she had a child before ... a woman with such a problem can never have a baby unless treated by a traditional healer.'*
P2: *'A woman may conceive but nzoka can cause a pregnancy to move and hide at the back and disappear completely.'*

These reproductive system abnormalities may be seen as having different underlying causes. The main causes can be grouped as those having religious or spiritual origins; those associated with sexual behaviour and STDs; and those related to contraception. In all groups there were mixed discourses about the causes of infertility, including biomedical, social and religious discourses. In the younger age groups the influence of biomedical knowledge on explanatory models was much greater than in the older age groups. This became most obvious in the discussions about contraceptive use as a cause of infertility, as discussed below.

Several groups gave spiritual or religious explanations. Adult and older women attributed infertility to witchcraft.

'Sometimes a woman can miss her menses and feel something moving in her womb. But when she is examined, nothing is seen. Here in this village it is perceived that she has been bewitched. Her pregnancy is hidden at her back.' (Middle-aged woman)

In the group discussion with older women, ability to conceive and have children was entirely up to the will of God. The women frequently used the sentence *'Mpaji ni Mungu'* (God is the giver of children). Several secondary school boys associated infertility with *'mzimu'* (spirits of a dead person) or a curse by parents or elders in the community. The adolescent girls also mentioned the possibility of a curse by an aunt or some other relative as a cause of infertility.

Sexual behaviour and STDs

Several types of sexual behaviour were linked to the risk of infertility. These included early onset of sexual intercourse among girls, multiple partnerships for women (leading to STDs), and transgression of a postpartum sexual taboo. The notion of multiple partnerships leading to acquiring or passing on STDs dominated most group discussions, but was mostly mentioned in the context of secondary infertility. It is notable that most groups focused on the promiscuity of the woman herself. The possibility of a woman being infected by a promiscuous husband rarely came up: the cause of infertility was the woman's own behaviour. Men in particular tended to attribute infertility to women's promiscuous behaviour. The older women were the only group that blamed men for bringing infertility-causing diseases home to their wives.

Adolescent girls mentioned that the tubes of the female reproductive system could be blocked by an STD and delay in treatment was even noted as a cause. They said:

'It is because persons with STDs feel ashamed and stay too long without treatment and thus increase the risk of complications.'

However, their biomedical understanding of the relationship between STDs and infertility was incomplete, as it was for other explanatory models used by this group. In fact, most adolescent girls seemed to think that ovulation occurred during the menstruation.

'I do not understand why a woman continues to have menses even when the tubes are blocked.'

The early onset of sexual intercourse was singled out as an important cause of infertility problems. One group of middle-aged women discussed it as follows:

M: *'What other causes of infertility do you know?'*
P1: *'Some say if a girl starts having sex at an early age and with an adult man.'*
M: *'What age do you mean?'*
P1: *'Say 10 or 12 years.'*
M: *'What is the problem if a girl at the age of 12 has sex with an adult man?'*
P2: *'They allege that a man's penis is bigger than a girls vaginal depth.'*
M: *'So?'*
P2: *'As a result a girl's reproductive system gets spoilt, the womb is pushed upwards, slips off and gets bent.'*
P3: *'Thus, they say a woman is infertile because she has a 'mgongo umepinda' deformed womb.'*
P4: *'Yes, conception can hardly happen within a deformed womb.'*

The schoolgirls and the men also addressed early onset of sex. Men considered that the woman's eggs would be destroyed by early sex. The adolescent girls said that early onset of sex could expose them to an STD at an early age, which could spoil the reproductive system.

STDs and promiscuity were mentioned as important causes for secondary infertility, especially in discussions with men in all three age groups. Multiple sexual partners were linked to repeated STDs, which could affect the reproductive organs. Middle-aged men:

P1: *'If a woman has sex with several men she can get infected with diseases.'*
M: *'What kind of these diseases can cause infertility?'*
P1: *'Kaswende (syphilis) and kasogone or kisonono (gonorrhea).'*
M: *'How do these cause infertility?'*
P2: *'If a woman contracts STDs frequently she may suffer from abortions or the uterus gets affected.'*
P3: *'STDs like gonorrhea affect reproductive eggs in a womans body and hence cause infertility.'*
P4: *'Regular STD infection may spoil the uterus.'*

Adult men and women also mentioned transgression of a sexual taboo as a cause of infertility. In the Sukuma language the term *'wiliyanongo'* was used. *Nongo* is used to refer to a woman having sex too early postpartum with a man other than the husband or the man who made her pregnant. This was thought to lead to mixing of different blood types in the woman's body, which could lead to blood clotting in the womb and prevent new conceptions. The duration of the postpartum period with risk of *wiliyanongo* is about 3-6 months. A woman is however allowed to resume sex with her husband before 2-3 months postpartum; this is not expected to cause any problems.

Contraception

Beliefs, rumours and fears about the side effects of modern contraceptives abound in sub-Saharan Africa (Bogue, 1983; Caldwell and Caldwell, 1987). For instance, in a recent study in Kenya focus group discussions and in-depth interviews with women of reproductive ages documented the multiple concerns of women about side effects of modern contraceptives (Rutenberg and Watkins, 1996). While many of these rumours and beliefs seem anecdotal, studies across the continent lead one to believe that these beliefs are quite widespread.

One of the most serious concerns of women is infertility. French researcher Anne Retel-Laurentin (1974) pointed to the link between infertility and family planning based on her work on Central Africa as early as the 1950s. She argued that family planning programmes would be much more successful if they were to address concerns about infertility, especially in populations where infertility is common.

In several group discussions, the use of contraceptives was mentioned as a cause of infertility, especially barrenness. Older women and older men did not discuss contraceptives much: quite a few of them said they did not know much about these drugs.

'It (contraception) is not very clear to us as we only learn about contraceptives through women.' (Older man)

Older women said:

P1: *'I hear nowadays women, including our daughters, use medicine to avoid pregnancy.'*
M: *'Has any of you ever seen those medicines?'*
P2: *'Because we disapprove the use of these medicines, our daughters do not show them to us. You'd only be surprised to find her getting fat, its because she is using contraceptives. Surprisingly, we find some losing weight and then they stop bearing children.'*
P3: *'Most of those who use those medicines do not bear children, they end up being ill. Most women using contraceptives are taking them without proper dosage, as a result they die! Some of them are simply given by friends without proper instructions ... and they end up having problems.'*
M: *'What happens in the woman's body after taking contraceptives?'*
P2: *'See, we do not use these things, so we cannot tell you.'*

The discussions with the secondary school girls focused extensively on their concerns about the link between contraceptives and infertility. In particular, the girls appeared to incorporate pieces of biomedical knowledge (animal hormones in pills, mercury in intra-uterine devices) into their beliefs about side effects of contraceptives. For virtually every method the girls mentioned, they also provided beliefs about side effects, all with a biomedical slant. This is illustrated by excerpts from group discussions with adolescent girls:

'Pills are made from animal hormones and if those enter the human body they cause problems.'

'If you take pills for a long time, some of them do not get diffused into the body and tend to remain. This then causes some numbness and the reproductive organs can even rot, and later this results into problems, like involuntary abortions.'

'I have heard women taking these pills. They start putting on weight, sometimes they may not get their menses for about three months, sometimes when she gets her menses excessive bleeding occurs. I think this happens when the woman has taken an overdose of contraceptive pills and this causes reproductive problems.'

'Injections can kill the reproductive eggs.'

'I want to talk about the loop. This is something like a rope and on the lower side there is a metal that is said to contain mercury. If this mercury comes in contact with the walls it causes cancer of the womb. And the woman may not get pregnant forever.'

'If the tubes are cut, they can never be connected again. Some seem to think that some women are deceived and told that reversal is possible.'

'Some of the condoms have lubricants that have stayed too long and expired or their storage has been poor contrary to the manufacturers condition. Because of that, some users encounter problems, especially women, they get cancer of the reproductive organs from the lubricants of the condoms. Others can burst or tear and remain in the vagina.'

'If a girl has had a lot of abortions she is not able to get pregnant again.'

Adolescent girls also mentioned traditional contraceptive methods. According to a Masai girl, these methods - including wearing 'pigi', a bead-like string made from a stem of specific traditional contraceptive plant, worn around the waist - are provided by the grandmother. These methods were thought to be effective and no side effects were known. The main concern was that a girl would remain infertile, if the grandmother died before giving the medicine to end the contraceptive effect.

Induced abortion was also cited as a cause of infertility among women. When probed about how abortion can cause infertility, it was explained that most abortions took place among young women, and were carried out in 'dark corners' in an unprofessional manner. During the discussions with schoolgirls, it was also reported that abortions are performed using a mixture consisting of boiled tea leaves and chloroquine tablets. It was described how abortion could lead to infection of the reproductive organs or genital injury, causing damaged reproductive organs and subsequent infertility. This was also mentioned in other groups (adolescent boys, adult women, adult men).

Male infertility

All groups mentioned male infertility as a possible cause of infertility. However, only women's groups felt that women are too often blamed when the cause is the infertility of the husband. Older women said:

M: *'From what we hear from you, women are blamed more often than men for not having children. Why is this so?'*
P1: *'Aii! Isn't it because they are the ones who bring diseases to women.'*
M: *'Earlier you said there is no man who is infertile. Now you are giving a different response. Please explain.'*
P2: *'mm There are! There are!'*
M: *'So there are also infertile men?'*
P3: *'There are. Only that the infertility status of men is not disclosed. If my husband was infertile it would be me and my mother who would know, and maybe my real sisters who will not tell others.'*
P4: *'Ehee, there are some men in the village who are well-known to be infertile as they may marry even thrice but cannot make their wives pregnant. And those women marry other men and they conceive and bear children. If a man in that category latter marries again and it happens that his new wife conceives, everybody in the village knows that he has been assisted by secret arrangements.'*

The main causes mentioned for male infertility were impotence and lack of seed. Some only mentioned impotence: men are 'safe' (fertile) as long as there is erection during sexual intercourse (middle-aged and older men).

The adolescent girls said that a man could become infertile due to an STD. The men explained why infertility is much more common among women than among men. Explanations included women's propensity to contract STDs, the early start of sexual activity in women, and the use of contraceptives.

Consequences of infertility

Many studies have reported the high value of children in African societies (Caldwell and Caldwell, 1987). Our study participants reiterated that having children is important to provide security in old age, to assure continuity of the lineage, to gain respect and power, and to give a sense of completeness, satisfaction and identity. A common Sukuma saying is *'Bana luli lubango lwa kaya'*, meaning children are the blessings of the home. Indirectly, this is used to indicate that families without children are not blessed.

Divorce was the primary consequence of infertility according to most groups. Most male participants responded that infertility was not something they could live with. Frequent responses in the group discussions were 'I would divorce her' and 'I would marry a second wife.' Interviews and discussion with women revealed a much more tolerant attitude, particularly among the younger women.

Women with infertility have a much lower social status in the community than fertile women: they are less respected, often harassed and denied basic rights. If their husband dies, infertile women are denied inheritance of whatever property or wealth belonged to the family. An older man also reported that:

'...in the past and to a lesser extent today infertile women could not be buried at the homestead or common cemetery, as this was thought to bring misfortune to the whole family. Instead she was buried in the bush, so that no one else from the family could inherit the barrenness.'

Some groups noted that the problem was due more to discrimination by the husband's family than to intramarital problems. The husband may sometimes accept the infertility of the wife, but his kin will not accept the barren woman. The discrimination by the husband's family is also clear in the women's life histories described in Chapter 8. An adolescent girl:

'I have a relative who has never had a child. She lives with her husband and he loves her but the man's relatives do not. They do not like to see her. They even have sent her several letters to that effect expressing dislike of her, and letters from her own relatives are torn before she has read them. There is hatred between her and her husband's sisters.'

The consequences of infertility were considered to be worse for a woman with no child at all than for a woman with secondary infertility. It was also pointed out that a man would be much slower to divorce a wife who had one child but did not conceive again, than a barren woman.

'A woman with at least one child is not a 'mgumba' (barren woman) and therefore not discriminated.' (Old man)

'But in some families even a woman with only one child is discriminated as the family would expect a good number of children. Especially if the only child is a daughter. The most preferable child in our culture is a boy. Indeed, in African culture a boy is a precious baby.' (Old woman)

Coping with infertility

The various groups proposed a range of coping strategies. Divorce was often mentioned. Even though polygyny is quite common among the Sukuma, the strategy of bringing another wife into a childless marriage was not a frequent response. One girl in the secondary school group discussion said she would divorce her husband if he could not give her children. Others would go for medical help, from both the modern and traditional health sectors. Most coping strategies suggested by women aim to solve the problem of male infertility. Adult women:

P1: 'If I would be married to a man and I do not conceive, I would first go to a traditional healer to confirm. If it is confirmed that I am ok, I'll stay with him for at least three years. If I still do not have a child I would resort to an outside lover (laughter). At the same time I continue having sexual intercourse with my husband. Once I become pregnant I will say that I am ill, I have to go a traditional healer somewhere. Meanwhile my pregnancy continues to advance. Then I come back to my husband, there won't be any problem. Later I get a child for my husband. Hasn't he begotten a child?'
M: 'What if the child resembles his real father and not the begotten one?'
P2: 'Ehee (laughter) still an explanation can be given that the child resembles one of his/her ancestors who might have died a decade ago!'

Older women also told us that in some families in-laws can make secret arrangements for their daughters in-law to have sex with another man so that she will conceive and have children. These children however will belong to the infertile husband, who is not aware of the secret arrangements.

Men were also asked if infertile men could allow their wives to have children from someone else, provided that it would remain a family secret. According to the men, this was not an option.

P1: *'That is not possible at all. If she cannot stay with me I would rather divorce her.'*
P2: *'If you allow a woman to sleep with another man, she will never respect you as the head of a family. It is painful to know that the children are not yours. I would not feel good. I think a woman is not even supposed to suspect that her husband has infertility problems. It is a shame.'* (Older men)

'Infertile women cannot stop their husband from marrying another woman because they are the ones with problems.' (Middle-aged man)

Only the younger respondents mentioned adoption of a child: other groups did not come up with this coping strategy. Adolescent girls suggested that orphans could be taken out of orphanages by infertile women. Another suggestion was that infertile men should marry infertile women and could ask for children from their relatives. A few ideas were given, again mostly by the younger respondents, on how to improve the status of infertile women in the community. The secondary school girls came up with three strategies: educate the community to change the traditions and customs that negatively affect the position of infertile women; establish an association of infertile women who have been chased away by their husbands, with objectives like adoption of orphans; and punishment for those who mistreat women who cannot bear children. Education for change also came up in the group discussions with middle-aged men and women.

Discussion

The analysis of group discussions with men and women in different age groups showed a number of competing and complementary discourses about infertility. Traditional explanations about womb position or the characteristics of the female eggs are still common, but easily blend with pieces of biomedical knowledge. This was most obvious in discussions with adolescent girls, who went into great detail, linking specific biomedical features of contraceptive methods to subsequent infertility. A second discourse relates to morals regarding sexual behaviour and STDs. Contrary to what has been observed in Pemba (Kielmann, 1998), where the moralizing discourse was considered a new development, there were also linkages between sexual behaviour and subsequent infertility in the past. This is illustrated by the *'wiliyanongo'*, a transgression of a postpartum sexual taboo. In other cases, respondents appear to be describing more recently developed links between sexual behaviour and infertility, for example, the promiscuous behaviour of women. However, no group mentioned an association between promiscuity and recent changes in sexual behaviour.

Side effects of modern contraceptives have been a neglected issue, which may have affected and still affects acceptance rates of modern methods of family planning.

This has also been demonstrated in a study on the other side of Lake Victoria (Rutenberg and Watkins, 1998). Our study clearly shows that 'educating' adolescents and others by providing inadequate health education and information is a step in the wrong direction. Limited knowledge about how contraceptives work appear to have made existing beliefs and rumours more scientific and perhaps more credible to women and men in the communities. There is a need to address reproductive health, including family planning, in a thorough manner within the school system and also through the health system. If adolescents' access to health services is low, special efforts to reach this age group could have great rewards for reproductive health programmes.

The group discussions also revealed substantial gender differences in attitude towards infertility. This was most obvious when the consequences of infertility were discussed. Even though there is considerable awareness of the existence of male infertility, the consequences for the inability to have children are put squarely on women's shoulders. The society has developed several mechanisms to avoid blaming men for not having children, except perhaps when impotence is the cause. It was also striking that the mens' groups did not consider the possibility that a woman can be infected by a promiscuous husband; instead they pointed to female sexual behaviour and contraceptive use as important causes of infertility. Data on sexual behaviour from surveys in the same populations indicate that married men much more frequently have extramarital sexual partners than women, although underreporting by women may play a role. However, it is unlikely that reporting bias is responsible for the entire gap between men and women. Therefore, a significant part of a married woman's risk of contracting an STD and becoming infertile comes from her own husband. This was not acknowledged by the men in our study.

The consequences of secondary infertility are less dramatic than those of primary infertility. The group discussions indicated that women who have already borne a child, but are unable to bear another, are more fortunate than barren women. The social stigma is less pronounced and it was thought that women with secondary infertility have a lower chance of divorce or rejection by their in-laws.

This study shows there still is a strong negative attitude towards infertility, which perpetuates social injustice toward infertile women. It denies women of some basic human rights, e.g. the right to be respected and the right to inherit property. There is a need for community education on infertility, and the very constructive and thoughtful contributions of adolescent secondary school girls in this study are a positive sign. In general, adolescent boys and men did not show a positive attitude: much of the educational efforts may have to be directed at males. These efforts must include raising awareness that male infertility is part of the problem, emphasizing the role of reproductive tract infections and the need for timely treatment, emphasizing the adverse effects of early onset of sex (e.g. prior to the menarche), and stressing the need to respect and support childless women.

Acknowledgements

This study was carried out in the context of the Tanzania-Netherlands project to support AIDS control in Mwanza Region (TANESA), which is funded by the Netherlands' Minister for Development Cooperation. We wish to thank our TANESA colleagues, Robert Wa-Shija, Yusufu Kumogola, Ida Bisanga, Mark Urassa and Flora Wilson, for their field work. We appreciate the assistance of Deo Luhamba who made it possible for us to include older Sukuma people. This chapter was presented as a paper at a UNAIDS/USAID/MEASURE Evaluation/CDC meeting on 'Infertility, STDs and HIV monitoring: problems and prospects', Arlington, Virginia, December 14-15 1998.

Bibliography

Bogue D (1983), 'Normative and psychic costs of contraception'. In: Bulatao RA and Lee RD (eds), *Determinants of fertility in developing countries*: Academic Press, New York: 151-192.

Caldwell JC and Caldwell P (1987), 'The cultural context of high fertility in Sub-Saharan Africa'. *Population and Development Review* 13: 409-37.

Feldman-Savelsberg P (1994), 'Plundered kitchens and empty wombs: fear of infertility in the Cameroonian grassfields'. *Social Science and Medicine* 39: 463-474.

Gerrits T (1995), 'Social and cultural aspects of infertility in Mozambique'. *Patient Education and Counseling* 31: 39-48.

Inhorn M and Buss KA (1994), 'Ethnography, epidemiology and infertility in Egypt'. *Social Science and Medicine* 39: 671-86.

Kielmann K (1998), 'Barren ground: contesting identities of infertile women in Pemba, Tanzania'. In: Lock M and Kaufert PA (eds), *Pragmatic Women and Body Politics*, Cambridge University Press, Cambridge, New York: 127-163.

Neff DL (1994), 'The social construction of infertility: the case of the matrilineal Nayars in South India'. *Social Science and Medicine* 39: 475-85.

Retel-Laurentin A (1974), 'Sub-fertility in black Africa: the case of the Nzakara in Central African Republic', In: Adadevoh BK (ed.), *Subfertility and infertility in Africa*, Caxton Press, Ibadan: 69-80.

Rutenberg N and Watkins SC (1996), 'The buzz outside the clinics: conversation and contraception in Nyanza Province, Kenya'. *Studies in Family Planning* 28: 290-307.

Biga, thought to be intended as an aid to conception (Mossi, Mali)

8 'No child to send': context and consequences of female infertility in northwest Tanzania

Marjolein Gijsels, Zaida Mgalla and Lilian Wambura

Leader:	*Daughter of Nyalama*
	What a good thing you did mother!
Chorus:	*Daughter of Nyamala you did a good thing to give birth to Doto,*
	Today mother, we go to congratulate the mother of this child!
Leader:	*Daughter of Nyalama*
	Daughter of Shizwalo
Chorus:	*Daughter of Nyalama, daughter of Shizwalo, today your upbringing,*
	Today have shown their value
	Our children go and make a home
Leader:	*Daughter of Nyalama*
	Daughter of Shizwalo
Chorus:	*Daughter of Shizwalo your teachings,*
	today have shown their value
	Our children go and make a home
Leader:	*Father Doto*
	and mother Susana
Chorus:	*Father Doto and mother Susana,*
	maintain your good hearts
	Your home will be,
	blessed by God.
Leader:	*Father Doto*
	and mother Susana
Chorus:	*Father Doto and mother Susana,*
	maintain your good hearts
	your home will be
	blessed by God.

Kisukuma song by the women's *ngoma* group '*Mwagazege*', at Nyakato, Mwanza

Anthropology has not devoted much attention to the problem of infertility, and most of the studies found in a literature search were outdated.[1] Infertility has been examined indirectly in the context of related issues such as fertility, marriage or divorce. Medical anthropology's neglect of reproductive morbidity has been recognized, and noted in the introduction to a special issue of Social Science and Medicine on infertility (Inhorn, 1994).

Although AIDS research, and the related attention to STDs, have helped to increase awareness of the extent of this problem, especially in the so called 'infertility belt' of Central Africa (Inhorn, 1994), we still lack an in-depth understanding of the cultural context and the social consequences of infertility. This chapter is intended as a contribution to such an understanding.

Methods

The life history

To gain insight into the socio-cultural context of infertility, we considered the 'anthropological life history' the most suitable approach in terms of both method and product. As a method, it provides a pattern for interaction that makes it acceptable for informants to discuss their problems. The narrative form is a pretext for retrieving some of the knowledge people possess but do not often reflect on or articulate explicitly because it is so widely shared and taken for granted. The life history is used not as a format for asking questions but to provide an occasion, or a catalyst, for the production of knowledge (Fabian, 1990: 7).

As an indigenous text, the life history has evoked critical reflections as part of the rethinking of ethnographic representation (Marcus and Fischer, 1986). Ortner (1984) indicates that there has been a strong tendency in anthropological accounts to spotlight the 'thingness' or objectivity of social forms once created. In this process the role of the author is obscured. Hence she pleads for an actor-oriented approach in which we are able to see that it is people who create meaningful history, not social and cultural systems as they impinge on a life, shape it, and turn it into an object (Ortner and Whitehead, 1981: 3).

On the other hand, there is the inclination to present mere scripts, to offer life histories as if they speak for themselves. Leaving them in the original voice follows from the assumption that life histories are, 'a direct representation of the informant's life, something almost equivalent of the informant's life' (Frank, 1979: 77). This is because the literary biography is taken as example, motivated by Western preconceptions about the role and nature of text. The life history is viewed as a fixed verbal text existing out there, ready-made and waiting for collection and analysis. In this way, it is used as a neutral tool from which the events of a person's life experience are reflected. However, the text is not the person, but a construction of the teller in interaction with the researcher. The story is, of course, determined by culture, class and gender; the tellers reproduce these contexts in a way that makes sense to them. Further, the narrative is structured by native traditions of storytelling and by specific forms that emerge through the interaction with the researcher. New ways of reading (i.e., interpreting) and writing life history texts will be needed to bypass these problems. We will analyse the documents in their own terms and focus on the tellers and how they interpret their situation and construct identity through telling.

When we listen to women's life histories we should acknowledge their own distinct 'feminine' way of expressing themselves. 'Feminist scholars have revealed that notions of objectivity are themselves androcentric, and that the higher levels of abstraction assumed to present a 'true' picture of 'reality' often represent neither truth nor reality for women' (Geiger, 1986: 338). The life histories we collected deal with tangible, domestic issues and day-to-day experiences and feelings. As personal accounts they are subjective documents that express the women's point of view. Like Martin (1987), we think that these context-specific, narrative and storylike accounts can reveal new understandings and lead to fresh insights.

Fieldwork

The study was conducted in Mwanza, the second largest town in Tanzania. It is situated on the southern shore of Lake Victoria in northwest Tanzania, where the Sukuma form the biggest ethnic group. Larsen and Raggers (Chapter 1) have found elevated levels of infertility in the area around Lake Victoria.

In total, we collected thirty life histories from women with infertility problems. We started our study at a women's centre in Mwanza town where we interviewed women in a small room. These women were bar workers, mostly rather independent and self-reliant. We also recruited respondents from the patients of a small dispensary, also in Mwanza. The head nurse was helpful, introducing us to her patients and letting us use her house for the interviews. These were ordinary, married women, glad to have found someone to discuss their problems with. The younger women were eager to talk but had the expectation of getting some real help.

We then went to Kisesa, a rural community about ten kilometres along the road which leads from Mwanza to Kenya. Initially we tried to talk to the women in a small office intended for these purposes, but they were very shy and sometimes reluctant. We also visited some women in their homes and, although they were very hospitable, they were never entirely free to talk. In some cases, the husbands requested that we wait for him so that he could participate in the interviews. In other cases, the woman was inhibited because we could be overheard by curious family members.

Infertility is defined here as the inability to give birth to a live child. A distinction is made between primary infertility, which refers to childlessness, and secondary infertility, which refers to the inability to bear a child subsequent to an earlier birth after a rather long period of exposure to the risk of pregnancy.

Three cases: Hamida, Sofia and Sharifa

In many societies throughout the world women who suffer from infertility experience grave hardships. Below we present three cases to give a first impression of the lived experiences of subfecund women in Mwanza.

Case 1: Hamida

Hamida is a bar worker. She often visits the women's centre because she is a peer health educator there. When she heard about our research she immediately presented herself, gratefully seizing the opportunity to talk to somebody who was interested in her problems. Hamida is 31 years of age. She was born out of wedlock and brought up by her grandmother. When she reached puberty the family decided it was time for her to get married. A neighbour introduced Hamida to the neighbour's brother-in-law, a soldier, but Hamida refused at first because she had heard that soldiers are cruel and was afraid that he would make her suffer. The neighbour eased her mind by saying that he was a Msukuma and that they do not mistreat their wives. The man came to propose and he agreed the brideprice with her family. He paid fifteen head of cattle. After the marriage he took her to the village of his parents. There he started to have affairs with other women. After dinner he used to put on his clothes and say he was going for a walk. When Hamida asked him where he was going he answered that it was none of her business. He stayed away all night and when he returned, Hamida prepared a bath for him. 'I thought it was normal, I was still a young girl,' she told us. What bothered her more was that he did not leave any money behind. A woman who worked in the fields with Hamida told her this was not a normal situation and, as soon as Hamida had saved the bus fare, she went back home to her parents. When her husband came after her, her parents asked him to account for his behaviour. He admitted everything but decided to take her back. She contracted gonorrhoea from him. From then on they started quarrelling. He could not understand why she would not rejoin him in his village. He started beating her and, on top of all these problems, she had not yet conceived after two years of marriage. His relatives had already been complaining for a whole year, and they told her husband to leave her because she was barren and, therefore, of no use. He divorced her and her parents returned his cattle. Hamida remained at home for two years. After that she got a job at a cotton ginnery. There she met a man and they moved to Mwanza town. She stayed with him for two years and he made her visit a traditional healer but to no avail. He became fed up and told her he could not continue living with her. After this she started working at a hotel owned by her aunt. The aunt took her to a traditional healer, again without success. In 1991 Hamida went to Geita, a small town about one hundred kilometres to the West of Mwanza, and after a month she met another man. The first thing she did was caution him that she could not have children. He said that he did not want her for children only: whatever happened was God's plan. So they started living together. The next year he took Hamida to a traditional healer but when she still had not become pregnant by the next year he started complaining and reproaching her for being barren. His family also advised him to leave her and take another woman.

She went to see another traditional healer who gave her medicines but she fell ill. Her condition became worse and her husband took her to the hospital where they decided to operate. That day her husband told her he had to go and look for some money. She did not want him to go but he reminded her that they did not have anything to eat, so she agreed. He never returned.

After the operation he arranged for Hamida's friend to take care of her. When she was dismissed from hospital she went to live with that friend. After recovery she sold her kerosene cooker to get some money for the bus fare to go and see her husband. The day she arrived they quarrelled and he shifted to another room in the house where he started to bring other women. She heard rumours that people had advised him to get rid of her for good, because her ovaries had been removed. This is how she found out. The doctor had not told her anything but had informed her husband. At this time there was a lot of shouting in the house and she decided to leave her husband. She went to visit her mother and then moved to Mwanza, where she started working in bars to earn some money. Now she has a boyfriend, a truck driver who travels a lot and who only comes to see her once in a while. He is married with a child. When he is in the area she is not even sure he will come to see her. That is why she is thinking about a man who asked her to come and live at his place as a second wife. But she hesitates. She will tell him about her problems, but what will happen later? Will he forget what she has told him, and will the suffering start all over again?

Case 2: Sofia

Sofia entered the house where we were waiting for her, announcing: 'I have the same problem that everybody has in this place'. Sofia is a traditional healer. She inherited her skills from her late grandmother, who inhibited her studies after primary school. Sofia said the grandmother caused severe headaches and blindness whenever Sofia tried to do something other than become a practising traditional healer. Her grandmother appeared to her in dreams, passing on her knowledge of herbal medicines, showing her where to find them and how to apply them to patients who would come to her the next day. Other medicine men said that it was the traditional medicine of her grandmother which prevented her from having children, but Sofia does not believe this. However, she cannot heal herself: 'A healer doesn't heal herself', she says. 'It would cause her harm to use her own medicines.' She is tired of going to hospitals where they wrongly diagnose her as being pregnant and do not have a solution for her problems. She is also tired of going to traditional healers, who have even made her drink faeces to induce vomiting so that she would be 'purified'.

She has been married for twelve years. One day, her brother-in-law came with a packet for her. It looked like a present, nicely wrapped. When she opened it there was faeces in it. He told her that it was her baby and that she should breast feed it. When her husband came home later and she told him what had happened, he said he was also fed up that she could only fill up the latrine with shit. Later her husband's maternal uncle came and told him to leave Sofia or they would ostracize him. From that moment her husband started to drink; he insulted her every day. She could not stand it anymore so they separated. Sofia earns good money nowadays. She owns a few houses and is proud of it. The only thing she misses, however, is a baby. She therefore selects her boyfriends from married men who already have children. The neighbourhood gossips about her trying a man for a few months and then exchanging him for another one when she does not become pregnant.

Case 3: Sharifa

Sharifa is a Moslem woman, dressed in black and wearing a long scarf over her head. She finished school and three years later, in 1980, became pregnant. She had a healthy daughter who is now fifteen. Two years later she became pregnant again but when the child was three years old he died of cerebral malaria. In 1988 she moved to Magu, a small district town 120 kilometres from Mwanza, where she met a man. They got married and had a baby boy together. When the child was two years old Sharifa started trading in fish; she went to Dar es Salaam often. Meanwhile she left the child with an aunt, who did not take care of him properly. He was given the leftover food, lost weight and had kwashiorkor. The only thing she could do was pray for him: eventually he died. She never became pregnant again. Her next husband complained and caused a lot of trouble as a result. He was from Pemba and had paid 20,000 shillings for her as his third wife. When, after a few months of marriage, he lost hope of having children with Sharifa, he told her he had received a message that her child had been run over by a car and that she should leave for Mwanza immediately. When she arrived there she found her child healthy. No one knew anything about a car accident. Her parents wrote a letter to Pemba asking the husband to explain himself, but Sharifa is still waiting for his response.

These stories illustrate that reproductive failure of any kind has serious social consequences and that it almost always leads to divorce. Women are stigmatized, and sometimes even ostracized, as was Sofia. In their desperate search for help, many women consult one traditional healer after another, accepting whatever is prescribed even at the risk of their health. Furthermore, there is the personal sadness and accompanying frustration of lacking children.

Cultural context

One's place in society

We know that in Africa children are highly valued and that big families are seen as a necessity. Not a single woman we interviewed did not want children.

One woman expressed this as: *Every woman cries for children.*

These norms are reflected in teknonymy, the practice, in traditional Swahili culture, of referring to the parent by the name of the firstborn, for example, '*mama Neema*'. In Sukumaland the parental relationship is indicated in the opposite way. There, a man is addressed by his father's name: he may be called '*Ng'wana Nenetwa*' which means '*the son of Nenetwa.*' It is necessary to refer to people in this way to show respect. These reproductive ideals are also expressed in rituals or poetry, as can be seen in the song at the start of this chapter. The song is sung by the female relatives of the woman who has delivered a child. They address her as their daughter. Somewhere in the song, they also address the father of the child and it becomes clear that they have a baby girl. They recite the new set of family relationships, mother, father and daughter, which are created by the birth of the first child. This establishment of relations and their respective hierarchical positions is very important in the progress of the reproductive process. In this light, the almost unanimous answer to the question of why, specifically, infertile people miss children starts to make sense.

I have to send my neighbour's child to fetch something for me.
I need a child, I send myself (when I need something), I don't even have anybody to send.

Or when we asked one of the women why her husband needs a child, she asked us rhetorically:

Could he really stay alone without a child you can send?

'A child to send' (*mtoto wa kutuma*) is a widely understood cultural concept. A dependant person from whom you can ask services adds to your status. Also, it means that one belongs somewhere in the domestic cycle. Lacking these services produces anxiety, because it shows that you have no place in the cycle.

Insurance for old age

One of the main motivations for having children was the expected support they can provide in old age:

When you grow old the child has the obligation to support you.

Another woman expressed her doubt about children she raises but who are not her own:

Can another woman's child help me when I grow old?

The elderly are usually reintegrated in the household of their children, or at least materially supported by them. Not having children means a woman will have to rely on her own family later in life.

Continuation of the lineage

Children are important in continuing the lineage. They perpetuate the life cycle in which the unborn, the young, the old and the dead are seen as united in a cycle of mortality-immortality (Robertson, 1991: 69). Rites of passage such as births, weddings and funerals take on the greatest importance since they stand for vital transitions in the reproductive cycle. People are respected as elders and then venerated as ancestors: their graves become important symbols of the continuity of the family corporation. This explains why dying without children is such an unbearable thought to many people. Such thoughts surfaced several times in the interviews.

Even one child would help me, he would cry for me when I die. But if I were to die now, there is only my mother. That is why I always pray to die before my mother.

There was one woman with infertility problems who had waited for an operation. Then she received the news that she was HIV positive. When she told her mother, her mother advised her:

Go back to the hospital and have the operation anyway. If you decide not to do so, then take traditional medicines so you can get a child. If you die, shall we not all die? It is better to have a child than to die childless.

One man told us: *There is that goal, to produce children means that the cemetery may be complete.*

Economic value

In communities where large tracts of land often have to be cultivated by relatively small numbers of people, reproduction is geared to economic activities. In these areas men are concerned with securing immediate access to labour and the production of descendants who will sustain the family corporation (Robertson, 1991: 57). They are in constant competition for able-bodied and fertile women. The agricultural instrument ubiquitously used in Africa also contributes to this situation: the hoe makes full use of women's labour and has changed remarkably little even in the modern era of commercial farming (Boserup, 1970). This need for labour helps account for the prevalence of polygyny in Africa. The more women a man accumulates the more legitimate descendants he will have, thereby ensuring a considerable workforce. Polygyny has been the privilege of wealth as well as a means to wealth (Mair, 1971: 153). The stories women told us about their first marriages fit this picture exactly, especially the tales of women from rural areas. Once puberty was reached the family started to look for a suitor, and the girl was hurried into marriage. There was no time to waste, and the new family started to look forward to the pregnancy of their daughter-in-law. When, after a few months, the girl was not yet pregnant, there was reason to be worried.

Almost all women we interviewed come from large families where eight, eleven or even fourteen children were not unusual. Now, one generation later, most of them do not see having this many children as their ideal. Apart from some desperate women who would be grateful to have at least one, most of the women interviewed reported four as the desired number. When we asked them why they did not want as many children as their parents, the standard answer was 'this was from the past, nowadays life is hard' (*maisha magumu*). There is also the more direct concern of having children to help in daily subsistence. When they are small they help with minor tasks around the house and look after their younger sisters and brothers; when they are a little older they work in the fields and tend the herds.

Marriage is exchange. It is about the transfer of the productive and reproductive capacities of a woman to her husband's family. In Sukumaland the bride's family often receives large amounts of goods, cows or cash, the 'bridewealth', which depends on what the two families have negotiated with respect to the girl's value. The most significant resource transfers may come after the marriage, endorsing the reproductive and productive progress of the union (Robertson, 1991: 58).

As one informant expressed it: *without having produced children you are still loose. … the natural and primary goal in marriage is to get children.*

Only with the birth of a child is the marriage validated. Girls are welcomed for the material gain they bring in the form of bridewealth and boys are welcomed for political reasons, such as the perpetuation of the lineage (Goody, 1976: 90).

Utasa and ugumba

In Swahili, a distinction is made between childlessness or primary infertility (*utasa*) and secondary infertility (*ugumba*), again reflecting the cultural concern with the number of children. We began our interviews with women recruited on the basis of our request for women who had 'infertility problems' (*matatizo na uzazi*). We received the most divergent stories, ranging from women who had never had a child to women who already had four daughters but now desperately wanted a son. All considered themselves to be in the category of infertile women. Each of them was very unhappy about their inability to conceive, as having no child was the least desirable position in a society in which 'a woman's most important role is to bear children.'[2] Hamida tells us how she felt when the doctor told her she would never be able to bear children.

Hamida: *I only felt pain when he told me for the first time. I trembled all over, I felt as if I were not in this world, as if I were nothing. I didn't see the point of remaining in this world, without a child and so many problems because of this.*
Interviewer: *This world is not only for bearing children, Hamida.*
Hamida: *But whenever I remember I feel very sad.*
Interviewer: *Some get children, but they become thieves or rude people.*
Hamida: *Even when he becomes a thief but he is healthy, it consoles you.*

When a woman has her first baby her identity changes. She can function in the community as a normal person without the social condemnation that someone without children would experience. Helena only had one child, who is now 22 years old. Since then she has never been pregnant. Helena's mother-in-law reconciles herself to the situation.

She says: *At least she has got a name, mama Atieno; that is enough.*

But one child is not a safeguard from disapproval of her situation: her sister-in-law, who herself has nine children, troubles her with the same old comments that she causes loss to her brother and that he had better marry someone else. This sentiment indicates that people do not think it is enough to have only one child.

Helena has a strong desire for more children and tells us: *Only one is bad.*
Another woman explained: *Take me for example. I have one child, yet according to our traditions one child is like I don't have any. It is like I have not conceived at all. And later, if it happens that I would get married to another man who doesn't have children yet and I fail to bear a child with him, he would be very unhappy. He would even think that it was better to marry someone who had not conceived at all before.*

When a woman's husband dies or leaves her because she does not become pregnant, there is always the pressure to remarry. Not many women choose to stay alone, as they would then be called *nshimbe*. *Nshimbe*[3] is a term that is mostly used in a derogatory sense. When the woman eventually remarries, sooner or later the wish for children will arise, as it is the primary goal of marriage. As most women made clear in their stories, the husband will be very disappointed if his wife does not become pregnant, despite her warnings of these problems before marriage. Situations like these help us to understand why women who already have one or more children are in such desperate need of another. This is especially the case when they remarry.

There is another reason why women with secondary infertility may feel miserable and consider themselves as good as childless. In the case of divorce, such a woman will have to leave her child behind with the man who has paid bridewealth for her. For example, Shakira had a baby boy with her second husband, who used to drink and beat her. She decided to leave him, and the boy remained with his father. Later she met another man with whom she had a baby girl. She then had a second baby girl, who died. When Shakira went to a traditional healer to find out why her baby had died, he told her that her family-in-law had bewitched the baby because they wanted a boy instead of a girl. Her aunt advised her to leave, so she left. Now she has been living with a man for four years, but they are still waiting for a child.

Interviewer: *But at least you have children. Why do you put yourself in this group of women with infertility problems? You have children.*
Shakira: *That is because the boy is not with me but with his father and the girl also has her father. Both have been taken away. I am alone. I have children but I am alone and lonely. I don't have children.*

These same patriarchal norms account for the women's preference for boys. For a woman, the most reliable persons in old age appear to be her sons.[4] As Shakira explains:

Shakira: *I need a boy.*
Interviewer: *Why a boy?*
Shakira: *He will help me when he gets married.*
Interviewer: *Can you send a boy to cook? I think a daughter will help you to wash clothes, to cook.*
Shakira: *A boy can cook. My first born is big now and when he comes I don't cook. He cooks for me.*
Interviewer: *So you feel that Betty [her daughter] is enough?*
Shakira: *Betty belongs to others. She can get married. A son will also get his home but he will remember me when I am old and help me.*
Interviewer: *Can a girl not help you?*
Shakira: *A daughter will have to ask her husband for something to take to her mother. When mother needs new clothes or something else she will first have to ask permission to get it for her.*

Explanations and cures

The women utilized different sources to explain their infertility, as well as for therapy. Some went to hospitals and others consulted traditional healers. Most combined biomedical with ethnomedical interpretations to help understand their problems. Most of the women were not aware of the connection between STDs and infertility. When we asked if they had ever had an STD, many told us they had. Most had contracted STDs from unfaithful husbands, but they never seemed to trace their current difficulties back to this. The cause of infertility, they suggested, was the use of contraceptives over a long period. Some mentioned that not every type of blood matched (*damu hazipatani*).

Many traditional healers in this area specialized in infertility problems (Pool and Washija, Chapter 10). Their most common diagnosis is related to *mchango* (*nzoka* in Kisukuma), which means 'snake' or 'worm' and is a key concept in local etiology. According to this belief, the body contains snakes or worms, which have to be kept in balance by taking good care of the body and keeping it healthy. When something goes wrong the *mchango* will make itself felt in the form of pains or other ailments. Witchcrafts, for instance, can influence the *mchango*: a curse can disturb the balance and rouse the *mchango* under certain circumstances. For example, one woman suffered from a curse caused by her deceased grandmother. She had a *mchango* that attacked the foetus and destroyed it from the moment she became pregnant. But a *mchango* can manifest itself under much more ordinary circumstances too. It can be cured by drinking herbs, smearing them onto the skin, bathing with them or inserting them into bodily orifices. The other common cause of infertility was *mgongo umepinda*. Literally, this means 'the back is bent'. This was explained as follows: the womb and reproductive organs were repressed by other organs and as a result did not have enough space to develop; they remained very small at the side of the back. This malformation was thought to be caused by the early onset of sexual intercourse among women, especially before puberty. Mothers warn their young daughters that the penis of a man can push their reproductive organs to the back, which will later lead to infertility.

Most women said they had visited innumerable traditional healers in the hope of getting help for their problems. When they hear about someone who has a good reputation in this field they are prepared to travel to other parts of the country if they have the money. The different traditional healers they end up consulting in this way approach care in one of two ways: they may work with herbal medicines or focus more on rituals.

Male versus female perspectives

When a man is infertile, his wife will get the blame. Men are protected from blame by patriarchal ideology. Manhood is linked to sexual desire and ability to father children. It gives men esteem, respect and, therefore, power over their wives, family and in society at large. If men are unable to father children it is so shameful that they said:[5]

I would rather be dead.
This is a reason for suicide.
There is no need to get married again.

In the past, when boys reached puberty they were carefully watched; family members could even enquire about their sexual reputation. If the boy eventually got married and the family's suspicion that he was infertile was confirmed, arrangements could be made. For example, the mother-in-law could arrange that her daughter be approached for sex by another man, such as the husband's relative. If she became pregnant, she would never disclose how it happened, and she and her husband would carry on with their lives and have a child. Even today, boys are observed.

One man told us: *When the boy's father has not noticed him showing interest in girls he is likely to ask what is wrong with him. It is good if the boy is, on some occasion, blamed for mischief with girls.*

This same view is reflected in the comments of one woman: *A woman is only for the husband, the husband is for everyone. A man needs variety, one day he likes his ugali with chicken the other day with mchicha and then another day with fish. Never challenge a man, 'What kind of a man are you.' He will rape you.*

Sleeping around is a sign of a man's virility and socially it receives less criticism than for a woman. There is also a general belief that a man cannot be infertile, that the cause always lies with the woman.

One man expressed it like this: *A man knows that infertility is a woman's problem.* Another man said: *Three quarters of the reproduction process happens inside the woman, she is the person responsible for all this.* Another argued: *It is only women who have infertility problems.*

Interviewer: *How do you know that?*
Man: *Have you ever seen a man with difficulties in that area?*
Interviewer: *Have you done research on this topic?*
Man: *No, but I never encountered a man with such problems, it is always the women.*

During our research we talked to two women who suspected that their husbands were the cause of their problems. One of the women's stories is illustrative: Asha had three children from her first marriage. When she divorced she had to leave the two oldest with her husband, but because the youngest one was too small, Asha took the child with her. Now she has been married to another man for five years. They still have not had children. Her husband had been married for two years to a woman who also did not conceive. Initially, when she did not become pregnant her husband took Asha to traditional healers. When she went to a gynaecologist in the hospital he told her that there was nothing wrong with her. But her sisters-in-law blamed her for not having children and they brought a young girl to their brother as his second wife. After two years of marriage there were still no children and now they are taking the girl to traditional healers. When Asha asked her husband why he did not go to the hospital he answered that he had already gone for a check up and that everything was all right. Besides, he already had children outside marriage whom he supported financially. He therefore saw no reason to doubt his 'fitness'. Still, Asha suspects that these are not his children but that the woman pretends, for the economic support she receives, and also to save him from social stigma.

Men are afraid of losing their power over their wives and other family members. When a man cannot reproduce it is said that he is not a proper man, and that he cannot fulfil his male tasks properly. A man who is infertile will be challenged by his wife, and she will take control saying, 'No no, you're not a man, leave everything to me.' It may be a public secret that a man cannot father children and this may be obvious to the parents and his wives. However, it will not be admitted; his wives will act as a shield and divert the blame.

Women, on the other hand, reported not considering divorce as their first option if their husband proved infertile. They said they would stay with their husband as long as he was good to them and gave them economic support.

Social consequences

Divorce

When a woman does not get pregnant fast enough, and the husband or the in-laws become impatient, they can decide to divorce her and they will claim back the cows they have paid for her. The main reason that women with infertility problems came and talked with us was the hope of getting help and saving their marriages. Marriage is under constant threat when infertility is suspected.

One woman expressed her fear: *Now my parents-in-law like me very much but there will come a time that they will hate me. They will lose their patience.* Another woman's parents-in-law gave her the following advice: *Keep on trying. If your husband can heal you, you stay. He will look for medicines for you. When he refuses, then go away so that the bridewealth can be refunded to us.*

The men we interviewed on this topic all gave the same answer to our question of what they would do if their wife failed to conceive. All of them, regardless of differences in education, answered that they would take another wife.

Respondent: *I would marry another wife.*
Interviewer: *Would you retain the first wife or would you leave her?*
Respondent: *No, it is not good to chase a woman away even if she is barren. We don't like doing that. She will be there. And you talk to her and agree that it is impossible to stay like this, she will allow you to marry another wife.*
Interviewer: *Won't she refuse?*
Respondent: *Some stubborn ones will refuse.*
Interviewer: *What would you do if she refuses?*
Respondent: *Then we give up and divorce.*
Interviewer: *She leaves, or you bring another one then it is up to her to decide if she stays.*
Respondent: *Yes, you bring another one by force, if she wants to she can stay, if she doesn't want to, that's it.*

We can learn from the accusations women hear from their husbands, in-laws or the neighbours.

Lucy's husband tells her: *Women who don't bear children are a terrible problem (shida tupu).* Her co-wife comments: *She only eats (anakula tu).*
Betty finds out that the neighbours talk about her: *That one doesn't bear children (hazai), she only gets fat without getting pregnant.* She also tells us what her future will look like if she does not conceive: *You will be shocked to find a new wife who gets children and I will be hit and kicked out because I am eating his food for nothing (unakula tu bure).*
Lilian's sisters-in-law tell her husband: *She doesn't bear children (hazai), she is wasting your time (anakupoteza muda).*
After two years of marriage Esther's husband tells her sister: *I cannot stay with a woman who doesn't bear children, this woman is deficient (hafai).* She herself poses us the rhetorical question: *When cows are given for you and you get chased, what profit (faida) do you have?*
Pendo's in-laws advise her husband: *Chase her away (umfukuze), she doesn't bear children (hazai); she is wasting your time (anakupoteza muda).*

Betty tells us about her experience of having a baby after many years of struggling to get pregnant, and others join in:

Interviewer: *It is good that you at least have got one.*
Betty: *(It is) profit (nafuu).*
Dunia tells us: *They laugh at you. If one has paid bridewealth will he stop telling you? You will hear your sisters-in-law!*
Interviewer: *So if one marries and pays bridewealth he wants you to have children?*
Dunia: *You must have children. That is the profit (faida), children, for the bridewealth he paid.*
Interviewer: *So if you don't have children they see it as a loss (hasara)?*
Dunia: *It is a loss (hasara).*

These reproaches all boil down to the same thing: to have children is profit and the inability to have children is loss. *Faida, nafuu* and *hasara* are purely economic terms and are applied in the context of marriage to remind us that the woman owes children to her husband and his family. After all, it was to obtain the reproductive services of the woman that they invested the family capital. It then becomes understandable that not getting anything in return is seen as a terrible loss. The woman loses her value (*hafai*: she is no good) and also her esteem (*ni shida tupu*: she is a terrible problem). Once this is established (*hazai*: she doesn't bear children) the only way to get the capital back is to get rid of the woman as quickly as possible (*umfukuze, anakupoteza muda*: chase her away, she is wasting your time) who has become a burden anyway, a mere consumer (*anakula tu bure*: she is only eating for nothing).

Neglect

In some cases, no divorce will be demanded but the woman will be neglected, which will also eventually lead to separation. In this case, the decision to leave will be up to the woman.

Esther told us about her first marriage: *He stayed in another town where he had other women. He never sent me even a little money or some soap. It was as if I was born at his home (i.e., living with her parents-in-law). One day my neighbours told me that I was a fool to continue living there, as if I was married to my in-laws. The next day I took a bucket as though I was going to draw water. When I reached the well I ran away.*

Teddy told us, crying: *When I asked him for money he told me I had to fend for myself. Or he took something from the house, saying that he had to feed the children he has with my co-wife. Can I be happy, really?*

Juliana told us: *In the past my husband took me to traditional healers, but now he has given up on me and refuses to give me money. He took another woman and brought her home. He has given some of my things, like my watch, to her. There was a lot of commotion at home; how could she take my property and wear it?*

Marriage and polygyny

Only a few women with infertility problems had managed to stay married. They lived in polygamous unions after their husbands had added a second, fertile wife. These infertile women are vital to the functioning of the household:

Lucy still stays with her husband, she tells us at what price: *He brought another woman with whom he had three children. She was very quarrelsome, not one day passed without shouting or fighting. She left and came back and left and came back. Finally she left for good leaving the children with me. She said, 'This woman is only eating for free so her work will be to take care of the children.' Later my husband again took another woman who lives somewhere else. They have one child together. He spends a lot of time there. He leaves me and I don't know when he will come back again and in the meanwhile I have to manage with the children. He leaves money for them, but when I am worried he tells me to go to his parents for help. When he complains about me I sometimes tell him to take me back to my parents, but until now he has never done this.*

Here it is obvious that Lucy is indispensable: otherwise the task of educating her husband's children would fall on his mother. Lucy makes herself useful, and that is why she is still tolerated and not yet divorced or neglected. However, this is not a satisfactory solution for these women, as they are still blamed for their infertility and are treated as instruments for keeping the household running. In these women's stories the lack of emotional involvement by the husbands in their wives' fate is striking.

Betty predicted her future: *There will come a time that they will tell him to divorce me and I will be like an 'aunt' my friend [i.e., she will never be a mother]. There will be no more love for me. There will be only abuse which will cause me high blood pressure. If a baby is born and happens to fall down they will ask me why he is falling. Then you can only look at them.*

This example, as well as the stories of Juliana and Teddy in which the husband withdraws all material support, shows that these women are discarded: they do not receive any more attention from their husband or his family. It seems as if the conjugal relationship is based less on affection than on the transactional component that was the initial motivation for the marriage.

Fostering

Some form of adoption of children exists. Frequently it happens that a child will be sent to a family member who is in need of help. For example, a person may be ill and need someone to look after younger children. Sometimes an older brother takes his younger brother or sister under his wing because he can afford to send them to school. These children can stay for extended periods. One woman with infertility problems had never had a child, but her brother gave her one of his daughters to keep her company. She said that she considered the girl as her own.[6] However, when we suggested this possibility to other women with infertility problems, they answered that they would never dare to ask family members for such a favour, as they would be laughed at because they were not able to produce their own children. In case of a conflict between husband and wife, when the wife has been sent back home to her parents and becomes pregnant by another man while she is there, the children are assumed to be the lawful offspring of the husband, if he decides to take the woman back. In such a case, the biological father could be accused of adultery if he claimed the child. This could be seen as another form of adoption, though it is not considered as such.

Conclusion

Infertility is a tragedy in a woman's life. Marriage is expected, and the main aim of marriage is reproduction. Bridewealth is the payment for the productive and reproductive services of the woman to the husband's family. When a marriage is contracted, the couple is expected to have children as soon as possible. The desire to have children is very strong, for women as well as for men; there is no one who chooses a life without them. Femininity and masculinity are measured by fertility.

Factors like infant mortality, short life spans due to poor medical care, and the economic utility of children due to the lack of geriatric institutions and financial provisions for care are the reasons for the emphasis on the number of children. Children are the evidence of status in the domestic hierarchy and are expected to support their parents in old age. Domestic organization depends heavily on the authority of parent over child. People are therefore concerned with high fertility.

To be totally without children has the most consequences for a woman. It puts her identity and status at risk, and it is almost always fatal to her marriage. Secondary infertility, however, is also experienced as a serious problem, particularly in case of divorce, after which the child remains with the father in accord with patriarchal norms. Social pressure forces women to remarry and try to have children.

A woman who cannot conceive is considered to cause 'loss' to her husband. Reproduction is thought of in economic terms. The husband and his family sees a woman with infertility problems as deficient, and will decide to return the woman to her family. The bridewealth must then be returned. Divorce, neglect by the husband or withdrawal of economic support are the direct consequences for an infertile woman. If men have infertility problems they are protected by patriarchal society; their problem will be hidden from outsiders and the wives will receive the blame.

Infertility may also be a risk factor for HIV and STDs. Infertile women have to cope with unfaithful husbands more often than other women, because these men are under pressure to prove their fertility outside marriage. Women with infertility problems are frequently abandoned by their husbands and have to make their own living. Often bar work and prostitution are the only options. Many have a history of several marriages and divorces, and in their desperate quest for children they are more likely to exhibit risky sexual behaviour.

The institution of polygyny among the Wasukuma is not a satisfactory solution for an infertile woman. She will first have to prove herself indispensable to the household while the other, fertile, wife receives all the respect and attention. Rather, the form of adoption that exists among family members appears to be a better mechanism for coping with infertility in this particular African context.

Acknowledgement

The study was conducted in the context of the Tanzania-Netherlands project to support AIDS control in Mwanza Region, Tanzania (TANESA), a project funded by the Netherlands' Minister for Development Cooperation.

Notes

1. We found: David and Voas, 1981; Meuwissen, 1966; and Barlovatz, 1955.

2. This was a recurring remark throughout the interviews.

3. In English 'spinster' is a similar term, but this only refers to women who have never been married. *Nshimbe* denotes unmarried women, whether they have been married before or not.

4. In this regard Robertson (1991: 58) remarks: 'In her middle years, when she has accomplished her reproductive tasks for her husband's family, a woman is most at risk of losing direct

access to the productive resources needed for her own continued survival. Her declining physical capacity makes her more dependent on relatives of her own.'

5. This section is based on the life histories of the women. In addition, we conducted some interviews with men covering their ideas on infertility, which supplied the expressions quoted. Their opinions confirmed what was suggested by women's life histories.

6. Separate research involving interviews with sixty women over thirty years of age with one or two children in a rural area just outside Mwanza town found 17% who had initially reported a child as their own, while the in-depth interview showed that it was a child of another family member.

Bibliography

Barlovatz MD (1955), 'Sterility in Central Africa'. *Fertility and Sterility* 6: 363-373.

Boerma JT, Urassa M and Isingo R (1996), 'Infertility and its Association with Sexual Behaviour, STD and HIV Infection in Tanzania'. *IUSSP seminar on innovative approaches to the measurement of reproductive health*, Manila, Phillipines.

Boserup E (1970), *Woman's role in economic development*, Allen & Unwin, London.

David N and Voas D (1981), 'Societal causes of infertility and population decline among the settled Fulani of Northern Cameroon'. *MAN* 16: 644-64.

Fabian J (1990), *Power and performance. ethnographic explorations through proverbial wisdom and theatre in Shaba, Zaire*. University of Wisconsin Press, Madison.

Frank G (1979), 'Finding the common denominator: a phenomenological critique of life history method'. *Ethos* 7: 69-94.

Geiger S (1986), 'Women's life histories: method and content'. *Signs* 11: 334-351.

Goody J (1976), *Production and reproduction: a comparative study of the domestic domain*, Cambridge University Press, Cambridge.

Inhorn M (1994), 'Interpreting infertility: medical anthropological perspectives'. *Social Science and Medicine* 39: 459-461.

Larsen U (1993), 'Levels, age patterns and trends of sterility in selected countries south of the Sahara'. *IUSSP General Conference Proceedings*, Montreal: 593-603.

Marcus GE and Fisher M (1986), *Anthropology as a cultural critique: an experimental moment in the human sciences*, University of Chicago Press, Chicago.

Mair L (1971), *Marriage*. Penguin, Harmondsworth.

Martin E (1987), *The woman in the body: a cultural analysis of reproduction*. Beacon Press, Boston.

Meuwissen JH (1966), 'Natality and marital infertility in Ghana'. *Tropical and Geographical Medicine* 18: 153-6.

Ortner S (1984), 'Theory in anthropology since the sixties'. *Comparative studies in society and history* 26: 126-66.

Ortner S and Whitehead H (1981), *Sexual meanings: the cultural construction of gender and sexuality*, Cambridge University Press, New York.

Robertson AF (1991), *Beyond the family: the social organization of human reproduction*, Polity Press, Oxford.

Ngide, used by childless women to induce fertility
(Turkana, Kenya)

9 Mchango, menses and the quality of eggs: women's perceptions of fertility risks

Denise M. Roth Allen

'Mimi kweli, nitamnyesha mtoto?' ('Will I ever really breast-feed a child?')
A Tanzanian woman laments her inability to conceive

'I was so happy [during labour]. I couldn't believe I was finally having a baby. The whole time I was pushing, I kept asking myself, Is this really me giving birth?'
A Tanzanian friend on her first birth experience after four miscarriages

Risk is a common concept in studies of health and illness. The definition of risk usually determines the type of health interventions that will be proposed. In much of the international public health literature on maternal health, for example, risks are often defined in terms of the direct and indirect medical factors that contribute to the high levels of maternal mortality seen in many of the world's poorer countries. Two examples of health care interventions that aim to address risks to maternal health are, first, the provision of prenatal care to identify women at risk of birth complications and, second, the use of family planning to reduce the health consequences associated with too many or too closely spaced pregnancies (WHO, 1996a).

This chapter presents data from an anthropological study of the cultural construction of risk during pregnancy and childbirth. This provides a means of examining an alternative set of risk factors and solutions associated with fertility and maternal health outcomes in 'Bulangwa', a small, culturally heterogeneous community in west-central Tanzania.[1] In contrast to the international and national concern with the health risks associated with 'excessive' fertility (Herz and Measham, 1987; Kaisi, 1989; WHO, 1996b), this chapter focuses on women's concerns about the risk of 'unsuccessful' fertility. As the two quotations that open the chapter suggest, the notion of 'unsuccessful fertility' reflects a range of fertility-related conditions - from those that prevent conception to those that prevent a woman from carrying a pregnancy to term.

In addition to considering how women in this small community define risks to their own fertility or that of their family members, we shall look at ways some of those risks are diagnosed and treated outside the biomedical context. As the following pages show, risks in this context are said to have spiritual as well as physical properties which, unless prevented or counteracted, could have disastrous effects on the procreative ability of both women and men and hence on their ability to achieve the valued social position of 'parent' within the community.

This chapter is based on the premise that an understanding of the context in which health problems occur is essential if health outcomes are to be improved (Bibeau, 1997; Yoder, 1997). In the setting of the community of 'Bulangwa' specifically, we shall see that the context of fertility and maternal health outcomes is rich, though complex. This context draws simultaneously upon a widespread acknowledgement of ancestral and non-ancestral influences upon fertility, on local beliefs about bodily processes, and on individual perceptions of the ability of biomedicine to effectively address their concerns about reproduction. Although the ways these beliefs and practices affect fertility and maternal health outcomes is difficult to quantify, it is nevertheless important that they are documented, acknowledged, and incorporated into health care programming. Such acknowledgement is essential if biomedical interventions offering reproductive health care within particular local settings are to remain relevant to realities and constraints of people's everyday lives.

I begin with a brief presentation of some of the ethnographic literature on the culturally and linguistically related Sukuma and Nyamwezi peoples, the predominant ethnic groups living in west-central Tanzania (Brandström, 1986). In particular, I shall focus on the ways various authors have discussed the central place of fertility and parenthood in Sukuma and Nyamwezi culture and the significant part ancestral spirits can be said to play in the fertility of their living descendants.

The second part of the chapter will introduce Mwana Nyanzanga, a woman whose work I observed during twenty-two months of fieldwork. Mwana Nyanzanga refers to herself both as a *mganga wa wanawake* (a healer of women) and as a member of an ethnic group that is neither Sukuma nor Nyamwezi.[2] Although she is not Sukuma herself, the majority of her clientele are. Many of them come to her from surrounding villages in search of treatment for a variety of fertility-related problems as well as to give birth. Through my observations of her work I was able to identify categories of infertility problems as they emerged in her healing practice. I intersperse my discussion of these observations with the results of two group interviews with women who lived in the same village as Mwana Nyanzanga, and also with results from my formal interviews with 154 women about their experiences with pregnancy and childbirth.[3] These latter interviews illustrate the ways the categories of risk addressed by Mwana Nyanzanga in her healing practice are relevant to the general population of women in Bulangwa. Most of the local terms used are Swahili, the national language of Tanzania; when Sukuma terms are used this is noted in the text.

Fertility and parenthood in 'Sukuma-Nyamwezi thought and reality'

According to the anthropologist Per Brandström (1990: 167), although there is no single word in the Sukuma language to express the notion of fertility, 'the fact of life, its generation, maintenance and regeneration, stands ... at the core of Sukuma-Nyamwezi thought and imagery.'[4] These themes of generation and regeneration are present in a variety of contexts: in aspects of agricultural life and the relation of the people to the land; in social and reproductive relations between men and women; and in ritual life as regards the relationship between the living and the dead.

Given the absence of a single word to convey the concept of fertility, Brandström states that discussions of fertility require the use of metaphor, analogy, or a series of descriptive phrases. Drawing from his own research and that of past ethnographers of the Sukuma and Nyamwezi peoples, he shows how agricultural metaphors are used to capture male and female roles in the reproductive process (Brandström, 1990; Bösch, 1930). From the perspective of his male informants, the female role in the reproductive process is passive; women are the containers for men's seed, while pregnant women are merely 'sacks filled with sorghum' (Brandström, 1990: 170). He notes, however, that women wittily contest men's representations of their role as passive. Women see themselves as the major players in the reproductive process, since they conceive and give birth to children. Brandström suggests that it is precisely this continuous and unresolved competition of words between men and women that illustrates not only the differences between male and female roles in reproduction, but also their complementarity (Brandström, 1990: 170-1).

With regard to notions of parenthood and kinship, Brandström (1991) explains how the union of the core symbols of fatherhood (*buta*) and motherhood (*migongo*)[5] represent the totality of all kin related through blood and womb. *Buta*, or bow, represents male qualities as well as the living or dead paternal relatives (the 'left' side); *migongo*, or back, refers to female qualities and the living or dead maternal relatives (the 'right' side). These symbols of parenthood represent the individual strengths of each side; when joined together they represent the two halves that make a person whole, as illustrated in the concept of kinship (*budugu*). In other words, both the living and the dead are included in a person's 'kin' (*badugu*).

Relatives who have died, however, differ from the living in significant ways. Most importantly, they have the power to positively or negatively affect the lives of their living descendants. Through that power they are transformed into entities known as *masamva* or *mizimu* (Brandström, 1990; Blöhm, 1933; Bösch, 1930; Cory, 1960; Hendriks, 1988). Ancestral power was believed to be particularly significant in the context of fertility, the success or failure of which was considered to be directly linked to interventions by ancestral spirits (Tanner, 1958). According to Kang'wezi (1974), ancestors make their displeasure and specific demands known by possessing one or more of their living descendants, a phenomenon he refers to as 'being visited by relatives (*kunsangwa badugu, mahugi, or masamva*)'. Kang'wezi also notes that women - especially those aged 35 and over - are seen as being particularly vulnerable to this form of ancestral displeasure. He suggests that women so 'visited' often show the signs of 'a person badly needing a mental sanatorium': they cry, howl, shout and talk in some strange language, and kick their legs as if they were dying.

During my interviews with women about their experiences during pregnancy and childbirth, I also asked them about possession by spirits. Fifty-eight per cent of the 154 women interviewed believed women were much more likely to experience possession then men, 31% believed that men and women experienced possession to the same extent, while only 7% believed that men experienced possession more often than women. When I first began asking about possession, I did not realize that various categories of possession existed, nor that the spirits were portrayed as having 'ethnicities' or 'genders'. My aim was simply to get a sense of how many women had experienced possession. These ethnic and gender distinctions did not occur to me until women themselves mentioned them in response to my question as to how they initially knew they were possessed. Some women told me they had started speaking the Maasai or the Taturu language or that they had asked for a sheep. When I asked about the significance of the sheep, I was told that it was the offering requested by ancestors from a mother's side (matrilineal ancestors). Other women told me a sheep was the offering that *female* ancestors demanded. Some women expressed the belief that women could only be possessed by matrilineal ancestors, while others told me women could also experience possession by their patrilineal ancestors. According to some women in the study, patrilineal ancestors demanded that a goat be kept or slaughtered in their honour (Tanner, 1958). Women in the survey also spoke about possession by Muslim spirits (*majini* plural, *jini* singular). *Majini* were not considered ancestral spirits, but rather outsiders who 'came' primarily from Mecca or Oman (Boddy, 1989; Janzen, 1992; Giles, 1989). Although possession by a *jini* was much more common among the Muslim population in the community, non-Muslims were also known to experience this form of possession.[6]

Mwana Nyanzanga (the non-Sukuma healer whose work will be examined in more detail below) once told me that although she believes ancestors can affect a woman's fertility and pregnancy outcome, she refuses to treat her client's health problems by prescribing ritual offerings to their ancestors as part of the cure. For example, she would not tell her clients to keep a sheep or wear a copper bracelet, the usual offerings to a person's matrilineal ancestors. She believed ancestral offerings as a form of treatment were dangerous in two distinct ways. First, attention to ancestors could lead to death, as in the case of a man she knew who was initiated as a healer and then drowned while ritually bathing in the river. Second, a healer might mistakenly identify an illness as ancestor-induced when in fact it was caused by sorcery.[7] She saw this misidentification of etiology as a serious risk, believing it could lead to death by delaying 'proper' treatment of the afflicted person. In instances where her clients' ancestors appeared to be actively inhibiting their cure, she first symbolically 'tied the ancestor up' (*kufunga mzimu*) by momentarily placing a necklace made of materials with spiritual properties around the persons neck. She told me this worked by making the ancestor 'lie down' or 'sleep' (*ilale kwanza*), allowing her herbal treatment to begin, uninhibited by the feisty ancestor.

She then described to me the case of one of her Sukuma clients. This particular woman had come to her several years before with childbearing problems. Although the woman experienced no problems in becoming pregnant or giving birth, her children always died within their first year of life. The relatives who accompanied the woman told Mwana Nyanzanga her problem was caused by an ancestor. Upon hearing this, Mwana Nyanzanga told the woman's relatives that she didn't treat illnesses by paying attention to ancestral spirits because she was a Christian (*Mimi ni Mkristo!*). Later that same night, after they had all gone to bed, the woman - or rather, her ancestor - began shouting, 'Bring me my sheep! Bring me my sheep!' (*Nileteni kondoo yangu, nileteni kondoo yangu !*). Mwana Nyanzanga refused. She recounted to me in Swahili what she had told the woman's relatives in Sukuma: 'Me, I don't want to bring someone her sheep. I don't want to, nor have I ever seen that when a person goes to a hospital for treatment, she goes with a sheep. I've never seen that! I don't like it at all that ancestral spirits say they want to be brought a sheep!'[8] Nevertheless, she did tie up the woman's ancestor and continued with her herbal treatment. The woman now has two grown children, Elizabeth and David.[9] However, despite her proclaimed aversion to dealing with ancestral spirits, Mwana Nyanzanga herself invokes the names of her female matrilineal ancestors when she uses particular spiritual medicines.

As the above example shows, the treatment of fertility concerns in a culturally heterogeneous context highlights the fluid nature of cultural beliefs and practices. Even though people may draw upon widely held cultural notions, these beliefs and practices are not static; there is room for negotiation. Although the woman and her relatives were convinced that the source of her problem lay with a displeased ancestor, they were willing to follow the advice of a non-Sukuma healer who, although she acknowledged the possibility of ancestral intervention, nevertheless refused to address this displeasure in the manner to which they were accustomed.

Although the possibility of ancestral spiritual influence on fertility outcomes was widely acknowledged in 'Bulangwa', it is important to note that it was not seen as the *only* cause of fertility-related problems, nor did it appear to be the predominant one. The other fertility-related concerns that emerged in my discussions with women can be classified into two distinct, but not mutually exclusive, categories of risk: physical and spiritual. As we will see below, physical risks appear to be a direct result of bodily processes, whereas spiritual risks refer to outside influences that affect bodily processes.

Specific infertility risks

Physical risks to fertility

Wombs, eggs, and seed
Women in 'Bulangwa' used a variety of terms to convey the notion of fertility.[10] Although these terms were most often applied to women's ability to conceive and bear children, some also referred to men's ability to father children. For example, both male and female infertility can be expressed in general terms, as in 'not having the ability to procreate' (*hana uzazi*). Further, a woman might be referred to as 'not having eggs' (*hana mayai*) whereas an infertile man might be referred to as 'not having seed' (*hana mbegu*). A variety of terms specifically describe varying degrees of women's fertility. A woman's general fertility (*uzazi*) may be described as 'far away' (*uzazi wa mbali*) if she has difficulty conceiving, or 'close' (*uzazi wa karibu*) if she has no difficulty conceiving. *Mgongo* (again, literally the back or the back part of the body), is also used in the context of fertility.[11] A woman who has difficulty becoming pregnant or experiences unwanted delays between pregnancies is described as having a 'hard' or 'difficult' back (*mgongo ngumu*), whereas those women who become pregnant without difficulty or perhaps even too quickly are referred to as having an 'easy' or 'light' back (*mgongo upesi*).

The position of a woman's cervix or womb may be seen as the cause of her infertility. In terms of the cervix, which Mwana Nyanzanga referred to as 'the door to the womb' (*mlango ya kizazi*), infertility can occur if the 'door' is facing in the wrong direction. The proper position of the door was directly in the middle, ready to receive the man's seed (*Ni lazima ikai kati-kati, tayari kupokea mbegu za mwanaume*). Conception was seen as impossible if the 'door' was facing straight up, straight down, or completely towards the back. Infertility could also occur if a woman's entire womb was 'off to the side' (*kizazi cha upande*) or 'missing' altogether (*hana kizazi*).

The term *mlango* (door) was also used to refer to the vaginal opening. *Itale*, a Sukuma word, refers to a condition in which the vagina is covered by an extremely thick membrane. Although I never saw a case of it myself, I learned about this condition in my interviews with women who had undergone training to become 'traditional' birth attendants (Roth, 1996: 154-61). *Itale* was linked to infertility not only because it made sexual intercourse physically impossible but also because it was often accompanied by a very late onset of puberty. Many women who have this condition, I was told, do not develop breasts. Although this condition was not talked about openly, when I asked people to describe the symptoms, the descriptions were always similar. In the past, I was told, this condition was 'cured' by piercing the thick membrane with an arrow (*isonga* in Sukuma), whereas nowadays parents take their child to the hospital.[12] In my formal survey, *itale* or 'never developing breasts' (*maziwa hayioti* in Swahili) was listed by three people as one of the causes of infertility.

The notion of fertility was also expressed in terms of a woman having or not having eggs (*mayai* in Swahili, *magi* in Sukuma; Varkevisser, 1973). With regard to infertility, a woman's eggs were described as being cold (*baridi*), covered (*kufunikwa*), cooked (*kupikwa*), few (*machache*), far away (*mbali*) or completely finished (*kumaliza mayai*). Herbal remedies are used to enhance the quality of a woman's eggs or to 'repair' eggs that have been damaged. However, if a woman is unfortunate enough to be born without eggs, or with only a few, there is nothing, ritual or medicinal, that can be done to treat the specific problem.

'Late' pregnancies

A woman's infertility might also be expressed in terms of time: she may describe herself, or be described by others, as being 'late' in becoming pregnant (*amechelewa kupata mimba*) or in giving birth (*amechelewa kuzaa*). In my formal survey, 29% of the 151 women who were asked if they had ever been late becoming pregnant said they had. But 'late' is relative: what is considered late for one person may not be late for another. When I asked 20 women during a group interview to clarify what 'late' meant for them, they generally agreed that 'late' could be defined as not becoming pregnant within the first six months of a marriage or of starting a relationship with a man. Mwana Nyanzanga, on the other hand, defined 'late' as not becoming pregnant within five months to a year of marriage, while an Arab woman in my community told me that she sought treatment for infertility when she failed to become pregnant within the first three months of her marriage. The doctor who ran a weekly fertility clinic at the mission hospital defined a woman as medically infertile if she experienced involuntary infertility for three years in succession.

The forty-three women in my survey who had experienced 'late' pregnancies gave a range of answers as to how they knew they were 'late'. These are presented in Table 1. The responses ranged from a woman who had never been pregnant but wanted to be, to a woman who was intentionally late by calculating her 'safe days'. Thirty per cent of the responses appeared to coincide with the doctor's definition of 'medically infertile', i.e., in a relationship for more than three years without becoming pregnant. The category 'neighbour or friend pregnant before her' may represent the societal pressure put on women to bear children. The two women who gave this particular response spoke about it as a source of anxiety. Some women also linked being 'late' to taking oral contraceptives. As will be seen below, several women interviewed cited a perceived threat to their future fertility as the reason they had discontinued birth control, or avoided it altogether.

Mchango and the menstrual cycle

Physical causes of infertility were also linked to a condition known in Swahili as *mchango* and in Sukuma as *nzoka*.[13] In either language this concept covers a range of health problems that include, but are not limited to, colic in new-born infants, general digestive problems in the old and young, epileptic fits in young children, menstrual discomfort in women, and impotence in men. A key characteristic of *mchango* is that it is said to have physical as well as spiritual origins and to be more responsive to local herbal or spiritual remedies, rather than biomedical interventions. Many in the community self-treat for these conditions without seeking the assistance of local healers.

The treatment of *mchango*-induced infertility problems is different, however. Instead of self-treatment, women either go to local healers who are specialists in herbal or ritual cures for infertility, or they buy herbal remedies for infertility from vendors who sell the ingredients in the marketplace. Herbal treatment for infertility problems appears to occur quite frequently: 54.8% of the 154 women interviewed stated that at some point in their lives they had used an herbal remedy to help them conceive or to prevent miscarriage.

Infertility that is caused by *mchango* is seen as being closely linked to a woman's menses. Women, in fact, pay a lot of attention to the physical aspects of their menstrual cycle - timing, duration and flow, as well as any associated physical discomfort.

Table 1 Responses to 'How did you know you were late getting pregnant?'

Definition of 'late'	N of women who responded	% of all responses
Never pregnant[a]	1	2.3
In relationship <1 year, not pregnant	4	9.3
In relationship 1-2 years, not pregnant	7	16.3
In relationship 3-5 years, not pregnant	13	30.2
In relationship >5 years, not pregnant	7	16.3
General problems getting pregnant	2	4.7
Neighbour or friend pregnant before her	2	4.7
Infertility after miscarriage or death of infant	2	4.7
Linked to breast-feeding	1	2.3
Not pregnant after weaning	2	4.7
Infertile period after stopping oral contraceptives	1	2.3
Intentional infertily: knows 'safe days'	1	2.3
Total	43	100.0

[a] More than three women had never experienced pregnancy, but only one answered this question. Others may have seen their situation not as being late but rather as being generally infertile

Even divinations for women, whether they involve chicken entrails or a twig from a *minyara* bush, usually begin with some comment on the general state of their menses. Any irregularities in the menstrual cycle are seen as an indication that a woman does, in fact, have *mchango* and therefore may experience fertility problems in the future. Menses that last more than three days, that occur too early, too late or are characterized by a heavy flow, are all cause for concern. Herbal remedies are usually prescribed to return the menses to their normal state.

The timing of a woman's menses is calculated in one of two ways.[14] Most of the women interviewed who did not know how to read told me they kept track of their menses by noting the corresponding phase of the moon at the onset of bleeding. These women spoke of their menses as occurring when the moon is to the west (*magharibi*), to the east (*mashariki*) or directly above (*kati-kati*). Using these lunar phases, the women know if they are pregnant or if their menses are irregular. One of the vendors at the herbal market in Shinyanga town told me that a woman who has difficulty conceiving, and whose cycle occurs when the moon is straight above, is one of the most difficult cases of infertility to cure. His treatment of this specific type of infertility occurs in stages. He first gives the woman an herbal remedy to change the timing of her cycle so that the onset of her menses will take place when the moon is either in the west or in the east. Only when this change has taken place will he begin to give the woman an herbal remedy to treat her infertility.

Women who know how to calculate their menses by calendar dates. For these women, a 'normal' cycle is supposed to occur on the same date every month. If a woman's menses begin on the twelfth of every month, they must continue to occur on the twelfth of subsequent months, although a difference of one or two days is not cause for great concern. When I told the woman who first explained this to me that sometimes my own cycle begins on different dates, she told me that I had *mchango* and should start using medicine to return it to normal.

Pain associated with the menstrual cycle was also seen as an indication that a woman was suffering from *mchango*. Several of the women interviewed referred to this particular category of *mchango* by its Sukuma name *buhale*. *Buhale* was characterized by its defining features - sharp, stabbing pains in the lower abdomen, vagina or rectum. *Buhale* is apparently one of the most dreaded forms of *mchango* because it is seen as able to cause a miscarriage, turn the woman's uterus around, or 'explode' her eggs. A woman suffering from *buhale* might also experience very light menses, a condition that is believed to decrease her chances of conceiving.

When I asked a Tanzanian physician at the regional hospital if he had ever heard of the illness *mchango*, he told me that he had heard of it. In his opinion, however, it was one way women spoke about the symptoms of pelvic inflammatory disease, a condition that can result when sexually transmitted diseases are left untreated (Dixon-Mueller and Wasserheit, 1991). The possibility that *mchango* was related to venereal disease had also occurred to me previously, and I had already raised it with the women themselves. However, although some women recognized that untreated venereal diseases could result in infertility, they perceived *mchango* to be an altogether different condition, since it manifested itself in a variety of ways, among people of all ages.

Infertility caused by immoral behaviour

Infertility was also seen as a consequence of immoral behaviour. Women who had previously tried to abort a pregnancy, or young girls who started having sex at a very early age, might find their future fertility in jeopardy. In the latter case, the wombs of sexually active young girls were believed either to slip out of place, or to be squeezed. In addition, many women reported the seed of older men who have already fathered children to be dangerous. Because the man's semen is considered to be 'hot', it has the capacity to ruin immature eggs if it comes in contact with the womb of a young girl who has not yet given birth.

Some women noted that the semen of men who had slept around a lot was a particularly lethal source of infertility for women in general, even for those women who had already given birth. One woman specifically stated that if a woman slept with a man who had had many sexual partners, her womb would dry up and disappear altogether. Infertility linked to a woman's promiscuity or to that of her partner was also spoken of as the source of one form of *mchango*. Though the reader might think, as I did, that this latter category of *mchango* is actually venereal disease in disguise, whenever this analysis was offered as a possible explanation people emphatically disagreed. Venereal disease (*ugonjwa wa zinaa*), acknowledged by everyone I spoke to as a source of infertility, is seen as something altogether different from *mchango*. Someone explained the difference to me in the following manner: 'Gonorrhoea is gonorrhoea. *Mchango* is *mchango* (*Kisonono ni kisonono. Mchango ni mchango*)'.

Spiritual risks to fertility

Sorcery-induced infertility

Women also spoke about spiritual risks to their fertility. Of the 137 women whom I specifically asked about the link between sorcery and infertility, 72.4% agreed that sorcery could indeed cause infertility, 9.5% said it was impossible, and 13.1% said they did not know. I was told that sorcery could be used by blood relatives, disgruntled or jealous neighbours, co-wives, past lovers or former husbands (Renne, forthcoming; Sargent, 1982). Ten women specifically noted that care should be taken with regard to a woman's menstrual cloth; if stolen, it could be used in sorcery against her and result in her future infertility. Several women told me that a woman should not leave her menstrual cloth out the open to dry after washing, as anyone - male or female - could steal it. Another woman told me that a person could block a woman's menses, and thus fertility, by stealing her menstrual cloth and burying it a place where grass would not grow. Sorcery-induced infertility was also believed to be the result of someone gaining access to a woman's postpartum blood, underwear, or the cloth used to clean the genitals after sexual intercourse. As their use in sorcery could block a woman's future fertility, great care is supposed to be taken to safeguard these items. Fertility was also believed to be susceptible to other types of sorcery medicines, which might be put into the food of an unsuspecting woman, placed at a crossroads she is likely to pass, or placed on a chair on which she is likely to sit (Varkevisser, 1973).

Of those women who agreed that sorcery was a possible cause of infertility, some specifically stated it was seen as the likely cause *only* if a woman had previously given birth. In other words, if a woman had never been pregnant, sorcery was not the source of her infertility; she was just 'born that way' or her infertility was seen as 'God's work' (*kazi ya Mungu*). Disgruntled ancestors were also seen as one source of infertility, though among the women in the survey who had used local herbal or spiritual remedies to cure their infertility, only four stated they had specifically been told by a healer that their infertility was caused by an ancestor.

Infertility caused by blood incompatibility
Although some forms of *mchango* were linked to sexual intercourse, the resulting infertility apparently had nothing to do with disease transmission as described in the biomedical literature. Rather, this particular form of infertility is talked about as if a spiritual, rather than physical, form of disease transmission had taken place. Like physical disease transmission, spiritual transmission can occur via the blood. For example, some infertility is explained in terms of a man and woman's blood being incompatible (*damu haipatani; damu inakosakana*). As two different Sukuma men explained to me, the blood of the two people is, in essence, engaged in warfare. One Sukuma man, who made reference to the fact that young Sukuma men and women have usually had several sexual partners prior to marriage, explained it this way: the woman's blood gets mixed up with the blood of everyone she has slept with, and the man's blood gets mixed with the blood of everyone he has slept with. When these two people, in turn, sleep with each other, their separate 'bloods' have to fight it out and come to terms with the other; *mchango* occurs when their separate 'bloods' are unable to come to terms. The other Sukuma man, a vendor at the herbal market in Shinyanga town, gave me a slightly different version of the warfare metaphor: he explained that the man's blood is battling the blood of all the men that the woman has ever slept with.

Although women also mentioned blood incompatibility in connection with infertility, I never heard them speak of it as warfare but only as general incompatibly. Although a man and a woman may not be able to conceive a child together, I was often told, they may each experience no difficulty having children later with a different partner. This 'new-found fertility' is the result of the compatibility of the new couple's blood. When I pressed for clarification of the concept of 'blood compatibility', a middle-aged

Sukuma woman offered the explanation that finally helped me to understand the concept. She told me that it was similar to what happens when people are asked to give blood for family members or friends at the mission hospital. Hospital staff have to examine the blood of many people before they find a person whose blood is compatible with the person needing a transfusion.

Male fertility

People in 'Bulangwa' also acknowledged the possibility of male infertility, a condition that many linked to the quality of a man's seed.[15] When I asked Mwana Nyanzanga for clarification, she explained that although the quantity of a man's ejaculate (his 'water' or 'seed') may be large, it might not produce offspring because it was watery in colour and consistency. One of the male vendors interviewed at the herbal market in Shinyanga town told me that infertility in males might also be the result of a man having 'cold', rather than 'hot', semen. We had been talking about infertility in general, and how it was decided whether the source of the 'problem' lay with the man or the woman. He told me that specific signs and symptoms indicated that the origin of the fertility problem lay with the man. First, the quantity of 'water' (ejaculate) would be large and, second, it would not be hot but cold. There appears to be no cure for this form of male infertility; it is simply the will of Almighty God (*Hamna dawa. Ni kazi ya Mwenyezi Mungu*).

There are other commentaries on male fertility; these refer not to a man's seed, but rather to his virility in general. According to women in two separate group interviews, impotence among males (*hanisi* in Swahili), appears to be a common occurrence. There are different causes of impotence and each has its own cure. One of these is the illness schistosomiasis (*kichocho* in Swahili), which is said to cause impotence as a side effect. These women acknowledged that schistosomiasis can be treated with modern medicine and that once the man is cured of illness he is also usually cured of impotence.

Another form of male impotence is seen to be the result of sorcery. A woman who suspects her husband or lover of having a mistress may seek out medicine that renders her man impotent in any illicit encounter. *Mchango* is also seen as a cause of impotence, but this category of impotence can be treated with herbal remedies. Such *mchango*-induced impotence occurs in degrees: a man may be completely impotent, or he may just experience difficulty maintaining an erection.

Unwanted fertility

Although the women in 'Bulangwa' talked about the risk of infertility in many different ways, their concerns with ensuring 'successful fertility' did not mean that they wanted to have as many children as biologically possible. For example, examination of a subset of 104 premenopausal women (taken from the formal survey of 154 women) found 49% who wanted to have more children but also 38% who stated they did not want any more children at all. Despite their claims, only 23 of the 104 premenopausal women had ever tried a modern contraception method, and of these only seven were currently using a method of family planning. These numbers are rather low given the fact that family planning is available at 'Bulangwa's' government clinic.

In my general conversations with women about their non-use of birth control, they often stated that irregular periods, fears of getting *kansa* (cancer), or perceived risks to their future fertility were the reasons they had either decided to discontinue the use of a chosen birth control method or had chosen to avoid the use of family planning methods altogether. This concern about birth control methods and their perceived risks to health also emerged in the formal survey among the subset of 104 premenopausal women. Sixty-two per cent of the 16 women who were no longer using birth control told me they had stopped using it because it was causing health problems. And among the 81 women who had never used a modern method of family planning, 15.4% said they believed birth control caused health problems, 9% stated that they just did not wish to use it, 9% said they still wanted to get pregnant, 3.8% said their husbands forbade it, and 50% stated 'I just didn't use it' ('*Sikutumia tu*'), without giving a specific reason.

Conclusions

At the beginning of this chapter I suggested that an essential first step towards improving health outcomes is understanding the context in which health problems occur. In this chapter I have tried to delineate that context as it relates to the fertility concerns of women in a small, rural community in west-central Tanzania.

Gaining an understanding of women's health concerns and practices as they relate to the reproductive process is important at several levels. For example, in contrast to the international emphasis on the health risks to women of 'excessive' fertility, this chapter has shown that some women in west-central Tanzania appear just as concerned, or more concerned, with risks to their successful fertility. As a result, they are often quite active in seeking treatment to enhance their fertility or to ensure that they carry their pregnancies to term. These women's concerns indicate that health care interventions that seek to improve the health status of women by enabling them to space their pregnancies must also address women's concerns about safeguarding their fertility.

We have also learned that many women in the rural area, irrespective of their level of literacy, pay a lot of attention to their bodily processes, particularly to the various aspects of their menstrual cycle, such as its timing, duration, flow, and any associated physical discomfort. Any irregularity is seen as an indication that something is amiss, and herbal and spiritual remedies are used in the hope of returning the menses to their cycle. In turn, this diligence is linked to women's concerns with safeguarding their fertility. Little, if anything, is known about the biomedical equivalent of some of these conditions: for example, what are the biomedical equivalents of *mchango* and *buhale*? It is quite possible that women's concerns with preventing and treating these conditions are an indication that a variety of gynaecological problems - such as reproductive tract or sexually transmitted infections, pelvic inflammatory disease and/or uterine tumours - are prevalent in the community and are not being adequately treated (Younis *et al.*, 1993).

It is also clear that certain categories of conditions were perceived as not amenable to biomedical treatment, at least not initially; as a result hospitals and clinics were often the last places where treatment was sought, if it was sought at all. These results suggest that in some community settings research that attempts to measure the level of reproductive and gynaecological health problems must expand beyond the clinical setting. Such research should include identifying how risks to reproductive health are defined from the perspective of women, men, and healers alike (Inhorn, 1994). Defining the context of fertility concerns might also necessitate linking-up with local healers to gain insight into the range of fertility-related problems for which they are consulted and which they treat.

Acknowledgement

The research on which this article is based was made possible through the generous support of the Joint Committee on African Studies of the Social Science Research Council and the American Council of Learned Societies, with funds provided by the Rockefeller Foundation and by a Fulbright-Hays Doctoral Dissertation Research Training Grant. I am particularly indebted to my Tanzanian friends and neighbours in the community of 'Bulangwa' and its surrounding villages, especially to the women who shared their stories with me, without whom this research would not have been possible.

Notes

1. To protect the privacy of the people who took part in this research, pseudonyms are used for names of the community and individuals.

2. Although her father was born of 'mixed' parentage (a Sukuma father and non-Sukuma mother) and her mother of non-Sukuma parents of one ethnicity, Mwana Nyanzanga identifies with the ethnic group of her mother and her paternal grandmother.

3. To test the generalizability of my informal interviews and observations, during the last few months of my fieldwork I interviewed 199 women about general aspects of their reproductive lives and their experiences during pregnancy and childbirth. I selected 108 women from a list of households in 'Bulangwa', and 46 women from a list of households in the village where I conducted my observations of Mwana Nyanzanga's work. In addition, I interviewed 35 women attending the regional family planning clinic in Shinyanga Town, as well as 10 women who sought treatment at Mwana Nyanzanga's home. As neither of these latter groups of women were residents of 'Bulangwa' or of Mwana Nyanzanga's village, they have been excluded from the present analysis.

4. The son of missionaries, Brandström grew up in west-central Tanzania among what he defines as the Sukuma-Nyamwezi people. His scholarly work among this group spans a period of over twenty years, dating from his undergraduate thesis in 1966 on the place of religion in the Sukuma-Nyamwezi context, to his Ph.D. thesis in 1990 on thought and reality in the Sukuma-Nyamwezi 'universe'.

5. At my field site the back was referred to as *ngongo*.

6. Treatment for illnesses caused by Muslim spirits required a different type of treatment, namely, participation in an *ngoma*, or ritual drumming, session. This type of treatment was considerably more expensive, and did not take place in 'Bulangwa' but in Shinyanga town (see Roth, 1996).

7. *Uchawi* is the Swahili term for both sorcery and witchcraft, two different but related concepts. In 'Bulangwa' both sorcerers and witches (either of whom could be male or female, kin or non-kin) were feared for their ability to negatively affect fertility outcomes through the use of harmful medicines. Nevertheless, there are major differences between sorcerers and witches. Witches (as opposed to sorcerers) were also described as having the power to steal people's souls and turn them into zombies. It was commonly 'known' that these zombies were then used as a source of free labour on the witches' farms, which were always said to be located in far away villages. Witches were also said to have the ability to make themselves invisible and cause harm without being seen. People become witches by agreeing to kill a family member, usually a blood relative. The ability of both sorcerers and witches to affect a person's fertility is the reason I use the more general term sorcery through this text.

8. *Nikawambia kwamba, Mimi sitaki kuletea kondoo ya mtu. Na sitaki, mimi sijaona kwamba mtu amekwenda kuuaguliwa hospitali, amekwenda na kondoo! Sijaona. Mimi sitaki kabisa haya mizimu ya kusema niletewa kwa kondoo*

9. She names all the babies delivered by her, and almost all are given Christian names, such as James, Mary, John, Moses, etc. She even named one of the new-borns Filipo after myself and my father, because I was known in that particular village as *Mwana Filipo* or Phillip's child. It is possible that the children she names may be renamed upon returning home. Nevertheless, several people in that particular village were known by their Christian names, all of whom she had delivered.

10. In this section I use the Swahili terms used by Sukuma and non-Sukuma people alike.

11. *Mgongo* (*ngongo* in Sukuma) was also used both in Swahili and in Sukuma to refer to the lower intestinal tract. For example, to describe gas in the lower intestines a person might say that their *mgongo* was crying or making noise (*mgongo unalia*). Women also used this phrase to describe the sound air pockets in the vaginal tract make after giving birth. The prevention of that particularly embarrassing sound was one of the major reasons cited by women for getting hot sponge baths during the postpartum period.

12. Tanner also makes reference to this condition in his 1955 article on marriage practices among the Northern Sukuma: 'A few women have their marriages delayed because there is some physical obstruction in the vagina, which is usually dealt with surgically.' (Tanner 1955: 129).

13. *Nzoka* is a general term in Sukuma, and literally means 'snake'. The definition of *mchango* in a Swahili dictionary is 'worms'. However, these definitions are simplistic renderings of the meaning of the term. Reid (1969: 68-70) has discussed the term *nzoka* in terms of Sukuma notions of illnesses in general as well as in regard to pregnancy and infertility problems specifically among the Sukuma (ibid.: 79-80).

14. Of the 154 women in the formal survey who were asked how they kept track of their menses, 62.7% said they looked at the moon, 37% said they looked at the date and one said she used both methods; another said she couldn't calculate because her menses were always irregular.

15. Much of what I learned about male infertility was initially in the context of two group interviews. There were approximately twenty women in each group. After learning something I had never heard before, I checked this new piece of information out with friends or healers in the community. They always verified what women had said in the group. I also spoke with Mwana Nyanzanga and with vendors of herbal remedies in Shinyanga town.

Bibliography

Bibeau G (1997), 'At work in the fields of public health: the abuse of rationality'. *Medical Anthropology Quarterly* 11: 246-55.

Blöhm W (1933), *Die Nyamwezi, Gesellschaft und Weltbid*, Friedericksen, De Gruyter and Co., Hamburg.

Boddy J (1989), *Wombs and alien spirits: women, men and the Zar cult in northern Sudan*, University of Wisconsin Press, Madison.

Bösch F (1930), *Les Banyamwezi, peuple de l'Afrique Oriental*, Bibliotheca Anthropos, Münster.

Brandström P (1986),'Who is a Sukuma and who is a Nyamwezi?' *Ethnic Identity in West-Central Tanzania* 27, University of Uppsala, Uppsala.

Brandström P (1990), 'Seeds and soil: the quest for life and the domestication of fertility in Sukuma-Nyamwezi thought and reality'. In: Jacobson-Widding A and van Beek W (eds), *The creative communion: African folk models of fertility and the regeneration of life*, Almqvist and Wiksell International, Stockholm.

Brandström P (1991), 'Left-hand father and right-hand mother: unity and diversity in Sukuma-Nyamwezi thought'. In: Jacobson-Widding A (ed.) *Body and space: symbolic models of unity and division in African cosmology and experience*, Almqvist and Wiksell International, Stockholm.

Cory H (1960), 'Religious beliefs and practices of the Sukuma/Nyamwezi tribal group'. *Tanganyika Notes and Records* 54: 13-26.

Cory H (nd), *The Sukuma and Nyamwezi*, Mimeograph.

Dixon-Mueller R and Wasserheit J (1991), *The culture of silence: reproductive tract infections among women in the Third World*, International Women's Health Coalition, New York.

Giles L (1989), *Spirit possession on the Swahili coast: peripheral cults or primary texts?*, Ph.D. Thesis, University of Texas at Austin, Texas.

Hendriks J (1988), *Imani za jadi za Kisukuma*, CID Editions, Nantes, France.

Herz B and Measham AR (1987), *The Safe Motherhood Initiative: proposal for action*, World Bank, Washington, DC.

Inhorn MC (1994), 'Interpreting fertility: medical anthropological perspectives'. *Social Science and Medicine* 39(4): 459-461.

Janzen J (1992), *Ngoma: discourses of healing in Central and Southern Africa*, University of California Press, Berkeley.

Kaisi M (1989), *The Safe Motherhood Initiative in Tanzania*, Ministry of Health, Dar es Salaam.

Kang'wezi DMC (1974), 'The relationship between the ancestors, clan utani, and land ownership among the Sukuma: a case study of Nyashimba community in Shinyanga'. Research paper, University of Dar es Salaam.

Reid M (1969), *Persistence and change in the health concepts and practices of the Sukuma of Tanzania, East Africa*, Ph.D. thesis, Catholic University of America.

Renne E (forthcoming), 'Cleaning the Inside and the regulation of menstruation in southwestern Nigeria'. In: Renne E and van de Walle E (eds), *Ambiguous intentions: the means and meanings of menstrual regulation*, University of Chicago Press, Chicago.

Roth DM (1996), *Bodily risks, spiritual risks: contrasting discourses on pregnancy in a rural Tanzanian community*, Ph.D. dissertation, University of Illinois, Urbana-Champaign.

Sargent CF (1982), *The cultural context of therapeutic choice: obstetrical care decisions among the Bariba of Benin*, D Reidel Publishing Co., Dordrecht, Holland.

Sargent CF (1982), *The cultural context of therapeutic choice: obstetrical care decisions among the Bariba of Benin* D. Reidel Publishing Co., Dordrecht, Holland.

Tanner RES (1955), 'Maturity and marriage among the northern Basukuma of Tanganyika', *African Studies* 13: 123-133.

Tanner RES (1958), 'Sukuma ancestor worship and its relationship to social structure'. *Tanganyika Notes and Records* 50: 52-62.

Varkevisser CM (1973), *Socialization in a changing society: Sukuma childhood in rural and urban Mwanza, Tanzania* (Translation), DA Bloch, Center for the Study of Education in Changing Societies, Den Haag.

Yoder PS (1997), 'Negotiating relevance: belief, knowledge, and practice in international health projects'. *Medical Anthropology Quarterly* 11: 131-46.

Younis N, Khattab H, Zurayk H et al. (1993), 'A community study of gynecological and related morbidities in rural Egypt'. *Studies in Family Planning* 24(3): 175-86.

WHO (1996a), *Mother-baby package: implementing Safe Motherhood in countries*, World Health Organization, Geneva.

WHO (1996b), *The midwife in the community: education material for teachers of midwifery*, World Health Organization, Geneva.

Wood, wrapped with rope, which has lots of knots. Each knot stands for a disease and is touched by the healer and the patient to aid the healing process. Presumably each knot represents a specific disease. Unfortunately which disease they represent is no longer known. (Yombe, Congo, former Zaire)

10 Traditional healers, STDs and infertility in northwest Tanzania

Robert Pool and Ndatulu Robert Washija

Sexually transmitted diseases (STDs) are one of the most important public health problems in Africa. They are closely related to the spread of HIV and their treatment has been demonstrated to substantially reduce the incidence of HIV infection (Grosskurth et al., 1995). In many parts of sub-Saharan Africa people explain STDs in supernatural terms and seek traditional treatments (Green, 1992a; Green, 1992b; Green et al., 1993; Niang et al., 1996; Meyer-Weitz, 1998). The reasons for this vary: in some areas the largely supernatural, popular aetiology of STDs lies behind this preference (Green et al., 1993) while in other areas the attitude of biomedical health care providers, the lack of privacy in clinics and the stigma attached to STDs have been reported as important in a decision to consult traditional healers (Kikonyogo et al., 1996; Gebre et al., 1996; Ayuku et al., 1996; Roets et al., 1996; Dallabetta et al., 1993).

Given the widespread preference for traditional treatment of STDs and that, to an objective observer, this treatment generally appears inadequate (Green, 1992a), it has been argued that attempts to reduce the incidence of STDs will fail unless they include both biomedical healthcare providers and traditional healers. For this reason, various collaborative programmes have been initiated (Green et al., 1994; Mahlalela et al., 1996; Kikonyogo et al., 1996; King and Homsy, 1997).

In spite of the apparently monolithic picture of preference for traditional treatment for STDs in Africa, studies in Kenya and Cameroon suggest that traditional treatment is not widely utilised and that most patients in these areas do seek biomedical treatment, whether formal and informal (Moses et al., 1994; Trebucq et al., 1994; Crabb et al., 1996). It is therefore important to establish the precise contribution of traditional healers in the treatment of STDs, as well as to understand popular STD nosology and aetiology in different areas before planning specific interventions.

STDs play an important role in infertility (Mayaud, Chapter 2), which is a serious public health issue and a serious social problem in sub-Saharan Africa (Gysels et al., Chapter 8; Roth, Mgalla and Boerma, Chapter 9). Several studies have indicated that infertile women often use traditional health services. In Tanzania, women who visited an infertility clinic in an urban hospital reported that, on average, they had previously visited three traditional healers for infertility treatment (Favot et al., 1997). A four-country study of traditional healers showed that infertility was considered the primary domain of traditional healers rather than modern health services in Kenya, Nigeria and South Africa (Green, 199?:14). In Mozambique, 33 of 34 infertile women had visited traditional healers once or several times, while only half had visited the hospital (Gerrits, 1997). Visits to traditional healers were not cheaper than access to modern health services. In Pemba island, Tanzania, most infertile women had consulted more than three healers and healers were found to play a pivotal role in local discourses on infertility (Kielman et al., 1998). Frequent use of traditional healers for infertility was also reported in Rwanda and the Gambia (King et al., 1992; Sundby et al., 1998).

Setting and methods

As part of demographic surveillance around Kisesa, a rural ward consisting of six villages about 20 km outside Mwanza town in northwest Tanzania, all practising *waganga* (traditional healers) in the ward were identified and interviewed in 1995. The 26 men and 12 women in this group of healers were asked which diseases they treated, what their specialization was, whether they treated STDs or AIDS and how many patients they saw per month. They were also asked whether they would be prepared to discuss their activities further. Twenty-six responded positively and 11 of these, together with seven *waganga* from Mwanza town, were included in an in-depth study of the background of the *waganga*, the types of illness treated (with a particular focus on STDs and infertility), traditional aetiology, and referral. The study was also aimed at assessing the willingness of *waganga* to collaborate with the biomedical sector in the treatment or prevention of STDs and AIDS.

This was a convenience sample of *waganga* who were present at the time of the study. Many of them travel frequently, either to pay short visits to particular patients or to visit disciples in remote areas where they may reside for months. In total, 18 *waganga* were interviewed: 16 men and 2 women. All were Sukuma; their average age was 59 years. They were interviewed in-depth on a number of occasions. The interviews were recorded in the vernacular, transcribed verbatim and translated.[1] They were then subjected to a detailed analysis using the QSR NUD*IST software package for qualitative data analysis.

In 1994-1995 a survey of all eligible persons aged 15-44 years was carried out in Kisesa ward (Boerma *et al.*, 1999). Men and women were asked if they had experienced genital discharge or a genital ulcer during the past 12 months. If so, the respondent was asked whether treatment had been sought and, if so, what sources of treatment had been used.

Sukuma healers

A distinction is made between herbalists (*waganga*) and diviners (*bafumu*). Most diviners practice herbal medicine, though not all herbalists practice divination. As a result, in everyday conversation the term '*waganga*' (sing. *mganga*) is used as a general term for both. A distinction can also be made between 'traditional' and 'modern' *waganga*. In general, the 'traditional' *waganga* divine and treat witchcraft-related illnesses, in addition to treating naturally caused illnesses with herbs. The 'modern' *waganga* (of whom there was only one in the study) are herbalists alone and tend to interpret their practice 'scientifically': they know the Latin names of the herbs they use, write papers, attend conferences and so forth.

The *waganga* in this study all had relatives who were or had been *waganga*. Most came to take up medicine either through the experience of a serious illness, during which ancestors revealed to them that they must start practising medicine, or as a result of ancestors making this clear during dreams at other times. Usually the ancestor was a deceased grandparent or great grandparent who had also been a *mganga*. During dreams, the ancestor explained the causes of illnesses and revealed the treatment required. The *waganga* claimed that they dreamt which patients were going to visit them and which herbs they would need to gather for the treatment. Through dreams the ancestor often informed the incipient *mganga* that he or she must become the apprentice of an established *mganga*, and told him/her where to find this teacher. Learning therefore had two sources: the supernatural instruction from an ancestor, through dreams, and the worldly teaching of another *mganga*.

I started bufumu at home. Neither of my parents practised medicine, though some other relatives do. My dead grandfather, who had been nfumu, came to me, I was at home. Thereafter I started having dreams about the type of herbs to use. Later I also went to look for my father-in-medicine [teacher]. I was about 29. He told me that my father in medicine was at Nyamatongo [another village across the lake], that he would open the door of uganga for me. He told me his name and that I would meet him in a certain house. (38 year old male mganga)

I wasn't taught, not at all; it is traditional, inborn. I simply started treating after I had finished performing the rituals demanded by my ancestors. I don't have any father in medicine from whom I learned. None. Both grandfathers and my father are waganga. Even my mother was a mganga. I wasn't taught at all, you see? Only my ancestors' spirits used to come to me, and they told me all things. Then I started divining. A person comes and you tell him his problems. I have the medicine, because these ancestors have taught me everything: 'do this, do that. If a person has stomach problems, go and look for such and such herbs'. And right away I do that. You see? You wake up only to find that everything has been revealed to you, thereafter you go to the forest to search for medicine. (61 year old female mganga)

Waganga often had many followers and assistants; some stayed in the teacher's compound to learn and assist, while others were spread over a wide area and had their own practices. The *waganga* travelled often and far, visiting pupils and followers while resident pupils and followers took care of their practice at home. Some had a number of homes with resident wives and assistants, and circulated among them. Some had large compounds with various huts in which in-patients resided during treatment, which sometimes lasted many months. During this period patients were adopted into the household and assisted with domestic chores.

The *waganga* reported that they treated a wide variety of illnesses and other misfortunes. Most specialised in a small number of ailments, varying from two or three to about ten. Specializations included genital disorders, asthma, swelling of the body and all kinds of witchcraft-related illnesses. STDs and infertility problems were commonly reported specializations. None of the *waganga* specialised in treatment for AIDS and only two reported actually treating it.

Twenty five of the 38 *waganga* surveyed named STDs as one of their specializations (17/26 men, 8/12 women); 17/38 (7 men and 10 women) specialised in treating infertility problems. The most common illnesses treated by the 18 *waganga* who participated in the in-depth study were infertility and various witchcraft-related illnesses. Most of the *waganga* in the in-depth study stated they saw patients with STDs only sporadically, even though most (16/18) said STDs were one of their specializations.

The average number of patients that the 38 *waganga* reported treating each month varied from two to 200, with a mean of 17.

Traditional Sukuma aetiology

As in many sub-Saharan African cultures, traditional Sukuma aetiology is characterized by a basic threefold distinction: illnesses may be natural or God-given, caused by witchcraft or caused by the ancestors.

Common, usually non-fatal, illnesses, such as diarrhoea, fevers, coughs, stomach ailments, are generally considered to be natural unless there is some serious and unexpected complication; for example, if an illness which is normally brief and acute becomes chronic in spite of treatment, or if a healthy person suddenly dies of an illness that is normally not fatal. In the latter case, witchcraft (*bulogi*) would be suspected.

Belief in both witchcraft and the ancestors operates on a more remote level of causation; people's thoughts turn to them only when developments take an unexpected turn and other, ordinary causal factors have been excluded.

The ancestors may allow acute or serious illness to strike, or they may prevent success in various undertakings such as business or agriculture, rather than directly causing illness and misfortune. They do this to either punish or warn a person in connection with some negligence relating to traditional or ritual obligations. Witches, on the other hand, may cause illness or death directly through various means, such as by placing medicine on a path so that the victim steps on it and becomes ill, or by poisoning his food. Unexpected deaths, in particular, are attributed to the activities of witches. For example, of 141 adult deaths reported in Kisesa during a verbal autopsy study, slightly more than 46% were attributed to witchcraft by relatives (Boerma et al., 1997).

Apart from deeper levels of causation, the most important causal factor in everyday explanations of common illnesses is nzoka, which means 'snake' in Kisukuma. The Kiswahili equivalent is mchango, which is translated into English as 'worm'.[2] Although people describe the mchango or nzoka realistically - as a snakelike creature that lives in each person's abdomen (biomedical health workers equate the michango with intestinal worms) - it seems likely that it is more a metaphor for the balance between health and disease rather than a real living creature. When we asked Sukuma waganga to describe the nzoka, they said it was a real snakelike creature living in the body. However, when we asked whether, if we went into the hospital for an operation and the surgeon cut open our abdomen he would see the nzoka, they became confused and said probably not.[3]

The nzoka is said to live in the body, mainly the abdomen, and move around under the influence of various stimuli. If it experiences these stimuli as unpleasant, it may manifest itself by making noises or causing pain or illness. In the case of illness, people may say that the nzoka has climbed up or risen from being dormant (kulinwa nzoka). Thus, exposure to cold may lead the nzoka to rise up into the chest and cause respiratory tract infections, referred to as nzoka ya lubazu (lubazu = ribs) or nzoka ya mshikuba (mshikuba = chest). Eating the wrong food or drinking dirty water may irritate the nzoka so that it causes cramps and noises in the stomach or abdomen, or even vomiting or diarrhoea; for example, diarrhoea may be referred to as nzoka ya kuhalisha or nzoka ya kupanza in Kisukuma.

Nzoka is associated with various genital symptoms. Nzoka ya bagosha (bagosha = men) refers to swelling or pain in the groin, reddening of the testicles, or swelling of the scrotum. Nzoka ya buhale (buhale = women) refers to swelling in the groin, or continuous or irregular menstrual flow. Nzoka ya kigosha is often translated as 'hernia'. In addition to nzoka, people may attribute all kinds of illness, from diarrhoea to AIDS, to 'germs' (madudu).

There are also all sorts of factors, behavioural and coincidental, that are thought to bring a person into contact with a causal agent. For instance, someone may get an STD or AIDS because of promiscuous sexual behaviour, a sore throat because he always drinks cold beer, or bilharzia because he bathes in the lake where the water is dirty.

All of the factors discussed above may be related to each other in causal chains. A woman may be infertile either because she neglects her obligations to the ancestors and they prevent her from bearing children or because the nzoka has been disturbed by medicines that were placed in her path by a jealous relative. Similarly, if a man is promiscuous, has a partner with an STD and becomes ill, the illness may have occurred directly, because he has become infected with *madudu* ('germs') or indirectly, because his *nzoka* protests at the pollution of his body. Again, a child might drink dirty water, causing the *nzoka* to become agitated and induce diarrhoea. When people consider the cause of a specific case of illness, witchcraft, the ancestors and *nzoka/mchango* are central aetiological concepts.

Sexually transmitted diseases (STDs)

Table 1 presents the sources of treatment among men and women who reported an STD (either genital discharge or genital ulcer or both) in the last year during a cross-sectional survey in 1994-95. Fourteen percent of men and nine percent of women reported an STD in the last year. A very high proportion of the treatment patterns were fairly similar among both sexes, except that women more frequently did not use any source (22% of women and 11% of men).

Table 1 Reported treatment utilization among men and women who reported a genital ulcer or genital discharge in the year preceding the survey, Kisesa, 1994-95.

	men	women
Number of respondents	2715	3105
Number with an STD in last year	387	273
% with STD in last year	14.3	8.8
% used government health facility	20.7	17.2
% used private health facility	18.4	12.8
% visited traditional healer	46.2	45.0
% went to shop	13.7	8.4
% asked friend	1.8	1.8
% used other source	1.8	1.5
% no treatment	10.6	22.3

Respondents could report more than one source

Most of the *waganga* in the study said they treated a number of diseases, referred to collectively as *bunyolo* in Kisukuma and *magonjwa ya zinaa* in Kiswahili, terms that could be translated roughly as 'sexually transmitted diseases' in English. When talking about *bunyolo*, the *waganga* always named the same three diseases: k*aswende*, *kabambalu* and *kasogone* (*kaswende*, *kabambaru* and *kisonono* respectively in Kiswahili). If English terms are used then both the *waganga* and the biomedical health workers translate *kaswende* and *kasogone/kisonono* as syphilis and gonorrhoea respectively. No English term for *kabambalu* is in popular use, though health workers tend to translate it as 'lymphogranuloma venereum'. There is only a partial overlap in the meanings of the English and vernacular terms. The Kiswahili *magonjwa ya zinaa* literally means 'diseases of adultery', but the term actually refers to the location of symptoms rather than their aetiology. That is, it refers to various symptoms located in the genital area rather than to sexually transmitted diseases *per se*. Thus, non-sexually transmitted genital discharge would be included under this term, while sexually transmitted hepatitis B would not. Occasionally other forms of *magonjwa ya zinaa* or *bunyolo* were mentioned, such as *nailoni*, which is characterized by a nylon-like thread coming out of the penis. If this thread is cut, the patient is said to die.

Although there is some individual variation regarding some symptoms of these illnesses, there is a very general consensus on the major symptoms. *Waganga* say that *kasogone/kisonono* is characterized by the genital discharge of pus, sometimes also by the passing of blood in the urine. The main symptom of *kaswende* is genital ulcers. *Kabambalu* is characterized by swelling of the lymph nodes in the groin, which are said to burst and become ulcerated. Most of the *waganga* interviewed could describe the symptoms from experience, as they examined patients physically. The symptoms are the same for men and women. All the *waganga* were aware that these diseases could also be present asymptomatically.

If not treated these diseases were all thought to be fatal, though informants differed on the period of time between infection and death: this was said to vary from several weeks to many months.

What happens if you don't treat bunyolo?
You die, you die. If you get infected with mabambalu the lymph nodes in the groin swell and later they burst. When this has happened the whole part including the intestines have been affected and you die.

How long would it take if a person is not taking medicines?
It can take some days, up to two months.

How do these diseases develop when you don't treat them?
You die.

How long does it take? For example, kisonono, if you don't treat it?
If you stay one month without treating the disease it weakens you, it makes your stomach rot, and your nzoka get attacked. So after one month without medicine, the second month you die.

How long would it take a person who has kaswende until he dies?
It all depends on the person's blood [health]. It can take three months.

With kabambalu you feel pains when you urinate, and the lymph nodes swell on both sides, and the mchango rumbles all the time. If you leave it untreated you'll find both sides burst, and it goes deep into the bones and thereafter you die.

How long does it take from the time you become ill?
It takes about one week.

In spite of the *waganga's* insistence that STDs could be fatal, in 141 verbal autopsy interviews in Kisesa, relatives never attributed a death to an STD. This may reflect a fundamental difference of opinion between *waganga* and the general population, but it is more likely to be due to the fact that STDs either remain undetected (at any rate as far as the deceased's relatives are concerned) or that most STDs are probably treated sooner or later (i.e. before they become 'fatal').

Although these diseases were often described as being related to agitation of the *nzoka*, the interviewed *waganga* were unanimous that they were ultimately sexually transmitted. Most thought they could only be transmitted sexually, though one thought that sitting on a chair recently occupied by someone with *kaswende* could also pass on the germs (*madudu*). Male *waganga* tended to talk about men getting STDs from women, forgetting that those women must have been infected by men.

You can't get them from bewitching: kaswende or kichocho[4] or kabambalu. You only get these from women. They're never from bewitching. You treat them also in hospitals, by injections, and they quickly dry up.

If you have a partner who has an STD, what are the chances of you catching it; is it easy to get it?
If you have sex with him/her you must get infected.

You said that these diseases are transmitted sexually but also that they are caused by nzoka; what is the relationship between the two?
Because after they've had sex the nzoka is disturbed it starts losing its way. It leaves its dwelling place, then it changes and becomes a mdudu, thereafter it starts eating up the blood, it spoils it.

Because *waganga* were aware that a potential partner could have an STD without manifesting any symptoms, they claimed that prevention is difficult. No one mentioned the possibility of condom use. In fact, two *waganga* (the two women) had never even seen a condom. A subsequent demonstration was met with much laughter and amazement. Some of the *waganga* did advise patients with an STD to avoid having sex until they were cured. Some also advised patients to remain with one partner to avoid contracting STDs.

Once you know that he has the disease [STD] you say to him: 'please, now you should stop having sex with these women until you are cured.'

Infertility

The *waganga* distinguished three kinds of reproductive impairment (*uzazi*):
- a women is unable to bear any children at all (primary infertility);
- she has one or two children and wants more, but can not become pregnant (secondary infertility);
- she becomes pregnant but repeatedly miscarries, has stillbirths or the children die shortly after birth.

Women with secondary infertility were the most common of the three categories seen by the *waganga* in our study.

Seventeen of the 38 *waganga* surveyed named infertility problems as one of their specialities. Infertility appeared to be a predominantly female speciality: 11/12 female *waganga* in the survey specialised in infertility compared with 6/26 male *waganga*. All reported seeing more patients with infertility problems than with STDs. Some *waganga* reported seeing up to 4 patients with infertility problems in a single day, with monthly averages of between 5 and 20 patients.

Three major causal factors are thought to be involved in infertility: the ancestral spirits (*mizimu*), *nzoka* and witchcraft. These factors may be linked in causal chains.

For one who has had one or two children but can't have more, it is a question of witchcraft. Then the nzoka is disturbed, you see; it's disturbed after she has stepped on those medicines of witchcraft. It could be her aunt, or simply her mother who may be experimenting with her witchcraft medicine.

The kizazi [uterus] becomes contracted. I can treat those who've stopped bearing. Especially those due to mchango, the sort that forces the reproductive organs to move inwards.

It might be caused by her ancestors (mizimu). They must perform some rituals, then her ancestors will cure her of the infertility problem.

There are also a variety of more immediate and mechanical causes, which may or may not be related to the more distant causal factors such as ancestors, *nzoka* and witchcraft. These include contractions of the uterus, the uterus moving, 'fat' or incompatibility between sex partners.

If she has mchango only, you give her medicine. If you see that she's fat but wanting to bear children you first give her medicine to clear the fat on her reproductive organs. Because when she's fat the eggs are buried.

It's possible that her problem is due to the uterus moving to the side of the back.

The size of the male and female organs is also an important factor: they have to match.

Although some *waganga* agreed with the widely held view that infertility is a female problem and that men could not be infertile, others insisted the problem could lie with either sex. There was no clear distinction between male and female *waganga* in this respect.

Do you only treat women or do you treat their husbands as well?
I must see the husband first. I think you know there are cases in which it is the man who is infertile? (38 year old male mganga)

Ever since I started treating I have never come across a man who is infertile. I won't tell lies in that respect: there's no man who's infertile. If it's a woman it's due to contraction of the uterus, or that she had an STD during youth. (73-year-old female mganga)

I will treat them both when both man and woman have the same problem. But when it's only the man, I will have to use some diplomacy to avoid breakdown of their marriage. (61-year-old female mganga)

But if a woman comes with such a case we also ask her if her husband is all right. Because you can think that perhaps it's her mistake but it could be the mistake of the husband. (44-year-old male mganga)

All interviewed *waganga* saw a connection between STDs and infertility. As they all claimed that untreated STDs were inevitably fatal, it may be assumed they meant that STDs which had been cured left the sufferer infertile.

They [STDs] affect reproductive organs. Once they enter these organs they cause destruction. For some they cause irreparable destruction.

Bunyolo [STDs] disturb the nzoka and lead to infertility.

Usually it [infertility] is caused by 'venereal diseases'. There's no other thing. Because there are very few who are born barren. For example, gonorrhoea destroys the reproductive eggs, as does syphilis.

Basically two factors are responsible for women to have children and then stop: mchango and mizimu (ancestral spirits). Or she has had an illness [STD] before.

Treatment and referral

Although many claimed to specialize in treating STDs, most of those who participated in the in-depth study did not seem to see many STD patients. One *mganga* said he saw about such 20 patients per month. This was the highest, but it may be an exaggeration, as most clinics would not see this many STD patients. All others said they rarely saw such patients: some reported one or two a month; others had not seen a single patient with an STD in the last year. When they did see them, the disease was already well developed. The *waganga* claimed patients waited as long as possible before seeking professional treatment, whether traditional or biomedical. They gave two main reasons for this. First, when a person has an STD it is thought to be shameful, so he or she avoids making it known for as long as possible. The first recourse is to seek advice from a friend and initiate self-medication, either with traditional herbal remedies or antibiotics bought over the counter. *Rangi mbili* ('two colours,' as antibiotic capsules are popularly called) are widely available over the counter and in Tanzania are a popular means of treating almost any ailment. If self-treatment does not have any effect, and if the disease is causing much discomfort, then the person may seek professional help. Second, when this stage is reached, many people prefer to seek biomedical treatment in the form of antibiotic injections. All *waganga* agreed that STDs could best be treated in hospital by injections; the small number of patients seen by some of them was due, according to their own explanation, to the efficacy of biomedical treatment.

Traditional treatment for both STDs and infertility is mainly herbal (either taken orally or inserted into the vagina); some ritual treatment is used as well, particularly for infertility. We saw no evidence of the use of pharmaceuticals or injections by the *waganga* we studied, though we did not investigate this systematically. These *waganga* thought infertility, especially if it related to witchcraft or *mizimu* (ancestors), was better treated traditionally, and there were many stories of patients being cured. Contrary to what is usually the case in African traditional medicine, the *waganga* in our study did not appear to be interested in the ultimate supernatural causes of their patients' infertility problems. Instead, they focused only on what they perceived to be the immediate, naturalistic cause. This was despite the fact that supernatural causes were a vital part of their own explanatory model of the problem.

I take her to the place where she stepped over those bewitching medicines, and I remove it from her. I send back the illness from where she picked it, so that it comes out of her. I take it out, there in the field, from where she picked it.
What happens to the person who bewitched her?
Well, my concern is to treat and cure my patient only. I have nothing to do with the witch; it is up to him/her. My concern is this person's well being.

All *waganga* we interviewed claimed that if they thought they could not treat a patient, or that their treatment was not working, they would refer the patient to another *mganga* or to the hospital. There did not appear to be serious rivalry among *waganga*, in spite of their relatively large numbers. All talked about referring patients and asking colleagues for advice in the case of difficult diagnoses or diseases that did not respond to treatment. This collaboration and interaction was illustrated during the research by frequent visits of colleague *waganga*. Interviews were often interrupted by not one but several other *waganga* paying a visit to the *mganga* being interviewed. Consequently interviews were often collective affairs. This interaction must also contribute to the relative uniformity of views on symptoms, treatment, etc.

   The *waganga* did not reject biomedicine and clearly saw traditional and modern medicine as complementary, each having their own specializations. They insisted that acute diseases, serious infections and STDs were better treated in hospital, and that chronic and minor ailments, *nzoka* and witchcraft related illnesses and various mental problems were better treated traditionally.

You know the hospital is ideal for curing these diseases [STDs]. And if I also see that this disease is beyond my ability and that the patient could be lacking initiative, I send him straight to the hospital.

How do you treat them [STDs]?
I go to the forest to get some herbs, I come back and prepare them. I then clean the patient. I clean the ulcers with warm water and soap. I clean it until I see some blood coming out, then I know that the dirt has come out. I then apply some medicine, I sprinkle it on the ulcers. Within three days it dries. I give him/her some oral medicines also. For kisonono I have some roots; I collect them from the forest. I boil them and store them in bottles. I make sure that after he has finished that dose the illness is also out, free from his stomach. And I clean his bowels using another medicine, and his urinary system, for four to five days. If you attend to kabambalu early it is cured; though it's difficult when ulcers have developed, much more difficult.

And when people don't get better with your treatment what do you do with them?
After treating him for two days only and without success and having observed all symptoms, I refer him to the hospital. That's already a difficult stage and I tell him openly to please go the hospital.

The *waganga* in the study were very eager to collaborate with biomedical providers. All expressed dissatisfaction that when they had patients whom they thought would be treated better in hospital, they did not know how and where to refer them. *Waganga* were also eager to learn from biomedicine.

Discussion

In spite of some general misconceptions, such as that untreated STDs are inevitably fatal, knowledge of STDs was relatively high, particularly regarding aetiology and prevention. Although the vernacular terms are not completely identical in meaning to the biomedical terms for STDs, the descriptions of symptoms and syndromes were relatively consistent among the *waganga*, probably due to the high degree of mobility and interaction among these healers. As in many African cultures, supernatural causes appear to be important explanations for fatal illness. However, STDs are firmly situated in the naturalistic category (infection, *nzoka*, sexual transmission). Infertility, though also often explained in naturalistic terms, is more often ascribed to supernatural causes, such as witchcraft or the influence of ancestors.

Although most of the *waganga* in the in-depth study claimed to see relatively few patients with STDs, the fact that 45% of the female and 46% of the male respondents in the survey reported consulting a traditional healer for a genital ulcer or genital discharge in the last year suggests that traditional healers are an important source of treatment for STDs in this area. Although only one of the *waganga* in the in-depth study claimed to see substantial numbers of STD patients, the numbers in the in-depth study were small: it may be that a relatively small number of *waganga* who specialize in STD treatment actually see most of the patients. We also have insufficient data on the hierarchy of resorting to treatment. Treatment-seeking behaviour often entails a quest during which care seekers try various therapy options until they have obtained a satisfactory cure. More information is needed on the relative positions of traditional healers and biomedical care providers in this process.

Waganga also seem to play a significant role in the treatment of infertility, most commonly secondary infertility. Treatment is mainly herbal, and a high degree of success is claimed. In Kenya, Katz and Katz (1983) found some evidence that treatment of barrenness by traditional healers was fairly successful. They suggested success could be attributed to reductions in the inhibiting effect of stress on fertility. Significantly, *waganga* in Kisesa did not always consider infertility to be an exclusively female problem; it was the two female *waganga* who said it was impossible for a man to be infertile. All *waganga* in the in-depth study saw a connection between infertility and STDs.

Most studies have reported willingness on part of the traditional healers to refer patients to, or collaborate with, modern medicine (Warren, 1982; Green *et al.*, 1984; Green, 1992a). This also applies to the *waganga* in this study. There was a great deal of respect for the work and skills of fellow *waganga* as well as for biomedicine, and there appeared to be much openness and willingness to collaborate with and learn from both fellow *waganga* and biomedicine. The *waganga* saw traditional and biomedicine as complementary. They often expressed frustration at not knowing how and where to refer patients they felt unable to treat. There was much referral to colleagues, especially if a *waganga* thought he/she could not cure the patient.

In several countries AIDS and STD programmes have begun to include collaboration with traditional healers (Green, 1994: 25-26; Mahlalela *et al.*, 1996; Kikonyogo *et al.*, 1996; King and Homsy, 1997). Most programmes aim to enhance traditional healers' skills as promoters of condoms and health educators for HIV infection and other STDs, to prevent care-related transmission of HIV by traditional healers and to encourage referral to modern health services.

Although not all the *waganga* in this study treated large numbers of patients with STDs, some of them did. They also appear to have extensive networks, even stretching into neighbouring regions, and to see many patients. They are therefore an obvious potential source of AIDS/STD education, as well as condom distribution and promotion. Collaboration with biomedicine would further enhance their status in the community (Green, 1992a) and give such messages added impact. *Waganga* could also play a useful role in the psycho-social and cultural aspects of infertility (Katz and Katz, 1983).

Notes

1. The vernacular in Mwanza Region is Kisukuma; the national language is Kiswahili. The educated classes are familiar with English and English terms are quite common in medical settings. This led to extensive code switching and interchanging of terms during interviews.

2. Reid (1982) has discussed the concept of *nzoka* in the context of Sukuma aetiology, and Van Overveld and Kuipers (1995) have described *nzoka* in relation to respiratory infections in children among the Sukuma. Bjerke (1989: 222) has described the concept of *nzoka* among the neighbouring Zinza, and Green *et al.* (1993: 267-9) and Green *et al.* (1994) have discussed a very similar idea, *nyoka*, in Manica Province, Mozambique.

3. *Nzoka* as a metaphor for *equilibrium = health / imbalance = illness* has many similarities with the hot-cold metaphor in ancient Greek humoural medicine, as well as in contemporary Indian Ayurvedic and popular Latin Americal medicine (see for example Pool 1987).

4. *Kichocho* is usually translated into English as bilharzia, though like other local illness terms, this is not entirely accurate. The major symptom of *kichocho* is passing blood in the urine, and although this is a major symptom of bilharzia, it may also be related to other diseases. It is often referred to as an STD because the major symptom referred to is genitally situated.

Bibliography

Ayuku D, Bentley M, Egessa O, *et al.* (1996), 'Factors that facilitate and impede STD control in western Kenya'. XIth International Conference on AIDS, Vancouver: Abstract No. Th.C.4744.

Bjerke (1989), 'Witchcraft as explanation. The case of the Zinza'. In: A. Jacobson-Widding and D. Westerlund (eds) *Culture, Experience and Pluralism. Essays on African Ideas of Illness and Healing.* Uppsala: Almqvist & Wiksell International, pp. 219-134.

Boerma JT, Ngalula J, Isingo R, *et al.* (1997), 'Levels and causes of adult mortality in rural Tanzania with special reference to HIV/AIDS'. *Health Transition Review* 7 (suppl. 2): 63-74.

Boerma JT, Urassa M, Senkoro K, Klokke AH, Zaba B and Ng'weshemi JZL (1999), 'Spread of HIV in a rural area of Tanzania'. *AIDS 1999*, 13: 1233-1241.

Crabbé F, Carsauw H, Buvé A, Laga M, Tchupo JP and Trebucq A (1996), 'Why do men with urethritis in Cameroon prefer to seek care in the informal sector?' *Genitourinary Medicine* 72: 220-222.

Dallabetta G, Allen H, Helitzer-Allen D and Kendall C (1993), 'Sexually transmitted infections (STI) in Malawi: local perceptions, knowledge and behaviour'. IXth International Conference on AIDS, Vancouver: Abstract No. PO-DO1-3404.

Favot I, Ngalula J, Mgalla Z, Klokke AH, Gumodoka B and Boerma JT (1997), 'HIV infection and sexual behaviour among women with infertility in Tanzania: a hospital-based study'. *International Journal of Epidemiology* 26: 414-9.

Gebre A, Teshome W, Tennagashaw M, Workneh F, Dallabetta G and Field ML (1996), 'Health seeking behaviours for STDs in four Ethiopian communities: their relevance for designing treatment and prevention programmes'. XIth International Conference on AIDS, Vancouver: Abstract No. Th.C.4382.

Gerrits T (1997), 'Social and cultural aspects of infertility in Mozambique'. *Patient Education and Counseling* 31: 39-48.

Green EC (1992a), 'Sexually transmitted disease, ethnomedicine and health policy in Africa'. *Social Science and Medicine* 35: 121-130.

Green EC (1992b), 'The anthropology of sexually transmitted diseases in Liberia'. *Social Science and Medicine* 35: 1457-1468.

Green EC (1994), *AIDS and sexually transmitted disease in Africa: bridging the gap between traditional healing and modern medicine*, Westview Press, Boulder, Colorado and Oxford, UK.

Green EC, Jurg G and Dgedge A (1993), 'Sexually transmitted diseases, AIDS and traditional healers in Mozambique'. *Medical Anthropology* 15: 261-281.

Green EC, Jurg G and Dgedge A (1994), 'The snake in the stomach: child diarrhea in central Mozambique'. *Medical Anthropology Quarterly* 8(1): 4-24.

Green EC and Makhubu L (1984), 'Traditional healers in Swaziland: toward improved cooperation between the traditional and modern health sectors'. *Social Science and Medicine* 18: 1073.

Grosskurth H, Mosha F, Todd J, *et al.* (1995), 'Impact of improved treatment of sexually transmitted diseases on HIV infection in rural Tanzania: randomised controlled trial'. *Lancet* 346: 530-536.

Katz SS and Katz SH (19XX), 'An evaluation of traditional therapy for barrenness'. *Medical Anthropology Quarterly* 394-405.

Kielmann K (1998), 'Barren ground: contesting identities of infertile women in Pemba, Tanzania'. In: Lock M and Kaufert PA (eds), *Pragmatic women and body politics*, Cambridge University Press, Cambridge, UK: 127-163.

Kikinyongo N, Kasattiro A, Mutebi M, *et al.* (1996), 'Sharing HIV/AIDS education in the communities: a Kampala traditional healer's experience'. XIth International Conference on AIDS, Vancouver: Abstract No. Th.C.4543.
King R and Homsy J (1997), 'Involving traditional healers in AIDS education and counselling in sub-Saharan Africa: a review'. *AIDS* 11 (suppl A): S217-225.

Mahlalela X, Mini C, Ngcokoto Arabaji E and Sonnischen C (1996), 'Experience of capacity building in HIV/AIDS education and prevention with South African traditional healers: the Nompumelelo Phambili traditional healer's project'. XIth International Conference on AIDS, Vancouver: Abstract No. We.D.3717.

Meyer-Weitz A, Reddy P, Weijts W, van den Borne B and Kok G (1998), 'The socio-cultural contexts of sexually transmitted diseases in South Africa: implications for health education programmes'. *AIDS Care* 10 (suppl 1): 39-55.

Moses S, Ngugi EN, Bradley J, *et al.* (1994), 'Health care-seeking behaviour related to the transmission of sexually transmitted diseases in Kenya'. *American Journal of Public Health* 84: 1947-51.

Niang CI, Ryan C, Ghee A, Ndoye I and Dallabetta G (1996), 'Health seeking behaviour for STDs in Senegal: findings of a targeted intervention research study'. XIth International Conference on AIDS, Vancouver: Abstract No. Th.C.4747.

Overveld E van and Kuipers M (1995), 'Snakes and infections in the chest'. *Memisa Medisch* 3: 56-64.

Pool (1987), 'Hot and cold as an explanatory model: the example of Bharuch District in Gujarat, India'. *Social Science and Medicine* 25(4): 389-399.

Reid (1982), 'Patient/healer interactions in Sukuma medicine'. Yoder S (ed.), *African Health and Healing Systems: Proceedings of a Symposium*. Los Angeles, CA: Crossroads Press, pp. 121-158.

Roets L, Lurie M, Mini C and Field ML (1996), 'Health seeking behaviours for sexually transmitted diseases and the social context of commercial sex in a gold mining community: a case study of Welkom, South Africa'. XIth International Conference on AIDS, Vancouver: Abstract No. Th.C.4745.

Sundby J, Mboge R and Sonko S (1998), 'Infertility in the Gambia: frequency and health care seeking'. *Social Science and Medicine* 46: 891-9.

Trebucq A, Louis J-P, Tchupo J-P, Migliani R, Smith J and Delaporte E (1994), 'Treatment regimens of STD patients in Cameroon: a need for intervention'. *Sexually Transmitted Diseases* 2: 124-126.

Warren DM (1982), 'The Techiman-Bono ethnomedical system'. In: Yoder S (ed.), *African health and healing systems*, Crossroads Press, Los Angeles: 39.

Nowadays fertility dolls or *Aku'amma* are used more and
more by little girls as a doll to play with. But this was
originally a secondary use (see also p.188)
(Ashanti, Ghana)

11 Health and traditional care for infertility in the Gambia and Zimbabwe

Johanne Sundby and Aileen Jacobus

The UN International Conference on Population and Development (ICPD) has stressed the need for infertility services as an integral part of reproductive health services for all the women of the world. Despite the idealistic tone of this statement, infertility is not a priority in the reproductive health services of developing countries. Resources are often preferentially focused on infectious disease control or primary health care rather than infertility. Services related to infertility will have an even lower priority if 'reproductive health' in a country still implies population control rather than a woman's right to bear children.

For most couples in the developing world today, access to modern infertility treatment is less than for any other type of health care (Rowe and Farley, 1990). This lack of access is striking in comparison with the advances in infertility treatments in countries with established market economies, where advanced baby-making technology has become commonplace (Aral and Cates, 1983). This chapter discusses challenges involved in meeting peoples' needs for infertility services in settings with very limited resources. It is argued that although the highest standard of infertility treatment may be beyond the reach of health systems in developing countries, there is potential for the improvement of infertility services within existing resources and programs. Materials from ongoing research on infertility in Zimbabwe and the Gambia are used to illustrate the problems encountered and some possible improvements. Studies from both countries provide insights into the challenges of addressing infertility as an element of comprehensive reproductive health programmes in developing countries.

Infertility studies

The Gambia

The Gambia is a small West-African country with a population of just over one million people. The total fertility rate (TFR) is more than six children per woman. As in other parts of West Africa, the desire for children is high (Bledsoe et al., 1994). HIV prevalence was low in eight antenatal clinic surveillance sites in 1994 (0.6%), but prevalence of other sexually transmitted diseases (STDs) is thought to be much higher (UNAIDS, 1998). GNP per capita is estimated at $ 320 per year. While primary care is the cornerstone of the Gambian health services, the referral system is less developed than in many other developing countries.

A full investigation into the causes of infertility has not been conducted in the Gambia. Here, as elsewhere, STDs are presumed to be a significant contributor to infertility. Elevated levels of circulatory antibodies against both gonorrhoea and chlamydia in infertile as compared to fertile women have been documented in the Gambia (Mabey et al., 1985). A survey was conducted by the Maternal and Child Health Unit in the Gambian Ministry of Health to determine the frequency of infertility and care-seeking behaviour for infertility. Researchers visited randomly assigned geographical areas in the Gambia, where women were interviewed. Screening questions allowed researchers to assess whether women were infertile: the women thus designated completed a longer semi-structured interview, which covered marital and fertility history and care-seeking behaviour related to infertility. In addition to these field interviews, focus group discussions and interviews were conducted with public and private health care professionals in the same areas to determine practices and attitudes of doctors and nurses with regard to infertility (Sundby et al., 1998). Finally, traditional healers, traditional midwives and members of a traditional group for infertile women were interviewed. A description of the methodology and main study results can be found in Sundby *et al.* (1998) and Sundby (1997).

Zimbabwe

Zimbabwe is a southern African country with a population of more than 11 million people, with a well-established primary health care system. The total fertility rate (TFR) has declined in recent years: from 5.5 in 1988 to 4.3 in 1994 (Central Statistical Office, 1994). Antenatal care surveillance sites have reported HIV prevalence rates of 30% or more in urban and rural areas of Zimbabwe, with border towns suffering even higher rates. Other STDs are also thought to be common and are the leading causes of infertility in males (Mbizvo *et al.*, 1994). Pregnancy-related complications and malnutrition may also contribute to infertility in Zimbabwe. GNP per capita is estimated at $ 560 per year.

We are involved in two studies concerning infertility in Zimbabwe. In a case-control study based in three sites in Harare (Harare General Hospital, Parareniyatwa Hospital and Spielhaus Family Planning Clinic) couples seeking infertility services are administered a structured questionnaire, adapted from the WHO clinical manual for infertility investigations. The purpose of the study is to determine care-seeking behaviour of infertile couples, as well as risk factors and major medical causes for infertility. To 1998, a total of 325 case couples and 204 fertile female controls have been enrolled into the study. The second study, piloted in 1998, is a survey of infertile women identified through local health workers, with additional interviews of traditional healers and village health workers in Masvingo, a rural district of Zimbabwe.

Infertility and women's lives

Infertile women face serious difficulties as regards their status and role in society (Adepoju and Oppong, 1994). In many African societies, the birth of children bestows upon a woman her right to a share of the man's property or wealth. Throughout the whole of Africa, infertility creates a burden that can profoundly affect women's social status and mental or physical health. For example, under the law in Zimbabwe, childless women who are widowed or divorced may have no right to inherit property from their husband. In many African countries, infertility is legal grounds for divorce (Hellum, 1995 and 1999; Jensen, 1996; Inhorn, 1994; Mutambirwa, 1984). In the Gambia, Muslim law states that a couple who have been married for seven years without a child should be divorced (Skramstad, 1995). Our research in the Gambia, as well as in Zimbabwe, provides instances of infertile women who have been abandoned by their husbands and families. It also gives examples of infertile women, abandoned or not, who are seeking new partners to help them get pregnant. More than 25% of infertile Zimbabwean women had experienced divorce, as compared with 8% of the fertile sample.

There is a tendency for women to seek new partners to help them get pregnant (Skramstad, 1995; Sonko, 1994). In cases of infertility, childbearing may be considered more important than marital fidelity. There is some evidence of communities either condoning or overlooking extramarital affairs if an infertile woman is trying to get pregnant. For example, in Zimbabwe, the rural pilot study revealed a practice which allowed 'sperm donation' to be arranged within the family, without the husband's knowledge. The donor would be sworn to secrecy, at risk of being banned from the male *dare* (village court).

A large volume of research links psychological disorders to infertility, although most evidence suggests that infertility causes suffering, and not the other way around (Sundby, 1994). Consequences of infertility in Africa tend to be severe, especially for women. A study in West Africa found that infertility causes severe stress and anxiety, that infertile women frequently search for ritual and medical assistance, and that infertile women forfeit their rights to live in their father's home. Infertile women are termed 'persons apart' and described as having a 'meaningless life' (Enel *et al.*, 1994). According to the Women's Health Project in Johannesburg, South Africa, infertile women are denied respect and social standing and feel unsure about their social security. The severe consequences of infertility in Africa may be an outgrowth of a limited role and lack of opportunities for the African woman outside of childbearing. Among the 325 women in the urban Zimbabwe sample, 41% stated that they felt deeply worried and depressed by their infertility, 20% experienced pressure from in-laws or relatives, and 6% stated that they felt like a social outcast.

Both the social and biomedical roles of males in infertility in Africa are under-researched. Although men have been named as possible sources of childlessness in some research studies, generally the woman is blamed (Skramstad, 1995). Social stigma related to male infertility is also high; infertile men often disguise their problem and claim to have children 'elsewhere' (Skramstad, 1995; Sonko, 1994). For example, in the Gambian study, one man refused a sperm test on the grounds that he had a child in Sierra Leone. Mbizvo *et al.* (1994) found that although male infertility or impotence is known to be a causal factor in infertility among some people in Zimbabwe, the woman nevertheless took the blame for lack of children in the family.

A difference in male and female reactions to a diagnosis of infertility was observed in the study in Zimbabwe. When asked, 'Would you be willing to continue in a childless marriage or would you rather find another partner and a chance to prove fertility?", the majority of women (90%) in the urban study said they would not divorce their husbands. In the rural pilot study, the following reasons were among those given for not divorcing:
- *lobola*: because the man had paid lobola (bride wealth, usually consisting of cows given to the bride's family), women often felt they had no right to leave the husband. Taking such decisions is not for them alone, as their families are a part of the process. Some had since lost their parents and had no relatives who could afford to replace the cattle if they left;
- cultural dictates: some women felt their families would be put to shame if they took the initiative to leave their husbands: traditionally men leave women, not the other way around. This paralleled the idea that infertility is most often the responsibility of the women;
- husband's decision: some felt a decision about divorce should be made by the husband rather than the wife. These women were willing to accept whatever decision the husband made, whether this involved taking a new, fertile wife, or making decisions relating to seeking health care or infertility services;
- religious grounds: others cited religious grounds as a reason to stay in a marriage, rather than divorcing.

Men answered this question differently. Almost all men responded that if infertility were diagnosed they would replace their wives on the very same day. Some said they would take another wife, indicating that as a consolation the infertile wife could help choose the second wife, possibly one of her own sisters or nieces.

Barriers to seeking formal health care for infertility

According to WHO, more than half of infertile couples in developing countries do not seek formal medical care. In the survey in the Gambia, 40% of women had not sought help from formal medical services. In addition to the inherent limits of a resource-poor environment, health workers often give inadequate or inappropriate care to infertile couples (Blackwell et al., 1987; Inhorn, 1994).

Infertility, and the unhappiness that surrounds it, is found across all social strata in Zimbabwe, with the poorest people making up the majority of sufferers. The medical investigation of infertility is hampered by the inability of the low-income group to pay for services. However, the extent of the barrier due to cost of treatment is unclear, as some people choose to pay comparable or larger amounts for traditional treatments. Even the upper class, who are covered by Medical Aid Insurance, may be unable to use advanced facilities for infertility investigations due to cost. Recent political and economic developments in Zimbabwe have resulted in the suspension of health care subsidies by the government.

In the Gambia some of the reasons for not consulting health services for treatment of infertility were: hope that pregnancy will occur in the future unassisted by any type of treatment; a belief in 'God's will' rather than treatment; failure of husband to get involved, pay for services or comply with advice; lack of confidence in formal health care; and economic restrictions (Sundby, 1997). A general lack of health services in developing countries may also contribute to low usage rates, and modern medicine may not be acceptable to infertile couples. Delay in care may result from the reasons listed above. In the urban sample in Zimbabwe, 20% had waited more than four years before they sought care. Difficulties in travelling to the central region for appointments, financial constraints and failure to meet a preferred doctor were some of the constraints to seeking health care mentioned in Zimbabwe.

One barrier to providing infertility services is that many women are reluctant to talk about the problem. Often women seek infertility services by presenting somatic complaints, without revealing the real cause of their concern. According to several nurses in the Gambia, common complaints that may indicate infertility include generalised pain, abdominal pain, back pain, discharge, menstrual pain and painful urination. Sometimes the complaint is that the reproductive organs do not function properly or are 'sick'. Further symptoms often include fatigue, lack of appetite, headache, difficulty in sleeping and depression. It is common for infertile women to complain that their men are not 'strong enough', implying a problem with impotence or fertility of the husband. It can be a challenge for the health care provider to identify infertility as the underlying cause of the complaints. If the woman has no children or if a long time has elapsed since her last delivery, it may be appropriate to ask some probing questions about difficulties in conceiving a child. In the Gambia, two years between births is the culturally desired interval (Bledsoe et al., 1994).

Another barrier to providing infertility services is the unwillingness of husbands to participate in routine testing procedures. In Zimbabwe, very few men initially agreed to seminal testing. One-third of husbands refused the test, citing reasons such as a child outside the marriage. Of those tested, half presented with various degrees of severe spermatozoal disorders (oligoaesthenozoospermia). About 10% were unable to produce a sperm specimen at the clinic as they were not comfortable with masturbation. Very few women in Gambia brought their husbands when they went to receive infertility care, and in almost all cases the health care providers did not request the presence of the husband. Among the 325 Zimbabwean women who sought care in the tertiary system, where the husband's presence was requested by the health workers, most husbands were willing to attend; only 9% of the husbands were unwilling.

Ethical issues may arise: in 1997, three men sought confirmation of their fertility status at the andrology clinic in Harares Parareniyatwa Hospital. Two were azoospermic and had been aware of their condition for the past three years, following laboratory investigations. The third had had a vasectomy three years earlier and had not informed his wife. All of the wives of the men were pregnant. In these cases, costly, high level care was accessed in relation to paternity rather than infertility.

Traditional medicine as a barrier

Our research in the Gambia suggests a strong connection between infertility and traditional medicine, with infertility often attributed to possession by evil spirits. Fertility rituals are prominent among the Muslims of Gambia, where infertile and childless women make up a traditional women's group called the Kanyaleng. Many sacred sites all over the country provide refuge for childless and infertile women. Such traditional mechanisms may be a significant factor in the decision of many individuals and couples not to use formal health care services. In Zimbabwe, extensive use of traditional health care was documented in our rural pilot study. Approximately 20% of the urban sample reported they had sought services from traditional healers (ng'anga), faith healers, herbalists or a combination of these services. Other studies have reported that one of four consultations with traditional healers were for infertility (Hellum, 1999). Traditional advice may include intercourse with the brother of the husband (in Zimbabwe); or it may be said that the lobola or bride wealth was insufficient or that the 'blood lines' of the two families are incompatible. Although traditional explanations for infertility may relieve some of the blame on the woman, they may also push couples to purchase expensive ritual treatments that usually fail.

Pathways to care

In Zimbabwe, the modern health care system is based on a stepwise, referral-based structure. The first level of contact for infertile couples consists of village health workers and community-based family planning distributors. The most appropriate care at this level is counselling and referral. The Zimbabwe National Family Planning Council (ZNFPC) operates clinics around the country. These clinics include some mobile units that offer counselling for infertility and help with referral, as well as providing infertility services in their Harare clinics. ZNFPC is a parastatal organization that offers some subsidies on services. The most advanced level of care can be obtained in state-run referral hospitals, or from private providers. The most advanced centre for infertility care is in the specialised andrology unit at the University Hospital. Only a tiny fraction of couples who have a first encounter with lower levels of care reach this level. Paralleling this system of formal medicine is a well-developed system of traditional medicine.

An intricate maze of healthcare-seeking behaviour was seen among infertile women and couples in Zimbabwe, unrelated to educational level of the care seekers. Although individual responses to infertility and health care seeking behaviour varied significantly between couples and individuals, some common responses were observed. Initially, either one or both spouses will seek confirmation of infertility, usually without the knowledge of the partner. Communication may begin to break down due to the secrecy surrounding this decision. Severe stress leads to faultfinding by one or both individuals. Money and hopes are wasted on various types of 'cures.' As many respondents indicated, the process of seeking care for infertility becomes a vicious cycle of hope, a variety cures and blame.

Neither Zimbabwe nor the Gambia has a systematic or computerised record system within and between hospitals. Clients often visit multiple sources of health care, and thus go through the same procedure several times. Consequences include overmedication with a fertility-inducing drug (Clomiphene) or antibiotics, or multiple dilatation and curettages (D&Cs) in a single year. When clients weave in and out of modern health care systems and traditional medicine or use the two concurrently, both the health care providers and the client suffer.

First level infertility services

Although improved access to STD treatments, better nutrition and reduced levels of female circumcision may all help to reduce infertility among future generations, those who are presently infertile are forced to rely on existing services in their own countries. At village level local paramedical and traditional health care providers have very few biomedical interventions to offer infertile couples, apart from referral.

Interventions at the primary health care level are limited, but some simple steps can be followed to alleviate infertility. For example, a community nurse can counsel about the timing of intercourse, the need to involve the husband/partner in testing and services, and the need to be tested and treated for STDs. Further, she can give a referral to a higher level of care. A primary health care practitioner can also counsel the couple against potentially harmful services (including D&Cs or cervical electro-cauterization) that may be provided by, or recommended in, the private sector. Alternatives to child-bearing, such as child fostering, may also be discussed with patients.

Basic services and common interventions

According to WHO infertility treatment guidelines (1993), the first step in evaluating infertility is a systematic medical examination of both partners. In the Gambia, the most common interventions were D&C, provision of medicine such as drugs for STDs or oral contraceptives for a limited period of time, and - on a more limited scale - a hysterosalpingogram. Only 3% of couples in the study reported that the husband had a sperm test.

In Zimbabwe, the only institutions that offer comprehensive infertility investigations are the two-referral hospitals and the Spielhaus Family Planning Clinic. Because all three are in Harare, these advanced infertility services are almost completely inaccessible to the rural poor. The distance from Masvingo to Harare (300 km), and the delays in receiving care at the overcrowded Harare medical facilities, make the trip prohibitive for most villagers. General poverty in the health care system as well as the staggering burden of HIV/AIDS make counselling services for infertile couples almost non-existent.

Service in the modern health care system is often experienced as unsystematic, unfriendly and ineffective. In the Gambia, both women and health care providers commonly believed that D&C was a necessary component of infertility care. Structured interviews with samples of nurses from health centres and family planning clinics in the Gambia showed wide variations in knowledge about the treatment of infertility. Nurses trained in family planning have a better understanding of infertility than general community nurses, while trained nurse/midwives have a more thorough understanding of infertility care.

At a minimum, a primary level infertility examination should include screening and treatment of both partners for STDs, including suspected asymptomatic chlamydia infection if laboratory facilities are not available to confirm active infections. Observation of cervical mucus using wet smears can verify ovulation; if taken after a timed coitus, they can offer some information about sperm motility. This can only be done if microscopes are available. Nurses can also provide advice on diet in cases of suspected ovulatory dysfunction due to weight change; give treatment with one or two cycles of Clomiphene; and counsel on timing of intercourse. A microscopic examination of a sperm sample can also confirm the presence or absence of live motile sperm. If all of these approaches fail, then the couple should be referred to the next level.

Access to care in the Gambia is tied into resources. Even when free public services are available, travel expenses and the cost of drugs may be prohibitive. Active discouragement of inappropriate and costly interventions such as vaginal douching, D&C, prescription oral contraceptives and local antimicrobiological treatment may help couples to save money that can be used towards more effective services. Thus, the first point of contact should also explain service options and locations. Psychosocial counselling, including discussions with the husband or other family members, is appropriate.

Referral care

Most infertility treatment as well as advanced investigations must be accessed through a referral to hospitals or specialists. Hospital facilities vary from rural secondary care facilities to modern teaching hospitals in the capital. Hospitals or other facilities with laboratory capacity offer screening for sexually transmitted diseases (VDRL, gonorrhoea, bacterial vaginosis, yeast infections etc.). Testing for chlamydia can be problematic due to lack of laboratory infrastructure, trained laboratory technicians and the cost of the tests. A hysterosalpingogram to assess the status of the tubes and a sperm test are appropriate at this level of care. Reliable sperm tests may be difficult, since busy laboratories may find it difficult to read the sample within the two-hour time limit.

To support our study, a special infertility clinic was established in the Parareniyatwa referral hospital in Harare on allocated weekdays, where group counselling, sperm and blood tests and specialised X-ray services are among the services offered. A counselling guide has been written in conjunction with this clinic to standardize the services offered to infertility care clients. During the study, male sperm investigations and hormone assays were provided free, but clients had to pay for hysterosalpingograms, laparoscopy and surgical procedures such as tubal surgery or myomectomy. The clinic was highly successful, but with the introduction of counselling services in 1995 it became overburdened with new clients, due to the shortage of infertility services elsewhere in the country. From 1995 to 1997 over 450 couples/clients were seen.

The clinic uses an advanced computerized Hamilton-Thorne version microscope, donated by WHO, for seminal fluid analysis. This provides a more accurate diagnosis of sperm quality than the ordinary light microscope. Clients with azoospermia can receive a testicular biopsy to confirm the absence of spermatogenesis; they are subsequently referred to a urologist. Those with sperm activity can be referred to hospitals in South Africa, some of which offer *in-vitro* fertilization (IVF) and intra-cycloplasmic insemination at lower cost than in Zimbabwe, where *in-vitro* fertilization is only available in the private sector and at a very high cost. Treatment facilities for tubal surgery are also scarce and costly. In general in Zimbabwe the lack of laparoscopic diagnostics, refined hormone assay tests and other *in-vitro* services for detection of ovulation impedes the provision of infertility services.

In the Gambia, infertility ranks high among reasons for referral to the main hospital. No information about treatment outcome is available. Hysterosalpingograms are offered once or twice a week. Although this service is supposed to be available to all infertile couples seeking care, it is not known how many actually have access. Very few patients - only 4-6 per year - undergo surgery.

Given the dearth of both technical and financial resources, it may be necessary to train health care workers to help clients to cope with the fact of permanent infertility. In some cases, it is unethical to start costly investigations when the necessary equipment for treatment services are unavailable. In other cases, infertility may be easier for clients to cope with if biological explanations are given, especially those which remove some of the blame from the infertile woman.

Care in the private sector

Most developing countries have well equipped private gynaecological clinics in urban areas. A considerable number of infertility clients from the wealthier part of the population use private facilities despite the high cost of services. Although private clinics may provide high quality infertility care and counselling, there are many other private providers and facilities which provide inappropriate services at a high price. In the Gambia in 1994, some clients paid 100 dalassies (>10 US dollars) for a D&C, while in Zimbabwe the 1994 cost of a private sector *in-vitro* fertilization was as high as 40,000 Zimbabwean dollars per session (about 3000 $ US at the time). In some cases, dangerous practices such as D&C are overused, as reflected in our finding that twice as many patients in the Gambian study (25% of those who sought care) had a D&C as a hysterosalpingogram. It is possible that doctors and others performing the service perpetuate the use of D&C because it is lucrative. There appears to be little public knowledge about the limited value and potential hazards of D&C in infertility services; meanwhile its overuse has created public demand for this service.

Common harmful practices

The common expression for D&C in the Gambia is 'to clean the uterus.' As new abortion methods such as medically induced abortions and vacuum curettage have evolved, the use of procedure has become quite limited in most developed countries. Though simple, in the hands of an inexperienced medical or paramedical person D&C can be a dangerous procedure. If performed without pain relief, without proper cleaning of the instruments and without follow up, it becomes increasingly risky. When an untrained person performs D&C, there is a risk that the sharp curette will perforate the uterine wall. When the procedure is performed with infected instruments or in women who are already suffering from a uterine infection, complications become more likely.

Despite all of these hazards, D&C is widely used in many developing countries as a medical method for treating infertility, as demonstrated by Inhorn (1994) in Egypt. A sign in an operating theatre in a rural Tanzanian hospital prohibits D&C, illustrating the known hazards using D&Cs to treat infertility. Yet across Africa patients request D&C and doctors perform it; both believe it cleans the uterus - the 'dirty womb' - and so helps it to return to normality. This condition of a 'dirty womb' has been described as 'germs' or 'products of a ghost.' While it is perhaps forgivable that indications of D&C are not fully understood by people in indigenous cultures, it is disturbing that medical practitioners give a diagnosis of 'pollution of the womb' rather than bacterial infection.

Vaginal douching, or cleansing, is another culturally influenced practice based on the concept of a 'dirty womb'. It can contribute to recurrent vaginal infections and possibly infertility by introducing pathological bacteria into the vagina. In Egypt (Inhorn, 1994), the practice of electro-cauterization of the cervix, removing the normal cervical cylinder epithelium ectopia, is an additional practice that has no value and harm the woman.

Discussion and conclusions

Infertility in Africa is unquestionably an important public health problem with ties to both the provision of medical services and social issues (Larsen and Raggers, Chapter 1; Mayaud, Chapter 2; Boerma et al., Chapter 6). Clients do not see these as separate concerns. On the contrary, they often seek care in modern and traditional sectors simultaneously, and discuss causes and consequences as intertwined. Given this mix, it may be appropriate to integrate or collaborate with traditional healers in infertility treatment.

Different solutions to infertility are offered in different venues, but the underlying factors are often the same: without a child, the value of the woman's life is diminished; she will seek all possible solutions to alleviate the problem. Husbands, partners and other family members tend to be less involved in care seeking, but their interpretation of the situation may severely affect the women's future and current role in the family.

Unfortunately, the current services at the local level do not have a full package of infertility services to offer, so women or couples have to travel long distances to receive full services. At this level it is important for nurses or other staff to be able to provide adequate basic services: history taking, counselling about infertility treatments, screening for STD symptoms, and treatment of both partners if an STD is detected or suspected.

Due to the low success rate and high cost of infertility services, health care providers may profit more from the provision of these services than the clients themselves (Inhorn, 1994). Because people are willing to pay, both health care providers and untrained individuals provide services, whether or not they are effective. Infertility is a serious issue for these women and couples: it has an important role in their negotiations for a place in society and access to their spouse's resources. Generally speaking, there is a hierarchical culture around most medical services in developing countries. Within this culture, the health care worker has a monopoly on power and knowledge; the opinion of the client is not valued. Given this, and the low status of most women seeking care for infertility, there is almost no pressure from clients to improve the quality of care. Even in the best circumstances, medical treatment may have limited success. For example, *in-vitro* fertilization has a success rate no higher than one in six or seven couples (Okonofua, 1996). The low success rate of formal medicine, especially given substandard health facilities in Sub Saharan Africa, may contribute to patient's reluctance to use formal medical services for infertility treatment.

In this chapter, we have outlined interventions that could be included in a minimum care package for infertility services at different levels of health care in developing countries. A better understanding of constraints on care seeking and of the emotional and social needs of clients, combined with improved knowledge of appropriate infertility interventions, can facilitate improvements even in resource-poor settings.

Bibliography

Adepoju A and Oppong C (1994), *Gender, work and population in sub-Saharan Africa*, ILO, Geneva, James Currey, (London) and Heinemann, (Portsmouth N.H.).

Aral S and Cates W (1983), 'The increasing concern with infertility: why now?' *Journal of the American Medical Association* 250: 2327-31.

Blackwell R, Carr B, Chang R, *et al.* (1987), 'Are we exploiting the infertile couple?' *Fertility and Sterility* 48: 735-9.

Bledsoe C, Hill A, D'Alessandro U and Langerock P (1994), 'Constructing natural fertility: the use of western contraceptive technologies in rural Gambia'. *Population and Development Review* 20: 81-113.

Central Statistical Office (Zimbabwe) and Macro International, Inc.(1994), *Zimbabwe Demographic and Health Survey 1994*, Central Statistical Office and Macro International Inc., Calverton, Maryland.

Enel C, Pison G, and Lefebvre M (1994), 'Migration and marriage change: a study of Mlomp, a Joola village in southern Senegal'. In: Bledsoe C, Pison G (eds), *Nuptiality in sub-Saharan Africa*, Clarendon Press, Oxford, UK: 92-116.

Hellum A (1995), 'Population policy, childlessness and legal pluralism: one example from Zimbabwe'. In: Austveg B and Sundby J (eds), *Population policies toward year 2000*, Tano, Oslo, Norway.

Hellum A (1999), *Women's human rights and legal pluralism in Africa: mixed norms and identities in infertility management in Zimbabwe*, Tano, Oslo.

Inhorn M (1994), *Quest for conception*, University of Pennsylvania Press, Philadelphia, Pennsylvania.

Jensen A (1996), *Fertility - between passion and utility*, PhD Thesis, NIBR, Oslo.

Mabey D, Ogba Selassie G, Robertson J, Heckels J and Ward M (1985), 'Tubal infertility in the Gambia: chlamydia and gonococcal serology in women with tubal occlusion compared with pregnant controls'. *Bulletin of the World Health Organization* 63: 1107-13.

Mbizvo M, Danso M, Tswana S, Bassett E, Marowa L and Mbengeranwa L (1994), 'Reduced semen quality and risk behavior amongst men consulting a referral STD clinic'. *Central Africa Journal of Medicine* 40: 170-75.

Mutambirwa J (1984), *Shona pathology religio-medical practices*. PhD Thesis, University of Zimbabwe, Harare.

Okonufua FE (1996), 'The case against new reproductive technologies in developing countries'. *British Journal of Obstetrics and Gynaecology* 103: 957-962.

Rowe P and Farley T (1990), 'Prevention and management of infertility'. *Research in human reproduction*, World Health Organization, Geneva.

Skramstad H (1995), 'Fertilitet i Gambia'. In: Austveg B and Sundby J (eds), *Befolkningspolitikk mot år 2000*, Tano, Oslo, Norway.

Sonko S (1994), 'Fertility and culture in Sub-Saharan Africa: a review'. *International Social Sciences Journal* 46: 397-411.

Sundby J (1994), *Infertility: causes, care and consequences*, PhD Thesis, University of Oslo, Oslo.

Sundby J (1997), 'Infertility in the Gambia: modern and traditional health care'. *Patient Education and Counselling* 31: 29-37.

Sundby J, Sonko S and Mboge R (1998), 'Infertility in the Gambia: frequency and health care seeking'. *Social Science and Medicine* 46: 891-99.

UNAIDS (1998), *Epidemiological Fact Sheets on HIV/AIDS and Sexually Transmitted Diseases*, Geneva.

World Health Organization (1993), *Manual for the standard investigation and diagnoses of the infertile couple*, Geneva.

Index

Herpes and infertility 72, 153
Histology 82
HIV/AIDS 210, 263
    Causes/associations 46, 90, 144, 153, 184, 219, 242
    Counselling 176
    Incidence 87, 179, 180, 183-184, 242
    And infertility 13, 16, 17, 20, 72, 78, 87, 95, 140-141, 156, 176-185, 219
    Prevalence 16, 46, 179, 180, 183-184
    Prevention 13, 27, 90, 140, 243, 248, 252-253
    STD/I on HIV, effect of other 46, 90, 153, 184, 242
    Testing 176
    Treatment 253
Holland, Successful AIDS campaign in 93
Hormonal function 73, 76-77, 78, 123
    PID-related 78
Hospital services 18, 94, 213, 228, 229, 234, 250-253, 262-265
Human papilloma virus 72
Hyperprolactinaemia, Abnormal levels of 77
Hypopituitarism 77
Hysterosalpingogram 263
Hysterosalpingography 77, 83, 94, 112
Iatrogenic infection
    Causes 82-83
    And infertility 72, 82-83, 94
    And PID 82-83, 94
    Prevention 94
Infant morbidity 72
Infant mortality 14, 72, 87, 219
Infant sequalae 79
Infecundity 72
Infertility
    Age patterns 14, 16, 18-19, 26-48, 110, 118-119, 125, 127-130, 136-141, 152-170, 176, 180, 181, 182, 183, 192, 198
    Awareness 13
    Definitions 13-15, 26, 27-28, 72, 110, 118-119, 152, 158, 178, 190, 206, 229
    Fertility rate, And the effect on 18-20, 26-66, 75, 118-143, 152-155, 159-170, 176
    Geographic 'belt' 16, 26, 36-37, 86, 118, 167, 204
    Incidence 19, 47, 118, 124, 125, 132, 136, 140
    Male perspective and risks 13-14, 15-16, 20-21, 27, 47, 72, 73, 87-89, 95, 123, 152, 190, 195-196, 197-198, 214-215, 218-219, 228, 233
    Male versus female perspectives 190-199, 214-215, 218-219
    And patriarchal ideology 211-219
    Prevalence/levels 14-15, 18, 19, 26-48, 118-143, 152-170
    Public health significance 13, 21, 48, 72, 73, 90, 153, 169-170, 176, 242, 266
    Sexual behaviour, related 13, 15, 16-17, 19, 20, 46-48, 123, 125, 136-137, 140-141, 152, 155, 156, 168-169, 176-185, 191-193, 196, 198-199, 213-215, 218-219, 231, 245, 248
    Socio-economic perspective 20, 90, 158-159, 210-211, 215-217, 219